AF848268

# CULTURAL HERITAGE IN INTERNATIONAL INVESTMENT LAW AND ARBITRATION

Can states adopt protectionist cultural policies? What are the limits, if any, to state intervention in cultural matters? A wide variety of cultural policies may interfere with foreign investments, and a tension therefore exists between the cultural policies of the host state and investment treaty provisions. In some cases, foreign investors have claimed that cultural policies have negatively affected their investments, thereby amounting to a breach of the relevant investment treaty. Investment treaty arbitration constitutes a sophisticated means of dispute settlement. As a result, foreign investors choose to take their disputes to investment treaty tribunals when such disputes nevertheless contain obvious cultural issues. This study maps the relevant investor–state arbitrations concerning cultural elements and shows that arbitrators have increasingly taken cultural concerns into consideration in deciding cases brought before them, eventually contributing to the coalescence of general principles of law demanding the protection of cultural heritage.

VALENTINA VADI is a reader in international economic law at Lancaster University. She was previously an Emile Noël Fellow at the Jean Monnet Center for International and Regional Economic Law, New York University, and a Marie Curie Fellow at Maastricht University. Her main areas of research are in international economic law and international cultural law.

# CULTURAL HERITAGE IN INTERNATIONAL INVESTMENT LAW AND ARBITRATION

VALENTINA VADI
*Lancaster University and New York University*

CAMBRIDGE
UNIVERSITY PRESS

**CAMBRIDGE**
**UNIVERSITY PRESS**

University Printing House, Cambridge CB2 8BS, United Kingdom

Published in the United States of America by Cambridge University Press, New York

Cambridge University Press is part of the University of Cambridge.

It furthers the University's mission by disseminating knowledge in the pursuit of education, learning, and research at the highest international levels of excellence.

www.cambridge.org
Information on this title: www.cambridge.org/9781107038486

© Valentina Vadi 2014

This publication is in copyright. Subject to statutory exception and to the provisions of relevant collective licensing agreements, no reproduction of any part may take place without the written permission of Cambridge University Press.

First published 2014

Printed in the United Kingdom by Clays, St Ives plc

*A catalogue record for this publication is available from the British Library*

ISBN 978-1-107-03848-6 Hardback

Cambridge University Press has no responsibility for the persistence or accuracy of URLs for external or third-party internet websites referred to in this publication, and does not guarantee that any content on such websites is, or will remain, accurate or appropriate.

DAMAGED

A mia madre

# CONTENTS

# FOREWORD

It is my pleasure to present to the reader this monograph by Valentina Vadi, which she prepared during the years 2011–2013, as a Marie Curie post-doctoral fellow of Maastricht University's Faculty of Law. Valentina Vadi has recently published a book on *Public Health in International Investment Law and Arbitration* (2012), which is based on her PhD dissertation, which she successfully defended at the European University Institute in Florence. In the present book, Valentina Vadi explores another area in which investment law meets the concern of states and local communities to protect important non-market values. After the public health concern explored in her previous book, here Valentina Vadi examines the cultural heritage concern. Whereas transnational economic activity is a source of cultural exchange between countries and can promote greater cultural liberty, tensions between investment and culture also frequently arise. This book shows how legitimate concerns for the protection of the cultural heritage or cultural identity of the host state may lead to limitations of transnational economic activity, which are then adjudicated by arbitral tribunals or other fora where such investment disputes are settled. What is remarkable in Valentina Vadi's approach to the study of these issues, is the equal ease with which she analyses the domains of international investment law and international cultural law. The first two chapters, in fact, give a succinct presentation of those two sub-fields of international law, thereby setting the scene for the other chapters in which the multiple tensions and conciliations between them are analysed in great detail, and in a style which combines legal rigour with elegance and clarity. I warmly recommend this book to the reader interested in the legal aspects of economic and cultural globalization.

*Bruno De Witte*
*Professor of European Union Law,*
*Maastricht University and European University Institute, Florence*

# PREFACE

The original idea for this book came about in 2007 during the time I spent as a researcher at the European University Institute in Florence, Italy. Not only is Florence a World Heritage site of ineffable beauty but it was also a financial capital during the Renaissance period, home to philosophical inquiry and capital flows, religious iconoclasm and supreme artistic expression, power struggles and influential political thinking. Money and beauty undeniably attract the interest of many; and my investigation started at the crossroads between two major fields of international law dedicated to the study of these concepts: international investment law and international cultural law. Coming across a large number of culture-related investment treaty arbitrations, I began to wonder why so many culture-related cases had been arbitrated before investment treaty tribunals. Since 2007 my investigation has focused on how arbitral tribunals have adjudicated these disputes and what implications this emerging jurisprudence could have for international law.

On a more personal level, the book reconciles two streams of passionate interest: interest in law and the social sciences, and interest in art and architecture that my mother – architect and professor of art history – passed on to me. This book is a tribute to the beauty of Florence and other heritage sites all around the world – to their inhabitants, and to those who struggle for the protection of their heritage as a fundamental component of their human rights. May the protection of cultural heritage flourish further and promote respect for human dignity and peaceful dialogue among nations.

*V.V.*
*New York, 1 November 2013*

# ACKNOWLEDGEMENTS

In writing this book, I have benefited from the inspiration of many people. I thank Francesco Francioni, Hildegard Schneider, Gus Van Harten, Ana Filipa Vrdoljak and Bruno De Witte for their mentorship, guidance and support. I also gratefully acknowledge the Marie Curie Fellowship granted by the European Commission for the furtherance of this study. The research leading to these results has received funding from the European Union Seventh Framework Programme. The book reflects my views only and not necessarily those of the Union.

Parts of this book were presented at conferences and seminars held in: Beijing, Boston, Buckingham, Florence, Glasgow, Groningen, Lancaster, London, Maastricht, Minneapolis, Montreal, Onati, Prague, Rome, Siena, Singapore, Southampton, Turin, Washington D.C. and York. Convening four international conferences on law and culture – one at the European University Institute in 2008, one at New York University (Villa La Pietra) in 2010 and two at Maastricht University in 2013 – also helped me to frame discourse and engage in interdisciplinary approaches. I greatly benefited from the comments received on these occasions. In particular, I thank Alexander Bauer, Judith Carter, Claire Cutler, Emily Den, Antonietta di Blase, Federico Lenzerini, Amanda Perry-Kessaris, Sol Picciotto, Sarah Sargent, Della Scott-Ireton, M. Sornarajah, Peter Van den Bossche, Laura Westra and Jacques Werner for their comments on earlier parts of my research. I also thank my colleagues Suzanne Jongste and Esther Crombach for inspiring me in so many fruitful ways. I am grateful to Sinead Moloney, Finola O'Sullivan, Elizabeth Spicer and Nienke van Schaverbeke at Cambridge University Press for accompanying this book from proposal to publication.

On a personal note, I thank my fiancé Gianluca for his love and support, and my parents, Lidiana and Carlo, and grandmother, Lora, for encouraging me in every possible way.

*V.V.*
*New York, 1 November 2013*

# TABLE OF INSTRUMENTS

# TABLE OF CASES

## Investment Arbitration

This table contains an alphabetical listing of all arbitral awards cited in the text. The awards are cited to a print source, where this was available at the time of this writing. Unreported awards and notices of intent are cited by giving a docket number, where one has been used. The majority of such awards can be accessed electronically on one or more of the following websites: www.worldbank.org/icsid (the official ICSID website); www.state.gov (the official site of the Government of the United States); http://ita.law.uvic.ca and, in the case of claims under NAFTA, www.naftaclaims.com.

## International

## Regional

## National

*Tahoe-Sierra Preservation Council v. Tahoe Regional Planning Agency*, 535 US, 302, 330 (2002) 72

*The Blackwall*, 77 U.S. 1 (1869) 144

*Tikiri Banda Bulankulama v. Secretary, Ministry of Industrial Development*, S. C. Application No. 884/99 (F/R), (2000) SAELR 7 (2) 1, available at www.elaw.org/node/1295 109

*United Artists' Theater Circuit, Inc. v. City of Philadelphia*, 635 A.2d 612 (Pa. 1993) 71

*United States v. Gettysburg Electric Railway Co.*, 160 US 668 (1896) 70

*United States v. Wheeler*, 435 US 313 (1978) 209

*Village of Euclid v. Ambler Realty Co.*, 272 US 365 (1928) 70–1

*Yanner v. Eaton* (1999) 166 ALR 258 (Australia) 227

# ABBREVIATIONS

| | |
|---|---|
| AB | Appellate Body of World Trade Organization |
| AJIL | American Journal of International Law |
| BIT | Bilateral Investment Treaty |
| BYIL | British Yearbook of International Law |
| CCD | Convention on the Protection and Promotion of the Diversity of Cultural Expressions |
| CJEU | Court of Justice of the European Union |
| CPUCH | Convention on the Protection of Underwater Cultural Heritage |
| CUSFTA | Canada–US Free Trade Agreement |
| DCF | discounted cash flow |
| EC | European Communities |
| ECHR | European Convention of Human Rights |
| ECtHR | European Court of Human Rights |
| ECJ | European Court of Justice |
| ECT | Energy Charter Treaty |
| EIA | environmental impact assessment |
| EJIL | European Journal of International Law |
| EPA | Economic Partnership Agreements |
| EU | European Union |
| FCN | Friendship, Commerce and Navigation |
| FDI | foreign direct investment |
| FET | fair and equitable treatment |
| FTA | Free Trade Agreement |
| GA | General Assembly |
| GAOR | Official Records of the General Assembly |
| GATS | General Agreement on Trade in Services |
| GATT | General Agreement on Tariffs and Trade |
| GYIL | German Yearbook of International Law |
| Harvard ILJ | Harvard International Law Journal |
| HRQ | Human Rights Quarterly |
| IACtHR | Inter-American Court of Human Rights |
| IAR | Investment Arbitration Reporter |
| Iran–US CTR | Iran–US Claims Tribunal Reports |
| IBRD | International Bank for Reconstruction and Development |
| ICC | International Chamber of Commerce |

| | |
|---|---|
| ICCPR | International Covenant on Civil and Political Rights |
| ICESCR | International Covenant on Economic, Social and Cultural Rights |
| ICH | intangible cultural heritage |
| ICJ | International Court of Justice |
| ICLQ | International and Comparative Law Quarterly |
| ICMM | International Council on Mining and Metals |
| ICOMOS | International Council for Monuments and Sites |
| ICSID | International Centre for the Settlement of Investment Disputes |
| ICSID Convention | Convention on the Settlement of Investment Disputes between States and Nationals of Other States |
| ICSID Review-FILJ | ICSID Review Foreign Investment Law Journal |
| ICTY | International Criminal Tribunal for the former Yugoslavia |
| IFC | International Finance Corporation |
| IIA | Investment Investment Agreement |
| IISD | International Institute for Sustainable Development |
| ILC | International Law Commission |
| ILJ | International Law Journal |
| ILM | International Law Materials |
| ILO | International Labour Organization |
| ILR | International Law Review |
| IMF | International Monetary Fund |
| ITN | Investment Treaty News |
| ITO | International Trade Organization |
| IUCN | International Union for the Conservation of Nature |
| IYIL | Italian Yearbook of International Law |
| JIEL | Journal of International Economic Law |
| JIL | Journal of International Law |
| JWIT | Journal of World Investment and Trade |
| JWT | Journal of World Trade |
| LDC | least developed country |
| MAI | Multilateral Agreement on Investment |
| MFN | most favoured nation |
| MSA | Master Settlement Agreement |
| NAAEC | North American Agreement on Environmental Cooperation |
| NAFTA | North American Free Trade Agreement |
| NGO | Non-Governmental Organization |
| NT | national treatment |
| OAU | Organization of African Unity |
| OECD | Organization for Economic Cooperation and Development |
| PCA | Permanent Court of Arbitration |

| | |
|---|---|
| PCIJ | Permanent Court of International Justice |
| RGDIP | Revue Générale de Droit International Public |
| RIAA | Reports of International Arbitral Awards |
| SCC | Stockholm Chamber of Commerce |
| SIEL | Society of International Economic Law |
| TDM | Transnational Dispute Management |
| TRIMS | Trade-Related Investment Measures |
| TRIPS | Trade-Related Intellectual Property Rights |
| UCH | underwater cultural heritage |
| UDHR | Universal Declaration of Human Rights |
| UKTS | United Kingdom Treaty Series |
| UNCITRAL | United Nations Commission on International Trade Law |
| UNCLOS | United Nations Convention on the Law of the Sea |
| UNCTAD | United Nations Conference on Trade and Development |
| UNDRIP | United Nations Declaration on the Rights of Indigenous Peoples |
| UNESCO | United Nations Educational, Scientific and Cultural Organization |
| UNGA | United Nations General Assembly |
| UNIDO | United Nations Industrial Development Organization |
| UNTS | United Nations Treaty Series |
| VCLT | Vienna Convention on the Law of Treaties |
| WHC | World Heritage Convention |
| WIPO | World Intellectual Property Organization |
| WIR | World Investment Report |
| WTO | World Trade Organization |
| YIL | Yearbook of International Law |

# Cultural heritage in international investment law and arbitration

## Introduction

Can states promote economic development without infringing their cultural heritage? Culture represents inherited values, ideas, beliefs, and traditions, which characterize social groups and their behaviour. Culture is not a static concept but rather a dynamic force, which evolves through time and shapes countries and civilizations. As such, culture has always benefited from economic exchange. Globalization and international economic governance have in recent times spurred a more intense dialogue and interaction among nations: thus, they offer unprecedented opportunities for cultural exchange. In parallel, foreign direct investments can promote cultural diversity and provide the funds needed to locate, recover and preserve cultural heritage.

Nonetheless, globalization and international economic governance can also jeopardize cultural diversity and determine the erosion of cultural heritage. While trade in cultural products can lead to cultural homogenization and even to cultural hegemony, foreign direct investments have an unmatched penetrating force with the ultimate capacity to change landscapes and erase memory. At the same time, the increase in global trade and foreign direct investment (hereinafter FDI) has determined the creation of legally binding and highly effective regimes that demand states to promote and facilitate trade and FDI. An *international economic culture* has emerged that emphasizes productivity and economic development at the expense of the common weal.

This book aims to explore the 'clash of cultures' between international investment law and international cultural law. When countries pursue economic growth, their policy-makers may have an incentive to lower cultural standards to promote economic activities.[1] The host state 'may

[1] This phenomenon is also known as a 'race to the bottom'. The literature is extensive. See e.g. N. Meisel, *Governance Culture and Development: A Different Perspective on Corporate Governance* (Paris: OECD, 2004), p. 41.

have a financial stake in the project, making it reluctant to take any action that would diminish its profitability . . . And even if officials are genuinely concerned about the impacted peoples and the environment, they may assign them a lower priority than development goals.'[2] If states nonetheless maintain a high level of cultural heritage protection, disputes may arise as foreign investors can claim that such policies affect their economic interests thereby breaching investment treaty provisions. As a wide variety of cultural policies may interfere with foreign investments, tension exists between the cultural policies of the host state and investment treaty provisions. In some cases, foreign investors have claimed that cultural policies negatively affected their investments, thereby amounting to indirect expropriation. In other cases, the investors have alleged discrimination and/or violation of other investment treaty provisions. In sum, there is a variety of potential areas of conflict between investor rights and cultural policies.

If a dispute arises between the foreign investor and the host state, several fora are available. However, foreign companies may prefer not to recur to local courts and human rights courts (which require the exhaustion of local remedies), but to bring the case before investment treaty arbitral tribunals because of streamlined procedures and alleged independence. While cultural heritage law lacks an institutionalized dispute settlement mechanism, investment treaty arbitration constitutes a sophisticated means of dispute settlement.[3] As a result, foreign investors may choose to take their disputes to investment treaty tribunals when the disputes nevertheless contain obvious cultural issues.

Three examples may clarify the issues at stake. Characterized by an impressive complex of Gothic, Renaissance, Baroque and classical buildings, the historic town of Vilnius, in Lithuania, is listed on the World Heritage List as a cultural heritage site of outstanding universal value.[4] A Norwegian investor participated in a bid to build a parking area

[2] G. K. Foster, 'Foreign Investment and Indigenous Peoples: Options for Promoting Equilibrium between Economic Development and Indigenous Rights', *Michigan JIL* 33 (2012), 655–6.

[3] See e.g. A. Newcombe and L. Paradell, *Law and Practice of Investment Treaties: Standards of Treatment* (Aalphen an den Rijn: Kluwer Law International, 2009), pp. 3 ff.

[4] Convention concerning the Protection of the World Cultural and Natural Heritage, Paris, 16 November 1972, in force 17 December 1975 (1972) 11 ILM 1358. For commentary, see F. Francioni (ed.), *The 1972 World Heritage Convention: A Commentary* (Oxford University Press, 2008).

under the historic centre of the town.[5] However, cultural heritage impact assessments required by law revealed that the project submitted by the investor could jeopardize the cultural heritage of the city because it included excavation under the cathedral. Therefore, the project was rejected on cultural heritage grounds and another project was selected which did not include excavation under the cathedral. Against this background, the investor filed an investor–state claim on the grounds of discrimination. Was it legitimate for the municipality of Vilnius to prefer another contractor in order to limit the perceived risk of damaging its cultural heritage?

Another example involves maritime cultural heritage. An investment dispute involved the salvage of an ancient shipwreck discovered in the Straits of Malacca by a British salvor, a company that specialized in the recovery of ancient shipwrecks.[6] The company had signed a contract with Malaysia which gave the latter the right to obtain only a limited percentage of the recovered artefacts, while the salvor would retain the rest, to sell at the auction house Christie's. According to the salvor, however, the host state had breached the salvage contract, retaining more artefacts than those allocated in the contract. Therefore, he brought the case before an investment treaty arbitral tribunal. Two questions arose in this context. Was the salvage contract between the salvor and Malaysia a form of investment? If so, would international arbitrators take into account the cultural value of the goods?

A third example concerns religious freedom and cultural practices. An indigenous tribe has performed a spiritual pilgrimage throughout the Californian desert for centuries.[7] Its rights are recognized by statutory law. What happens if a foreign investor deems local regulations requiring the backfilling of open-pit gold mines as a form of indirect expropriation? Should the sacred landscape of the local community be devastated by open-pit gold mines? All the above-mentioned examples are real cases that have been decided before different investor–state arbitral tribunals. These cases are just a representative sample but there are many other investment arbitrations that clearly involve cultural entitlements.[8]

[5] *Parkerings-Compagniet AS v. Lithuania*, ICSID Case No. ARB/05/8, Award, 11 September 2007.

[6] *Malaysian Historical Salvors Sdn, Bhd v. Malaysia*, Award on Jurisdiction, ICSID Case No. ARB/05/10, 17 May 2007.

[7] *Glamis Gold Ltd v. United States of America*, ICSID Award, 8 June 2009.

[8] On this emerging jurisprudence, see e.g. F. Lenzerini, 'Property Protection and Protection of Cultural Heritage', in S. Schill (ed.), *International Investment Law and Comparative Public Law* (Oxford University Press, 2010); A. Froehlich, 'Cultural Matters in Investment

A number of questions arise in this context. *First*, is it legitimate for the state to adopt cultural policies? What are the limits, if any, to state intervention in cultural matters? *Second*, if the state adopts cultural policies, how do we set the boundaries between legitimate regulation (which is not compensable) and (compensable) violation of the investment treaty provisions? To what extent may investment treaty obligations collide with states' obligations to protect cultural heritage? *Third*, how have arbitrators dealt with these crucial policy issues? *Fourth*, while foreign investors have been recognized as 'international corporate citizens' and have been afforded direct access to investment treaty arbitration,[9] the procedural rights of the investment-affected communities have remained almost unchanged.[10] Is investor–state arbitration a suitable forum to protect public interests?

This book aims to provide a fresh approach to these questions, offering an in-depth analysis of the largely unexplored linkage between international investment law and cultural policies. While the clash between cultural policies and free trade has been broadly discussed by authors,[11] what is lacking is a systematic analysis of the relationship between cultural policies and international investment law. Given the broad policy implications that foreign investments provoke in host countries, in-depth scrutiny is needed. The aim of this study is to fill this gap in academic literature, and to contribute to the ongoing debate on the need for 'globalization with a human face'.[12]

Agreements and Decisions', in A. Reinisch and C. Knahr (eds.) *International Investment Law in Context* (Utrecht: Eleven International Publishing, 2008); A. Froehlich, 'L'enjeu de la culture dans son contexte économique international', in P. Meerts (ed.), *Culture and International Law* (The Hague: T.M.C. Asser Press Publishers, 2008); V. Vadi, 'Cultural Heritage and International Investment Law: A Stormy Relationship', *International J. Cultural Property* 15 (2008), 2.

9 P. Muchlinski, 'Global Bukovina Examined: Viewing the Multinational Enterprise as a Transnational Law Making Community', in G. Teubner (ed.), *Global Law Without a State* (Dartmouth: Aldershot, 2003), p. 79.

10 See N. Gal-Or, 'The Investor and Civil Society as Twin Global Citizens: Proposing a New Interpretation in the Legitimacy Debate', *Suffolk Transnational L. Rev.* 32 (2008–2009), 284.

11 See, for instance, J. Morijn, *Reframing Human Rights and Trade: Potential and Limits of a Human Rights Perspective of WTO Law on Cultural and Educational Goods and Services* (Antwerpen: Intersentia, 2010); P. van den Bossche and H. Schneider (eds.), *Protection of Cultural Diversity from a European and International Perspective* (Antwerpen: Intersentia, 2008); T. Voon, *Cultural Products and the World Trade Organization* (Cambridge University Press, 2007); P. Van den Bossche, *Free Trade and Culture* (Amsterdam: Stichting Boekmanstudies, 2008); R. J. Neuwirth, *The Cultural Industries in International Trade Law* (Hamburg: Kovac, 2006).

12 See J. Stiglitz, *Globalization and Its Discontents* (New York: WW Norton & Company, 2002); but see J. Bhagwati, *In Defense of Globalization* (Oxford University Press, 2004).

The book complements and improves upon the current literature in several ways. *First*, if investment law scholars have analysed some of the relevant cases, they have approached them from a mere investment law standpoint, leaving aside cultural arguments or merely citing them in passing. In sum, the cultural aspects of these cases have been neglected, while at the same time light has been shed on more conventional economic law topics, such as, inter alia, the definition of regulatory expropriation. Only recently has the linkage between international investment law and public policy objectives attracted scholarly analysis.[13]

*Second*, with regard to the existing literature on international investment law and other values,[14] the book takes the discussion into greater depth by focusing on the linkage between international investment law and culture. Culture is an inclusive concept, whose protection partially includes but also differs from the protection of environmental goods. *Third*, while there is a growing amount of literature on multinational corporations and the law,[15] the interplay between cultural heritage and investor rights has never been studied from a perspective internal to international investment law and arbitration. Thus, it is my belief that a thorough study is greatly needed.

*Fourth*, in a systemic perspective, this study complements the literature on the linkage between trade and culture by offering an updated and systematic analysis of the parallel linkage between investment and culture.[16] This scrutiny is needed because international investment law and arbitration complement the existing international trade regime in many ways. Although there is no single multilateral investment treaty, authors have stressed the emergence of an international investment regime.[17] In this context, investor–state arbitration constitutes a major

[13] See, e.g. S. Subedi, *International Investment Law: Reconciling Policy and Principle* (Oxford: Hart Publishing, 2008).

[14] See e.g. J. Viñuales, *Foreign Investment and the Environment in International Law* (Cambridge University Press, 2012); L. Cotula, *Human Rights, Natural Resources and Investment Law in a Globalized World* (Abingdon: Routledge, 2011); K. Tienhaara, *The Expropriation of Environmental Governance* (Cambridge University Press, 2009); S.F. Puvimanasinghe, *Foreign Investment, Human Rights and the Environment* (Leiden: Martinus Nijhoff, 2007).

[15] On multinational corporations and the law, see e.g. S. Picciotto, *Regulating Global Corporate Capitalism* (Cambridge University Press, 2011); P. Muchlinski, *Multinational Enterprises and the Law*, 2nd edn (Oxford University Press, 2007).

[16] On trade and culture, see note 11 above.

[17] See e.g. S.W. Schill, *The Multilateralization of International Investment Law* (Cambridge University Press, 2009).

development in international law and facilitates the access of foreign investors to justice.[18] At the same time, it may jeopardize the cultural policies of the host state if read in 'clinical isolation' from international public law.[19] Thus, an analysis and critical assessment of the interplay between the international investment regime and cultural heritage are urgently needed.

Finally, this book complements the existing literature on international cultural law.[20] While authors have explored the role of UNESCO in international cultural law rule-making,[21] little attention has been paid to the adjudication of disputes related to cultural heritage.[22] The book offers an extensive overview and critical assessment of the investor–state arbitrations that have involved cultural heritage.

As there is an increasing tension between two different sets of normative values, which is shown by the boom of relevant international disputes, this study aims to (1) map in a systematic and complete fashion the relevant investor–state arbitrations in order to give policy-makers, arbitrators, stakeholders and the public at large a complete survey of the existing arbitral case law concerning cultural elements; and (2) propose legal methods to reconcile these different values both *de lege lata* (i.e. interpreting the existing legal instruments) and *de lege ferenda* (amending the existing law or proposing the adoption of different legal provisions). In this sense, this study investigates whether or not culture can be mainstreamed into international investment law and arbitration, and if so, how. At the same time, this book cautions against an uncritical

[18] See generally J. Paulsson, *Denial of Justice in International Law* (Cambridge University Press, 2005).

[19] The term is borrowed from Appellate Body Report, *US Gasoline, United States Standards for Reformulated and Conventional Gasoline*, WT/DS2/AB/R, adopted 20 May 1996, at 16.

[20] See, e.g. J. A. R. Nafziger, R. K. Paterson and A. Dundes Renteln (eds.), *Cultural Law: International, Comparative and Indigenous* (Cambridge University Press, 2010); C. Forrest, *International Law and the Protection of Cultural Heritage* (Abingdon: Routledge, 2010); B. Hoffmann (ed.), *Art and Cultural Heritage: Law, Policy and Practice* (Cambridge University Press, 2006).

[21] See, e.g., A. Yusuf (ed.), *Standard-Setting in UNESCO: Normative Action in Education, Science and Culture* (Leiden: Brill, 2007).

[22] Most scholars have focused on the national case law. See e.g. S. von Schorlemer, 'Compliance with the UNESCO World Heritage Convention: Reflections on the Elbe Valley and the Dresden Waldschlösschen Bridge', *German YIL* 51 (2008), 321–90; B. W. Boer, 'World Heritage Disputes in Australia', *Journal of Environmental Law and Litigation* 7 (1992), 247–79. Other authors have focused on the regional case law. See e.g. H. Nathan, 'Creating an Ever Closer Union: The European Court of Justice and the Threat to Cultural Diversity', *Columbia J. of Transnational Law* (2008), 166–207.

merger and acquisition of cultural entitlements in international investment law and arbitration: it is submitted that while the state must comply with investment treaty provisions, certain cultural entitlements are linked to human dignity and to other human rights and may present higher status.

The key objective of the study is to find ways to reconcile economic development with cultural heritage protection. The underlying thesis of this work is that reconciliation is possible, and that development should be conceived as a broad concept inclusive not only of mere economic growth, but also of human flourishing and well-being to which cultural elements are crucial. This analysis contributes to the current discourse on global governance and the legitimacy of international investment law and arbitration, and strengthens the growing cognizance of the importance of effective protection of cultural heritage and diversity for peaceful relations between nations.

## Chapter plan

The book proceeds as follows. The first part of the book aims at defining the two fields of international cultural law and international investment law. The first chapter introduces the notion of cultural heritage and examines its regulation at the international law level. The second chapter briefly explores the rationale behind the protection of foreign direct investment and the elements of investment rules that will be of particular importance when considering their impact on cultural policies.

The second part of the book investigates the interplay between the protection of foreign direct investment and cultural policies in international investment law and arbitration, focusing on specific sectors such as the governance of world cultural heritage, underwater cultural heritage, cultural diversity, intangible heritage and indigenous heritage. In particular, the third chapter will scrutinize the areas of conflict between the protection of world cultural heritage and foreign direct investment. Chapters 4, 5 and 6 explore the interplay between foreign direct investment and underwater cultural heritage, cultural diversity, intangible heritage and indigenous cultural heritage. A rich collection of arbitrations provides evidence that the regime established according to investment treaties does not strike an appropriate balance between the different interests concerned, and that international law has not yet developed any institutional machinery for the protection of cultural values through investment dispute settlement.

The third part of the book analyses the available means for promoting consideration of cultural heritage in international investment law and arbitration, and suggests new methods and approaches. Chapter 7 is divided into two parts. The first part explores the possible synergies between foreign direct investment and cultural policies, suggesting the use of available mechanisms to better reconcile cultural values and investor rights. Viewed *de lege lata*, investment treaties should not be considered as self-contained regimes, but as an important component of public international law. Accordingly, this book argues that international investment law has to be consistent with international law and, therefore, must also be interpreted in accordance with customary rules of treaty interpretation. In the interpretation of investment treaties, arbitrators should take relevant international law into account. Traditional tools of treaty interpretation may contribute to reconciling foreign investment and cultural heritage in a harmonious fashion, as well as to the *humanization* of international investment law. The second part of Chapter 7 focuses on the mechanisms that *lex ferenda* can reconcile the protection of cultural heritage and the promotion of foreign direct investment including cultural exceptions. The conclusions will then sum up the key findings of the study.

## Methodological framework of the book

This book crosses traditional boundaries between academic disciplines to explore an area of inquiry at the crossroads between economics and culture. Therefore it presents both interdisciplinary and multidisciplinary aspects. Because of the interdisciplinary character of the research project, methods and insights of different disciplines and traditional fields of study are taken into account. In particular, reference is made to studies elaborated under the aegis of the UNESCO, in cultural economics literature and in cognate disciplines such as international relations, anthropology and art history.

Against this background, the analysis maintains a primarily legal character and rests on sound theoretical and empirical methodological grounds. The book rests on a firm theoretical standpoint, elaborated by Hart.[23] A 'moderate external point of view'[24] is adopted that combines 'explanation' (which implies the distance of the scientist, commitment to objectivity and focus on causality) with 'comprehension' (understanding

[23] H. L. A. Hart, *The Concept of Law* (Oxford: Clarendon Press, 1961). [24] *Ibid.*, pp. 86–8.

the inner logic of the object of study), and provides the rational structure on which the scientific nature of the approach is based. This approach does not follow a mere positivist stance, but considers the legal norms as the results of balance of interests. This is very appropriate to the study of international law which is the outcome of intense political processes and negotiations.

While the interrelationship between cultural policies and investor rights may be studied from a variety of different perspectives and institutional settings, this book adopts an 'internal' approach with respect to international investment law and arbitration. The choice of this approach is not meant to imply that the institutional setting of international investment law is to be preferred to other approaches for reconciling the interests at stake. On the contrary, it is acknowledged that other fora, like the International Court of Justice and regional human rights courts, represent useful alternatives. However, looking at the linkage between cultural policies and foreign direct investment from an inside view of international investment law allows a reflection on the emerging investment treaty arbitrations. Although investment treaty arbitration may not constitute the most ideal forum for the settlement of disputes with cultural elements, a rich case law has emerged in recent years. Therefore, an analysis and critical assessment of this emerging jurisprudence is necessary.

The experimental aspect of the work is based on the adoption of a double track. On the one hand, the book focuses on the impact of investors' rights on the five different but related categories of culture: (1) world cultural heritage; (2) underwater cultural heritage; (3) cultural diversity; (4) intangible heritage and (5) indigenous cultural heritage. Specific chapters of the book will be dedicated to an analysis of the interplay between international investment law and the relevant cultural policies governing each of these aspects, except for the linkage between cultural diversity and intangible heritage on the one hand, and foreign investment on the other, which will be discussed in Chapter 5 due to the conceptual closeness between cultural diversity and intangible heritage. Elements of intangible heritage will also be examined in the context of Chapter 6 dedicated to indigenous heritage. The way in which the work is organized aims to allow the reader to immediately identify thematic areas of interest.

On the other hand, within each of these tracks, the analysis proceeds by adopting investment law categories; and the relevant case studies are analysed according to the traditional elements of investment law. Thus, the book questions whether certain economic activities relating to the conservation of cultural heritage may constitute a form of investment; or whether certain regulations aimed at protecting cultural heritage may be deemed to amount to an expropriation and/or a violation of other standards vis-à-vis foreign investors. By adopting a double track, the methodological differences between the legal systems regulating foreign investments and cultural heritage respectively are acknowledged.

The choice of case studies that are factually rich is deliberate, in order to provide a proper context and to enable the reader to draw his or her own conclusions about the norms at play. This contrasts with the way in which cases are generally mentioned within international investment law and arbitration; investment law scholars and practitioners usually omit the statement of the facts, or they offer them sparsely to enucleate the *ratio decidendi*. While such a fact-elusive approach is most appropriate for those who scrutinize investment law per se; it may not be appropriate for inter-disciplinary and contextual analysis connecting international investment law and arbitration to other areas of the law. Only by providing the reader with proper context can he or she appreciate the full interaction between international investment law and the protection of cultural heritage.

There are, of course, limitations with this case method. For instance, only those investment treaty arbitrations and conflicts which received media attention or were available to the public could be scrutinized. There were cases in which there was not enough information to analyse. More generally, investment treaty arbitration constitutes a *post factum* dispute settlement mechanism mainly triggered by a foreign developer after a state has adopted cultural policies. Therefore, the cases are not representative of all threats to cultural heritage posed by foreign direct investment. However, they are still valuable for illuminating trends in international law.

Many conflicts of interests between developers, government actors and residents affected by projects are settled at a domestic level.[25] In some cases, even if state authorities are genuinely concerned about the impact on local communities, they balance the protection of cultural heritage against developmental goals, and forms of quantitative assessment

[25] See e.g. A. Perry-Kessaris, '*Anemos*-ity, *Apatheia*, *Enthousiasmos*: An Economic Sociology of Law and Wind Farm Development in Cyprus', *Journal of Law and Society* 40(1) (2013), 72 (discussing the development of wind farms in Cyprus and mentioning 'the cultural implications of a wind farm towering over an eighteenth-century mosque').

lead to the exploitation of natural resources and hence the destruction of significant cultural heritage.[26] In other cases, the identification of what is worth being protected can be a difficult political, aesthetic and social judgement. In a few cases, the official taste may diverge from international canons. Evidentiary problems may arise especially with regard to the demonstration of the importance of rural and indigenous heritage. In such cases, oral evidence of indigenous or local cultural practices is necessary.[27] Nonetheless, this type of evidence is often evaluated like any other.[28] Until recently, archaeological discourse has been dominated by non-indigenous stakeholders and 'some aspects of past land use fall completely outside the realm of Western understanding'.[29] For instance, given their focus on tangible heritage, 'archaeologists have often inadequately recognized trails, sacred sites, and other meaningful indicators of human presence and land use'.[30]

Finally, in post-conflict zones governments may favour development projects to the preservation of archaeological sites. For instance, Mes Aynak, an entirely buried Buddhist city – decaying remains of a wealthy and cosmopolitan culture that thrived in Afghanistan in the early centuries AD – is about to be destroyed for the planned development of a copper mine by a Chinese mining consortium which

[26] See e.g. *Kitkatla Band v. British Columbia (Minister of Small Business, Tourism and Culture)* 2002 SCC 31. File No. 27801. In this case, the Kitkatla Band challenged the legality of the permit authorizing the cutting of culturally modified trees during logging operations in British Columbia. Culturally modified trees – i.e. trees which bear the marks of past aboriginal use for artistic or ceremonial purposes or for indicating boundaries or trails – are part of indigenous cultural heritage. The Court held: 'heritage conservation schemes . . . must strike a balance between conservation and other societal interests which may require the destruction of heritage objects or sites . . . No heritage conservation scheme can provide absolute protection to all objects or sites that possess some historical, archaeological or cultural value to a society. To grant such an absolute protection would be to freeze a society at a particular moment in time.' *Ibid.* ¶ 45. For commentary, see C. Bell, 'Protecting Indigenous Heritage Resources in Canada: A Comment on *Kitkatla Band v. British Columbia*', *International Journal of Cultural Property* 10(2) (2001), 252 (pinpointing that 'Aboriginal perspectives . . . [we]re subordinated to what [wa]s considered "proper utilization of provincial lands and resources"').

[27] *Kitkatla Band v. British Columbia*, ¶ 46 (holding that '[oral evidence of Aboriginal values] should be assessed with understanding and sensitivity to the traditions of a civilization which remained an essentially oral one').

[28] *Ibid.*

[29] G. P. Nicholas, 'Decolonizing the Archaeological Landscape', *American Indian Quarterly* 30 (2006), 350–80, 351 and 354.

[30] *Ibid.* 361.

bought a 30-year lease on the entire site. According to the local authorities, the development of the copper mine could lead to the economic resurgence of the country as the valley contains potentially US$100bn worth of copper.[31] However, the copper cannot be extracted without destroying the entire hill on which the ruins are located.[32]

The intended readership for this book is that of specialists in the field of international law, cultural heritage scholars, policy-makers and practitioners. The book is of particular relevance to those working in the areas of the interplay between international economic law and national policies, international human rights, multinational corporations and the law, and global governance. In order to make the analysis relevant to the different targeted audiences, the language has deliberately been kept technical, but efforts have been undertaken to avoid assumptions and to achieve clarity and cohesion. As a result, this study will be of relevance for a wide audience, including but not limited to: international law scholars, investment law arbitrators and practitioners, and state officials, as well as cultural heritage experts and other interested audiences.

[31] W. Dalrymple, 'Mes Aynak: Afghanistan's Buddhist Buried Treasure Faces Destruction', *The Guardian*, 31 May 2013.

[32] E. Graham-Harrison, 'Mes Aynak Highlights Afghanistan's Dilemma over Protecting Heritage', *The Guardian*, 23 May 2013.

# PART I

## Cultural heritage and foreign direct investments: defining and connecting the two fields

# 1

# Cultural heritage in international law

*Vita brevis, ars longa*[1]

## Introduction

Culture is a multifaceted concept which represents inherited values, ideas, beliefs, and knowledge, which characterize social groups and their behaviour. The United Nations Educational, Scientific and Cultural Organization (UNESCO)[2] has defined culture as: 'the distinctive traits, including the total spiritual, material, intellectual and emotional traits that characterize a society or social group, and that include, in addition to arts and literature, their ways of life, the manner in which they live together, their value systems, and their traditions and beliefs.'[3] However, culture, as such, is not a static concept but rather a dynamic force, which evolves through time and crosses borders.

The interplay between law and culture is an ancient one, which can be traced back to the early being of mankind. As noted by Koren, in the history of Greece, Rome, the Middle Ages and the Renaissance and Baroque periods, evidence confirms the attempts by local legislators 'to confront the difficulties of preserving the heritage'.[4] For instance, the

1 Hippocrates, *Aphorismi Hippocratis (Hippocrates' Aphorisms)* (Amsterdam: Hendrik Wetstein, 1685) Section I, 1 ('Life is short, art endures'). Although 'art' (Latin: *ars*, Greek: τέχνη) is better interpreted as 'technique, craft' and not as 'fine art', Hippocrates being a doctor and this being the start of a medical text, the text here is translated more freely.

2 Constitution of the United Nations Educational, Scientific, and Cultural Organization (UNESCO Constitution), London, 16 November 1945, in force 4 November 1946, (1945) 4 UNTS 275.

3 Preamble to UNESCO's Universal Declaration on Cultural Diversity, Paris, 2 November 2001 (2002) 47 ILM 57.

4 G. Koren, 'Limitations in Enforcement of International Conventions: Implications for Protection of Monuments and Sites', in *Estrategias relativas al patrimonio cultural mundial. La salvaguardia en un mundo globalizado. Principios, practicas y perspectivas* (Madrid: ICOMOS, 2002), p. 90.

Athenians preserved Theseus' ship in the harbour as a memorial, replacing the old planks as they decayed with new and stronger timber, something which made the Greek philosophers debate whether the ship remained the same or whether it had become another boat.[5] In Olympia, the wooden pillars of the temple of Hera had been replaced with new pillars of marble.[6] In Rome, the emperor Theodoric the Great appointed an *architectus publicorum* to oversee the restoration of all important monuments in Rome, already the object of spoil and pillage.[7] Concerns about the destruction of Roman heritage and antiquities led to the appointment of Raphael as Commissioner of Monuments, with the role of overseeing all activities connected to ancient ruins. According to some, 'This can be considered as the first step towards the modern involvement of the state in the protection of monuments.'[8] Renaissance architects dedicated a more systematic interest in historic buildings and Leon Battista Alberti dedicated a chapter of his landmark treaty on building techniques to the restoration and maintenance of such buildings.[9]

However, for centuries cultural resources have been seen often as extras. As noted by Sax, 'the remains of old churches would unceremoniously be torn down to make way for new ones, and statues and columns were for centuries routinely recycled as building materials.'[10] Only in the twentieth century have cultural resources come into mainstream international law and policy,[11] moving from the margins to the forefront of legal debate. Although the 1907 Hague Convention concerning the law and customs of

[5] Plutarch, *Rise and Fall of Athens: Nine Greek Lives* (I. Scott Kilvert transl.) (New York: Penguin Books, 1960). The ship had to be maintained in a seaworthy state, for, in return for Theseus's successful mission, the Athenians had pledged to honour Apollo every year thereafter. Thus, pilgrims used to sail from Athens to the island of Delos, one of Apollo's most sacred sanctuaries, on a yearly basis.

[6] Koren, 'Limitations in Enforcement of International Conventions', p. 90.

[7] See generally J. Jokilehto, *A History of Architectural Conservation* (Oxford/Boston: Butterworth-Heinemann, 1999).

[8] D. D'Ayala and M. Forsyth, 'What is Conservation Engineering?', in M. Forsyth (ed.), *Structures and Construction in Historic Building Conservation* (Oxford: Blackwell Publishing, 2007), p. 3.

[9] L. B. Alberti, *De Re Aedificatoria* 1485 (transl. by J. Rykwert, R. Tavernor and N. Leach), *On the Art of Building in Ten Books* (Cambridge, MA: MIT Press, 1988).

[10] J. L. Sax, 'Heritage Preservation as a Public Duty: The Abbé Grégoire and the Origins of an Idea', *Michigan L. Rev.* 88 (1989–90), 1150.

[11] See generally P. Meerts (ed.), *Culture and International Law* (The Hague: T.M.C. Asser Press, 2008).

war protected historic monuments from bombardments,[12] and the 1931 Athens Charter marked the symbolic beginnings of international cultural cooperation in the preservation of artistic and historic monuments,[13] the first convention to introduce the notion of cultural property and to deal with it exclusively was adopted only after the Second World War, in response to the war's devastations.[14]

Against this background, the chapter proceeds as follows. First, it defines the concept of cultural heritage, sketching out its theoretical origins and contours in international law. The concept of cultural heritage is used in a broad fashion capturing a variety of cultural forms and expressions. This conceptual tool is particularly useful for mapping the different cultural offsprings and elucidating the regime complex which governs them at the international law level. Second, the chapter sketches the regulatory framework which governs cultural resources at the international level identifying five main paradigms or analytical lenses through which it can be scrutinized: (1) the property paradigm; (2) law and economics approaches; (3) human rights approaches; (4) the good cultural governance paradigm; and (5) the linkage paradigm. This book mainly adopts the last paradigm, in that it focuses on the specific interplay between cultural heritage and international investment law; nonetheless the other paradigms are briefly explored in this chapter in order to offer the reader a brief but systemic overview of the different layers of regulation that govern cultural heritage at the international law level. Third, the chapter addresses the linkage between culture and development. The chapter concludes with a reflection on the possible clash of cultures between international cultural law and international investment law.

[12] Convention (IV) respecting the Laws and Customs of War on Land and its annex: Regulations concerning the Laws and Customs of War on Land, The Hague, 18 October 1907, in force 26 January 1910; AJIL Supp. Vol 2 (1908) p. 90, Article 27; Convention (II) with Respect to the Laws and Customs of War on Land and its annex: Regulation concerning the Laws and Customs of War on Land: 29 July 1899, 32 Stat. 1803, 1 Bevans 247, in force 4 September 1900, Article 27; Hague Convention IX concerning Bombardment by Naval Forces in Time of War, 3 Martens Nouveau Recueil (ser. 3) 604, 205 Consol. T.S. 345, in force 26 January 1910, Article 5.

[13] The Athens Charter for the Restoration of Historic Monuments, Adopted at the First International Congress of Architects and Technicians of Historic Monuments, Athens 1931, available at www.icomos.org/en/charters-and-texts?id=167:the-athens-charter-for-the-restoration-of-historic-monuments.

[14] Hague Convention for the Protection of Cultural Property in the Event of Armed Conflict, Article 1, 14 May 1954, in force 7 August 1956, 249 UNTS 240.

## *1.1 Defining cultural heritage*

This book adopts a broad notion of cultural heritage as a concept encompassing a number of cultural resources. In this broad sense, cultural heritage includes five legal components: (1) world heritage (natural and cultural sites of outstanding and universal value); (2) cultural diversity (including a variety of cultural expressions); (3) intangible cultural heritage (traditions, folklore etc.); (4) underwater cultural heritage (objects that have been underwater for more than one hundred years); and (5) indigenous cultural heritage. The last category obviously partially overlaps with the other categories (world cultural heritage, cultural diversity, intangible cultural heritage and even underwater cultural heritage) and one could argue that there is no need to create an additional 'indigenous cultural heritage' category within the general concept of cultural heritage. Nonetheless, the category of indigenous cultural heritage deserves special scrutiny and attention because of its specific features. In fact, indigenous cultural heritage differs from the general notion of cultural heritage in that: it presents a holistic nature; it is related to land and natural resources; it involves collective and intergenerational custodianship; and it is based on customary law.[15]

Such categories may overlap as certain goods may belong to two or more categories. For instance, cultural landscapes inhabited by indigenous peoples are a form of indigenous cultural heritage; at the same time they may represent world heritage (if they present outstanding and universal value) and a form of intangible cultural heritage for their historical associative values. Analogously, maritime landscapes such as the Straits of Malacca constitute a World Heritage site and may include underwater cultural heritage.

Although such categories may overlap, their distinctiveness helps to frame legal discourse on the protection of cultural heritage. Thus, the structure of this book reflects this legal taxonomy and specific chapters are dedicated to the interplay between foreign direct investment and world cultural heritage, underwater cultural heritage, cultural diversity and intangible cultural heritage as well as indigenous cultural heritage. The scrutiny of the interplay between intangible cultural heritage and foreign direct investment in international investment law and arbitration is conducted in Chapters 5 and 6, which are dedicated to cultural

[15] See A. F. Vrdoljak, 'Reparations for Cultural Loss', in F. Lenzerini (ed.), *Reparations for Indigenous Peoples: International and Comparative Perspectives* (Oxford University Press, 2008), p. 199.

diversity, intangible heritage and indigenous heritage respectively, due to the close linkage and partial overlaps between these categories.

Cultural heritage is a multifaceted concept embodying both tangible and intangible cultural resources, capturing a variety of cultural forms and expressions and encompassing the various legal definitions in a holistic fashion. In order to properly conceptualize it, a useful starting point is the examination of its two elements: 'culture' and 'heritage'.

As mentioned, culture represents inherited values, ideas, beliefs and traditions which characterize social groups and their behaviour. Earlier studies distinguished between 'Culture' (with a capital) and 'culture' (lower-case), that is, between 'high arts and *belles lettres*' on the one hand, and culture in an anthropological sense, that is, the practices and traditions of a specific group on the other.[16] More recent studies have identified a tripartite meaning of culture: first, culture indicates the tangible outcome of cultural activities; second, culture means the process of artistic and scientific creativity; third, and in an 'anthropological' sense, culture refers to the way of life of a certain group that distinguishes it from other groups.[17] This composite definition has the theoretical merit of capturing the multifaceted concept of culture and has been gradually reflected in the UNESCO instruments which present a trend from protecting only masterpieces to protecting culture as a way of life and a process of artistic creation. For instance, the UNESCO Declaration on Cultural Diversity, defines culture as 'the set of distinctive spiritual, material, intellectual and emotional features of society or a social group . . . [I]t encompasses, in addition to art and literature, lifestyles, ways of living together, value systems, traditions and beliefs.'[18]

The term 'heritage' refers to something inherited from past generations, maintained in the present and bestowed for the benefit of future generations. Cultural heritage thus refers to the stock of culturally significant values and items belonging to a particular unit – individuals, communities or nations. Although questions can arise (and have arisen) as to the inclusion of given assets, the concept of cultural heritage expresses the idea of an abundance of culturally significant tangible

[16] L. V. Prott, 'Cultural Rights as Peoples' Rights in International Law', in J. Crawford (ed.), *The Rights of Peoples* (Oxford: Clarendon Press, 1988), p. 94.

[17] A. Eide, 'Cultural Rights as Individual Human Rights', in A. Eide *et al.* (eds.), *Economic, Social and Cultural Rights: A Textbook* (Boston: Martinus Nijhoff, 1995), pp. 230–1; R. Stavenhagen, 'Cultural Rights and Universal Human Rights', in Eide *et al.* (eds.), *Economic, Social and Cultural Rights*, pp. 65–6.

[18] UNESCO Declaration on Cultural Diversity, preamble.

and intangible items. Items which possess no value in the market may nonetheless qualify as cultural heritage and deserve protection at the international law level. In fact, there is a measure of incommensurability between culture and the market: some cultural items are not marketable because their value is incommensurable and far exceeds any possible economic valuation. Therefore, cultural heritage is not synonymous with the prosperity of nations, albeit the protection of cultural heritage may be a factor of sustainable development.

Cultural heritage can be an engine of growth and welfare, being central in wealth creation and people's lives, enriching their existence in both a material and immaterial sense. Cultural economic sociologists highlight 'the importance of culture inside actual economies, to utilise cultural wealth . . . to advance national prosperity'.[19] On the other hand, making a sustainable use of the valuable cultural resources that every society possesses and bringing them within the reach of everyone determines cultural empowerment, a tool for reducing disparities and enhancing individual capabilities.[20]

Here the expression 'cultural heritage' is preferred to that of 'cultural capital'. In economics, the concept of cultural capital conceives cultural goods as capital assets, and as instrumental to the production of further cultural goods and services.[21] However, this approach reifies culture as an object, separate from the people who interact with it, and suggests static, material and purely quantitative accumulation. Instead, cultural heritage is an expression which accommodates the dynamic nature of culture as an ever-changing force and alludes to the concept of common weal. As Coombe puts it, 'Culture considered as a resource encompasses a wider range of values than the purely economic emphasis that culture conceived of as an asset tends to project. These values include social cohesion, community autonomy [and] political recognition . . .'[22] In sum, the protection of cultural heritage encompasses human flourishing and dignity, as an alternative to materialistic rhetoric, and is a complement to sustainable growth.

[19] N. Bandelj and F. F. Wherry, 'Introduction: An Inquiry into the Cultural Wealth of Nations', in N. Bandelj and F. F. Wherry (eds.), *The Cultural Wealth of Nations* (Stanford, CA: Stanford University Press, 2011), p. 19.

[20] General Comment 21, ¶¶ 68–9.

[21] See D. Throsby, 'Cultural Capital', *Journal of Cultural Economics* 23 (1999), 3–12.

[22] R. Coombe, 'The Expanding Purview of Cultural Properties and Their Politics', *Annual Review of Law and Social Science* 5 (2009), 394.

Finally, cultural heritage encapsulates the concept of intragenerational and intergenerational equity, since cultural resources are to be maintained 'for some sort of common good'.[23] As one of the founders of modern international law once stated, depriving people of monuments of art is tantamount to declaring oneself 'an enemy to mankind'.[24] The tenet that the conservation of the artistic and archaeological property of mankind is one that interests the community of states was affirmed in the 1931 Athens Charter. The idea that cultural resources are of 'general interest to humanity' is also found in the 1954 Convention for the Protection of Cultural Property in the Event of Armed Conflict,[25] and the UNESCO Constitution.[26] The Rome Statute of the International Criminal Court[27] recognizes that the cultures of 'all peoples are united by common bonds, their cultures pieced together in a shared heritage' and that 'this delicate mosaic may be shattered at any time'.[28] A constant theme in UNESCO standard-setting is 'its emphasis on the need to protect cultural heritage for the sake of humanity – it is not trying to protect cultural monuments for their own sake nor . . . does it see them as more important than human beings themselves'.[29] At the same time, the protection of such cultural heritage must be seen as a component of international cooperation, 'reinforc[ing] the bonds between peoples which promote peace'.[30] All the nations of the world have cultural resources, albeit in different fashions and variable proportions. Cultural sociologists warn that it would be a mistake to measure cultural heritage by quantity or quality, stressing that the stock of cultural resources may change over time,[31] and that 'any region or nation in the world has latent cultural wealth'.[32]

[23] A. A. Bauer, 'New Ways of Thinking about Cultural Property: A Critical Appraisal of the Antiquities Trade Debate', *Fordham Int'l L. J.* 31 (2007–2008), 700.

[24] E. De Vattel, *The Law of Nations*, Book 3 Chapter 9, ¶ 168, J. Chitty (ed.) (Philadelphia: T. and J. W. Johnson & Co., 1883) quoted by R. Goy, 'La destruction intentionelle du patrimoine culturel en droit international', *RGDIP* 109 (2005), 273.

[25] Convention for the Protection of Cultural Property in the Event of Armed Conflict, preamble. 14 May 1954, 249 UNTS 240.

[26] Constitution of the United Nations Educational, Scientific and Cultural Organization, Paris, 16 November 1945, in force 4 November 1946, 4 UNTS 275, Article I(2)(c).

[27] Statute of the International Criminal Court, 17 July 1998, in force 1 July 2002, 37 ILM 999 [hereinafter ICC Statute].

[28] ICC Statute, preamble.

[29] P. J. O'Keefe and L. V. Prott, *Cultural Heritage Conventions and Other Instruments* (London: Institute of Art and Law, 2011), p. 8.

[30] *Commonwealth v Tasmania* (Franklin River Dam Case) [1983] 158 CLR 1 at 176.

[31] Bandelj and Wherry, 'Introduction: An Inquiry into the Cultural Wealth of Nations', pp. 2–8.

[32] *Ibid.*, at 8.

Cultural heritage does not refer to any form of collective, communal or internationalized property; rather this expression refers to the fact that the protection of cultural heritage promotes community interests and the common weal. Therefore, the concept of cultural heritage sensibly differs from the notion of common heritage of mankind.[33] The areas which are designated as 'common heritage' cannot be appropriated and/or be subject to claims of sovereignty; rather they are *res publica* governed by an international authority, and the profits derived from the exploitation of the common heritage are to be shared equitably and for the benefit of mankind.[34] If the concept of common heritage – which has been elaborated in relation to the status of resources in common spaces, notably the deep seabed and the moon[35] – has been used in some international cultural law instruments,[36] this indicates a general interest of the international community in the conservation and enjoyment of cultural resources, rather than excluding sovereignty and/or property over the same. The concept of common heritage in international cultural law does not have the same meaning as that used in the international law of the sea and in space law. In the cultural sector, such concept would be akin to the concept of *common concern of mankind*, developed in relation to environmental goods. Issues of common concern of humanity are those expressing a general interest that transcends state boundaries and requires collective action in response.[37] For instance, World Heritage sites, unlike the common heritage of mankind, remain subject to the territorial sovereignty of the territorial state, and property rights are left

[33] See R. Urueña Alvarez, 'La protección del patrimonio cultural en tiempo de guerra y de paz', *Cuadernos de Estudios Empresariales* 14 (2004), 260.

[34] K. Baslar, *The Concept of the Common Heritage of Mankind in International Law* (The Hague: Kluwer Law International, 1998), p. xxi; G. Nicholson, 'The Common Heritage of Mankind and Mining: An Analysis of the Law as to the High Seas, Outer Space, the Antarctic and World Heritage', *New Zealand J. of Environmental L.* 6 (2002), 178.

[35] For instance according to Article 136 of the UNCLOS the deep sea bed and ocean floor beyond the limits of national jurisdiction and its resources are the common heritage of mankind. United Nations Convention on the Law of the Sea, 10 December 1982, in force 28 July 1994 (1994) 33 ILM 1309. Analogously, Article 11(1) of the 1979 Moon Treaty provides that the moon and its resources are the common heritage of mankind. Agreement Governing the Activities of States on the Moon and Other Celestial Bodies, 5 December 1979 (1979) 18 ILM 1434.

[36] See e.g. the preamble of the Convention on the Protection of Underwater Cultural Heritage. Convention on the Protection of Underwater Cultural Heritage, 2 November 2001, in force 2 January 2009, 41 ILM 40.

[37] D. Shelton, 'Common Concern of Humanity', *Iustum Aequum Salutare* 5(2) (2009), 33–40.

untouched by the World Heritage Convention (WHC).[38] At the same time, state sovereign rights and private property rights must be exercised in such a way as to respect international law obligations requiring the state to protect cultural heritage sites located in its territory in the general interest of its population and the international community.

The notion of common heritage of humanity amounts to a 'revolution . . . in international relations' and presents controversial elements.[39] While it is favoured by developing countries – because if minerals found in the deep seabed are considered to be common heritage, then profits from the resources would have to be shared with the rest of the world – critics of this view, including the United States, argue that the concept of common heritage of mankind is 'founded on wishful thinking . . . and a serious philosophical misunderstanding of property rights and the true common heritage of humanity'.[40] By contrast, cultural heritage is not a revolutionary concept, but rather a useful conceptual framework and well-established legal category which reflects current trends and developments of international cultural law and its interactions with other fields of law.

## *1.2 The legal paradigms*

Cultural resources are governed by a legal matrix including national, regional and international regulatory frameworks and articulated in five theoretical and legal streams: (1) the property paradigm; (2) law and economics approaches; (3) human rights approaches; (4) the good cultural governance paradigm; and (5) the linkage paradigm.

The property paradigm approaches cultural goods focusing on their ownership. While the property paradigm as a tool for governing cultural goods has been predominant in the past, it now seems to be losing ground because of its inadequacies in dealing with the complexities of cultural phenomena. Given that law and economics approaches have provided useful insights on global common goods, this chapter also addresses the question as to whether cultural resources can be deemed to be global public goods. In addition, given the nexus between cultural heritage, human dignity and human rights, reference will be made to

[38] Convention concerning the Protection of the World Cultural and Natural Heritage (WHC), 16 November 1972, in force 17 December 1975, 1037 UNTS 151, 11 ILM 1358.

[39] A. Pardo, 'Ocean, Space and Mankind', *Third World Quarterly* 6 (1984), 559.

[40] See A. M. Cottrell, 'The Law of the Sea and International Marine Archaeology: Abandoning Admiralty Law to Protect Historic Shipwrecks', *Fordham Int'l. L. J.* 17 (1993–1994), 675.

human rights approaches. In parallel, international cultural law, as mainly elaborated under the aegis of the United Nations Educational, Scientific and Cultural Organization (UNESCO)[41] and in the form that has emerged in past decades, has provided parameters for good cultural governance. Finally, the linkage paradigm has explored the linkage between international cultural law and other fields of law such as international economic law.

This book mainly adopts the good cultural governance and the linkage paradigms, in that it focuses on the specific interplay between the protection of cultural heritage on the one hand and the promotion of foreign direct investment on the other in international investment law and arbitration, possibly contributing to the theoretical debate on the fragmentation or unity of international law.[42] Nonetheless, for the sake of analytical completeness, this chapter briefly explores these different paradigms to illuminate the meaning and content of a few terms and concepts that will be used throughout the book. The use of such a theoretical and legal framework also promotes the awareness of alternative and/or complementary viewpoints, addressing the field broadly at the point where diverse regulatory and theoretical traditions meet.

## 1.3 *The cultural property paradigm*

For centuries cultural outputs have been protected as a form of property.[43] According to this structure, movable cultural goods are personal property, cultural sites are real property,[44] and intangible cultural goods

41 UNESCO Constitution, 16 November 1945, in force 4 November 1946, 4 UNTS 275 (1945).

42 See e.g. R. Hofmann and C. J. Tams (eds.), *International Investment Law and General International Law* (Baden: Nomos, 2011); B. Simma, 'Foreign Investment Arbitration: A Place for Human Rights?', *ICLQ* 60 (2011), 573; B. Simma and T. Kill, 'Harmonizing Investment Protection and International Human Rights: First Steps towards a Methodology', in C. Binder, U. Kriebaum, A. Reinisch and S. Wittich (eds.), *International Investment Law for the 21st Century: Essays in Honour of Christoph Schreuer* (Oxford University Press, 2009); P. M. Dupuy, 'Unification Rather than Fragmentation of International Law? The Case of International Investment Law and Human Rights Law', in P. M. Dupuy, F. Francioni and E. U. Petersmann (eds.), *Human Rights in International Investment Law and Arbitration* (Oxford University Press, 2009); J. D. Fry, 'International Human Rights Law in Investment Arbitration: Evidence of International Law's Unity', *Duke J. of Comparative and Int'l L.* 77 (2007), 77–150.

43 J. Blake, 'On Defining the Cultural Heritage', *ICLQ* 49 (2001), 61.

44 Sax, 'Heritage Preservation as a Public Duty', 1142–5.

can be (but are not necessarily) a form of intellectual property.[45] Not only does the cultural property paradigm cross the boundaries between properties – real, personal, and intellectual – but it also crosses the boundaries between international, regional and domestic law. Due to the fact that the property paradigm is well established in most legal traditions, cultural property has mainly been regulated by the same provisions as other property, subject in some instances to derogations due to the cultural features of the protected good.

The cultural property paradigm is the most traditional way to govern cultural phenomena at the international law level. The 1954 Hague Convention on the Protection of Cultural Property in the Event of Armed Conflict defines cultural property as 'movable or immovable property of great importance to the cultural heritage of every people, such as monuments of architecture, art or history, whether religious or secular; archaeological sites . . .; works of art; manuscripts, books and other objects of artistic, historical or archaeological interest'.[46] Other international law instruments protecting cultural property followed, including the 1970 Convention on the Means of Prohibiting and Preventing the Illicit Import, Export and Transfer of Ownership of Cultural Property[47] and the 1999 Second Protocol to the Hague Convention of 1954 for the Protection of Cultural Property in the Event of Armed Conflict.[48]

However, recent shifts in international law highlight that the cultural property protection paradigm has increasingly been perceived as inadequate and that other approaches are gaining pre-eminence.[49] Admittedly, cultural property embodies 'several layers of incompatibility from within'.[50] First,

45 See R. Coombe, 'The Expanding Purview of Cultural Properties and their Politics', *Annual Review of Law and Social Sciences* 5 (2009), 394; S. Scafidi, 'Intellectual Property and Cultural Products', *Boston University Law Rev.* 81 (2001), 793–842; R. Coombe, 'First Nations' Intangible Cultural Heritage Concerns: Prospects for Protection of Traditional Knowledge and Traditional Cultural Expressions in International Law', in C. Bell and R. Paterson (eds.), *Protection of First Nations' Cultural Heritage: Laws, Policy and Reform* (Vancouver: University of British Columbia Press, 2008).

46 Hague Convention for the Protection of Cultural Property in the Event of Armed Conflict, Article 1.

47 Convention on the Means of Prohibiting and Preventing the Illicit Import, Export and Transfer of Ownership of Cultural Property, 14 November 1970, 823 UNTS 231.

48 Second Protocol to the Hague Convention of 1954 for the Protection of Cultural Property in the Event of Armed Conflict, 26 March 1999, 38 ILM 769.

49 See, e.g. M. Frigo, 'Cultural Property v. Cultural Heritage: A Battle of Concepts in International Law?', *International Review of the Red Cross* 86 (2004), 367–78.

50 K. A. Carpenter, S. K. Katyal and A. R. Riley, 'In Defense of Property', *Yale L. J.* 118 (2009), 1038.

the cultural property paradigm is based upon two potentially conflicting elements: 'culture' which encapsulates collective values; and 'property' which is an individual right.[51] The cultural property model has been perceived as not entirely satisfying as it tends to prioritize the interests of the right holder vis-à-vis those of society despite the fact that 'the fate of some objects is momentous for the community at large'.[52]

Second, the property model also presents a formalistic and rigid structure which may be inadequate to address incommensurable and inalienable aspects of culture.[53] For instance, the Lakota refuse to accept monetary compensation for the loss of the Black Hills – a sacred place which was removed from their ownership in the late nineteenth century.[54] Furthermore, some authors contend that 'Within cultural property discourse, the idea of property has so colonized the idea of culture that there is not much culture left in cultural property.'[55] In this sense, the expansive character of the notion of property has even led some scholars to deem cultural property not sufficiently dissimilar from ordinary property to justify its distinct regulation.[56]

Third, questions have arisen as to whether intangible forms of cultural heritage are adequately protected by intellectual property. The notion of cultural property is rooted in the Western intellectual tradition;[57] and 'Western societies prize material possession over process'.[58] However, other societies, for instance indigenous peoples, refuse a compartmentalized vision of culture; rather they adopt a holistic approach to nature and culture. Therefore, intellectual property is unable to capture the importance of cultural processes such as rituals and folklore and the anthropological meaning of culture as a way of life.[59]

[51] P. Gerstenblith, 'Identity and Cultural Property: The Protection of Cultural Property in the United States', *Boston University Law Rev.* 75 (1995), 567.

[52] J. Sax, *Playing Darts with a Rembrandt: Public and Private Rights in Cultural Treasures* (Ann Arbor, MI: University of Michigan Press, 1999), p. 4.

[53] N. Mezey, 'The Paradoxes of Cultural Property', *Columbia Law Review* 107 (2007), 2005.

[54] R. Tsosie, 'Land, Culture and Community: Envisioning Native American Sovereignty and National Identity in the 21st Century', *International Social Science Review* 2 (2001), 185–7.

[55] *Ibid.*

[56] See E. A. Posner, 'The International Protection of Cultural Property: Some Skeptical Observations', *Chicago JIL* 8 (2007), 213.

[57] K. Last, 'The Resolution of Cultural Property Disputes: Some Issues of Definition' in International Bureau of the Permanent Court of Arbitration (ed.), *Resolution of Cultural Property Disputes* (The Hague: Kluwer Law International, 2004), p. 55.

[58] S. Harding, 'Value, Obligation and Cultural Heritage', *Arizona State L. J.* 31 (1999), 309.

[59] See, inter alia, R. Coombe and J. Turcotte, 'Indigenous Cultural Heritage in Development and Trade: Perspectives from the Dynamics of Cultural Heritage Law and Policy' in C. Beat

Finally, as Blake has pointed out, 'Implicit . . . in the use of the term "cultural property" is the idea of assigning to it a market value, in other words the "commodification" of cultural artefacts and related elements by treating them as commodities to be bought and sold.'[60] While classic economic theories of property are based on the assumption of fungibility, cultural phenomena may present unique features that cannot be replaced.[61]

Against this background, in the past decades, the concept of cultural heritage has emerged.[62] The shift to cultural property as world 'heritage' occurred with the WHC. While respecting the national sovereignty and the property rights provided by national legislations,[63] the states parties recognized that 'world heritage' – i.e. natural and cultural sites of outstanding universal value – should be protected in the interest of humanity as a whole.[64] The more recent UNESCO instruments also refer to cultural heritage rather than cultural property.[65]

Cultural heritage is a protean concept that is difficult to define. Further ambiguity arises from the fact that the various language versions of the term do not convey exactly the same meaning,[66] and each international instrument provides its own definition of the concept to delimit its scope of application.[67] Finally, like the concept of cultural property, cultural heritage owes its indefinite nature to its cultural component, and its reliance on disciplines such as art history, archaeology, anthropology and others.[68]

The concept of heritage does not replace the notion of cultural property but constitutes an addition to the same. The concept of 'heritage' is distinguished from that of 'property' for three different albeit related reasons. First, cultural heritage embodies a sense of legacy, expressing

Graber, K. Kuprecht and J. C. Lai (eds.), *International Trade in Indigenous Cultural Heritage* (Cheltenham: Edward Elgar Publishing, 2012), pp. 272–305.

60 Blake, 'On Defining the Cultural Heritage', 66.

61 Carpenter, Katyal and Riley, 'In Defense of Property', 1038.

62 See e.g. L. V. Prott and P. J. O'Keefe, '"Cultural Heritage" or "Cultural Property?"', *Int'l J. of Cultural Property* 1 (1992), 307.

63 WHC, Article 6. 64 WHC, Articles 1 and 2.

65 See e.g. the Convention on the Protection of Underwater Cultural Heritage and the Convention for the Safeguarding of Intangible Cultural Heritage. Convention on the Protection of Underwater Cultural Heritage, 2 November 2001, in force 2 January 2009, 41 ILM 40; Convention for the Safeguarding of the Intangible Cultural Heritage, 17 October 2003, in force 20 April 2006, 2368 UNTS 3.

66 Frigo, 'Cultural Property v. Cultural Heritage', 370. 67 *Ibid.*, 375. 68 *Ibid.*, 376.

a public interest to be protected irrespective of ownership.[69] Cultural heritage conservation contributes to a sense of identity as well as to intergenerational and intragenerational equity. As Prott and O'Keefe highlight, 'Heritage creates a perception of something handed down; something to be cared for and cherished. These cultural manifestations have come down to us from the past; they are our legacy from our ancestors. Today there is a broad acceptance of a duty to pass them on to our successors . . .'[70] Second, cultural heritage is best viewed as including cultural property rather than replacing the same concept.[71] This view is also reflected in the 1954 Hague Convention which refers to cultural property as 'property of great importance to the cultural heritage'.[72] In fact, the notion of heritage includes both tangible and intangible elements.[73] Third, as Blake puts it, cultural heritage is an inclusive notion, which 'has grown beyond the much narrower definitions included on a text-by-text basis'.[74] At the same time, it constitutes an important corrective to many of the limitations inherent in applying the concept and law of property to culture.[75]

The emergence of the concept of cultural heritage has not entailed the abandonment of the property paradigm. Adopting an evolutionary interpretation of treaties, some international courts and tribunals have interpreted property as inclusive of immaterial and collective elements. For instance the Inter-American Court of Human Rights has interpreted the sense and scope of the right to property, under Article 21 of the American Convention, as entailing collective entitlements and indigenous heritage.[76] More generally, even property law scholars deem that property should be conceived of as a system of social relations that takes

[69] See F. Francioni, 'Culture, Heritage and Human Rights: An Introduction', in F. Francioni and M. Scheinin (eds.), *Cultural Human Rights* (Leiden/Boston: Martinus Nijhoff, 2007), p. 5.

[70] Prott and O'Keefe, '"Cultural Heritage" or "Cultural Property?"', 311.

[71] Blake, 'On Defining the Cultural Heritage', 66.

[72] Hague Convention for the Protection of Cultural Property in the Event of Armed Conflict, 14 May 1954, in force 7 August 1956, 249 UNTS 240, Article 1.

[73] F. Lenzerini, 'Intangible Cultural Heritage: The Living Culture of Peoples', *EJIL* 22 (2011), 103–8.

[74] Blake, 'On Defining the Cultural Heritage', 64.

[75] Prott and O'Keefe, '"Cultural Heritage" or "Cultural Property?"', 312.

[76] IACHR, *Case of the Mayagna (Sumo) Awas Tingni Community v. Nicaragua. Merits, Reparations and Costs*, Judgment of 31 January 2001, series C No. 79, ¶ 149. IACHR, *Case of the Yakye Axa Indigenous Community v. Paraguay. Merits, Reparations and Costs*, Judgment of 17 June 2005, Series C No. 125, ¶¶ 124, 131.

into account the rights of owners and the public,[77] and that the concept of property should be broadened to encompass the concept of stewardship or non-owners' fiduciary obligations toward cultural resources.[78]

Without delving into the complexities of property theory, this book adopts the concept of cultural heritage rather than that of cultural property, following current treaty practice. When dealing with cultural heritage the main concern of this book is not that regarding the question of who owns culture; rather it is the question as to whether cultural heritage is adequately protected vis-à-vis economic interests in international investment law and arbitration.

### *1.4 Cultural heritage as a global public good*

Cultural heritage can be scrutinized adopting approaches from law and economics. Such approaches refer to the application of the methods of economics to legal problems, and/or the use of economic concepts in the context of legal analysis.[79] Economic analysis of law has been extremely influential especially in the last quarter of the twentieth century, and has been applied to many branches of law including international law.[80]

Adopting such an approach, one may question whether cultural heritage can be categorized as a global public good, given the collective benefits it provides and its positive intergenerational and intragenerational spillovers.[81] Global public goods present two main features: (1) they present an element of publicness; and (2) they have a global nature.[82] With regard to the first feature, although the concept of public goods traces its roots back to antiquity, originating in the writings of Plato, Aristotle and Cicero (*res publica*),[83] the current meaning of 'public goods' as goods that are

[77] J. W. Singer, *Entitlement: The Paradoxes of Property* (New Haven, CT: Yale University Press, 2000), pp. 95–139.

[78] Carpenter, Katyal and Riley, 'In Defense of Property', 1022.

[79] See generally R. A. Posner, *Economic Analysis of Law*, 6th edn (Aspen Publishers, 2003).

[80] See generally S. R. Ratner and A.-M. Slaughter, 'Appraising the Methods of International Law: A Prospectus for Readers', *AJIL* 93 (1999), 291–302; J. L. Dunoff and J. P. Trachtman, 'Economic Analysis of International Law', *Yale JIL* 24 (1999), 1.

[81] See T. Sandler, 'Intergenerational Public Goods', in I. Kaul, I. Grunberg and M. A. Stern (eds.), *Global Public Goods: International Cooperation in the 21st Century* (New York: UNDP, 1999), p. 20.

[82] I. Kaul, I. Grunberg and M. A. Stern, 'Defining Global Public Goods', in Kaul, Grunberg and Stern (eds.), *Global Public Goods*, p. 2.

[83] M. Velasquez, C. Andre, T. Shanks and M. Meyer, 'The Common Good', *Issues in Ethics* 5 (1992), 1.

non-rivalrous and non-excludable derives from the economic literature.[84] Non-rivalry is the ability of multiple consumers to consume the same good; and non-excludability means that no one can be excluded from using the good. Common examples of public goods can be found in lighthouses, clean air and environmental goods.[85] With regard to the second feature of global public goods, their global character is given by the fact that their benefits are almost universal in terms of countries, peoples and generations.[86]

A number of cultural goods present the features of (global) public goods as they provide collective benefits and intergenerational and intra-generational spillovers. For instance, a poem can be read by many people without reducing the enjoyment of that good by others. Similarly, cathedrals, mosques, synagogues and equivalent buildings of cultural significance constitute public goods 'to the extent that, first, no-one can be excluded from the complex combination of benefits that they give, including identity formation and architectural beauty, and, second, the appreciation of them by some does not reduce the possibility of others receiving the same benefits'.[87] In the same fashion, a World Heritage site can be visited by some without reducing the enjoyment of the site by others. However, cultural goods may also belong to private owners, and some aspects of cultural heritage conservation can be privatized – for example, access to a site can be restricted and money charged. Thus, only some components of cultural heritage can be categorized as public goods in a strict economic sense.

If one adopts a legal notion of public goods as goods which are shaped and constituted by law, and which benefit and matter to all states or humankind as a whole, cultural goods can be considered public goods, because their benefits extend to both developing and industrialized countries, rich and poor, and to people of different cultures.[88] The conceptualization of cultural resources as an international public good or cultural heritage of mankind is evident in a number of international law instruments, such as the 1954 Hague Convention for the Protection

[84] P. Samuelson, 'The Pure Theory of Public Expenditure', *Review of Economics and Statistics* 36 (1954), 387.

[85] R. H. Coase, 'The Lighthouse in Economics', *Journal of Law and Economics* 17 (1974), 357–76.

[86] Kaul, Grunberg and Stern, 'Defining Global Public Goods', p. 3.

[87] S. Deneulin and N. Townsend, 'Public Goods, Global Public Goods and the Common Good', *International J. of Social Economics* 34 (2007), 19–36.

[88] F. Francioni, 'Public and Private in the International Protection of Global Cultural Goods', *EJIL* 23 (2012), 719.

of Cultural Property in the Event of Armed Conflict, which recognizes that 'damage to cultural property belonging to any people whatsoever means damage to the cultural heritage of all mankind, since each people makes its contribution to the culture of the world'.[89] Similarly the 1972 World Heritage Convention acknowledges that 'deterioration or disappearance of any item of the cultural or natural heritage constitutes a harmful impoverishment of the heritage of all the nations of the world'.[90] Even cultural rights present a collective dimension: while human rights treaties define cultural rights as individual rights, their enjoyment is necessarily linked to the other members of a given cultural community.[91]

As public goods, cultural goods cannot easily be provided by the 'invisible hand' of the market. While private markets financed by admission revenue, sponsorship and donations can foster the recovery and protection of cultural goods, market forces alone may not supply or ensure the adequate protection of such goods efficiently.[92] As a seminal study highlighted, 'there will be cases where the market can work reasonably efficiently and cases where it may not'.[93] In some cases, cultural goods are characterized by market failures as their value is mainly historical or archaeological rather than economic. For instance, if the economic value of a building is less than the value of the land plus the value of what can be recovered from the demolition of that building, then – adopting pure economic efficiency criteria – demolition would be the most efficient use of the property.[94] Furthermore, some types of cultural activities may gradually become obsolete vis-à-vis new forms; the fact that they are not marketable does not imply that they do not hold cultural value. Finally, in other cases, an excessive commercialization of cultural resources can jeopardize their conservation; for instance, overcrowding may result in degradation or physical damage to heritage sites.[95] In case of market

89 Hague Convention for the Protection of Cultural Property in the Event of Armed Conflict, 14 May 1954, in force 7 August 1956, 249 UNTS 240, preamble.
90 WHC, preamble.
91 Y. Donders, 'Culture and Human Rights', in P. Forsythe (ed.), *Encyclopedia of Human Rights* (Oxford University Press, 2009), p. 445.
92 United Nations Industrial Development Organization, *Public Goods for Economic Development* (Vienna: UNIDO, 2008), p. 6.
93 A. Peacock, 'Preserving the Past: An International Economic Dilemma', *Journal of Cultural Economics* 2 (1978), 2.
94 See R. D. Hale, 'Economic Aspects of Historic Preservation', *Journal of Cultural Economics* 2 (1978), 45.
95 A. L. Barfelz, 'The Little Island that Could: How Reforming Cultural Preservation Policies Can Save Easter Island and the World's Heritage', *Mich. St. Int'l L. Rev.* 20 (2011), 154.

failures, government intervention is necessary to govern cultural goods for the common weal.[96] In turn, international regulation allows states to address the shortcomings of national regulation.[97] Finally, international regulation is needed because 'nations and regions may not fully, or sufficiently, appreciate the value of cultural and natural sites as a global public good'.[98]

According to mainstream economic literature, two main problems affect the provision of public goods: (1) free riding; and (2) the prisoner's dilemma.[99] Free riding refers to the powerful incentive to avoid contributing personal resources to common endeavours. Let us consider the following example. Ancient shipwrecks constitute an important source of knowledge and the recent UNESCO Convention on the Protection of the Underwater Cultural Heritage requires their conservation. While a number of states have ratified the Convention, other states are reluctant to do so, fearing that by ratifying the Convention they could jeopardize the 'salvage' industry, that is, the number of companies that after locating shipwrecks claim property or a salvage award recovering their expenses through the sale of the recovered artefacts. While the salvage industry seems to be a profitable one, underwater cultural heritage is a finite resource; and once the goods are sold they are lost forever. If a state behaves as a pure *homo oeconomicus*, i.e. rational and narrowly self-interested human, it will seek to 'free ride' by allowing others to commit themselves to a binding regime, and then allow its nationals to exploit scarce and finite underwater resources. If the free-rider problem cannot be solved, valuable cultural resources will remain unprotected and over-exploited.[100] Hardin reformulated this problem, calling it the 'tragedy of the commons': where the pursuit of individual self-interest can jeopardize natural resources that should sustain current and future generations.[101]

The prisoner's dilemma refers to a situation in which cooperation would lead to a better outcome, but individual players driven by self-interest prefer a less desirable outcome.[102] In the imagined scenario

[96] UNIDO, *Public Goods for Economic Development*, p. 1.

[97] A. Efrat, 'A Theory of Internationally Regulated Goods', *Fordham Int'l L. J.* 32 (2008–2009), 1467.

[98] B. S. Frey and L. Steiner, 'World Heritage List: Does it Make Sense?', *International Journal of Cultural Policy* 17 (2011), 567.

[99] Kaul, Grunberg and Stern, 'Defining Global Public Goods', p. 6.

[100] See T. Cowen, 'Public Goods', in D. E. Anderson (ed.), *The Concise Encyclopedia of Economics*, 2nd edn (Monterey, CA: Liberty Fund Inc., 2005).

[101] G. Hardin, 'The Tragedy of the Commons', *Science* 162 (1968), 1244.

[102] Kaul, Grunberg and Stern, 'Defining Global Public Goods', pp. 7–8.

two prisoners are held in separate cells and so are unable to agree on a common line of defence.[103] In the meantime the prosecutors give the prisoners the following three options: (1) if both prisoners deny the charge they will each get one year in prison; (2) if one confesses while the other denies, the one who collaborates will be rewarded with freedom, while the other will spend five years in prison; (3) if both confess, each will spend three years in prison.[104] Both prisoners select the option of confessing in the attempt to minimize the higher risk.[105] Lacking the ability to communicate, they also lack the possibility to cooperate and thus to optimize their chances.[106]

The prisoner's dilemma clarifies that parties to a regime may have an incentive to deviate from it, unless mechanisms are established to facilitate communication and cooperation.[107] For instance, states may have economic incentive to deviate from the World Heritage Convention, which demands the conservation of World Heritage sites, when a particular heritage site presents mineral resources and is thus suitable for mineral exploitation. However, the risk that a particular site be delisted from the World Heritage List and inserted in the List of World Heritage in Danger constitutes a mechanism of blame and shame, and a number of states have taken action to prevent delisting because of consequential loss of reputation.[108]

Conceptualizing cultural heritage as global common good is useful in that it emphasizes the positive spillovers and common benefits that derive from cultural assets. The paradigm also provides useful theoretical tools for examining state conduct and the pervasive role of private actors in the cultural domain. However, the use of approaches from law and economics is not meant to be resolutive but to be a component in a broader analysis. Fundamental criticisms have been levelled at law and economics approaches. For instance, economic analysis does not capture the importance of non-economic concerns which characterize legal systems,[109] and often assumes the existence of unique optimal results.[110]

[103] *Ibid.*, p. 7. [104] *Ibid.* [105] *Ibid.* [106] *Ibid.* [107] *Ibid.*, p. 8.

[108] According to Ohlin, states make strategic decisions in light of strategies selected by other states, thus generating Nash equilibria and, ultimately, a stable social contract. See J. D. Ohlin, 'Nash Equilibrium and International Law', *Cornell L. Rev.* 96 (2010–2011), 869.

[109] See e.g. R. C. Ellickson, 'Bringing Culture and Human Frailty to Rational Actors: A Critique of Classical Law and Economics', *Chicago Kent L. Rev.* 65 (1989), 23; R. A. Epstein, 'Law and Economics: Its Glorious Past and Cloudy Future', *University of Chicago L. Rev.* 64 (1997), 1167; G. J. Stigler, 'Law or Economics?', *Journal of Law and Economics* 35 (1992), 455–68.

[110] W. Samuels, *The Legal-Economic Nexus* (Abingdon: Routledge, 2007), pp. 23–4.

### 1.5 *Human rights approaches*

Cultural heritage can be (and has been) scrutinized through the lens of cultural rights and other human rights. Although a right to cultural heritage does not yet belong to the human rights pantheon, one may deem that rights relating to cultural heritage are inherent in cultural rights. Cultural rights are deemed to include the interplay between individuals and their cultural expressions, including cultural heritage.[111] Furthermore, the protection of cultural heritage is deeply linked to human dignity and cultural identity promoting the enjoyment of other human rights. Such linkages are acknowledged, for instance, by the Council of Europe Framework Convention on the Value of Cultural Heritage for Society (Faro Convention)[112] which recognizes that 'every person has a right to engage with the cultural heritage of their choice, while respecting the rights and freedoms of others, as an aspect of the right to participate freely in cultural life'.[113] Analogously, the 1981 Banjul Charter of the Organization of African Unity (OAU)[114] refers to the right of all people to 'their economic, social and cultural development with due regard to their freedom and identity and in the equal enjoyment of the cultural heritage of mankind'.[115] The United Nations Declaration on the Rights of Indigenous Peoples (UNDRIP)[116] provides that indigenous peoples 'have the right to . . . maintain, protect and have access . . . to their religious and cultural sites', and 'the right to maintain, control, protect and develop their cultural heritage'.[117]

More generally, a human rights-based approach to cultural heritage centres on the human dimension of heritage discourse expressing 'the need to put people and human values at the centre of an enlarged and cross-disciplinary concept of cultural heritage'.[118] UN Independent Expert on Cultural Rights, Farida Shaheed, highlighted that: 'Access to and enjoyment of cultural heritage as a human right is a necessary and

[111] See General Comment 21, ¶ 15 (b).

[112] Council of Europe Framework Convention on the Value of Cultural Heritage for Society, 27 October 2005, CETS No. 199 (hereinafter Faro Convention).

[113] Faro Convention, preamble.

[114] African Charter on Human Rights and Peoples' Rights ('Banjul Charter'), adopted by the Organization of African Unity (OAU) in 1981, 21 ILM 58.

[115] Banjul Charter, Article 22.1.

[116] United Nations Declaration on the Rights of Indigenous Peoples (UNDRIP), G.A. Res. 61/295, UN Doc. A/RES/61/295, adopted by the General Assembly on 13 September 2007, 46 ILM 1013 (2007).

[117] UNDRIP, Articles 12(1) and 31.

[118] Faro Convention, preamble.

complementary approach to the preservation/safeguard of cultural heritage. Beyond preserving/safeguarding an object ... in itself, it obliges one to take into account the rights of individuals and communities in relation to such objects ... and, in particular, to connect cultural heritage with its source of production. Cultural heritage is linked to human dignity and identity. Accessing and enjoying cultural heritage is an important feature of being a member of a community, a citizen and, more widely, a member of society.'[119]

A necessary corollary of a human rights-based approach to cultural heritage is that any meaningful protection of cultural heritage needs to respect fundamental human rights and freedoms. In this sense, the Faro Convention acknowledges that 'everyone, alone or collectively, has the responsibility to respect the cultural heritage of others as much as their own heritage' and that 'exercise of the right to cultural heritage may be subject only to those restrictions which are necessary in a democratic society for the protection of the public interest and the rights and freedoms of others'.[120] If a conflict arises between cultural entitlements and other human rights, international law instruments address this tension in favour of internationally proclaimed human rights.[121] Cultural entitlements are neither absolute nor unlimited.

Notwithstanding early case law and the formal entry of cultural rights into the human rights pantheon after the Second World War,[122] cultural rights have been neglected for a long time and have been less developed than civil, political, economic and social rights.[123] In the human rights discourse, cultural rights are considered to be the 'second generation', in contrast to civil and political rights, which are referred to as the 'first generation' of human rights.[124] Furthemore, while the expression 'economic,

119 UNGA, HRC, Report of the Independent Expert in the Field of Cultural Rights, Farida Shaheed, 21 March 2011, UN Doc.A/HRC/17/38, para. 2, available at www.unesco.org/new/fileadmin/MULTIMEDIA/HQ/CLT/images/Report%20of%20Farida%20Shaheed.pdf.

120 Faro Convention, Article 4.

121 Convention for the Elimination of All Forms of Racial Discrimination, Article 7; Convention on the Elimination of All Forms of Discrimination against Women, Article 5. International Convention on the Elimination of All Forms of Racial Discrimination, in force 4 January 1969, 660 UNTS 195. Convention on the Elimination of All Forms of Discrimination against Women, in force 3 September 1981, 1 UNTS 1249, p. 13.

122 See, for instance, Universal Declaration of Human Rights (UDHR), G.A. Res. 217 A, UNGAOR, 3rd Sess., UN Doc. A/810 (1948), adopted on 10 December 1948, Article 22.

123 See J. Symonides, 'Cultural Rights: A Neglected Category of Human Rights', *International Social Science Journal* 158 (1998), 559.

124 M. A. Baderin and R. McCorquodale, 'The International Covenant on Economic, Social and Cultural Rights: Forty Years of Development', in R. G. McCorquodale and

social and cultural rights' is commonly used, 'in most cases the concern appears to be limited to the economic and social rights'.[125]

The International Covenant on Civil and Political Rights (ICCPR)[126] recognizes the cultural rights of ethnic, religious and linguistic minorities.[127] Given the fact that cultural rights 'connect or overlap other categories of human rights', being strictly related to freedom of expression, freedom of religion, freedom of association and private and family life to mention a few, cultural entitlements have received a general albeit indirect protection by the Covenant under related provisions.[128] Other international law instruments, including the International Covenant on Economic, Social and Cultural Rights[129] and the Universal Declaration on Human Rights do refer to cultural rights, including a number of different entitlements, such as: the right to education; the right to participate in cultural life; the right to enjoy the benefits of scientific progress; the freedom for scientific research; and the possibility for individuals to speak their own dialects, to name a few.[130]

The reasons why cultural rights are a less developed legal category vis-à-vis other human rights are complex and have a legal and political nature. From a legal standpoint, cultural rights remain difficult to define,[131] as they relate to culture that has a fluid and elusive nature and adopts different forms across time and space. Definitions of culture, thus, rarely succeed in capturing its essence. From a political standpoint, governments have feared that cultural entitlements could determine claims of self-determination

M. A. Baderin (eds.), *Economic, Social and Cultural Rights in Action* (Oxford University Press, 2007), pp. 3–24.

[125] A. Eide, 'Cultural Rights as Individual Human Rights', in A. Eide *et al.* (eds.), *Economic, Social and Cultural Rights: A Textbook* (Dordrecht: Martinus Nijhoff, 1995), p. 229.

[126] International Covenant on Civil and Political Rights (ICCPR), 16 December 1966, in force 23 March 1976, 6 ILM 368 (1967).

[127] ICCPR, Article 27.

[128] For instance, in the case of *Francis Hopu and Tepoaitu Bessert v. France*, the claimants complained that 'the construction of [a] hotel complex on the contested site would destroy their ancestral burial grounds, which represent an important place in their history, culture and life, and would arbitrarily interfere with their privacy and their family lives, in violation of articles 17 and 23 [of the Covenant]'. *Francis Hopu and Tepoaitu Bessert v. France*, Communication No. 549/1993, UN Doc. CCPR/C/60/D/549/1993/Rev.1. (1997) at ¶ 10.3.

[129] International Covenant on Economic, Social and Cultural Rights (ICESCR), 16 December 1966, in force 3 January 1976, 993 UNTS 3.

[130] E. Stamatopoulou, *Cultural Rights in International Law* (Leiden/Boston: Martinus Nijhoff Publishers, 2007), p. 110.

[131] A. Yupsanis, 'The Concept and Categories of Cultural Rights in International Law: Their Broad Sense and the Relevant Clauses of the Human Rights Treaties', *Syracuse JIL and Commerce* 37 (2009–2010), 210.

and ultimately jeopardize the national unity.[132] Furthermore, during the Cold War, economic, social and cultural rights tended to be debated in ideological terms. While the West used to stress civil and political rights, the Soviet bloc stressed (in principle if not in practice) economic, social and cultural rights. The distinction between the two sets of rights was based on the perceived characterization of civil and political rights as entailing negative obligations on the part of the state, and economic, social and cultural rights as requiring positive duties.

In the past decades, however, cultural rights have undergone a renaissance. UN treaty bodies have highlighted the indivisibility and interrelatedness of all human rights, recognizing that 'without affording full guarantees for . . . cultural rights . . . the protection offered . . . by other rights can become practically meaningless'.[133] Both sets of rights – economic, social, and cultural rights on the one hand, and civil and political rights on the other – entail a series of positive and negative state obligations. For instance, the right to take part in cultural life requires from the state party both abstention (i.e. non-interference with the exercise of cultural practices and with access to cultural goods and services; the obligation not to destroy cultural heritage),[134] and positive action (i.e. ensuring access to and preservation of cultural goods).[135] As Stamatopoulou puts it, 'the assignment of a right to the category of civil and political rights or economic, social and cultural rights has a heuristic, ordering and classifying purpose; nevertheless, a stricter conceptualization would produce a *continuum* of rights, in which the place of each right would be determined by the symbolic weight of the positive or negative obligations' components outlined in it.'[136]

[132] See A. F. Vrdoljak, 'Self-Determination and Cultural Rights' in F. Francioni and M. Scheinin (eds.), *Cultural Human Rights* (Leiden/Boston: Martinus Nijhoff Publishers, 2008), pp. 41–78.

[133] UN Economic and Social Council, Commission on Human Rights, Final Report of the Special Rapporteur of the Sub-Commission on Prevention of Discrimination and Protection of Minorities (D. Türk), The Realization of Economic, Social and Cultural Rights, 3 July 1992, UN Doc. E/CN.4/Sub.2/1992/16.

[134] V. E. Abramovich, 'Courses of Action in Economic, Social and Cultural Rights: Instruments and Allies', *International Journal of Human Rights* 2 (2004), 183.

[135] United Nations, Economic and Social Council, Committee on Economic, Social and Cultural Rights, General Comment No. 21, *Right of Everyone to Take Part in Cultural Life* (art. 15, para. 1 (a), of the International Covenant on Economic, Social and Cultural Rights), 21 December 2009, E/C.12/GC/21, available at www2.ohchr.org/english/bodies/cescr/docs/gc/E-C-12-GC-21.doc (accessed on 19 April 2013) at ¶ 6.

[136] Stamatopoulou, *Cultural Rights in International Law*, p. 12.

Finally, notwithstanding some earlier opinions to the contrary,[137] cultural rights are not political commitments of a programmatic character, rather they have a legal nature as they belong to national, regional and international law.[138] Their binding nature has been affirmed by the International Court of Justice[139] and the practice of domestic courts and international bodies.[140] The trend is likely to continue with the adoption by the United Nations General Assembly in 2008 of a complaints and inquiry procedure under the International Covenant on Economic, Social and Cultural Rights (ICESCR).[141] While the ICESCR used to have a relatively weak monitoring system,[142] – its implementation being monitored by the Committee on Economic, Social and Cultural Rights – in 2008, the General Assembly unanimously adopted an Optional Protocol to the ICESCR which gives the Committee competence to receive and consider communications.[143]

As to the content of cultural rights, obligations of states parties under the Covenant are not uniform or universal, but are instead relative to levels of development and available resources.[144] While the Covenant provides for 'progressive realization', thus acknowledging the constraints due to the limits of 'available resources', the concept of progressive realization 'must be read in the light of the overall objective . . . of the Covenant which is to establish clear obligations for States parties in respect of the full realization of the rights in question'.[145] For instance,

[137] See e.g. E. W. Vierdag, 'The Legal Nature of the Rights Granted by the International Covenant on Economic, Social and Cultural Rights', *Netherlands YIL* 9 (1978), 69–105.

[138] P. Alston and G. Quinn, 'The Nature and Scope of States Parties' Obligations under the International Covenant on Economic, Social and Cultural Rights', *HRQ* 9 (1987), 160.

[139] *Legal Consequences of the Construction of a Wall in the Occupied Palestinian Territory* (the Wall), Advisory Opinion of 9 July 2004, ICJ Reports 2004, p. 136, ¶ 112.

[140] F. Francioni, 'Culture, Heritage and Human Rights: An Introduction', in F. Francioni and M. Scheinin (eds.), *Cultural Human Rights* (Leiden/Boston: Martinus Nijhoff, 2008), p. 3.

[141] See M. Langford, 'Closing the Gap? An Introduction to the Optional Protocol', *Nordic J. of Human Rights* 27 (2009), 1–28.

[142] A. R. Chapman, 'A "Violations Approach" for Monitoring the International Covenant on Economic, Social and Cultural Rights', *HRQ* 18 (1996), 23–66.

[143] Optional Protocol to the International Covenant on Economic, Social and Cultural Rights, GA resolution A/RES/63/117, 10 December 2008. The Optional Protocol entered into force on 5 May 2013.

[144] *General Comment 3:The Nature of States Parties Obligations (Art. 2(1))*, Committee on Economic, Social and Cultural Rights, 5th Sess., 14 December 1990, ¶ 9.

[145] M. Ssenyonjo, 'Reflections on State Obligations with respect to Economic, Social and Cultural Rights in International Human Rights Law', *International Journal of Human Rights* 15 (2011), 971.

various obligations are of immediate effect (e.g. the obligation to eliminate discrimination in the enjoyment of cultural rights).

Cultural rights, like other human rights, impose three types or levels of state obligations: the obligations to respect, protect and fulfil.[146] The obligation to respect requires states parties to refrain from interfering with the enjoyment of cultural rights and includes, inter alia, the adoption of specific measures to allow everyone to have access to their own cultural heritage and to that of others.[147] States parties must also respect the rights of indigenous peoples to their cultural heritage and their spiritual relationship with their ancestral lands.[148] The obligation to protect requires states parties to take steps to prevent third parties from interfering in the exercise of cultural rights.[149] States parties are required to respect and protect cultural heritage in all its forms, in times of war and peace, and natural disasters, preserving and restoring historical sites, monuments and works of art, among others.[150] The obligation to protect also includes protection from illegal or unjust exploitation of indigenous peoples' lands by state entities or private or transnational enterprises and corporations.[151] Lastly, the obligation to fulfil requires states parties to take appropriate measures for the full realization of cultural rights.[152] The obligation to fulfil requires, inter alia, the adoption of cultural policies such as measures aimed at enhancing diversity through public broadcasting in minority languages or 'preserving and restoring cultural heritage'.[153]

Cultural rights present a dual dimension, as individual and collective entitlements. With regard to their individual dimension, cultural rights include a series of different entitlements, such as the right to education, the right to participate in cultural life, the performance of cultural practices, the possibility for individuals to speak their own dialects and languages, and the freedom for scientific research. With regard to their collective dimension, people need social interaction to exercise some of their cultural rights.

In addition, cultural rights have a minimum core content which corresponds to state obligations to ensure the satisfaction of, at the very least, minimum essential levels of cultural rights.[154] Non-derogable

[146] A. Eide, 'Economic and Social Rights', in J. Symonides (ed.), *Human Rights: Concepts and Standards* (Aldershot: UNESCO Publishing, 2000), pp. 109–74.

[147] General Comment 21, ¶ 49(d). [148] *Ibid.* [149] *Ibid.*, ¶ 50. [150] *Ibid.*, ¶ 50(a).

[151] *Ibid.*, ¶ 50(c). [152] *Ibid.*, ¶ 48. [153] *Ibid.*, ¶¶ 52(a) and 54(b).

[154] See generally A. Chapman and S. Russel (eds.), *Core Obligations: Building a Framework for Economic, Social and Cultural Rights* (Antwerp: Intersentia, 2002).

core obligations include, inter alia, the provision of the most basic forms of education,[155] the adoption of measures to ensure gender equality in the enjoyment of the right to take part in cultural life,[156] and the requirement of 'free and informed prior consent when the preservation of [indigenous peoples'] cultural resources, especially those associated with their way of life and cultural expression, are at risk'.[157] In this context, the Human Rights Committee (HRC) stated that 'the admissibility of measures which substantially compromise or interfere with the culturally significant economic activities of a minority or indigenous community depends on whether the members of the community in question have had the opportunity to participate in the decision-making process in relation to those measures, and whether they will continue to benefit from their traditional economy. The Committee considers that participation in the decision-making process must be effective, which requires not mere consultation but the free, prior and informed consent of the members of the community.'[158] Analogously, the Inter-American Court of Human Rights (IACtHR) held that the state has the duty to obtain the free, prior and informed consent of indigenous peoples in the case of large-scale investment projects that can have a major impact in traditional land.[159] Scholars have pointed out that although the question of who is to decide whether interferences are significant is unclear,[160] this constitutes a major evolution in the participatory rights of the indigenous communities affected by investment projects.[161]

## 1.6 *Good cultural governance*

International cultural law is a component of international law which includes those norms – whether customary, or treaty norms, or general principles of law – that require the protection of cultural heritage.[162]

155 General Comment 3, ¶ 10. 156 General Comment 21, ¶ 55(a). 157 *Ibid.*, ¶ 55(e).

158 HRC, *Angela Poma Poma v. Peru*, Communication 1457/2006, 27 March 2009, UN Doc. CCPR/C/95/D/1457/2006 (2009) ¶ 7.6.

159 IACtHR, *Case of the Saramaka People v. Suriname*, Judgment of 28 November 2007, Series C No. 172, ¶ 134.

160 E. Stamatopoulou, 'Monitoring Cultural Rights: The Claims of Culture on Human Rights and the Response of Cultural Rights', *HRQ* 34 (2012), 1185.

161 T. Ward, 'The Right to Free, Prior and Informed Consent: Indigenous Peoples' Participation Rights within International Law', *Northwestern Journal of International Human Rights* 10 (2011), 58.

162 See J. Nafziger, 'The Development of International Cultural Law', *American Society of International Law. Proceedings of the Annual Meeting* 100 (2006), 317–22.

International cultural law raises public awareness, fosters cooperation, and sets common standards reducing or preventing the negative externalities for society resulting from the uncontrolled use of cultural resources, such as the exploitation of mineral resources in cultural sites of outstanding and universal value, or the destruction of archaeological sites.

By adopting a number of international law instruments regarding cultural matters, UNESCO[163] has furthered international cooperation in the cultural sector and empowered states to adopt cultural policies, thus contributing significantly to the development of a legal matrix for global cultural governance.[164] UNESCO conventions, recommendations and declarations have laid down legal obligations, standards of conducts and benchmarks which offer useful criteria for identifying permitted and best practices for governing cultural resources.[165] As Dupuy highlights, these standards constitute the most recent analogue of the classical canons of good conduct such as 'the *bonus pater familias* of Roman law or of the *well-governed state* mentioned in the old Alabama arbitration (1872)'.[166] In this sense, UNESCO has shaped a body of law that helps states to develop *good cultural governance* and requires *due diligence* in the conduct of cultural policies.

However, international cultural law appears fragmented in both vertical and horizontal senses.[167] Vertical fragmentation is reflected in the coexistence of different layers of heritage protection, at the national, regional and international levels.[168] At the horizontal level, such fragmentation is

[163] UNESCO Constitution, preamble.

[164] C. Tjetje, 'The Changing Legal Structure of International Treaties as an Aspect of an Emerging Global Governance Architecture', *German YIL* 42 (1999), 36 (defining 'global governance' as an 'analytical model for a better understanding of the mechanisms of cooperative, multi-level approaches toward the management of common concerns of societies').

[165] P. J. O'Keefe and L. V. Prott, *Cultural Heritage Conventions and Other Instruments* (London: Institute of Art and Law, 2011), p. 5.

[166] P.-M. Dupuy, 'The Impact of Legal Instruments Adopted by UNESCO on General International Law' in Yusuf (ed.), *Normative Action in Education, Science and Culture*, 358. *Alabama Claims Arbitration*, Decision and Award made by the tribunal of arbitration constituted by virtue of the first article of the treaty concluded at Washington the 8th of May, 1871, between the United States of America and Her Majesty the Queen of the United Kingdom of Great Britain and Ireland, reported in J. Bassett Moore (ed.), *History and Digest of the International Arbitrations to which the United States has been a Party*, vol. 1 (Washington D.C.: Government Printing Office, 1898), p. 653.

[167] L. Casini, '*Italian Hours*: The Globalization of Cultural Property Law', *International Journal of Constitutional Law* 9 (2011), 373.

[168] *Ibid.*, 387.

evident in the varied sources of cultural heritage law. The incremental and ad hoc adoption of conventions and soft law instruments by UNESCO has led to a heterogeneous system in which 'more regimes are being established, depending on the kind of properties and on the public interest at stake'.[169] These different regulations are not necessarily well coordinated and at times overlap. For instance, the fact that each convention adopts its own definition of cultural property or cultural heritage does not contribute to the systematization of the field. Analogously, at the national and regional levels, the existence of fragmented legal frameworks gives rise to legal uncertainty, duplication of responsibilities, time delays and, ultimately, governance inefficiencies.[170]

As a plethora of national, regional and international law instruments imposes extensive obligations on states to respect and protect cultural heritage, some authors have argued that an emerging legal principle or norm of customary law requires states to protect cultural heritage in well-determined contexts, particularly in the event of armed conflict and military occupation.[171] Some cases point in this direction.[172] This argument is also based on the consideration that the protection of cultural heritage is firmly linked to the protection of fundamental human rights.[173]

With regard to the analogous question as to whether under customary international law there is a prohibition on the peacetime destruction of cultural property of particular significance for humanity as a whole, the point is much debated. Although not all the existing legal instruments are formally binding on states, they may contribute to the formation of the *opinio juris ac necessitatis*. For instance, Lenzerini argued that there is 'a general *opinio juris* on the binding character of the prohibition of acts of deliberate destruction of cultural heritage of major value for

[169] *Ibid.*, 373.

[170] See e.g. L. Kotzé and S. de la Harpe, 'The Good, the Bad and the Ugly: Using Good and Cooperative Governance to Improve Environmental Governance of South African World Heritage Sites: A Case Study of the Vredefort Dome', *Potchefstroom Electronic L. J.* 11 (2008), 27.

[171] See e.g. R. O'Keefe, 'Protection of Cultural Property under International Criminal Law', *Melbourne JIL* 11 (2010), 339; F. Francioni, 'Au-delà des traités: l'émergence d'un nouveau droit coutumier pour la protection du patrimoine culturel', *RGDIP* (2007), 19–42.

[172] See e.g. Eritrea Ethiopia Claims Commission, Partial Award – Central Front, Eritrea's Claims 2, 4, 6, 7, 8, & 22, 28 April 2004, available at www.pca-cpa.org/upload/files/Eritrea%20Central%20Front%20award.pdf. The Commission held that 'the falling of the Stela (of Matara) was a violation of customary humanitarian law' (*Ibid.*, ¶ 113).

[173] F. Francioni, 'Beyond State Sovereignty: The Protection of Cultural Heritage as a Shared Interest of Humanity', *Michigan JIL* 25 (2003–2004), 1213.

humanity'.[174] However, state practice in this field is far from uniform. While it may be held that *customary* international law is gradually emerging, the question as to whether such a norm already exists in international law is far from settled. Certainly, UNESCO law is contributing to the *gestalt* of treaty law and general principles of law in the area of cultural heritage protection. It remains to be seen whether culture-related awards can contribute to the emergence of such general principles of law requiring the protection of cultural heritage during times of peace and a fair balance between public and private interests involved in its protection.

UNESCO instruments do not 'expropriate' the states of their cultural sovereignty;[175] rather they 'shore up and back up states . . . in their regulatory responsibilities' and contribute to multilevel governance.[176] In general terms, states do not abandon, but rather, exercise their sovereignty when they enter into a treaty,[177] thereby triggering the basic rule of *pacta sunt servanda*.[178] According to general international law, a state must fulfil its obligations resulting from treaties but it is, in principle, free to select the means of implementing the treaty.[179] The means by which treaties and conventions are implemented are a matter for the domestic law of each state.[180] Furthermore, UNESCO instruments expressly affirm that states remain uniquely placed in protecting their cultural heritage.[181]

[174] F. Lenzerini, 'The UNESCO Declaration Concerning the Intentional Destruction of Cultural Heritage: One Step Forward and Two Steps Back', *IYIL* 13 (2003), 134. *Contra*, see e.g. R. O'Keefe, 'World Cultural Heritage Obligations to the International Community as a Whole?', *ICLQ* 53 (2004), 204 n.105.

[175] See N. Affolder, 'Mining and the World Heritage Convention: Democratic Legitimacy and Treaty Compliance', *Pace Environmental L. Rev.* 24 (2007), 36.

[176] J. K. Cogan, 'The Regulatory Turn in International Law', *Harvard ILJ* 52 (2011), 330.

[177] *See generally S.S. Wimbledon* (*United Kingdom v. Japan*), 1923 PCIJ (ser. A) No. 1, Judgment of 17 August 1923 (stating that the right to enter into international engagements is an act of state sovereignty). PCA, *Island of Palmas* Case (*United States of America v. the Netherlands*), 2 RIAA 829, at 839 (stating that sovereignty entails the obligation to protect the rights of other states – including those related to their nationals – within the state territorial borders).

[178] See Vienna Convention on the Law of Treaties (VCLT) 23 May 1969, 1155 UNTS 18232, Article 26.

[179] ICJ, *LaGrand Case* (*Germany v. United States*), Judgment of 27 June 2001, 2001 ICJ 466 (referring to 'means of [the state's] own choosing').

[180] PCIJ, *Certain German Interests in Polish Upper Silesia*, Judgment of 25 August 1925, PCIJ, Series A, No. 7, p. 19.

[181] Convention on the Protection and Promotion of the Diversity of Cultural Expressions (CCD), Paris, 20 October 2005, in force 18 March 2007, 2440 UNTS 311. CCD, Article 1(h); WHC, Article 4.

An important issue is that of whether international cultural law needs to place greater emphasis on dispute settlement mechanisms and deterrence in order to be more effective.[182] UNESCO treaties tend to lack compulsory adjudication and enforcement mechanisms. The proposals to establish a World Heritage Court or permanent arbitral tribunal for the settlement of disputes with cultural elements have not been successful, because cultural disputes are often perceived as political disputes. Will states ever relinquish their autonomy on issues that are related to cultural identity, nationhood and sovereignty? As one author points out, 'cultural heritage disputes are often multidimensional, involving not only complex legal issues, but also sensitive, not necessarily legal elements, of an emotional, ethical, historical, moral, political, religious, or spiritual nature'.[183] Finally, litigation may not be the proper context for settling this kind of dispute.

Because of the distinct features of cultural disputes, about fifty per cent of UNESCO treaty law lacks a dispute settlement provision *tout court*.[184] Arguably, UNESCO members preferred referring to diplomatic means of dispute settlement, rather than 'choosing a clear operational modus vivendi'.[185] Codifying compulsory dispute settlement mechanisms in the treaty text may make widespread ratification more difficult to achieve. The critical question then becomes whether it is better to have a strong treaty with fewer states parties, or a weak treaty with broader ratification. Given the increasing relevance of international cultural law, and the rise of cultural heritage-related disputes, further reflection is crucial.

However, the lack of compulsory dispute settlement and enforcement mechanisms should not lead to the conclusion that international cultural law has no binding character. UNESCO conventions are binding on the states which have ratified them. Implementation must be reasonable or proportionate with respect to the attainment of the relevant objectives, must comply with human rights, and is subject to monitoring. On the other hand, states should make better use of the international cultural law framework that is already in place. This means signing on and becoming party to the existing treaties; but greater commitment is also

[182] A. Milligan, 'Targeting Cultural Property: The Role of International Law', *Journal of Public and International Affairs* (2008), 102.

[183] S. Theurich, 'Art and Cultural Heritage Dispute Resolution', *WIPO Magazine* 4 (2009).

[184] S. Von Schorlemer, 'UNESCO Dispute Settlement', in A. A. Yusuf (ed.), *Standard-Setting in UNESCO: Normative Action in Education, Science and Culture Essays in Commemoration of the Sixtieth Anniversary of UNESCO* (Leiden/Boston: Martinus Nijhoff, 2007), p. 78.

[185] *Ibid.*

needed from those countries that are already signatories to the key conventions.

Given the lack of dedicated courts or tribunals, disputes with cultural elements have been adjudicated before national, regional and international courts and tribunals. At the international law level, the International Court of Justice (ICJ) has rarely adjudicated culture-related disputes. One such dispute is the case of the Temple of Preah Vihear[186] which has been recently revived.[187] The Court held that Thailand had to return the cultural property that had been removed from the site of the temple, an ancient sanctuary and shrine of considerable artistic and archaeological interest. In another dispute between Liechtenstein and Germany which concerned the return of cultural goods confiscated after the Second World War in the former Czechoslovakia, the Court declined jurisdiction *ratione temporis*.[188] In *Jurisdictional Immunities of the State*[189] Germany contended, inter alia, that by taking measures of constraint against Villa Vigoni, Italy violated Germany's jurisdictional immunity.[190] Villa Vigoni is a property of the German state located near Lake Como[191] and 'the seat of a cultural centre intended to promote cultural exchanges between Germany and Italy'.[192] The ICJ confirmed that immunity from execution applies to cultural property insofar as this is specifically used for non-commercial governmental purposes.[193] In the *Genocide* case, Bosnia and Herzegovina alleged, inter alia, that the Serbian forces' attempt 'to eradicate all traces of the culture of the protected group through the destruction of historical, religious and cultural property' inflicted on Bosnian Muslims conditions of life calculated to bring about their physical destruction.[194] However, in the Court's view, 'the destruction of historical, cultural and religious heritage c[ould] not be considered to constitute the deliberate infliction of

[186] *Case Concerning the Temple of Preah Vihear* (*Cambodia v. Thailand*), ICJ Judgment of 15 June 1965, ICJ Reports 1962, pp. 6ff.

[187] *Request for Interpretation of the Judgment of 15 June 1962 in the case concerning the Temple of Preah Vihear* (*Cambodia v. Thailand*), Request by the Kingdom of Cambodia for the Indication of Provisional Measures, 28 April 2011, available at www.icj-cij.org/docket/files/151/16472.pdf.

[188] *Certain Property* (*Liechtenstein v. Germany*), ICJ Judgment of 10 February 2005, ICJ Reports (2005), p. 6.

[189] *Jurisdictional Immunities of the State (Germany v. Italy: Greece Intervening)*, ICJ Judgment of 2 February 2012, available at www.icj-cij.org/docket/files/143/16883.pdf.

[190] *Ibid.*, ¶ 15. [191] *Ibid.*, ¶ 109. [192] *Ibid.*, ¶ 119. [193] *Ibid.*, ¶ 120.

[194] *Case Concerning Application of the Convention on the Prevention and Punishment of the Crime of Genocide* (*Bosnia and Herzegovina v. Serbia and Montenegro*) (Genocide case), ICJ Judgment of 26 February 2007, ICJ Reports (2007), p. 43, at ¶ 320.

conditions of life calculated to bring about the physical destruction of the group' and thus 'it d[id] not fall within the categories of acts of genocide set out in Article II of the Convention'.[195] In the *Area between Greenland and Jan Mayen*, the ICJ stated that the Arctic states could adjust maritime borders, considering the livelihood and needs of the local fishing communities, including the Inuit's needs.[196] Finally, in the *Navigational and Related Rights* case,[197] the ICJ deemed the subsistence fishing practices of the local peoples to be a customary right.[198]

Analogously, under the *Eritrea–Yemen Arbitration*, the Permanent Court of Arbitration (PCA) gave local communities non-exclusive access to maritime zones important to their livelihood.[199] Eritrea and Yemen had a dispute over the Mid-Sea islands in the Red Sea. While Eritrea contended that the islands were important to its people for religious and burial practices,[200] Yemen maintained that its people had long fished around the Mid-Sea islands.[201] The Arbitral Tribunal found that fishing was important for both countries, 'reflect[ing] deeply rooted and common social legal traditions that had prevailed for centuries among these populations'.[202] Therefore it concluded that local traditions were 'entitled to the respect and protection of law'.[203]

The absence of dedicated courts or tribunals has also caused a 'diaspora' of culture-related cases before other 'borrowed' specialized courts and tribunals. In addition to the cases adjudicated before the ICJ and the PCA, a number of culture-related cases have been adjudicated before human rights bodies and international economic fora, such as the World Trade Organization[204] panels and Appellate Body on the one hand and investment treaty arbitral tribunals on the other.

The jurisprudence of human rights courts and tribunals has increasingly dealt with cultural entitlements and the clash between property rights and the conservation of cultural heritage. A systematic analysis of this case law is outside the limited scope of this book; it must suffice to

195 *Ibid.*, ¶ 344.

196 *Maritime Delimitation in the Area Between Greenland and Jan Mayen* (*Denmark v. Norway*), ICJ Judgment, 14 June 1993, 1993 ICJ Reports, p. 38, ¶¶ 71–2 and ¶ 79.

197 *Dispute Regarding Navigational and Related Rights* (*Costa Rica v. Nicaragua*), ICJ Judgment of 13 July 2009, ICJ Reports 2009, p. 213.

198 *Ibid.*, ¶¶ 134–44.

199 *Eritrea Yemen Arbitration*, Award of the Arbitral Tribunal in the Second Stage of Proceedings (Maritime Delimitation) (*Eritrea v. Yemen*), PCA, 15 November 1994, 40 ILM p. 983.

200 *Ibid.*, p. 991. 201 *Ibid.*, p. 994. 202 *Ibid.*, p. 995. 203 *Ibid.*, p. 1000.

204 Agreement Establishing the World Trade Organization, 15 April 1994, 33 ILM (1994).

mention that the European Court of Human Rights (ECtHR) has adjudicated a number of cases in which private individuals alleged that their private property rights had been infringed by state cultural policies. In these cases, the ECtHR has tried to weigh up the different interests at stake, balancing property rights against the need to protect of cultural values. In this sense, the Court can be seen as favouring a concept of good cultural governance, according to which the protection of cultural heritage is considered to be a public objective that is worthy of protection, so long as other human rights, including property rights are not disproportionately and/or arbitrarily affected.[205] In parallel, the Inter-American Court of Human Rights (IACtHR) has gone further, adopting an evolutive interpretation to the notion of property encapsulated in Article 21 of the American Convention.[206] In particular, the IACtHR has interpreted the right to property as embodying the collective entitlements of indigenous peoples to the lands they traditionally inhabit.

International economic fora have adjudicated a number of cases concerning cultural goods. Given the fact that international economic fora present a distinct culture,[207] it is important to examine this emerging jurisprudence through a cultural lens, as such cases are scrutinized by international economic law experts from an international economic law perspective. Textually, while international economic goods receive strong protection under international economic law, cultural values are afforded much weaker consideration (if any). For instance, Article IV of the GATT 1994 provides a specific exception for certain screen quotas in connection with movies.[208] Article XX(f) of the GATT 1994[209] contains a limited exception to allow measures imposed for the protection of national treasures of artistic, historic and archaeological value.[210] Only recently Article XX(a) of the GATT 1994, containing a limited exception to allow measures adopted to protect public morals, has been interpreted as covering cultural products.[211] Cultural concerns are rarely mentioned

205 See, e.g. *Beyeler v. Italy*, Application 33202/96, Judgment of 5 January 2000; *Sud Fondi Srl c. Italia*, Application no. 75909/01, ECtHR, Judgment of 20 January 2009.

206 American Convention on Human Rights, 22 November 1969, 9 ILM 673 (1970).

207 See D. Steger, 'The Culture of the WTO: Why It Needs to Change', *JIEL* 10 (2007), 483–95; A. Bjorklund, 'The Emerging Civilization of Investment Arbitration', *Penn State L. Rev.* 113 (2009), 1269.

208 GATT Article IV.

209 General Agreement on Tariffs and Trade 1994 (GATT 1994), 15 April 1994, Marrakesh Agreement Establishing the World Trade Organization, Annex 1A, 33 ILM 1153 (1994).

210 Article XX(f) of the GATT 1994.

211 See Chapter 5 below.

in investment treaties.[212] As the main focus of this book is on investment treaty arbitrations, the cases of other courts and tribunals will be mentioned by way of reference.

## *1.7 The linkage paradigm*

The linkage paradigm explores the connection between international cultural law and other branches of international law. An examination of culture-related cases before international investment tribunals can test the effectiveness of international cultural law. These arbitrations show whether international cultural law is really able to address emerging issues in relation to economic globalization and international economic governance. Furthermore, arbitral tribunals, when attracting culture-related disputes, risk overemphasizing economic values vis-à-vis cultural values due to their limited mandate. While the linkage between development and cultural concerns may endorse positive synergies, the relationship remains fundamentally ambiguous, as in certain circumstances economic activities may endanger cultural heritage. Despite decades of protection of cultural heritage in many states, widespread non-compliance by individuals and corporations and lack of enforcement have been the norm rather than the exception. International cultural law only emerged after the Second World War, in a piecemeal fashion, through a series of international conventions and the formation of customs, and lacking a dispute settlement mechanism. Whereas international investment law constitutes a well-developed part of public international law and presents sophisticated means of dispute settlement that have produced a growing body of jurisprudence. Given the increasing number of investment disputes containing cultural elements, the interaction between international investment law and cultural heritage law deserves further scrutiny.

Exploring the available culture-related arbitrations also tests the linkage between international investment law and general international law. More precisely, is international investment law a self-contained regime[213] or is it an integral and responsive branch of international law? The relationship between international law and international investment law has taken on a greater significance with the extraordinary

[212] See Chapter 7 below.

[213] *Case Concerning United States Diplomatic and Consular Staff in Tehran* (*United States of America v. Iran*), Judgment of 24 May 1980, ICJ Reports 1980, p. 3, at ¶ 86.

flourishing of investment treaties in recent years.[214] Investigating the linkage between investment law and international cultural law as a case study of the interaction between international investment law and international law shifts the discussion about fragmentation in international law from a static to a dynamic perspective. Are investment treaties compatible with states' obligations to protect cultural heritage? Is investor–state arbitration a suitable forum for the protection of public interests?

Although the international legal system has undergone a process of functional differentiation in many different areas, and in a formal sense, investment treaties differ little from other international treaties; the legal regimes they create are often at variance with the assumptions underlying traditional models. Not only do these legal regimes provide for the investor–state dispute settlement mechanism that constitutes a major departure from customary international law, offering aggrieved investors direct access to an international arbitral tribunal. At the substantive level, investment treaties also provide an extensive protection of investor's rights in order to encourage foreign direct investment. Thus, a potential tension exists when a state adopts regulation interfering with foreign investments as this may breach investment treaty provisions and foreign investors can seek compensation directly for the impact of such regulation on their business. In this sense, investment law may appear to be self-contained in many respects.

Adopting a unitarian approach,[215] this book supports the argument that international law, albeit decentralized, is not an anarchic amalgam of different norms, but has a structure similar to a system.[216] To say that there is *continuity* between international law and international investment law does not imply a sort of *pre-established harmony* between the system and its sub-system.[217] Rather, the appropriate equilibrium needs to be found by the interpreters who should act as cartographers of international law.

[214] See P. M. Dupuy, 'Unification Rather than Fragmentation of International Law? The Case of International Investment Law and Human Rights Law', in P. M. Dupuy, F. Francioni and E. U. Petersmann (eds.), *Human Rights in International Investment Law and Arbitration* (Oxford University Press, 2009), pp. 45–62.

[215] See, e.g. ILC's Fragmentation Study: '[n]o legal regime is isolated from general international law', and 'no regime is self-contained', at ¶¶ 193 and 192 respectively.

[216] See J. Pauwelyn, *Conflict of Norms in Public International Law* (Cambridge University Press, 2003), p. 9.

[217] These terms belong to the philosophical discourse. See G. Leibniz, *Discourse on Metaphysics* XIV (1686, reprinted 2007).

A series of problematic cases involving elements of cultural heritage has shown the increasing interrelatedness of foreign investment and economic development on the one hand, and cultural heritage on the other. A survey of these cases shows that international law has not yet developed any institutional machinery for the protection of cultural heritage through investment dispute settlement. However, in recent years, a jurisprudential trend has emerged that does take cultural heritage into consideration. This trend seems to confirm the power of centripetal forces leading to systemic integration and unity of public international law.

### 1.8 Culture and development

Culture can be a powerful driver for development.[218] Already in 1776, in the landmark *Wealth of Nations*, a canonic reading in the political economy field,[219] Adam Smith linked the wealth of nations to culture, albeit in an implicit fashion. In investigating what makes the polity flourish, Smith noted the transformational impact of cultural resources in a community, highlighting that investing in culture can contribute to the wealth of nations.[220] His reasoning was straightforward: if a person mainly invested in durable commodities such as 'useful or ornamental buildings', book collections, statues or paintings, his or her wealth would be continually increasing;[221] likewise, if a state invested in such commodities, its wealth would be continually increasing too.[222] While recognizing that such spending 'that is laid out in durable commodities gives maintenance to a great . . . number of people',[223] Smith emphasized that 'Noble palaces, magnificent villas, great collections of books, statues, pictures and other curiosities, are frequently both an ornament and an honour, not only to the neighbourhood, but to the whole country to which they belong.'[224]

More recently, cultural economic sociologists expressly coined the term 'cultural wealth of nations'.[225] As they put it, such a concept captures a relationship between culture and economy that can be envisioned 'not as two separate spheres but as connected worlds that always intermingle in various ways . . .'.[226] In a sociological sense, a nation's 'cultural wealth' has

218 UNGA, Resolution 57/249, *Culture and Development*, 20 February 2003, A/RES/57/249.
219 *Ibid.* 220 *Ibid.*, Book II, Chapter III, p. 37. 221 *Ibid.*, p. 38. 222 *Ibid.*, p. 39.
223 *Ibid.*, p. 41. 224 *Ibid.*, p. 39.
225 See Bandelj and Wherry, 'Introduction: An Inquiry into the Cultural Wealth of Nations', pp. 1–20.
226 *Ibid.*, pp. 6–7.

been deemed to include 'its cultural and natural heritage sites, its stock of art, and artifacts exhibited in . . . museums',[227] or 'the plentiful supplies of stories, symbols, traditions, reputations and artifacts that are collectively held and that confer benefits on those able to make legitimate claims to them in advancing their country's prosperity'.[228]

Cultural industries and the protection and sustainable use of cultural resources may foster economic development, enabling communities and individuals to respond to major economic and social changes. As development is seen 'as less like the construction business and more like education in the broad and comprehensive sense that covers knowledge, institutions and culture',[229] 'heritage conservation is no longer seen as an expense, but as an economic, social and cultural investment' as well as an essential component of development.[230]

There can be positive synergies between the promotion of foreign direct investment and the protection of cultural heritage. As public funding for the recovery and the conservation of cultural heritage is in lasting decline, new public-private modes of financing have been developed, including public-private partnerships, based on the cooperation between the public and private sectors. For instance, investment in the tourism business can lead to the generation of income for the host country and local communities; to this end the World Bank is funding projects and investments related to cultural heritage.[231] On the other hand, by offering a wider choice of cultural products, cultural industries can contribute to democratization processes and the expansion of individual freedom.[232]

Whether development is a binding right or whether it is an emanation of other rights are not settled issues; certainly a number of international law instruments refer to the right to development. For instance, Article 22 of the African Charter affirm that 'all peoples shall have the right to their economic, social and cultural development with due regard to their freedom and identity and in the equal enjoyment of the common

227 *Ibid.* 228 *Ibid.*, p. 2.

229 World Bank, *The Quality of Growth* (Washington D.C.: WB, 2000), p. xxiii.

230 X. Greffe, 'Heritage Conservation as a Driving Force for Development', in *Heritage and Beyond* (Strasbourg: Council of Europe, 2009), p. 103.

231 See e.g. C. E. Di Leva, 'The World Bank's Policy on Physical Cultural Resources', in B. Hoffmann (ed.), *Art and Cultural Heritage: Law, Policy and Practice* (Cambridge University Press, 2005), p. 245.

232 A. Sen, *Development as Freedom* (Oxford University Press, 1999).

heritage of mankind.'[233] Indeed, development can be conceived as a broad concept inclusive not only of mere economic growth, but also of human flourishing and well-being to which cultural elements are crucial. The Declaration on the Right to Development[234] stated that 'the human person is the central subject of development',[235] and considered that 'in order to promote development, equal attention and urgent consideration should be given to the implementation, promotion and protection of civil, political, economic, social and cultural rights'.[236] The right to development is deemed to comprise both procedural and substantive dimensions: 'the right to participate in the development process; and the right to a substantive improvement in well-being'.[237]

Several 'Culture and Development' UNGA Resolutions called for the mainstreaming of culture into development policies and strategies.[238] The linkage between culture and development is acknowledged in a number of international cultural law instruments. The Universal Declaration on Cultural Diversity acknowledges cultural diversity as 'a factor of development', stating that: 'Cultural diversity widens the range of options open to everyone; it is one of the roots of development, understood not simply in terms of economic growth, but also as a means to achieve a more satisfactory intellectual, emotional, moral and spiritual existence.'[239] The Convention on Cultural Diversity (CCD) emphasizes 'the need to incorporate culture as a strategic element in national and international development policies, as well as in international development cooperation, taking into account also the United Nations Millennium Declaration with its special emphasis on poverty eradication'.[240] While the importance of 'the link between culture and development for all countries, particularly for developing countries' is listed among the objectives of the CCD,[241] the 'principle of the complementarity of economic and cultural aspects of development' is included among the guiding principles of the CCD and 'the cultural aspects of development' are deemed to be 'as important as its

233 African Charter, Article 22.
234 Declaration on the Right to Development, UNGA Res. 41/128 of 4 December 1986, 21 ILM 58.
235 Declaration on the Right to Development, Article 2.1.
236 Declaration on the Right to Development, Preamble.
237 A. Korir Sing' Oei and J. Shepherd, 'In Land We Trust: The Endorois' Communication and the Quest for Indigenous Peoples' Rights in Africa', *Buffalo Human Rights Law Rev.* 16 (2010), 57.
238 See UNGA, Culture and Development, A/RES/66/208, 15 March 2012.
239 Universal Declaration on Cultural Diversity, Article 3.
240 CCD, preamble.
241 CCD, Article 1(f).

economic aspects, which individuals and peoples have the fundamental right to participate in and enjoy'.[242]

The relationship between culture and development can also be seen through the lens of sustainable development.[243] 'Sustainable' means that it 'meets the needs of the present generation without compromising the ability of future generations to meet their own needs'.[244] According to a restrictive interpretation, sustainable development would be an environmental law concept requiring the optimal use of the world's resources to protect and preserve the environment.[245] However, in recent times, the principle of sustainable development – restated not only in multilateral environmental agreements but also in international economic law instruments,[246] as well as in international cultural ones,[247] has been broadened to include some cultural elements[248] and culture has become the fourth pillar of sustainable development along with the social, economic and environmental dimensions. Accordingly, a sustainable approach to development would be one which takes into account economic, social, cultural and environmental factors, to produce projects and programmes whose results will not exhaust finite resources. The emphasis would be put on human needs rather than wants, and on inter- and intragenerational equity.[249]

Although the concept of sustainable development has gradually been codified in international law instruments, there is no consensus on its

[242] CCD, Article 2.

[243] See F. Francioni, 'Sviluppo sostenibile e principi di diritto internazionale dell'ambiente', in P. Fois (ed.), *Il Principio dello sviluppo sostenibile nel diritto internazionale ed europeo dell'ambiente* (Napoli: Editoriale Scientifica, 2007), pp. 41–62.

[244] World Commission on Environment and Development, *Our Common Future* (*Brundtland Report*) 4 August 1987, UN GA Res A/42/427 (1987).

[245] See *Declaration on Environment and Development (Rio Declaration)*, Principle 4, Report of the United Nations Conference on Environment and Development, UN Doc A/CONF. 151/6/Rev.1, adopted at Rio de Janeiro, 14 June 1992, 31ILM 874 (1992); *Agenda 21*, Report of the UNCED, I (1992) UN Doc. A/CONF.151/26/Rev. 1 (1992) 31 ILM 874, ¶ 39.1; *Declaration on the Human Environment* (*Stockholm Declaration*) Principle 13, 16 June 1972, UN Doc A/C 48/14 (1972) 11 ILM 1461 (1972).

[246] See e.g. the preamble to the Agreement establishing the World Trade Organization. Agreement Establishing the World Trade Organization, 15 April 1994, 33 ILM (1994).

[247] See e.g. Universal Declaration on Cultural Diversity, Article 11; Convention for the Safeguarding of Intangible Cultural Heritage, preamble, and Article 2; CCD, preamble and Articles 2, 13 and 14.

[248] S. Van Uytsel, 'Sustainable Development: Linking the Convention on the Diversity of Cultural Expressions to WTO?', SIEL Working Paper No. 2012/29, 22.

[249] *United States – Import Prohibition of Certain Shrimp and Shrimp Products*, WTO Panel Report, 20 September 1999, WT/DS58/R, at ¶ 129.

legal status. The fact that sustainable development is mentioned in both soft law and hard law instruments suggests that the international community is increasingly embracing the notion of sustainable development.[250] While some authors consider sustainable development to be a general principle of law,[251] others categorize the concept of sustainable development as non-binding.[252] In particular, such 'normative uncertainty coupled with the absence of justiciable standards for review, strongly suggest that there is as yet no international legal obligation that development must be sustainable'.[253] Instead, sustainable development would be an emerging soft law concept, which, albeit not binding, may be persuasive in the way that it influences the conduct of states[254] and may gradually achieve binding character and inspire international courts and tribunals.[255]

While the concept of sustainable development is inherently vague, it proposes a *method* or integrated and balanced approach to the different objectives of development and cultural protection. In this sense, it helps to build bridges between different sets of international law norms.[256] In his Separate Opinion to the judgment of the International Court of Justice in the *Case Concerning the Gabčikovo-Nagymaros Dam*, Judge Weeramantry noted that environmental and developmental objectives may collide, and stated that 'the law necessarily contains within itself the principle of reconciliation. That principle is the principle of sustainable development.'[257] Sustainable development constitutes a useful 'element

250 Van Uytsel, 'Sustainable Development', p. 18.

251 C. Voigt, *Sustainable Development as a Principle of International Law: Resolving Conflicts between Climate Measures and WTO Law* (Leiden: Martinus Nijhoff Publishers, 2009), p. 128.

252 T. Kono, 'UNESCO and Intangible Cultural Heritage from the Viewpoint of Sustainable Development', in A. A. Yusuf (ed.), *Standard Setting in UNESCO: Normative Action in Education, Science and Culture* (Leiden: Martinus Nijhoff, 2007), p. 237.

253 A. Boyle and D. Freestone, 'Introduction', in A. Boyle and D. Freestone (eds.), *International Law and Sustainable Development: Past Achievements and Future Challenges* (Oxford University Press, 1999), p. 16.

254 See e.g. D. Shelton, 'Law, Non-Law and the Problem of Soft Law', in D. Shelton (ed.), *Commitment and Compliance: The Role of Non-Binding Norms in the International System* (Oxford University Press, 2000), pp. 4–10.

255 P. Sands, 'International Law in the Field of Sustainable Development', *BYIL* 65 (1994), 303.

256 A. Khalfan and M. C. Cordonier Segger, 'Introduction', in A. Khalfan and M. C. Cordonier Segger (eds.), *Sustainable Development Law* (Oxford University Press, 2005), p. 1.

257 ICJ *Gabčikovo-Nagymaros Project*, Judgment 25 September 1997, ICJ Reports 1997. Judge Weeramantry Separate Opinion.

of the process of judicial reasoning' which may help adjudicators reconcile the different interests and values reflected in legal norms.[258] Furthermore, it may contribute to the coherence of the legal system and enhance its ultimate legitimacy entailing a holistic approach to the settlement of disputes.[259]

The conceptualization of sustainable development as the principle of reconciliation between economic development and cultural, environmental and social concerns, is confirmed by the text of recent investment treaties.[260] Some investment treaties recognize not only the importance of a favourable investment climate, but also the importance of other policy goals, such as environmental protection and sustainable development.[261] The codification of the principle in investment treaties requires its consideration in the context of the interpretation and application of the treaty.

## Conclusions

This chapter has adopted a broad notion of cultural heritage, exploring and systematizing international cultural law. It posits that such a concept includes five different legal categories: (1) world heritage; (2) underwater cultural heritage; (3) cultural diversity; (4) intangible cultural heritage; and (5) indigenous heritage. This concept, however, is more than the sum of its parts as it alludes to the importance of culture for the common weal. In the context of this book it is used as a synonym for cultural resources.

The different legal and theoretical paradigms underpinning international cultural governance have been briefly explored in order to offer the reader a brief but systemic overview of the different epistemic premises and regulatory tools that govern cultural heritage at the international law level. Finally, the chapter has focused on the relationship between culture and development, pinpointing that culture is the fourth pillar of sustainable development, along with the economic, social and environmental dimensions and that there can be synergy between the protection of cultural resources and sustainable development.

258 V. Lowe, 'Sustainable Development and Unsustainable Arguments', in A. Boyle and D. Freestone (eds.), *International Law and Sustainable Development: Past Achievements and Future Challenges* (Oxford University Press, 1999), p. 31.

259 *Ibid.*, p. 32.

260 See Chapter 7 below.

261 See e.g. North American Free Trade Agreement (NAFTA), 17 December 1992, in force 1 January 1994 (1993) 32 ILM 289, preamble.

# 2

## International investment law

### Introduction

International investment law constitutes an important part of public international law governing foreign direct investment (FDI).[1] The sources of international investment law include international investment treaties, customary rules of international law protecting the rights of aliens, general principles of law, and – as subsidiary means for the determination of rules of law – previous awards and judicial decisions, and legal scholarship. As there is still no single comprehensive global treaty, investor rights are mainly defined by almost 3,000 international investment agreements (IIAs)[2] that are signed by two or more states and are governed by public international law. Under such treaties, states parties agree to provide a certain degree of protection to investors coming from the other contracting party/ies, including compensation in case of expropriation, fair and equitable treatment, and full protection and security.

FDI can be defined as 'the transfer of tangible or intangible assets from one country into another for the purpose of their use in that country to generate wealth under the total or partial control of the owner of the assets'.[3] As contained in investment treaties, investment is an all-encompassing concept, including almost any kind of business activity. All assets of an enterprise, such as movable and immovable property, contractual rights, intellectual property rights, concessions, licences and similar rights, are included. Given the broad scope of the concept, some investment provisions include both a general clause and an illustrative

1 For an historical overview, see A. Lowenfeld, *International Economic Law*, 2nd edn (Oxford University Press, 2008), pp. 469–94; M. Sornarajah, *The International Law on Foreign Investment*, 3rd edn (Cambridge University Press, 2010), pp. 19–28; A. Newcombe and L. Paradell, *Law and Practice of Investment Treaties* (Alphen aan den Rijn: Kluwer Law International, 2009), pp. 3–57.

2 UNCTAD, *World Investment Report 2011* (Geneva: UN, 2011), p. 100.

3 Sornarajah, *The International Law on Foreign Investment*, p. 8.

list of investments covered, as well as a negative list of areas specifically excluded from the scope of the agreements.[4]

The reason for protecting and promoting FDI is twofold. On the one hand, historically, foreigners have been amongst the vulnerable sectors of societies – easy objects of reprisal, with neither a vote nor a voice in local political affairs.[5] Fundamentally, investment treaties aim at establishing a level playing-field for foreign investors and a sort of shield against their discrimination and mistreatment by the host state. On the other hand, the majority of economists and policy-makers in both developing and developed countries see FDI as an engine for promoting economic growth and development.[6]

At the procedural level, most investment treaties allow foreign investors to file arbitral claims directly against the host state. This is a major novelty in international law as investors are not required to exhaust local remedies and no longer depend on diplomatic protection to defend their interests against the host state.[7] The claims are heard by ad hoc arbitral tribunals whose arbitrators are selected by the disputing parties and/or appointing institutions. Depending on the arbitral rules chosen, the proceedings occur *in camera* and the very existence of the claim and the final award may never become public.

Due to the recent surge in investment treaty arbitrations, the specific features of investment governance and the overall effects they produce have come to the forefront of legal debate. Once deemed to be an 'exotic and highly specialised' domain,[8] investment treaty law and arbitration is now moving into the mainstream.[9] At the same time, it has raised a storm of criticism mainly due to the alleged lack of democratic insight, and its impact on the host state's sovereignty. Investors have

4 See, e.g. North American Free Trade Agreement (NAFTA) 17 December 1992, in force 1 January 1994 (1993) 32 ILM 289, Article 1101(2).

5 See J. Paulsson, *Denial of Justice in International Law* (Cambridge University Press, 2005).

6 J. Bhagwati, 'Why Multinationals Help Reduce Poverty', *World Economy* 30 (2007), 211–28; V.N. Balasubramanyam, M. Salisu and D. Sapsford, 'Foreign Direct Investment and Growth: New Hypotheses and Evidence', *J. Int'l Trade and Economic Development* 8 (1999), 27–40.

7 See section 2.3 below.

8 International Law Commission, Fragmentation of International Law: Difficulties Arising from the Diversification and Expansion of International Law, Report of the Study Group (Martti Koskenniemi) UN Doc. A/CN.4/L.682 (13 April 2006) ¶ 8.

9 S. W. Schill, 'W(h)ither Fragmentation? On the Literature and Sociology of International Investment Law', *EJIL* 22 (2011), 875.

increasingly challenged regulatory measures in key sectors relating to a number of public goods, including but not limited to water services, cultural heritage and public health.[10] The surge in investment treaty making and arbitrations has attracted the increasing attention of the media and the public, not to mention the ever growing academic focus on the field.

This chapter proceeds as follows. First, after briefly providing a historical background, it explores the normative framework which governs foreign direct investment, setting out the elements of investment rules that will be of particular importance when considering their impact on the protection of cultural heritage. Second, the chapter highlights the most salient features of investor–state arbitration referring to the different paradigms through which this mechanism can be scrutinized.[11] Third, the chapter briefly explores the backlash against investment treaty law and arbitration.[12] It then concludes that this area of law, albeit still under-theorized, promises to develop in conformity with international law and has the potential to contribute to its further development.

## *2.1 Historical background: multilateral failures and bilateral successes*

Efforts to constitute a set of global rules to protect investor rights and to settle potential disputes between host countries and investors have been pursued by industrialized countries for a long time.[13] A first attempt to create a unified global investment law was made at the Bretton Woods conference in 1944. The conference, which stemmed from the consensus among the major international actors on the importance of establishing international economic institutions to foster peace and economic growth, determined the inception of the charters of the International Monetary Fund (IMF)[14] and the International Bank for Reconstruction

[10] See e.g. V. Vadi, *Public Health in International Investment Law and Arbitration* (Abingdon: Routledge, 2012).

[11] See generally A. Roberts, 'Clash of Paradigms: Actors and Analogies Shaping the Investment Treaty System', *AJIL* 107 (2013), 45–94.

[12] See generally M. Waibel, A. Kaushal, K.-H. Chung and C. Balchin (eds.), *The Backlash against Investment Arbitration* (Kluwer Law International, 2010).

[13] See, e.g. R. Dattu, 'A Journey from Havana to Paris: The Fifty Year Quest for the Elusive Multilateral Agreement on Investment', *Fordham Int'l L. J.* 24 (2000–2001), 275–316.

[14] Articles of Agreement of the International Monetary Fund (IMF), 22 July 1944, in force 27 December 1945, 2 UNTS 40.

and Development (IBRD).[15] Although the participants at the conference contemplated the necessity of an International Trade Organization (ITO), the Havana Charter which included rules on investment never came into force.[16]

Although the World Trade Organization (WTO)[17] in some ways has become 'the missing leg' of the Bretton Woods 'stool',[18] the moves to adopt multilateral investment rules initiated at the Doha Ministerial Conference in 2001 had to be abandoned at the Ministerial Conference in Cancun in 2003, due to growing opposition from developing countries and strong criticism from the NGO community. Similarly, the Organization for Economic Co-operation and Development (OECD), a forum of thirty industrialized countries, attempted to establish a Multilateral Agreement on Investments (MAI),[19] but this effort collapsed because of the opposition from civil society. The shortcomings of the MAI were evident. It was a one-sided instrument, unilaterally prepared by OECD Countries to ensure higher standards of protection and legal security for foreign investors. It did not adequately take into account the developmental needs of the host states, omitting crucial environmental and social issues.[20] Furthermore, while France and Canada were pursuing the insertion of a cultural exception in the text of the proposed MAI, the United States opposed such a move. The disagreement on this very point contributed to the failure of the MAI.[21]

However, some authors have submitted that there are global rules on foreign investment.[22] On the one hand, many instruments under the

15 Articles of Agreement of the International Bank for Reconstruction and Development (IBRD) as amended in 1965, 606 UNTS 294.

16 Charter for an International Trade Organization (Havana Charter), Final Act of the United Nations Conference on Trade and Employment, held at Havana, Cuba from 21 November 1947 to 24 March 1948, UN Document E/Conf. 2/78.

17 Agreement Establishing the World Trade Organization, 15 April 1994, 33 ILM 1994.

18 See J. Jackson, *The World Trading System* (Cambridge, MA: MIT Press, 2002), p. 32.

19 OECD Multilateral Agreement on Investment, Consolidated Text and Commentary, Draft DAFFE/MAI/NM(97)2.

20 See S. Picciotto, 'Linkages in International Investment Regulation: The Antinomies of the Draft Multilateral Agreement on Investment', *University of Pennsylvania JIEL* 19 (1998), 731–68; S. Picciotto, 'Lessons of the MAI: Towards a New Regulatory Framework for International Investment', *Law, Social Justice & Global Development* 1 (2000), 1–6.

21 A. Kolliopoulos, 'La Convention de l'UNESCO sur la protection et la promotion de la diversité des expressions culturelles', *Annuaire Français de Droit International* (2005), 489.

22 S. W. Schill, *The Multilateralization of International Investment Law* (Cambridge University Press, 2009); R. Leal-Arcas, 'Towards the Multilateralization of International Investment Law', *JWIT* 10 (2009), 865–919.

aegis of the WTO deal directly with areas of foreign investment. While the Agreement on Trade Related Aspects of Intellectual Property Rights (TRIPS Agreement)[23] covers intellectual property, which is deemed to be a form of investment, the General Agreement on Trade in Services (GATS)[24] deals with the service sector and covers the provision of services through a commercial presence in another country. Also, the Agreement on Trade Related Investment Measures (TRIMS Agreement)[25] deals with performance requirements associated with foreign investment.

On the other hand, the provisions of the Havana Charter, although never ratified, have served as an inspiration to many national and regional investment provisions.[26] Notwithstanding the persistent failures at the multilateral level, successful negotiations on investment protection have been undertaken at the bilateral and regional levels and a growing number of wider economic agreements establishing free trade areas (FTAs) have incorporated provisions in the style of bilateral investment treaties (BITs) into an investment chapter. All these treaties are designed to clarify the standards of protection that will apply to investments from one country into another, and to provide a stable environment for such investments. Because of the similarities among these different investment treaties and the fact that they tend to be negotiated from a limited set of model BITs, it has been argued that investment treaties often bilateral in form but multilateral in practice, are incrementally building a *de facto* global investment regime. While some argue that investment treaties constitute a *corpus juris* or a system of governance,[27] others deem such treaties to be evidence of customary law.[28]

23 Agreement on Trade Related Aspects of Intellectual Property Rights (TRIPS Agreement), 15 April 1994, Marrakesh Agreement establishing the World Trade Organization, Annex 1C, 33 ILM 1997 (1994).

24 General Agreement on Trade in Services (GATS), 15 April 1994, Marrakesh Agreement Establishing the World Trade Organization, Annex 1B, 33 ILM 1167 (1994).

25 Agreement on Trade-Related Investment Measures (TRIMS Agreement), 15 April 1994, Annex 1A to the Marrakesh Agreement Establishing the World Trade Organization (WTO Agreement), 1868 UNTS 186.

26 See Havana Charter, Article 12.

27 J. W. Salacuse, 'The Emerging Global Regime for Investment', *Harvard ILJ* 51 (2010), 431.

28 J. E. Alvarez, 'A BIT on Custom', *NYU JIL & Politics* 42 (2010), 63; A. Lowenfeld, 'Investment Agreements and International Law', *Columbia J. of Transnational Law* 42 (2003–2004), 123–30. *Contra* see M. Sornarajah, 'A Coming Crisis: Expansionary Trends in Investment Treaty Arbitration', in K. Sauvant (ed.), *Appeals Mechanism in International Investment Disputes* (Oxford University Press, 2008), p. 44.

As investment treaties are 'the most important instruments for the protection of foreign direct investment',[29] there is a general expectation that the conclusion of such treaties will encourage FDI.[30] Therefore, investment treaties are being strategically pushed by both developed and developing countries albeit for different reasons. On the one hand, host countries – generally developing and least developed countries (LDCs) – assume broad obligations for the protection of foreign investors in order to attract foreign investments. According to Guzman, LDCs sign BITs because they 'face a prisoner's dilemma in which it is optimal for them, as a group, to reject the Hull Rule, but in which each individual LDC is better off "defecting" from the group by signing a BIT that gives it an advantage over other LDC in the competition to attract foreign investment'.[31] On the other hand, developed countries have adhered to these dealings to protect the economic interests of their nationals and possibly to obtain favourable standards.

Recently, investment treaties have increasingly been signed not only among industrialized countries on the one hand and developing countries on the other, but also among LDCs and emerging economies. Therefore, the traditional distinction between capital importers and capital exporters has become blurred as emerging economies – like India and China – have become capital exporters.[32] As the primary objective of would-be investors is to obtain the effective guarantee that the host state will not act opportunistically once the investment has been made, investment treaties seem to provide appropriate solutions to this problem. Therefore, such treaties have come to play a major role in the

[29] UNCTAD, *Bilateral Investment Treaties: 1959–1999* (Geneva: UNCTAD, 2000), p. 1.

[30] Earlier work did not provide support for such a positive impact. See M. Hallward-Driemeier, 'Do Bilateral Investment Treaties Attract Foreign Direct Investment? Only a Bit... And They Could Bite', Policy Research Working Paper No 3121 (Washington D.C.: World Bank, 2003). However, more recent research suggests that the empirically identified impact is positive. See A. Bénassy-Quéré, M. Coupet and T. Mayer, 'Institutional Determinants of Foreign Direct Investment', *World Economy* 30 (2007), 764–82; P. Egger and V. Merlo, 'The Impact of Bilateral Investment Treaties on FDI Dynamics', *World Economy*, 30 (2007), 1536–49; J. Tobin and S. Rose-Ackerman, 'Foreign Direct Investment and the Business Environment in Developing Countries: The Impact of Bilateral Investment Treaties', Yale Law and Economics Research Paper No. 293 (2005).

[31] See A. Guzman, 'Explaining the Popularity of Bilateral Investment Treaties: Why LDCs Sign Treaties that Hurt Them', *Vanderbilt Journal of Transnational Law* 38 (1997), 667.

[32] V. Vadi, 'Converging Divergences: The Rise of Chinese Outward Foreign Investment and Its Implications for International (Investment) Law', *Yearbook of International Investment Law* 2011 (2012), 705–24.

growing competition to attract FDI and to provide conditions regarded as necessary to make countries attractive for foreign investment.

### 2.2 *Substantive standards of protection*

While investment treaties differ in their details, their scope and content have been standardized over the years, as negotiations have been characterized by an ongoing sharing and borrowing of concepts.[33] Moreover, the inclusion of the most favoured nation clause in most BITs drives convergence in treaty interpretation, and arbitral tribunals have constantly drawn upon earlier cases – which, albeit not binding, constitute a *de facto* persuasive precedent – leading to the coalescence of a *jurisprudence constante*.[34] Therefore, some authors have highlighted the development of a *common lexicon* of investment treaty law.[35]

Typically, investment treaty provisions deal with the scope and definition of foreign investment, non-discrimination (both national treatment and most favoured nation treatment), minimum standards and fair and equitable treatment. Other common provisions in investment treaties concern the repatriation of profits and other investment-related funds or the promise to freeze the existing regulatory regime for the duration of the investment (stabilization clauses). A small number of investment treaties also include provisions prohibiting certain forms of performance requirements, i.e. obligations on investors to act in ways considered beneficial for the host economy, mostly relating to local content, joint ventures, technology transfer and employment of nationals.

Investment treaties rarely mention the specific consequences in the case of non-compliance, when the host state violates a substantive standard of treatment. In practice, arbitral tribunals have held states liable to compensate investors for breaches of treaty standards that result in injury, relying on the *Chorzów Factory Case*.[36] The amount of the compensation should 'wipe out all the consequences of the illegal act

[33] C. McLachlan, 'The Principle of Systemic Integration and Article 31(3)(c) of the Vienna Convention', *ICLQ* 54 (2005), 284.

[34] See A. K. Bjorklund, 'Investment Treaty Arbitral Decisions as Jurisprudence Constante', in C. Picker, I. Bunn, and D. Arner (eds.), *International Economic Law: The State and Future of the Discipline* (Hart Publishing, 2008), p. 265; G. Kaufmann-Kohler, 'Arbitral Precedent: Dream, Necessity or Excuse?', *Arbitration International* 23 (2007), 357.

[35] C. McLachlan, L. Shore and M. Weiniger, *International Investment Arbitration* (Oxford University Press, 2007), p. 6.

[36] PCIJ, *Case Concerning the Factory at Chorzów*, Judgment on the Merits, 13 September 1928, 1928 PCIJ (Ser. A) No. 17, at 27–8.

and re-establish the situation which would, in all probability, have existed if such act had not been committed'.[37]

### 2.2.1 Expropriation

Protection against unlawful expropriation and guarantees of compensation in the event of nationalization, expropriation, or indirect expropriation constitute the core of investment treaties and aim to restrain the host state behaviour imposing a discipline on governmental actions.[38] Under customary international law or investment treaties, states can expropriate private property; such expropriations are lawful provided that certain conditions are met.[39] For instance, according to Article 1110 of the North American Free Trade Agreement (NAFTA), 'No Party may directly or indirectly nationalize or expropriate an investment of an investor of another Party in its territory or take a measure tantamount to nationalization or expropriation of such an investment, except: (a) for a public purpose; (b) on a non-discriminatory basis; (c) in accordance with due process of law and Article 1105(1); and (d) on payment of compensation.'[40]

The concept of expropriation is broadly construed in investment treaties which do not only protect foreign assets from the direct and full taking of property, but also from *de facto* or *indirect* expropriation. While direct and overt expropriations have become rare – after the nationalization trend that marked the 1960s and 1970s[41] – indirect expropriation constitutes the typical form in which expropriations take place today. Indirect expropriation indicates measures that do not directly take investment property, but which interfere with its use, depriving the owner of its economic benefit. As Professor Stern highlights, 'The prism of indirect expropriation includes a broad array of very different measures that do not involve a transfer of the investment but result in a serious interference with it.'[42] Treaty provisions lack a precise definition of indirect expropriation and their language encompasses a

[37] *MTD Equity Sdn. Bhd & MTD Chile SA v. Republic of Chile*, Award, 24 May 2004, ICSID Case No. ARB/01/7, ¶ 238, available at http://italaw.com/documents/MTD-Award.pdf.

[38] Salacuse, 'The Emerging Global Regime of Investment', 445.

[39] P. Comeaux and N. Kinsella, *Protecting Foreign Investment under International Law* (New York: Oceana Publications, 1997), pp. 77–8.

[40] NAFTA, Article 1110.

[41] See A. Akinsanya, 'International Protection of Foreign Direct Investments in the Third World', *ICLQ* 36 (1987), 58–75.

[42] B. Stern, 'In Search of the Frontiers of Indirect Expropriation', in A. Rovine (ed.), *Contemporary Issues in International Arbitration and Mediation* (Leiden: Martinus Nijhoff Publishers, 2008), p. 35.

wide variety of state activity that could potentially interfere with investor property.[43] States tend to achieve the same result (of expropriation) by indirect means (hence indirect or disguised or *de facto* expropriation), interfering in the use of property or with the enjoyment of its benefits even where the property has not been seized and the legal title of the property is not affected.[44] For instance, the host state may target a foreign investor by imposing very high taxes or regulatory requirements which may make the foreign investment economically unviable. In *Starrett Housing v. Iran*, the Iran–US Claims Tribunal held that: 'Measures taken by a state can interfere with property rights to such an extent that these rights are rendered so useless that they must be deemed to have been expropriated, even though the State does not purport to have expropriated them and the legal title to the property formally remains with the original owner.'[45]

In particular, the central question raised by so-called indirect expropriation is how to draw the line between legitimate regulations that do not give rise to compensation and regulatory takings that do.[46] States have an inherent right to regulate domestic affairs,[47] including private property and business activities. Moreover, 'due to the proliferation of treaties, states are increasingly becoming subject to international obligations that require states to regulate'.[48] However, the exercise of such regulatory powers 'is not unlimited and must have its boundaries'.[49]

There is no settled approach to cases where investors allege that certain regulatory measures constitute a compensable form of expropriation. Thus, as Professor Schreuer points out, today the most difficult question for an arbitrator faced with an allegation of expropriation is not so much whether the requirements for a legal expropriation have been met, but

43 L. Y. Fortier and S. L. Drymer, 'Indirect Expropriation in the Law of International Investment: I Know When I See It, or *Caveat Investor*', *ICSID Review–FILJ* 19 (2004), 293–327.

44 OECD, 'Indirect Expropriation and the Right to Regulate in International Investment Law', Working Paper on International Investment No. 4 (2004), pp. 3–4.

45 *Starrett Housing Corp. v. Iran*, 16 Iran–US CTR (1983), at 112, 154.

46 V. Lowe, 'Regulation or Expropriation?', *Current Legal Problems* 55 (2002), 447.

47 *ADC Affiliate Ltd and ADC & ADMC Management Ltd v. Hungary*, Award, ICSID No. ARB/03/16, 2 October 2006, at 423.

48 S. Olynyk, 'A Balanced Approach to Distinguishing Between Legitimate Regulation and Indirect Expropriation in Investor–State Arbitration', *Int'l Trade and Business L. Rev.* 15 (2012), 269.

49 *ADC v. Hungary*, Award, at 423.

whether there has been an expropriation in the first place.[50] Useful criteria to distinguish regulatory measures from indirect expropriation include the degree of interference (the extent, gravity and duration of the deprivation), and the character of the governmental measure (i.e. the purpose and the context of the governmental measure). Principles like proportionality, reasonableness, non-discrimination and due process of law are seen as interpretative tools in assessing whether a regulatory measure amounts to a taking.[51]

For instance, after recognizing that the identification of an indirect expropriation requires 'a case-by-case, fact-based inquiry', the 2012 US Model BIT sets out a tripartite test to identify an indirect expropriation: (i) 'the economic impact of the government action [. . .]; (ii) the extent to which the government action interferes with distinct, reasonable investment-backed expectations; and (iii) the character of the government action.'[52] At the same time, the same Annex acknowledges that 'Except in rare circumstances, non-discriminatory regulatory actions by a Party that are designed and applied to protect legitimate public welfare objectives, such as public health, safety, and the environment, do not constitute indirect expropriations.'[53] This formulation was also present in the previous 2004 US Model BIT and has been imported into the text of other investment treaties due to the perceived authority of its source.[54]

In spite of its apparent simplicity, this wording does not dispel interpretative doubts and uncertainties. Would heritage conservation be a 'legitimate public welfare objective'? Although the Model BIT does not refer to the 'genealogy' of the test, the criteria are derived from the *Penn Central* case, a landmark US case on the takings clause and the protection of cultural heritage.[55] In this case, Penn Central, a US railroad corporation, planned to build 55 stories on top of its Grand Central

[50] C. H. Schreuer, 'The Concept of Expropriation under the ETC and Other Investment Protection Treaties', *TDM* 2 (2005), 3.

[51] A. Newcombe, 'The Boundaries of Regulatory Expropriation in International Law', *ICSID Review-FILJ* 20 (2005), 1–57 and S. Ratner, 'Regulatory Takings in Institutional Context: Beyond the Fear of Fragmented International Law', *AJIL* 102 (2008), 475–528.

[52] 2012 US Model BIT, Annex B, 4(a). [53] *Ibid.*, 4(b).

[54] See e.g. 2004 Canada Model BIT, Article 10. 2004 Canadian Model BIT (Foreign Investment Protection Agreement or FIPA), Agreement between Canada and ___ for the Promotion and Protection of Investments, available at http://italaw.com/documents/Canadian2004-FIPA-model-en.pdf.

[55] A. B. Sanders, 'Of All Things Made in America Why Are We Exporting the Penn Central Test?', *Northwestern JIL & Business* 30 (2010), 339–81.

Station in Manhattan.[56] After the New York City (NYC) Landmark Preservation Commission denied such elevation on historic conservation grounds, the railroad sued, contending that the elevation denial constituted a regulatory taking. The NYC Landmarks Preservation Commission eloquently stated: 'To protect a Landmark, one does not tear it down. To perpetuate its architectural features, one does not strip them off ... [We have] no fixed rule against making additions to designated buildings – it all depends on how they are done. But to balance a 55-story office tower above a flamboyant Beaux-Arts facade seems nothing more than an aesthetic joke. Quite simply, the tower would overwhelm the Terminal by its sheer mass ... Such examples [of urban design] are not so plentiful in New York City that we can afford to lose any of the few we have. And we must preserve them in a meaningful way – with alterations and additions of such character, scale, materials and mass as will protect, enhance and perpetuate the original design rather than overwhelm it.'[57]

The US Supreme Court rejected the claimant's argument. After stating that regulatory takings require 'ad hoc factual inquiries', the Court highlighted that three factors are of 'particular significance': (1) 'the economic impact of the regulation on the claimant'; (2) 'the extent to which the regulation has interfered with distinct investment-backed expectations'; and (3) 'the character of the governmental action'.[58] In applying this test to *Penn Central*, the Court stressed that the economic impact of the measure was mitigated by the possibility to transfer the air rights of the company to other parcels nearby;[59] the railroad could still use the terminal as it had been used before; and that the measure had a general character and public purpose, aiming at enhancing the quality of life for all.[60] The genealogy of the test suggests that by enhancing the quality of life for all, heritage conservation can be a legitimate public welfare objective within investment treaty arbitration.

### 2.2.2 The *sole effects* doctrine and the *police powers* doctrine

In observing the growing tide of arbitral jurisprudence, two main doctrines have emerged concerning indirect expropriation: the *sole effects* doctrine and the *police powers* doctrine.[61] While the first concentrates on the effects of the state measure on the foreign property, and thus favours

[56] *Penn Central Transportation Co. v. New York City*, 438 US 104 (1978), at 115–16.
[57] *Ibid.*, 118. [58] *Ibid.*, 124. [59] *Ibid.*, 137. [60] *Ibid.*, 134–7.
[61] M. Brunetti, 'Introduction', *International Law Forum de Droit International* 5 (2003), 151.

the investor's perspective,[62] the second focuses on the alleged goal of the state measure and thus favours the right of the state to regulate. Thus far, neither of the two doctrines can be characterized as dominant or as representing the mainstream of international thinking.

The sole effects doctrine focuses on the negative impact of regulation on the foreign investment. The underlying assumption of this doctrine is that regulatory measures are generally adopted for the public good and may impose some burdens on private property. However, if the burden imposed on certain properties is too overwhelming or almost entirely to deprive them of any economic benefit, the owner is entitled to compensation. The bona fide public purpose of the taking may be presumed, but it still requires compensation.[63] Several cases lend support to such a doctrine.[64]

The police powers doctrine gives weight to the purpose and the circumstances of governmental action. According to such doctrine, bona fide non-discriminatory regulation within the police powers of the state does not require compensation.[65] The doctrine focuses on the inherent authority of a government to impose restrictions on personal freedom and property rights for the sake of order, safety, security, health, morals and general welfare. Under international law, there is no comprehensive and categorical definition of police powers, but this concept is generally understood to include measures taken by government to protect public goods against harm or nuisance. According to such doctrine, 'harm prevention' ought not to be compensated, because the proscribed use was not part of the investor's title to begin with,[66] but 'benefit extraction' should, generally, be compensated.[67]

While some authors deem this theory to be a justification of state action which would otherwise amount to a deprivation that can be compensated or to an appropriation of property[68] – in sum, 'once applied, the police

[62] R. Dolzer, 'Indirect Expropriations: New Developments?', *NYU Environmental L.J.* 11 (2003), 90.

[63] B. Appleton, 'Regulatory Takings: The International Law Perspective', *NYU Environmental L.J.* 11 (2003), 35–48.

[64] See e.g. *Telenor Mobile Communications v. Hungary*, Decision on Jurisdiction, ICSID Case No. ARB/04/15, 13 September 2006, ¶ 67.

[65] A. Newcombe, 'The Boundaries of Regulatory Expropriation in International Law', *ICSID Review–FILJ* 20 (2005), 2.

[66] In this context, see *Lucas v. South Carolina Coastal Council*, 505 US 1003 (1992) 1027.

[67] S. Rose Ackerman and J. Rossi, 'Disentangling Deregulatory Takings', *Virginia Law Rev.* 86 (2000), 1435; J. L. Sax, 'Takings and the Police Power', *Yale L.J.* 74 (1964–1965), 36.

[68] Newcombe, 'The Boundaries of Regulatory Expropriation in International Law', 21.

powers doctrine excludes liability'[69]– others deem it to be a necessary corollary of property. For instance, Montt argues that such measures constitute an 'internal limit of property', as 'property rights are conferred ... by the legal system under the explicit or implicit condition of not causing harm to third parties'.[70] As Howard Mann and Konrad von Moltke note: 'Under the traditional international law concept of the exercise of police powers, when a state acted in a non-discriminatory manner to protect public goods such as its environment, the health of its people or other public welfare interests, such actions were understood to fall outside the scope of what was meant by expropriation ... Such acts were simply not covered by the concept of expropriation, were not a taking of property, and no compensation was payable as a matter of international law.'[71] The introduction of the police powers doctrine in investment treaty arbitration has been successful in a number of cases.[72]

The problem is that while international investment law acknowledges the police powers doctrine, there is no commonly accepted formula which enables a clear distinction to be drawn between non-compensable regulation and compensable taking.[73] As an arbitral tribunal put it, international investment law 'has yet to identify in a comprehensive and definitive fashion precisely what regulations are considered "permissible" and "commonly accepted" as falling within the police or regulatory power of States and, thus, non-compensable'.[74]

Doctrinal studies have attempted to clarify the distinction between indirect expropriation and the right to regulate. Notably, some authors and arbitrators have elaborated a twofold test to verify whether regulatory measures may be deemed to be indirect expropriation or a legitimate exercise of police power. According to the proposed procedure, *first*, it must be ascertained whether a deprivation of property has

[69] J. Vinuales, 'Foreign Investment and the Environment in International Law: An Ambiguous Relationship', *BYIL* 80 (2010), 64.

[70] S. Montt, *State Liability in Investment Treaty Arbitration: Global Constitutional and Administrative Law in the BIT Generation* (Oxford: Hart Publishing, 2009), pp. 192–3.

[71] H. Mann and K. Von Moltke, *Protecting Investor Rights and the Public Good: Assessing NAFTA's Chapter 11* (Winnipeg: IISD, 2003), p. 16.

[72] *Sedco, Inc. v. National Iranian Oil Co.*, 10 Iran–US CTR 180, 25 ILM 629 (1986); *Too v. Greater Modesto* (1989) 23 Iran–US CTR 378; *Saluka Investments BV v. Czech Republic*, UNCITRAL Partial Award (2006), ¶ 262.

[73] M. Sornarajah, *The International Law on Foreign Investment*, 3rd edn (Cambridge University Press, 2010), p. 368.

[74] *Saluka Investments BV (The Netherlands) v. Czech Republic*, UNCITRAL Partial Award 2006, ¶ 263.

occurred because of the effect of the measure taken. The answer to this question would be given through an essentially quantitative approach. *Second*, the conclusion that a given measure is potentially expropriatory may be modified through an essentially qualitative approach. In other words, this third position considers that 'one should take into account both sides of the coin and that the challenge is precisely to know where to draw the line in balancing the conflicting interests of investors and states'.[75] In conclusion, while the identification of indirect expropriation will depend on the case-by-case analysis of the specific facts, a balanced approach based on both qualitative and quantitative tests seems preferable to the sole effects doctrine.

In the absence of any direction in an investment treaty, one may wonder whether state measures imposing restrictions (including sometimes onerous restrictions) on the use of investor property are (or should be) exempted from potential allegations of indirect expropriation, on the basis of the police powers doctrine. As a selected number of cultural policies include measures to protect paramount interests, police powers can (and have been) successfully invoked (*ordre public culturel*). For instance, police powers can be invoked to prevent the export of cultural artefacts or national treasures and to preserve sites of historical and cultural significance.

### 2.2.3 Historic preservation and the takings analysis

As several expropriation provisions in international investment agreements are structured in accordance with the *Penn Central* tripartite test, it is worth examining some relevant national cases concerning the interplay between cultural policies and expropriation claims. This brief analysis is not meant to be exhaustive; on the contrary, comparative studies illustrating the different jurisprudential trends of various courts and tribunals worldwide on the interplay between public and private interests in heritage management is needed. Due to space limits, the specific origin of expropriation provisions in IIAs, and the fact that this book has an international rather than comparative focus, this section only explores a selected number of cases, mainly from US takings jurisprudence.[76]

[75] Stern, 'In Search of the Frontiers of Indirect Expropriation', p. 44.

[76] Reference to Asian, African, Australian and European cases will be made in other sections of the book. Again, these references are not meant to be exhaustive given the fact that the focus of the book is international rather than comparative.

The preservation of sites of historical and cultural significance and/or the enhancement of public welfare and the quality of life associated with redevelopment projects can be a legitimate public objective, which is one of the prerequisites for lawful expropriation. In the landmark case *United States v. Gettysburg Electric Railway Co.*,[77] the United States Supreme Court held that the preservation of a historical site served a legitimate objective and thus was within the government's power of expropriation.[78] The Court highlighted that 'the battle of Gettysburg was one of the great battles of the world ... the existence of the government itself ... depended on the result ... Such a use seems necessarily not only a public use, but one so closely connected with the welfare of the republic itself as to be within the powers granted Congress by the Constitution for the purpose of protecting and preserving the whole country.'[79] In *Berman v. Parker*,[80] the US Supreme Court confirmed that Congress had the power to compulsorily acquire a blighted neighbourhood in Washington D.C. and redevelop it, holding that the provision of a beautiful place for residents to live was within the concept of public welfare that states could promote pursuant to their police powers.[81]

In other cases, the police powers doctrine has been used to bar claims of indirect expropriation. As an author highlights, 'while health and safety were initially the main objectives of the police power, the definition of the term "general public welfare" has been expanded in the area of historic preservation'.[82] As Justice Scalia aptly put it, 'The transition from the early focus on control of "noxious" uses to contemporary understanding of the broad realm within which government may regulate without compensation was an easy one, since the distinction between "harm preventing" and "benefit-conferring" regulation is often in the eyes of the beholder.'[83] Historic preservation laws often explicitly state their objectives in terms of promoting the common weal by enhancing the beauty of the place and the quality of life of the local communities, fostering education in the cultural heritage, and attracting tourists.[84] In *Village of Euclid v. Ambler Realty Co.*,[85] a company challenged

[77] *United States v. Gettysburg Electric Railway Co.*, 160 US 668 (1896).
[78] *Ibid.*, 681–86. [79] *Ibid.*, 681–2. [80] *Berman v. Parker*, 348 US 26 (1954).
[81] *Ibid.*, 32.
[82] A. H. Manwaring, 'American Heritage at Stake: The Government's Vital Interest in Interior Landmark Designations', *New England L. Rev.* 25 (1990–1991), 311.
[83] *Lucas v. South Carolina Coastal Council*, 1024.
[84] Manwaring, 'American Heritage at Stake', 292.
[85] *Village of Euclid v. Ambler Realty Co.*, 272 US 365 (1928).

a zoning ordinance which precluded the commercial development of its property, claiming that the ordinance amounted to an unconstitutional taking of its property. The Court held that the ordinance was not an unconstitutional taking; rather it served the public welfare and was an expression of the police powers of the local authorities.[86] Analogously, in *Penn Central*,[87] the United States Supreme Court held that the protection of historic places is a legitimate public objective within the scope of the government's police powers,[88] and that the restrictions on private properties imposed by the *Landmarks Law* did not amount to a taking.[89] The Court noted that a reasonable use for the property still existed, and that the law was a valid exercise of the police powers for the benefit of the public welfare.[90] In *United Artists' Theater Circuit, Inc. v. City of Philadelphia*,[91] the Supreme Court of Philadelphia held that the designation of a theatre as a historic building was not a taking that required compensation. Such designation placed a number of restrictions on the owner's use of the property, including an obligation to preserve the building. However, it did not deprive the owner of any profitable use.[92] The police power authority to require owners to maintain historic properties in good repair is well settled.[93] Similarly, at the regional level, in *Matos Silva v. Portugal*, the European Court of Human Rights held that a law which created a nature reserve on land including that of the complainant's did not amount to expropriation, as the complainant's property rights had not disappeared and he could still productively work the land.[94]

Police powers arguments have been used to uphold regulation aimed at preserving the decorum of heritage sites. For instance, in *City of New Orleans v. Dukes*,[95] the United States Supreme Court upheld a New Orleans ordinance banning all pushcart food vendors in the French Quarter, holding that the legislation was rationally related to the legitimate state interest in preserving the appearance of the French Quarter.[96] In *A-S-P Associates v. City of Raleigh*,[97] the Supreme Court

[86] *Ibid.*, 387–8.
[87] *Penn Central Transportation Co. v. City of New York*, 438 US 104 (1978).
[88] *Ibid.*, 123–8. [89] *Ibid.*, 131, 138. [90] *Ibid.*, 105, 123–8.
[91] *United Artists' Theater Circuit, Inc. v. City of Philadelphia*, 635 A.2d 612 (Pa. 1993).
[92] *Ibid.*, 618.
[93] *Maher v. City of New Orleans*, 516 F.2d 1051, 1067 (5th Cir. 1975), certiorari denied 426 US 905 (1976).
[94] *Matos Silva v. Portugal*, 24 Eur. H.R. Rep. 573, ¶ 85 (1997).
[95] *City of New Orleans v. Dukes*, 427 US 297 (1976). [96] *Ibid.*, 304.
[97] *A-S-P Associates v. City of Raleigh*, 298 NC 207 (1979).

of North Carolina held that the regulation preserving the appearance of historic buldings was a valid and reasonable exercise of the police power promoting the public welfare.[98] In *Bohannan v. City of San Diego*, the Court of Appeals of California held that 'Preservation of the image of Old Town . . . contributes to the general welfare; gives the general public attendant educational and cultural advantages; and by its encouragement of tourism, is of general economic value. The purpose of the ordinance clearly is within an exercise of the police power . . .'[99] The Court concluded that: 'Regulations regarding and restrictions upon the use of property in an exercise of the police power for an authorized purpose, do not constitute the taking of property without compensation.'[100]

Conversely, if there is a transfer of property or a complete deprivation of use, a taking could be ascertained. For instance, in *Lucas v. South Carolina Coastal Council*,[101] the petitioner argued that the prohibition of building permanent structures on his beachfront property made his property valueless, thus constituting a taking.[102] While the South Carolina Supreme Court rejected the claim, holding that the regulation aimed at preventing harmful uses of property and public nuisance, the Supreme Court reversed, stating that denial of all uses of property amounted to a taking requiring just compensation.[103] The *Lucas* rationale relates to those cases in which a property owner can demonstrate that a property has become worthless due to the given regulation.[104]

Cultural policies 'must be reasonably related to objectives that promote public welfare to be a valid exercise of police power'.[105] The criteria of rationality, reasonableness and/or proportionality are used to evaluate government conduct.[106] For instance, the Polish Constitutional Tribunal held that a provision of the Polish 2003 *Protection and Care for Monuments Act* that required a landowner – who planned to carry out construction works concerning a building registered as a monument – to

[98] *Ibid.*, 216. [99] *Bohannan v. City of San Diego*, 30 Cal. App. 3d 416, 422.

[100] *Ibid.*, ¶ 7. [101] *Lucas v. South Carolina Coastal Council*, 2886.

[102] For commentary, see D. T. Cavarello, 'From *Penn Central* to *United Artists' I & II*: The Rise to Immunity of Historic Preservation Designation from Successful Takings Challenges', *Boston College Environmental Affairs Law Review* 22 (1994–1995), 606.

[103] *Lucas v. South Carolina Coastal Council*, at 2895.

[104] *Tahoe-Sierra Preservation Council v. Tahoe Regional Planning Agency*, 535 US, 302, 330 (2002).

[105] Manwaring, 'American Heritage at Stake', 318.

[106] *Nollan v. California Coastal Commission*, 483 US 825 (1987) and *Dolan v. City of Tigard*, 512 US 374 (1994).

cover all costs of archaeological research, was unconstitutional.[107] The Tribunal held that such duties were the sole obligation of the state. If these costs, which are usually substantial, were to be borne by the landowners, the latter would not be able to cover them and the public would be deprived of the enjoyment of and access to cultural property.[108] The Polish Constitution also provided that restrictions of ownership could not violate the core of the right to property, and that legislative measures must be adequate and proportionate to the goal that is to be achieved.[109]

In conclusion, this brief survey of relevant national cases shows that with regard to the interplay between conservation policies and private economic interests, a 'decision making algorithm as a tool for making or predicting judicial decisions' is not something that exists.[110] By contrast, the three-step test provided by *Penn Central* provides a useful analytical 'framework or structure for discussion' of the issues arising from conservation policies,[111] catalysing the attention of adjudicators regarding: (1) the effect of the given measure; (2) interference with legitimate expectations; and (3) public purpose. In some instances the Court 'construed the character of the governmental action deferentially'[112] by inquiring whether the conservation policy under challenge was 'reasonably related to the promotion of the general welfare'.[113]

### *2.3 The settlement of disputes between foreign investors and states*

While international investment law is a well-established area of public international law, investment treaty arbitration is a recent phenomenon.[114] When the International Centre for the Settlement of Investment Disputes (ICSID)[115] was established in 1966 no one could predict that investment

[107] Judgment of 8 October 2007, K 20/07, OTK-A 2007/9/102. For commentary, see M. Habdas, 'My Home is My Castle – But is my Castle Truly Mine? Polish Historical Immovables as Objects of Ownership', *Opinio Juris in Comparatione* 2(5) (2010), 5–6.

[108] *Ibid.* [109] *Ibid.*, at 9.

[110] E. R. Claeys, 'The *Penn Central* Test and Tensions in Liberal Property Theory', *Harvard Environmental Law Review* 30 (2006), 343 (internal citations omitted).

[111] *Ibid.* [112] *Ibid.*, 357. [113] *Penn Central*, at 131.

[114] See Newcombe and Paradell, *Law and Practice of Investment Treaties*, p. 45. See generally Z. Douglas, *The International Law of Investment Claims* (Cambridge University Press, 2009).

[115] Convention on the Settlement of Investment Disputes between States and Nationals of Other States, 18 March 1965, 575 UNTS 159 (hereinafter ICSID Convention or Washington Convention) Articles 1–3.

treaty arbitration would move 'from a matter of peripheral academic interest to a matter of vital international concern'.[116] Investor–state arbitration has become a standard feature in international investment treaties since the 1980s, and the mechanism has been increasingly used.[117] Under the mechanism, foreign investors may bring claims against the host state before international arbitral tribunals, which may be ad hoc or administered under the aegis of different institutions, such as the Permanent Court of Arbitration (PCA), the International Chamber of Commerce (ICC), ICSID and others.

This development has transformed the landscape of modern investment protection,[118] as customary international law and Friendship, Commerce and Navigation (FCN) treaties did not confer such a right on individuals.[119] Similarly, investment treaties that pre-dated the establishment of ICSID only provided for state against state disputes. According to the traditional paradigm of states as the only subjects of international law and the only ones having the capacity to raise international claims against other states in legal proceedings, customary law and FCN treaties used to leave the dispute settlement of investment-related disputes to national courts, or to the exercise of diplomatic protection by the state of origin of the given corporation. By exercising diplomatic protection, a state invokes – through diplomatic action or other dispute settlement mechanism – the responsibility of another state for an internationally wrongful act of that state, causing injury to a national of the former state.[120] A company could seek redress before the local courts of the host state; after which, failing a satisfactory outcome, it could seek diplomatic protection from the home state.[121] However, diplomatic

[116] S. D. Franck, 'Development and Outcomes of Investment Treaty Arbitration', *Harvard Int'l L.J.* 50 (2009), 435.

[117] From 1995 to 2011 the ICSID registered almost ten times as many claims as in the previous 30 years and the growth rate appears to be increasing. ICSID, *The ICSID Caseload: Statistics 2012–1* (Washington D.C.: ICSID, 2012). The ICSID renaissance is probably due to economic globalization and the proliferation of investment treaties. See D. Sedlak, 'ICSID's Resurgence in International Investment Arbitration: Can the Momentum Hold?', *Penn State Int'l L. Rev.* 23 (2004), 147.

[118] *See* C. McLachlan, L. Shore and M. Weiniger, *International Investment Arbitration: Substantive Principles* (Cambridge University Press, 2007), p. 5.

[119] *See* J. Collier and V. Lowe, *The Settlement of Disputes in International Law: Institutions and Procedures* (Oxford University Press, 1999), pp. 1–10.

[120] ILC Draft Articles on Diplomatic Protection, Article 1. See ILC Draft Articles on Diplomatic Protection (2006), GAOR, Sixty-first Session, Supplement No. 10 (A/61/10).

[121] I. Brownlie, *Principles of Public International Law*, 7th edn (Oxford University Press, 2008), p. 522.

protection constitutes a prerogative and not a duty for states, which can exercise it at their will. By resorting to diplomatic action or international judicial proceedings on behalf of one of its nationals, 'a State is in reality asserting its own right, the right to ensure in the person of its nationals respect for the rules of international law'.[122] When violations of treaty or customary law obligations are limited in scope and discriminate against a foreign investor only, its national state will be reluctant to initiate an international dispute because of political and *de minimis* considerations. Furthermore, even if the state were to bring an international claim for its own injury, it would be under no obligation to pay any reparations received to the national actually injured.

In contrast with this traditional paradigm, modern investment treaties do not require the intervention of the home state in the furtherance of the dispute. Foreign investors no longer depend on the discretion of their home states in the context of diplomatic protection, in deciding whether or not a claim should be raised against another state; and recourse to diplomatic protection has become residual. While in the 1970s, the ICJ in the *Barcelona Traction* case found it 'surprising' that the evolution of international investment law had not gone further in the light of the expansion of economic activities in the preceding half century,[123] in the more recent *Diallo* case, the Court has recognized the residual nature of the exercise of diplomatic protection and recourse to the Court in case of investment disputes.[124] In practice, this means that foreign investors have access to arbitration against the host state if there is a BIT between the home state and the host state. In the absence of such a legal instrument, foreign investors have access only to the traditional dispute settlement mechanisms, including the host state national courts, human rights courts and, if diplomatic protection is exercised, inter-state dispute settlement mechanisms.

Suggestively described as 'arbitration without privity',[125] the internationalization of investment disputes has, by guaranteeing a neutral forum, been conceived as an important means for adequately recognizing

[122] PCIJ, *Penevezys-Saldutiskis Railway Case* (*Estonia v. Lithuania*), Judgment 28 February 1938, PCIJ (Ser A/B) No. 76 (1939).

[123] *Barcelona Traction, Light & Power Company Limited* (*Belgium v. Spain*), Judgment of 5 February 1970, 1970 ICJ Reports 3, at ¶ 89.

[124] *Case Concerning* Ahmadou Sadio Diallo (*Guinea v. Democratic Republic Congo*), Preliminary Objections, Judgment of 24 May 2007, at ¶¶ 88–91, available at www.icj-cij.org/docket/files/103/13856.pdf.

[125] J. Paulsson, 'Arbitration without Privity', *ICSID Review–FILJ* 10 (1995), 256.

and protecting the assets of foreign investors from expropriation or other forms of interference by the host state. Through arbitration clauses the host state signatory to the treaty agrees in advance to arbitrate disputes over the treaty meaning and application at the investor's initiative. Such clauses are to some degree necessary to render meaningful the substantive investment treaty provisions.[126] As Böckstiegel points out, the traditional David–Goliath relationship between private investors and states has been replaced, at least procedurally, by a level playing-field, even if, in some circumstances, private claimants, such as large multinational companies, may well have more resources available than some small states who are respondents.[127] The rationale for internationalizing investor–state disputes lies in the assumed independence and impartiality of international arbitral tribunals, while national dispute settlement procedures are often perceived as biased or inadequate.[128]

### 2.4 *Main procedural features of investor–state arbitration*

The arbitral process in investment arbitration presents characteristics similar to those in a typical international commercial arbitration.[129] The composition of the tribunal is determined by the parties who generally choose law scholars or professionals. Arbitral rules require that arbitrators be independent.[130] While 'arbitrators . . . are expected to be both independent of the party appointing them and impartial . . . it is usually conceded that without violating in any way this theoretical obligation of independence, the arbitrator may quite acceptably share the nationality, or political or economic philosophy, or "legal culture" of the party who has nominated him – and may therefore be assumed from the very beginning to be "sympathetic" to that party's contentions or favourably disposed to its positions.'[131] Arbitrators have clear incentives to adopt a

[126] T. Wälde, 'The Umbrella Clause in Investment Arbitration: A Comment on Original Intentions and Recent Cases', *JWIT* 6 (2005), 185.

[127] See also K.-H. Böckstiegel, 'Enterprise v. State: the New David and Goliath?', *Arbitration International* 23 (2007), 93–104.

[128] See e.g. Newcombe and Paradell, *Law and Practice of Investment Treaties*, p. 24.

[129] N. Blackaby, 'Investment Arbitration and Commercial Arbitration (or the Tale of the Dolphin and the Shark)', in J. Lew and L. Mistelis (eds.), *Pervasive Problems in International Arbitration* (Kluwer Law International, 2006), pp. 217–33.

[130] J. Salacuse, 'The Emerging Global Regime for Investment', *Harvard ILJ* 51 (2010), 466.

[131] A. S. Rau, 'Integrity in Private Judging', *South Texas L. R.* 38 (1997), 507.

high standard of conduct because of reputation;[132] the arbitrator has an obligation to disclose eventual conflicts of interest; and the parties can challenge him or her if a conflict of interest is deemed to have arisen.

Confidentiality is one of the main features of the proceedings as hearings are generally held *in camera* and the documents submitted by the parties remain confidential in principle. Final awards may not be published, depending on the will of the parties. Even the names of the parties may not be disclosed, much less the details of the dispute.[133] While confidentiality well suits commercial disputes, it may be problematic in investor–state arbitration, because investment arbitrations may deal with public policy matters. The lack of transparency may hamper efforts to track investment treaty disputes, to monitor their frequency, and their settlement, and to assess the policy implications involved.

In recent years, efforts to make investment arbitration more transparent have been undertaken in different fora. In response to calls from civil society groups, the three parties to the NAFTA – Canada, the US and Mexico – have pledged to disclose all NAFTA arbitrations and to open future arbitration hearings to the public.[134] Similarly, ICSID rules provide for the public disclosure of dispute proceedings under their auspices.[135] Increasingly, investment arbitration tribunals have allowed public interest groups to present *amicus curiae* briefs or to have access to the arbitral process.[136] ICSID rules have undergone amendments, and now also grant ICSID tribunals discretion to allow interested third parties to make written submissions in arbitral proceedings.[137] These important moves, however, involve the conduct of the proceedings in a

[132] See A. Lowenfeld, 'The Party-Appointed Arbitrator in International Controversies: Some Reflections', *Texas ILJ* 30 (1995), 59–72.

[133] For instance, Article 46 of the 2010 Arbitration Rules of the Arbitration Institute of the Stockholm Chamber of Commerce (SCC Institute) provides that unless otherwise agreed by the parties, the SCC Institute and the Arbitral Tribunal shall maintain the confidentiality of the arbitration and the award. The new arbitration rules entered into force on 1 January 2010. The text is available at www.sccinstitute.com.

[134] NAFTA Free Trade Commission, *Statement of the Free Trade Commission on Non-Disputing Party Participation*, 7 October 2003, 16 WTAM (2004).

[135] See ICSID Regulation 22. The Administrative and Financial Regulations of ICSID are available at http://icsid.worldbank.org/ICSID/ICSID/RulesMain.jsp.

[136] See e.g. A. Kawharu, 'Participation of Non-Governmental Organizations in Investment Arbitration as Amici Curiae', in M. Waibel, A. Kaushal, K.-H. L. Chung and C. Balchin (eds.), *The Backlash against Investment Arbitration: Perceptions and Reality* (Netherlands: Kluwer Law International, 2010), pp. 275–95.

[137] ICSID Arbitration Rule 37. ICSID Arbitration Rules are available at http://icsid.world bank.org/ICSID/ICSID/RulesMain.jsp.

limited number of investment disputes. Indeed, the vast majority of existing treaties do not mandate such transparency, which means that a number of the proceedings are resolved behind closed doors.

Finally and perhaps more importantly, awards rendered against host states are, in theory, readily enforceable against host-state property worldwide, due to the widespread adoption of the New York[138] and Washington Conventions.[139] The decisions have only limited avenues for revision and cannot be amended by the domestic legal system or a supreme court.[140] Arbitration under the ICSID rules is wholly exempted from the supervision of local courts, with awards being subject only to an internal annulment process. The ICSID annulment process provides for a very limited review. ICSID annulment committees only have the ability to annul awards and send them back to the tribunal or to a new tribunal for a new decision, but cannot replace the decision with their own. The grounds for annulment are narrow and concern due process issues, for instance in cases where: the tribunal was not properly constituted; or it manifestly exceeded its powers; or there was corruption on the part of a member, a fundamental serious departure from a procedural rule, or the award did not state the reasons on which it was based.[141]

## 2.5 *Conflicting paradigms*

Given its hybrid features, investment treaty law and arbitration have been analogized to different legal systems.[142] *First*, arbitral tribunals have been analogized to other public international law tribunals. For instance, due to the transfer of adjudicative authority from national courts to arbitral tribunals, it has been argued that access to investor–state arbitration shares many characteristics of the direct right of action before human rights courts. However, arbitral tribunals do not only constitute an additional forum with respect to state courts, but also an alternative to the same. Thus, not only can foreign investors seek another decision after an eventual recourse to the national courts, but they are not

138 Convention on the Recognition and Enforcement of Foreign Arbitral Awards (New York Convention) 10 June 1958, 330 UNTS 38.

139 Convention on the Settlement of Investment Disputes between States and Nationals of Other States, Washington D.C., 18 March 1965, in force 14 October 1966, 575 UNTS 159.

140 New York Convention, Article V.

141 ICSID Convention, Article 52.

142 See Roberts, 'Clash of Paradigms: Actors and Analogies Shaping the Investment Treaty System'.

required to exhaust local remedies prior to pursuing an international legal claim. This is in stark counterpoint to international human rights treaties which oblige the claimants to turn to local courts in the first instance.

Arbitral tribunals have also been analogized to the WTO panels and the Appellate Body.[143] The case for drawing such an analogy is evident. On the one hand, arbitral tribunals and WTO dispute settlement panels do essentially share the same functions by settling international disputes in accordance with international economic law. Like WTO panels and the Appellate Body, arbitral tribunals are asked to strike a balance between economic and non-economic concerns. On the other hand, certain international trade treaties present an articulated regime that the investment treaties presuppose.[144] For instance, there is some coincidence in the subject matter of investment treaties and the TRIMS Agreement. Some authors support such an approach, as it would impede the dilution of multilateral norms while providing predictability.[145] However, while only states can file claims before the WTO panels and the Appellate Body, investor–state arbitration can be pursued by foreign investors directly without any intervention of the home state. Furthermore, arbitral tribunals can authorize the award of damages to the foreign investors, while remedies at the WTO only have prospective character and involve states only.

*Second*, given the fact that under most investment treaties, states have agreed to give arbitrators a comprehensive jurisdiction over what are essentially regulatory disputes, such review has been compared to a sort of administrative review.[146] Authors postulate the existence of a 'global administrative space': a space 'in which the strict dichotomy between domestic and international has largely broken down, in which administrative functions are performed in often complex

143 See generally T. Weiler (ed.), *Intersections: Dissemblance or Convergence between International Trade and Investment Law, TDM* 3 (2011).

144 C. Pfaff, 'Alternative Approaches to Foreign Investment Protection', *TDM* 3 (2006), 1–16.

145 L. Hsu, 'Applicability of WTO Law in Regional Trade Agreements: Identifying the Links', in L. Bartels and F. Ortino (eds.), *Regional Trade Agreements and the WTO Legal System* (Oxford: Oxford University Press, 2006), p. 551.

146 G. Van Harten and M. Loughlin, 'Investment Treaty Arbitration as a Species of Global Administrative Law', *EJIL* 17 (2006), 121; G. Van Harten, *Investment Treaty Arbitration and Public Law* (Oxford University Press, 2007); D. Schneiderman, *Constitutionalizing Economic Globalization: Investment Rules and Democracy's Premise* (Oxford University Press, 2008).

interplays between ... institutions on different levels'.[147] Under this theoretical framework, investor–state arbitration has been conceptualized as a global administrative law (GAL) creature,[148] which impels states to conform to GAL principles and to adopt principles of good governance.

In particular, Van Harten and Loughlin claim that investment arbitration can be analogized to domestic administrative review, since investment disputes arise from the exercise of public authority by the state and arbitral tribunals are given the power to review and control such an exercise of public authority.[149] While arbitration structurally constitutes a private model of adjudication, investment treaty arbitration can be viewed as public law adjudication, as it encompasses the full panoply of the state's regulatory relations with foreign investors.[150] Adjudication over a state's *acta jure imperii* implies a significant departure from the conventional use of international arbitration in the commercial sphere.[151] Arbitral awards ultimately shape the relationship between the state, on the one hand, and private individuals on the other,[152] determining matters such as the legality of governmental activity, the degree to which individuals should be protected from regulation, and the appropriate role of the state.[153] Indeed, many of the recent arbitral awards have concerned the determination of the appropriate boundary between two conflicting values: the legitimate sphere for state regulation in the pursuit of public goods on the one hand, and the protection of private property from state interference on the other.

However, the availability of investor–state arbitration should not be considered as a method of 'expropriating' the state of its judicial control over administrative matters. Instead, such an international mechanism should be viewed as complementary to the substantive guarantees provided by international investment treaties. International arbitration has traditionally involved horizontal relations between 'peers', that is, states

147 N. Krisch and B. Kingsbury, 'Introduction: Global Governance and Global Administrative Law in the International Legal Order', *EJIL* 17 (2006), 1.

148 Van Harten and Loughlin, 'Investment Treaty Arbitration as a Species of Global Administrative Law', 121.

149 *Ibid.*, 121–3.

150 G. Van Harten, 'The Public–Private Distinction in the International Arbitration of Individual Claims Against the State', *ICLQ* 56 (2007), 372.

151 Douglas, 'The Hybrid Foundations of Investment Treaty Arbitration', 221–2.

152 Van Harten, *Investment Treaty Arbitration and Public Law*, p. 70.

153 M. Sornarajah, 'The Clash of Globalizations and the International Law on Foreign Investment', *Canadian Foreign Policy* 12 (2003), 17.

versus states or private individuals versus private individuals. The fact that international investment treaty arbitration today addresses a diagonal relationship between host state and foreign investors reflects an evolution which is present in other sectors of international law such as human rights law. Therefore, if this mechanism is to parallel the local judicial review of the courts of the host state, it should not be conceived as a substitute for that, but as a different and additional forum expressly provided by international investment treaties. Investor–state arbitration is a creature of international law established by treaty, and as such it constitutes a consensual delimitation of state power.

*Third*, because of the procedural rules which govern it, investor–state arbitration has been analogized to commercial arbitration. As mentioned above, arbitrators are selected by the parties and/or an appointing institution and the hearings are held *in camera*. However, the distinction between international commercial arbitration and investment treaty arbitration is clear: while the former generally involves private parties and concerns disputes of a commercial nature, the latter involves states and private actors and may concern disputes of a public law nature.[154] This 'diagonal' dispute settlement mechanism is a major novelty in international law since international disputes have traditionally involved states only. In this sense, investment arbitration represents a successful means to ensure access to justice at the international level.[155]

These paradigms for categorizing investment treaty arbitrations all have merits and weaknesses; and may diverge and converge on specific aspects. Most notably, none of them – other than the international law and public law paradigms, due perhaps to their comprehensive nature – fully encapsulates the complex phenomenon of investor–state arbitration. There are compelling arguments for assimilating arbitrators to international judges. From a historical perspective, adjudication traces its roots to arbitration. From a functional perspective, both judges and arbitrators 'exercise the ultimate decision-making authority of the juridical sovereign in public law'.[156] Like judges, arbitrators are asked to safeguard vital community interests as well as to settle disputes in conformity with

[154] See J. Paulsson, 'International Arbitration is not Arbitration', *Stockholm International Arbitration Review* 2 (2008), 1–20.

[155] F. Francioni, 'Access to Justice, Denial of Justice, and International Investment Law', *EJIL* 20 (2009), 729–47.

[156] Van Harten, 'The Public–Private Distinction in the International Arbitration of Individual Claims against the State', 379–80.

'principles of justice and international law'.[157] As Crawford puts it, 'Investment law ... is about the way in which we bring the state under some measure of control, which is the main aspiration of general international law.'[158]

In sum, these paradigms are not normative; rather they are descriptive in nature and reflect and emphasize some aspects of investment treaty arbitration over others. They are a useful theoretical tool to better configure and understand investment treaty arbitration. While investment treaty arbitration is a relatively recent phenomenon and remains under-theorized, awareness of the existence of different paradigms promotes its better understanding and functioning. It is not within the scope of this book to provide further elaboration on these paradigms and the epistemic communities which adopt them, but it is worth pointing out that comparisons are not neutral; depending on the selected perspective the outcomes can be different.[159] Although no single paradigm is hereby singled out for analysis as the leading paradigm, the author mainly relies on the public international law paradigm; other paradigms are pinpointed by way of reference.

## 2.6 *The legitimacy crisis of international investment law and arbitration*

The rise in investment treaty arbitration and its impact on public goods has raised a number of criticisms. On the one hand, investor–state tribunals are ad hoc, constituted under different arbitral rules and without an appellate court to ensure consistency in dicta. The resulting risk of inconsistent awards has caused concern leaving many observers with the impression that international investment arbitration lacks structure and coherence.[160] On the other hand, given the fact that a number of arbitrations have affected public goods, ranging from access to water, to tobacco control, to cultural heritage management, some commentators

[157] VCLT, Preamble.

[158] J. Crawford, 'International Protection of Foreign Direct Investment: Between Clinical Isolation and Systematic Integration', in R. Hofmann and C. J. Tams (eds.), *International Investment Law and General International Law: From Clinical Isolation to Systemic Integration?* (Baden/Baden: Nomos, 2011), p. 22.

[159] V. Vadi, 'Critical Comparisons: The Role of Comparative Law in Investment Treaty Arbitration', 39 *Denver J. of Int'l Law & Policy* 1 (2010), 78.

[160] See S. Franck, 'The Legitimacy Crisis in Investment Treaty Arbitration: Privatizing Public International Law through Inconsistent Decisions', *Fordham L. Rev.* 73 (2005), 1537–8.

contend that international investment law and arbitration is constraining the regulatory autonomy of the state, potentially leading to the reverse discrimination of foreign investors and/or imprudently using private commercial dispute resolution tools to resolve public disputes.[161] Have international investment agreements 'become a charter of rights for foreign investors, with no concomitant responsibilities or liabilities, no direct legal links to promoting development objectives, and no protection for public welfare in the face of environmentally or socially destabilizing foreign investment'?[162] Has international investment law become a 'corporate bill of rights'[163] or a 'system of corporate rights without responsibility or liability'?[164]

Against this background, being fearful of becoming respondents in investment disputes, states have increasingly felt the need to protect their regulatory space and to limit arbitral discretion. While a few countries have withdrawn from the ICSID system,[165] others have omitted investor–state arbitration from the provisions of their treaties. For instance, the 2005 Australia–United States FTA does not include investor–state arbitration and Australia announced it will no longer include investor–state arbitration in its treaties with developing countries.[166] Others have adopted a preventive stance and have introduced general exceptions clauses in their investment treaties.[167]

Such criticisms, however, do not play a merely negative role; rather, they also have a positive function in that they can strengthen the system's legitimacy by raising important issues, stimulating debate and spurring novel approaches. For instance, due to the increasingly widespread publication of arbitral awards and sustained commentary the practice

[161] See generally M. Waibel, A. Kaushal, K.-H. L. Chung and C. Balchin, 'The Blacklash against Investment Arbitration: Perceptions and Reality', in M. Waibel, A. Kaushal, K.-H. L. Chung and C. Balchin (eds.), *The Backlash against Investment Arbitration: Perceptions and Reality* (Netherlands: Kluwer Law International, 2010), p. xxxviii.

[162] H. Mann, 'The Right of States to Regulate and International Investment Law: A Comment' in UNCTAD, *The Development Dimension of FDI: Policy and Rule-Making Perspectives* (New York/Geneva: UN, 2003), p. 212.

[163] T. Weiler, 'Balancing Human Rights and Investor Protection: A New Approach for a Different Legal Order', *TDM* 1 (2004), 2.

[164] Mann, 'The Right of States to Regulate and International Investment Law', p. 215.

[165] For instance, Bolivia, Ecuador and Venezuela have withdrawn from the ICSID Convention. See S. Ripinsky, 'Venezuela's Withdrawal from ICSID: What It Does and Does Not Achieve', *ITN*, 13 April 2012.

[166] See L. E. Peterson, 'In Policy Switch, Australia Disavows Need for Investor–State Arbitration Provisions in Trade and Investment Agreements', *IAR*, 14 April 2011.

[167] See Chapter 7 below.

of arbitral decision-making has converged, and precedents, albeit non-binding, matter. With regard to the criticism that international investment law and arbitration constitute a charter of corporate rights without responsibilities, it is worth pointing out that in protecting the property rights of foreign investors, international investment treaties do not have a revolutionary character. After World War II, property rights and the parallel right to compensation for expropriation, were enshrined in the Universal Declaration of Human Rights,[168] the first Protocol of the European Convention on Human Rights (ECHR),[169] the American Human Rights Convention,[170] and the Banjul Charter,[171] as well as in the Constitutions of many states.[172] Therefore, investment treaties reaffirm the right to property of a particular category of people, i.e. foreigners.

Even when considering property rights as human rights, limits and boundaries must be duly acknowledged. For instance, the ECHR recognizes 'the right of the state to enforce such laws as it deems necessary to control the use of property in accordance with the general interest or to secure the payment of taxes or other contributions or penalties'.[173] The American Convention on Human Rights similarly states that 'the law may subordinate [the] use and enjoyment [of property] to the interest of society'.[174]

Thus, the balance between private interests and the public at large is intrinsic to the same concept of property. In other words, the owner has the power to use what she owns; but she must use it lawfully. Therefore, a clear distinction needs to be made between the physical power to use the thing and the lawful use of the same. If we accept an absolutist conception of property, interference with the use of property becomes ipso facto a breach of the relevant BIT.

168 Universal Declaration of Human Rights (UDHR), GA Res. 217(III) UNGAOR UN Doc A/810 (1948), 10 December 1948, Article 17.

169 Article 1(1) of the First Protocol to the European Convention on Human Rights. Convention for the Protection of Human Rights and Fundamental Freedoms (the European Convention on Human Rights or ECHR) 4 November 1950, in force 3 September 1953, 213 UNTS 222.

170 Article 21.1 of the American Convention on Human Rights, 22 November 1969, 9 ILM 673 (1970).

171 Article 14 of the African Charter on Human and Peoples' Rights, 1520 UNTS 217.

172 See V. Vadi, 'Through the Looking Glass: International Investment Law through the Lenses of a Property Theory', *Manchester JIEL* 8 (2011), 47.

173 First Protocol to the European Convention on Human Rights, Article 1.2.

174 American Convention on Human Rights, Article 21.1.

However, this absolutist view is a misconception of property, as most constitutional systems and even human rights systems which protect property as a human right, also recognize the intrinsic limits of property and the need for its regulation.

## Final remarks

In analysing the content of investment treaties, what stands out as perhaps their most relevant feature is that countries seek to make the regulatory framework for foreign direct investment more transparent, stable and predictable and, thus, more attractive to foreign investors. The ratification of treaties necessarily involves states limiting their regulatory autonomy in exchange for certain benefits.[175] In this regard, however, investment treaties are more intrusive than trade agreements, as foreign investment takes place within the borders of a state. As one author puts it, 'While [investment] treaties may be a useful bulwark against egregious interference or expropriation of foreign-owned property, they may condition more subtle measures taken by governments . . . in the realm of regulation, taxation, legislation and judicial decision making.'[176] In addition, investment treaties provide foreign investors with direct access to the investor–state dispute settlement mechanism, which constitutes a revolutionary innovation causing a paradigm shift in international law. In this sense, the host state loses its exclusive territorial jurisdiction over disputes arising in its territory.

However, the right to regulate is a basic attribute of sovereignty under international law.[177] Traditionally, the sovereign powers of the state include the authority to adopt legislation, enforce judgments and enact those policies that it holds to be essential to promoting the basic needs of its citizens. In certain cases, states own not only a right to regulate, but also a duty to do so, because of international and/or regional obligations. In these cases, regulation has the function of ensuring the safeguard of internationally or regionally recognized values, and international

175 See generally W. Shan, P. Simons and D. Singh (eds.), *Redefining Sovereignty in International Economic Law* (Oxford: Hart Publishing, 2008).

176 L. E. Peterson, *The Global Governance of Foreign Direct Investment: Madly Off in All Directions* (Geneva: Friedrich Ebert Stiftung Publisher, 2005), p. 4.

177 M. Sornarajah, 'Right to Regulate and Safeguards', in UNCTAD, *The Development Dimension of FDI: Policy and Rule Making Perspectives* (New York/Geneva: UN, 2003), p. 205.

institutions that have 'rendered the erosion of sovereignty more legible, actually serve as a means to reassert sovereignty'.[178]

Therefore, according to some authors, investment treaty law and arbitration is facing a 'legitimacy crisis', as arbitral awards can affect public policy, but there is uncertainty over the relevance or irrelevance of norms external to investment law (such as human rights law) within investment treaty arbitration. Furthermore, while developing countries have deemed investment treaty arbitration politically biased against them, emerging economies and industrialized countries alike have also expressed some concerns about this mechanism. The emerging criticisms on the functioning of investment treaty arbitration in relation to public goods should be taken into account to allow the investment treaty system to develop in accordance with public international law. Paradoxically, although investment treaties share a philosophical affinity with civil and political rights, their application has determined a dramatic increase in support for economic, social and cultural rights worldwide with possible implications for the better incorporation of these latter three rights into the mainstream of international law.[179] Against this background, this study now explores the relationship between investor rights and cultural heritage in international investment law and arbitration.

[178] K. Raustiala, 'Rethinking the Sovereignty Debate in International Economic Law', *JIEL* 6 (2003), 841.

[179] C. H. Brower II, 'NAFTA's Investment Chapter: Initial Thoughts about Second Generation Rights', *Vanderbilt Journal of Transnational Law* 37 (2003), 1533–66.

# PART II

## When cultures collide: cultural heritage and foreign direct investment

# When cultures collide: cultural heritage and foreign direct investment

## Introduction

Cultural sovereignty, meaning the freedom of any state to choose its cultural model and to set relevant cultural policies, is an expression of state sovereignty. By virtue of state sovereignty, and in the words of the UN General Assembly, 'Each State has the right to freely choose and develop its political, social, economic and cultural systems.'[1] Even the ICJ has restated the concept, affirming that 'each state is permitted, by the principle of state sovereignty, to decide freely for example the choice of political, economic, social and cultural system, and formulation of foreign policy'.[2] Therefore, cultural policies have traditionally fallen within the domestic jurisdiction of the state.

Nonetheless, in the past sixty years there has been a gradual erosion of the *domaine réservé* of the states in the cultural sector, as international law has increasingly regulated cultural matters. As mentioned in Chapter 1, international cultural law shores up and backs up states in their regulatory responsibilities and contributes to multilevel governance. In parallel, human rights law has increasingly touched upon cultural matters. It is generally acknowledged that states can set their cultural policies as long as they respect *jus cogens* and relevant international law obligations.

With regard to the interplay between cultural policies and investor rights, states generally pursue cultural policies through top-down regulatory approaches. What happens if the regulation goes too far? As an archaeologist puts it, there is a risk that '[t]he relevant state authorities

1 Declaration on Principles of International Law Concerning Friendly Relations and Co-operation among States in accordance with the Charter of the United Nations, GA Res. 2625, UN GAOR Res., 25th sess., Supp. No. 28, at 123–4, UN Doc. A/8028 (1970).

2 *Case Concerning Military and Paramilitary Activities in and Against Nicaragua* (*Nicaragua v. United States*), Judgment, 27 June 1986, [1986] ICJ Reports 14, ¶¶ 202–9.

are seen as the nasty heritage police bothering house owners unnecessarily and preventing industrial development and economic growth by increasing construction costs'.[3] The cultural goal of a regulatory measure does not imply per se absence of discrimination or of any other breach of investment treaties. The jurisprudence of other international courts and tribunals is replete with cases of disguised discrimination, whereby foreigners are discriminated against through alleged cultural policies,[4] and/or disproportionate measures adopted to pursue cultural policies.[5]

Even when the adopted regulation is legitimate and taintless, questions arise with regard to the impact that such regulation will have on foreign property. In a seminal study of the matter, Rosalyn Higgins refined the question as the determination of who is to pay the economic cost of attending to the public interest involved in the measure in question. The pendulum swings between society as a whole, represented by the state, and the foreign investor. If the state never had to provide compensation to an investor deprived of property as a result of the exercise by the state of its regulatory power, the opportunity for abuse of such a rule would be evident and almost anything might be taken to be a significant part of a state's cultural heritage. Conversely, if the government always had to compensate investors deprived of their property as a result of the exercise by the state of its regulatory power, this would paralyse the regulatory activity of the state.

[3] C. Holtorf, 'What Does Not Move Any Hearts: Why Should It be Saved? The *Denkmalpflegediskussion* in Germany', *International J. of Cultural Property* 14 (2007), 48 (adding that 'this negative image is beautifully expressed by the following graffiti: "Gott schütze uns vor Staub und Schmutz, vor Feuer, Krieg, und Denkmalschultz"' which Holtorf translates as 'May God protect us from dust and dirt, from fire, war and the preservation of cultural heritage'. *Ibid.*, 52 (internal citations omitted)).

[4] For instance, the European Court of Justice (ECJ) found the conduct of municipal authorities in Italy introducing advantageous rates for admission to monuments and museums only for Italian nationals and residents as discriminatory. ECJ, Judgment of 16 January 2003, case C-388/01, *Commission of the European Communities v. Italian Republic.*

[5] For instance, in an early case, the ECJ found that the imposition of a progressive tax on the exportation of goods of artistic or historic interest 'had an effect equivalent to a customs duty on exportation and . . . was [therefore] contrary to Article 16 of the EEC Treaty', deeming that 'such measures have the sole effect of rendering more onerous the exportation of the products in question, without ensuring the attainment of the object referred to in that article, which is to protect the artistic, historic or archaeological heritage'. ECJ, *Commission v. Italy*, Case 7/68, Judgment of 10 December 1968, p. 430. On this case, see e.g. A. Biondi, 'The Merchant, the Thief and the Citizen: The Circulation of Works of Art within the European Union', *CMLR* 34 (1997), 1177–8.

Given the extraordinary increase of foreign direct investment flows in recent years, the privileged regime created by international investment law within the boundaries of the host state has increasingly determined a tension between investors' rights and cultural heritage protection.[6] While such tension has been adjudicated before different fora, the choice to limit the scope of analysis to investor–state arbitration is due to the peculiar characteristics of this mechanism and its extraordinary success in the past decades. The selection of this forum does not imply any a priori judgement on the preference of a dispute settlement mechanism vis-à-vis another. Instead, the selection of this perspective is due to the rich emerging 'case law' in this area and the fact that the linkage between cultural heritage and investor rights is relatively unexplored from this particular angle.

How have arbitrators dealt with cultural heritage-related cases? At first glance, the interaction between international investment law and international cultural law appears imbalanced. While international cultural law comprises embryonic dispute settlement mechanisms, international investment treaties now include sophisticated means of dispute resolution. However, this study shows that arbitrators have increasingly taken cultural concerns into consideration in deciding cases brought before them. While arbitral tribunals are tribunals of limited jurisdiction and thus cannot adjudicate on the violation of norms of international law outside the realm of international investment law, they have increasingly taken these other norms into account in evaluating the conduct of the host state. The fact that economic standards of valuation are not the only ones that are taken into account by arbitrators is remarkable.

While states are free to establish the cultural policies they deem appropriate, they are nonetheless bound to respect *jus cogens* and relevant international law obligations. In this sense, investment arbitration can encourage a more substantive 'rule of law' by external disciplines, subjecting international cultural law to rules of accountability, thus avoiding that cultural policies pose a disproportionate or unreasonable burden on the rights of individuals. The concept of rule of law is a principle of governance which requires, inter alia, equality before the law, fairness in the application of the law, legal certainty, avoidance of arbitrariness and procedural and legal transparency. The respect of the rule of law is a key element of state

[6] See e.g. A. Froelich, 'L'enjeu de la culture dans son contexte économique international', in P. Meerts (ed.), *Culture and International Law* (The Hague: Hague Academic Coalition, 2008), pp. 83–93.

capacity to comply with both international cultural governance and international investment governance.

From a cultural heritage law perspective, multilevel cultural governance may reinforce protection of cultural heritage; the broad ratification of the relevant UNESCO conventions indicates that the international community perceives the protection of cultural heritage as an important public interest. However, some investment treaty arbitrations that will be examined in the second part of this book show the vulnerability of indigenous and rural heritage to economic and developmental interests. In conclusion, while the review of domestic regulations can improve good cultural governance and the transparent pursuit of legitimate cultural policies, investment tribunals have limited jurisdiction: they cannot adjudicate on the eventual violation of international cultural law. The mechanism is triggered mainly by foreign investors. The affected communities are represented by the host state, but have few procedural rights in the context of the proceedings. In sum, concerns remain about the protection of cultural entitlements in international investment law and arbitration. Part III of the book will explore ways in which international cultural law and international investment law can be best reconciled and rendered complementary to the greatest extent possible.

# 3

# The world heritage and foreign direct investment

> There is a temple in ruins stands,
> Fashion'd by long forgotten hands:
> Two or three columns, and many a stone,
> Marble and granite, with grass o'ergrown!
> [. . .] What we have seen our sons shall see;
> Remnants of things that have passed away,
> Fragments of stone, rear'd by creatures of clay!
>
> Lord Byron, *Siege of Corinth* (st. 18)[1]

## Introduction

The tension between cultural heritage on the one hand, and foreign direct investment on the other, has come to the forefront of legal debate. This chapter focuses on the specific 'clash of cultures' between world heritage – that is cultural heritage *par excellence* – and foreign investment in international investment law and arbitration. Foreign investors have increasingly claimed before investment treaty arbitral tribunals that cultural policies negatively affected their investment, thereby amounting to indirect expropriation or other breaches of investment treaties.

The tension between investors' rights and cultural heritage protection raises a number of questions. Is any state measure justified by the fact that it allegedly aims to protect cultural heritage? Can governments use cultural policies to fail to comply with their investment-related commitments or to discriminate against foreign investors? What are the limits, if any, of cultural policies? Would a state be free to establish a *dictature culturelle* or totalitarian control over cultural life? Have arbitral tribunals paid any attention to cultural heritage? If so, how have they balanced investors' rights and the cultural policies of the host state? What implications, if any, can be drawn from these

[1] Quoted by Judge Bauer, *Autocephalous Greek-Orthodox Church of Cyprus and the Republic of Cyprus v. Golberg and Feldman Fine Arts, Inc.*, United States Court of Appeals for The Seventh Circuit, 917 F.2d 278, 1990 US App. Decision.

arbitrations with regard to the current debate on the unity or fragmentation of international law? Is international investment law a self-contained regime? Have arbitral tribunals conformed to existing adjudicative patterns of other courts and tribunals on cultural heritage issues? *Finally*, if one admits that adjudication is a bottom-up mode of governance, which has a fundamental importance with regard to the concrete implementation of a given legal regime, then it follows that the analysis of the adjudicative patterns of cultural heritage disputes also tests the effectiveness of cultural heritage law and, more specifically, the World Heritage Convention.

This chapter addresses these questions, exploring and critically assessing the recent awards on the interplay between the protection of world heritage and the promotion of foreign direct investment, and proceeds as follows. *First*, the multifaceted concept of world heritage will be defined and the main tenets of the UNESCO World Heritage Convention will be sketched out. *Second*, clashes of cultural and investment values are illustrated with reference to the relevant arbitrations. *Third*, a critical assessment exploring the relevance of these cases with regard to the debate on the unity or fragmentation of international law will be offered. *Finally*, some conclusions will be drawn.

## *3.1 The world heritage and its governance*

Considered 'the jewel of UNESCO treaties by international lawyers',[2] the World Heritage Convention (hereinafter WHC)[3] constitutes a turning point in the history of cultural governance, as it represents the first effort to govern world heritage in a comprehensive manner at the international level. The WHC protects cultural properties and natural sites of outstanding universal value and provides for international assistance with regard to the protection and conservation of world heritage.[4] Almost universally adopted, the WHC has proven to be 'the most successful and dynamic instrument' within the family of UNESCO conventions and has played a fundamental role in the conservation of world heritage.[5]

[2] S. von Schorlemer, 'Compliance with the UNESCO World Heritage Convention: Reflections on the Elbe Valley and the Dresden Waldschlössen Bridge', *German YIL* 51 (2009), 321–90.

[3] Convention concerning the Protection of the World Cultural and Natural Heritage (WHC), 16 November 1972, in force 17 December 1975, 11 ILM 1358. As of 19 September 2012, the states parties to the WHC are 190. whc.unesco.org/en/statesparties/.

[4] WHC, Article 13.

[5] F. Francioni and F. Lenzerini, 'The Future of the World Heritage Convention: Problems and Prospects', in F. Francioni (ed.), *The 1972 World Heritage Convention: A Commentary* (Oxford University Press, 2008), p. 409.

The idea of bringing together natural sites and cultural properties of outstanding and universal value came from the United States. A White House Conference in Washington D.C. in 1965 called for a World Heritage Trust.[6] The text of the Convention was the result of the consolidation of two separate texts.[7] One was drafted by the International Council for Monuments and Sites (ICOMOS) and focused on the protection of cultural heritage. The other was an initiative of the United States through the International Union for the Conservation of Nature (IUCN) to protect natural sites. Both the cultural heritage (monuments, architectural works, works of monumental sculpture and painting, groups of buildings and sites) and the natural heritage (natural features, habitats, natural sites or areas of outstanding universal value) are protected under the WHC provided they hold outstanding universal value.[8]

The WHC does not aim to protect all properties of great importance or value, but only a select 'world heritage', whose significance is so 'exceptional as to transcend national boundaries and to be of common importance for present and future generations of all humanity'.[9] Outstanding and universal value indicates 'the ability of the property to exercise universal appeal by virtue of its exceptional qualities, including its authenticity, its resonance in terms of human experience, and its capacity to interpret in an exceptional manner one of the eternal themes of the human conditions, such as the mystery of life, the struggle for survival, death, [and] the search for beauty'.[10] Over the years, the interpretation has moved from the 'best of the best' towards 'representative of the best',[11] and the concept of universality has been linked to 'the capacity to represent the diversity of the cultures and traditions of the world'.[12] According to the *Operational Guidelines*, to

[6] J. Turtinen, *Globalising Heritage: On UNESCO and the Transnational Construction of World Heritage* (Stockholm: Stockholm Centre for Organizational Research, 2000), p. 10.

[7] See L. V. Prott, 'UNESCO International Framework for the Protection of the Cultural Heritage', in J. A. R. Nafziger and A. M. Nicgorski (eds.), *Cultural Heritage Issues: The Legacy of Conquest, Colonization and Commerce* (Leiden: Martinus Nijhoff, 2009), p. 268.

[8] WHC, Articles 1 and 2.

[9] UNESCO, *Operational Guidelines for the Implementation of the World Heritage Convention*, WHC 12/01 (July 2012) (Paris: UNESCO, 2012), ¶ 49.

[10] F. Francioni, 'Preamble', in F. Francioni (ed.), *The 1972 World Heritage Convention: A Commentary* (Oxford University Press, 2008), p. 21.

[11] K. Rao, 'A New Paradigm for the Identification, Nomination and Inscription of Properties on the World Heritage List', *International J. of Heritage Studies* 16 (2010), 163.

[12] Francioni, 'Preamble', p. 21.

be deemed to have outstanding universal value, a property must also meet the conditions of integrity and/or authenticity and must have an adequate protection and management system to ensure its safeguarding.[13]

The WHC establishes a system of identification and registration of World Heritage sites in an international list providing for international assistance with regard to their protection and conservation.[14] States parties must identify sites within their borders which they deem to fall within the purview of the WHC and submit 'tentative lists' of such sites to the World Heritage Committee, an intergovernmental body consisting of twenty-one representatives of different governments elected by the General Assembly of all States parties.[15] After independent evaluation by either ICOMOS or IUCN, the World Heritage Committee then decides whether a property should or should not be inscribed on the World Heritage List.[16]

Properties which are on the World Heritage List can be included by the Committee on the 'List of World Heritage in Danger' ('Danger List') if they are 'threatened by serious and specific dangers' and major operations are necessary for their conservation.[17] Listed sites are prioritized when it comes to allocating funds. Sites may be deleted from the World Heritage List if the conditions for their inscription cease to exist. Although the WHC does not expressly regulate deletion, the World Heritage Committee has deemed this power implied in its competences: as it can inscribe properties on the World Heritage List, it can also delete them from the same list.[18]

The World Heritage Convention offers states parties a range of benefits in return for compliance, including cultural, economic, social and political benefits.[19] Cultural benefits include international visibility of World Heritage sites and the stimulation of cultural life. Ethnologists consider World Heritage sites to be 'status symbols' and 'highly desired symbolic capital'.[20] Placing 'globally dispersed phenomena from different times and places' on the World Heritage List allows such sites to 'take on new meaning in a global context'.[21]

[13] UNESCO, *Operational Guidelines for the Implementation of the World Heritage Convention* (Paris: UNESCO, 2012), ¶¶ 88, 86 and 78.

[14] WHC, Article 13. [15] WHC, Article 11(1). [16] WHC, Article 11(2).

[17] WHC, Article 11(4).

[18] See T. Scovazzi, 'Articles 8–11 World Heritage Committee and World Heritage List', in F. Francioni (ed.), *The World Heritage Convention: A Commentary* (Oxford University Press, 2008), p. 169.

[19] E. J. Goodwin, 'The World Heritage Convention, the Environment, and Compliance', *Colorado J. Int'l Environmental L. & Policy* 20 (2009), 167.

[20] Turtinen, *Globalising Heritage*, p. 3. [21] *Ibid.*, p. 4.

Economic benefits derive from the inclusion of a site on the World Heritage List as the latter entails a process of valorization of cultural sites or 'cultural capitalization'.[22] Through listing, world heritage is converted into economic capital, catalysing and multiplying potential economic benefits. The world heritage brand confers increased visibility on listed sites. In turn, the aura of representing 'the best of the best' promotes tourism and related economic activities.[23] In addition, the WHC promotes capacity building and provides for multilateral funding through the World Heritage Fund.[24] World Heritage sites become 'a magnet for international cooperation'[25] which, in turn, creates opportunities for funding from a variety of sources including UN agencies such as the United Nations Development Program.[26] Additional public benefits include enhancement of quality of life and job creation.

At a more political level, the World Heritage is a 'cosmopolitan political project'[27] which fosters the construction of humankind as 'one overarching community', and 'the becoming of the world as one single place',[28] not only contributing to the preservation of the sites, but also enabling a sense of unity and fostering 'a culture of peace'.[29] At the national level, the listing may help national authorities to prioritize the management of listed sites. As Goodwin points out, 'in development-versus-nature protection debates, international listing . . . may tip the balance in favour of protection' to avoid the exposure of the government to critical comment from the international community.[30]

As the WHC adopts a conservationist approach rather than a preservationist one,[31] the World Heritage sites may endure a range of uses that are ecologically and culturally sustainable. Furthermore, there is no express prohibition on economic activities such as mining within the

[22] A. Kowalski, 'When Cultural Capitalization Became Global Practice', in N. Bandelj and F. F. Wherry (eds.), *The Cultural Wealth of Nations* (Stanford, CA: Stanford University Press, 2011), p. 87.

[23] *Ibid.* [24] Articles 15 and 16 of the WHC.

[25] T. Kono and S. Wrbka, 'General Report', in T. Kono (ed.), *The Impact of Uniform Laws on the Protection of Cultural Heritage and the Preservation of Cultural Heritage in the 21st Century* (Leiden/Boston: Martinus Nijhoff, 2010), pp. 1–8.

[26] J. Phares and C. Guttman, *Investing in World Heritage: Past Achievements, Future Ambitions, A Guide to International Assistance* (Paris: UNESCO, 2002), p. 39.

[27] Turtinen, *Globalising Heritage*, p. 7. [28] *Ibid.*, p. 5. [29] *Ibid.*, pp. 19–20.

[30] Goodwin, 'The World Heritage Convention, the Environment, and Compliance', 170.

[31] C. Redgwell, 'The World Heritage Convention and Other Conventions Relating to the Protection of Natural Heritage', in F. Francioni (ed.), *1972 World Heritage Convention* (Oxford University Press, 2008), p. 380.

World Heritage sites in the text of the Convention.[32] However, in the conservation of (non-renewable) cultural resources a strong emphasis is put on maintenance and the exclusion of activities that may reduce heritage value.[33] For instance, the *Operational Guidelines* clarify that the protection and management of properties should ensure that outstanding universal value is maintained or enhanced in the future.[34] Wherever necessary for the proper conservation of the property, the *Operational Guidelines* require the provision of an adequate buffer zone surrounding the property.[35] These provisions express both *inter*-generational and *intra*-generational equity by permitting the sustainable use of the world heritage by present generations without reducing its cultural value thus benefitting both present and future generations.[36] In some cases, however, human use can be deemed to be incompatible with protection policies.[37]

In addition to their obligations to protect World Heritage sites in their territories, states parties also agree 'not to take any deliberate measures which might damage directly or indirectly' the cultural heritage of another state party.[38] Reportedly, the World Heritage Committee discussed the issue as to whether a home state should stop one of its nationals from mining in a host country's World Heritage site. The case concerned a mining project on Mount Nimba, a World Heritage site jointly nominated by Guinea and Côte d'Ivoire.[39] Should France stop the French company from activities potentially jeopardizing the integrity of the site? The question, however, was not answered, as the area of the mine was excluded from the World Heritage site.[40]

Each World Heritage site has cultural national roots and an international profile.[41] In fact, the protection of world heritage presents a latent

[32] N. Affolder, 'Mining and the World Heritage Convention: Democratic Legitimacy and Treaty Compliance', *Pace Environmental L. Rev.* 24 (2007), 58.

[33] B. Carter and G. Grimwade, 'Balancing Use and Preservation in Cultural Heritage Management', *International J. of Heritage Studies* 3 (2007), 45–53.

[34] *Operational Guidelines*, ¶ 96. [35] *Ibid.*, ¶¶ 103–4.

[36] C. Redgwell, 'Protecting Natural Heritage and Its Transmission to Future Generations', in A. A. Yusuf (ed.), *Standard-Setting in UNESCO, Normative Action in Education, Science and Culture* (Leiden: Brill, 2007), p. 276.

[37] *Operational Guidelines*, ¶ 119. [38] WHC, Article 6(3).

[39] Prott, 'UNESCO International Framework for the Protection of the Cultural Heritage', p. 269.

[40] *Ibid.*

[41] R. Anglin, 'The World Heritage List: Bridging the Cultural Property Nationalism-Internationalism Divide', *Yale J. L. & the Humanities* 20 (2008), 270.

antinomy or dialectic between private property and public interest on the one hand and state sovereignty and world community interest on the other. On the one hand, national regulation provides a first level of protection on the classical basis of the territoriality principle. As states wished to retain the ultimate control over heritage sites within their boundaries, they deliberately used the term 'world heritage' instead of 'common heritage' to reassert their sovereignty.[42] The WHC restates full respect for state sovereignty and for private property rights over World Heritage sites.[43] The achievement of World Heritage status neither implies the direct management of the site by UNESCO, nor the imposition of a single regulatory framework.[44] Rather, the broadly stated obligations allow states to adopt a broad range of conduct which can be deemed compatible with the Convention.[45] In fact, the 'ultimate control always remains with the state party in which the site is located, even if the site is on the World Heritage List'.[46]

On the other hand, the WHC constitutes a second level of governance providing a global response to the many threats facing the world heritage. The protection of world heritage no longer falls within the domestic jurisdiction (*domaine réservé*) of the states which are parties to the WHC.[47] The WHC sets out 'the duty of the international community to cooperate' to protect cultural heritage of outstanding and universal value,[48] enucleating the idea of a collective interest in the protection of such heritage. The *Operational Guidelines*, which are created and frequently revised by the World Heritage Committee, set out 'a code of good practices for effective implementation of the Convention'.[49] Although the *Operational Guidelines* are not binding

[42] G. Nicholson, 'The Common Heritage of Mankind and Mining: An Analysis of the Law as to the High Seas, Outer Space, the Antarctic and World Heritage', *New Zealand J. of Environmental L.* (2002), 195.
[43] WHC, Article 6(1).
[44] R. Bianchi and P. Boniface, 'Editorial: The Politics of World Heritage', *International J. of Heritage Studies* 8 (2002), 80.
[45] Affolder, 'Mining and the World Heritage Convention: Democratic Legitimacy and Treaty Compliance', 37.
[46] Nicholson, 'The Common Heritage of Mankind and Mining', 195.
[47] F. Francioni, 'The 1972 World Heritage Convention: An Introduction', in F. Francioni (ed.), *The 1972 World Heritage Convention: A Commentary* (Oxford University Press, 2008), p. 3.
[48] WHC, Article 6(2).
[49] Redgwell, 'Protecting Natural Heritage and Its Transmission to Future Generations', p. 277.

on states parties, they foster coherence in the administrative practice of the latter.[50]

The language of the World Heritage Convention raises the question as to 'whether there exists a "collective interest" of the international community as a whole in the protection of heritage'.[51] Some authors consider the protection of heritage to be an obligation *erga omnes partes*. This type of obligation is not owed to the international community as a whole, but to all parties to the WHC.[52] In the event that a state party fails to fulfil it, each of the other states parties can claim the cessation of the internationally wrongful act.[53] According to this view, third parties are not legally bound to protect world heritage unless they accepted this obligation, as treaties do not create rights for third states.[54] As restated under the Vienna Convention on the Law of Treaties,[55] *pacta tertiis nec nocent nec prosunt*.[56]

Other authors have stressed that under appropriate circumstances, the obligation to protect cultural heritage is *erga omnes*, that is, owed to the international community as a whole.[57] According to these authors, all states in the world have a legal interest in the compliance with the obligation to protect cultural heritage. While over time, the number of third states has radically decreased, authors have discussed the emergence of general principles of law and customary law demanding the protection of cultural heritage not only in times of war but also in peacetime.[58]

Although the WHC constitutes a significant step toward the international protection of cultural heritage, it does have certain drawbacks. *First*, as the WHC adopts a listing approach, it protects only those sites

50 See D. Zacharias, 'The UNESCO Regime for the Protection of World Heritage as Prototype of an Autonomy-Gaining International Institution', *German Law Journal* 9 (2008), 1849.

51 G. Carducci, 'Articles 4–7', in F. Francioni (ed.), *The 1972 World Heritage Convention* (Oxford University Press, 2008), p. 111.

52 R. O'Keefe, 'World Cultural Heritage: Obligations to the International Community as a Whole?', *ICLQ* 53 (2004), 190.

53 *Ibid.* 54 *Ibid.* 191.

55 Vienna Convention on the Law of Treaties (VCLT), Vienna, 23 May 1969, in force 27 January 1980, 1155 UNTS 331, 8 ILM 679.

56 VCLT, Article 34.

57 F. Francioni, 'Culture, Heritage and Human Rights: An Introduction', in F. Francioni and M. Scheinin (eds.), *Cultural Human Rights* (Leiden/Boston: Martinus Nijhoff Publishers, 2008), p. 11.

58 F. Francioni and F. Lenzerini, 'The Destruction of the Buddhas of Bamiyan and International Law', *EJIL* 14 (2003), 634.

expressly designated by the states parties and selected by the World Heritage Committee. The lists can be perceived as establishing a hierarchy in the heritage domain. Therefore, some authors critically describe the listing approach as elitist, making artificial distinctions between local value and universal value. It is extremely difficult to draw the line between what is of universal value and what has a mere local value with regard to heritage.[59]

Other international law instruments, including the 1962 Recommendation concerning the Safeguarding of the Beauty and Character of Landscapes and Sites,[60] the 1968 Recommendation concerning the Preservation of Cultural Property Endangered by Public or Private Works,[61] and the 1976 Recommendation concerning the Safeguarding of Contemporary Role of Historic Areas,[62] which have all been extremely influential, do not have a listing approach. In particular, the Recommendation concerning the Preservation of Cultural Property Endangered by Public or Private Works expressly mentions that: 'Measures to preserve cultural property should be extended to the whole territory of the State and should not be confined to certain monuments and sites.'[63] In addition, Article 12 of the WHC requires member states to protect those cultural properties that, although not included on the list, objectively satisfy the conditions and requirements for being considered as having outstanding and universal value.

The fact that some cultural properties are not included in the List does not mean that they do not hold outstanding and universal value. This argument is also proven by the fact that the List is not a closed inventory but it is still expanding on a regular basis. Furthermore, whether or not a site is listed may depend on the political will of governmental institutions to submit

59 P. Fowler, 'Cultural Landscape: Great Concept, Pity about the Phrase', in R. Kelly, L. Macinnes, D. Thackray, and P. Whitbourne (eds.), *The Cultural Landscape. Planning for a Sustainable Partnership between People and Place* (London: ICOMOS, 2001), p. 17.

60 UNESCO, Recommendation concerning the Safeguarding of the Beauty and Character of Landscapes and Sites, 11 December 1962.

61 UNESCO, Recommendation concerning the Preservation of Cultural Property Endangered by Public or Private Works, Paris, 19 November 1968.

62 Recommendation concerning the Safeguarding of Contemporary Role of Historic Areas, 26 November 1976, available at http://portal.unesco.org/en/ev.php-URL_ID=13133&URL_DO=DO_TOPIC&URL_SECTION=201.html.

63 Recommendation concerning the Preservation of Cultural Property Endangered by Public or Private Works, ¶ 3.

a given area for listing. For instance, the listing of the Old City of Jerusalem and its Walls was proposed by Jordan and was not in conformity with the letter of the WHC, which is based on territoriality and the consent of the state concerned.[64] Even before such listing, the outstanding and universal value of this site was uncontested.

However, recommendations are not binding instruments, and Article 12 of the WHC has been all but ignored in the concrete application of the Convention. Only rarely has the Committee called upon states parties to respect their responsibilities under the WHC with respect to properties not inscribed on the list and even when it has done so, its actions have been unproductive.[65]

*Second*, the World Heritage List has been criticized for lacking a 'grand design'.[66] On the one hand, the distribution of sites on the list across continents and countries is highly unequal. Even assuming that a completely equal distribution is 'an extreme position because it does not take into account the size of the country as measured by population or by geographical extension', Steiner and Frey pinpoint that 'some countries . . . have a large number of World Heritage Sites; others have a few sites, and a considerable number have none.'[67] This reflects negatively on the list whose coverage should be universal rather than regional.

On the other hand, since its creation, the World Heritage List has included more cultural sites than natural sites.[68] Among the cultural sites, three categories of cultural heritage (archaeological sites, historic

[64] See T. Scovazzi, 'Articles 8–11 World Heritage Committee and World Heritage List', in F. Francioni (ed.), *The 1972 World Heritage Convention* (Oxford University Press, 2008), pp. 172–3.

[65] F. Lenzerini, 'Article 12 Protection of Properties Not Inscribed on the World Heritage List', in F. Francioni (ed.), *The 1972 World Heritage Convention: A Commentary* (Oxford University Press, 2008), p. 208 (noting that the World Heritage Committee has underestimated the significance of Article 12 in implementing the practice of the Convention); but see P. J. O'Keefe, 'Foreign Investment and the World Heritage Convention', *International Journal of Cultural Property* 3 (1994), 263–4 (referring to an Australian case where Article 12 WHC was successfully invoked).

[66] S. von Schorlemer, 'Compliance with the UNESCO World Heritage Convention: Reflections on the Elbe Valley and the Dresden Waldschlössen Bridge', *GYIL* 51 (2009), 321–90.

[67] L. Steiner and B.S. Frey, 'Imbalance of the World Heritage List: Did the UNESCO Strategy Work?', University of Zurich Department of Economics, Working Paper No. 14 (2011), pp. 7–8 (noting that 47% of the sites are in Europe; 9% in sub-Saharan Africa; 7% in the Arab countries; 17% and 20% in the Americas and Asia Pacific respectively).

[68] *Ibid.*, p. 7.

towns, and religious monuments), which characterize European civilization, have predominated the list vis-à-vis cultural landscapes and rural heritage.[69] In order to redress these imbalances, in 1994 the World Heritage Committee adopted the *Global Strategy for a Representative, Balanced and Credible World Heritage List* to broaden the definition of World Heritage.[70] In 2000, the World Heritage Committee also adopted the *Cairns Decision* 'to further enhance the under-represented categories of sites and improve geographical coverage', limiting the number of nominations to be submitted by each state party to one; only those states parties that had no properties on the World Heritage List could propose two or three nominations.[71] Furthermore, despite the *Operational Guidelines* considering the enhancement of the role of local communities in the implementation of the Convention as a strategic objective,[72] anthropologists warn that 'women, the lower socio-economic classes and indigenous people together with local communities are still being marginalized by the World Heritage process.'[73]

*Third*, the World Heritage Convention lacks a dispute settlement mechanism. Although the states parties can have recourse to judicial or arbitral settlement of disputes if they so agree, the absence of a World Heritage Court can be a drawback as compulsory, binding, and effective dispute resolution mechanisms can promote compliance. So far, the proposals to establish a World Heritage Court or a permanent arbitral body for the settlement of disputes with cultural elements have not been successful.[74] Many considerations oppose the establishment of such a dispute settlement mechanism. Besides the challenge of defining a 'cultural heritage' dispute, states may prefer to keep control over issues that are related to cultural identity and nationhood. As cultural heritage disputes often involve not only complex legal issues, but also elements of historical, political or religious nature, litigation may not seem to be the proper context for settling this kind of dispute. Lastly, such disputes may require the consideration of ad hoc remedies including moral damages or apologies.

[69] M. Richon, 'UNESCO Rural and Vernacular Architecture: An Underrated and Vulnerable Heritage', *Futuropa* 1 (2008), 29.

[70] See http://whc.unesco.org/en/globalstrategy.

[71] See http://whc.unesco.org/en/cairns/. [72] *Operational Guidelines*, ¶ 26.

[73] C. De Cesari, 'World Heritage and Mosaic Universalism', *Journal of Social Anthropology* 10 (2010), 314.

[74] A. Galis, 'UNESCO Documents and Procedure: The Need to Account for Political Conflict When Designating World Heritage Sites', *Georgia J. Int'l & Comp. L.* 38 (2009–2010), 205.

Finally, the very 'soft character' of the WHC, i.e. 'the clear prevalence of rights and advantages over legal obligations that states parties derive from the Convention',[75] which has contributed to the success of the Convention, risks undermining its effectiveness. As Kowalski pointed out, the WHC 'was ... not crafted as an instrument of power. It was imagined by professionals of culture, environmentalists, and scientists as a pragmatic ... device to protect objects of symbolic and scientific interest.'[76] In practice, however, some states have questioned the binding nature of the WHC. For instance, Tasmania argued before the Australian High Court that the WHC did not impose an obligation on the Commonwealth to prohibit the construction of a dam in the Tasmanian Wilderness, a World Heritage site.[77] According to Tasmania, states should not be assumed to surrender the regulation of heritage in their territory to an international regime and hence to restrict their sovereignty. However, the Australian High Court remarked that WHC imposes real and substantive obligations.[78]

Even admitting the binding nature of the WHC, it does not set universally agreed standards of conservation against which to monitor compliance. The obligations present intrinsic vagueness, as they do not define a specific level of appropriateness of state conduct. States undertake to identify, protect and conserve World Heritage sites in their territories 'to the utmost of their own resources',[79] and 'endeavour, in so far as possible, and as appropriate', *inter alia*, to take appropriate measures for the identification and protection of world heritage.[80] However, it remains unclear what the convention means by protection and conservation.[81]

If a state violates its commitments under the convention, the World Heritage Committee 'can assume its role of guardian of the general interest of the convention' by listing a World Heritage site on the List of World Heritage in Danger (Red List or Danger List).[82] Although listing a site on the Danger List is supposed to secure priority in receiving

75 See F. Francioni and F. Lenzerini, 'The Future of the World Heritage Convention: Problems and Prospects', in F. Francioni (ed.), *The 1972 World Heritage Convention* (Oxford University Press, 2008), p. 409.

76 Kowalski, 'When Cultural Capitalization Became Global Practice', p. 84.

77 Prott, 'UNESCO International Framework for the Protection of the Cultural Heritage', p. 270.

78 *Commonwealth v. Tasmania* (1983) 158 CLR 1 ('*Tasmanian Dam Case*').

79 WHC, Article 4.

80 WHC, Article 5(d).

81 Goodwin, 'The World Heritage Convention, the Environment and Compliance', 191.

82 WHC, Article 11(4).

assistance, such inclusion has political repercussions as states perceive danger listing as 'humiliating and contrary to their best interest'.[83] In fact, they make efforts to avoid an in-danger listing to 'save face' and to maintain their reputation as reliable international actors.[84] In this sense, although the In Danger List is not meant to be punitive, it may work as a 'blame and shame mechanism' that can pull states towards compliance. For instance in 2004 Cologne Cathedral in Germany was listed on the Red List because of plans to erect several skyscrapers on the banks of the River Rhine.[85] The Committee decided to remove the site from the Red List only after the City of Cologne offered to scale down its plans.[86]

However, the placing of a site on the Red List may not deter countries to pursue activities in breach of the Convention. Even if a property is placed on such List, 'there is not much that the rest of the international community can do if that danger is exacerbated by action of the state concerned or with its sanction'.[87] The ultimate risk for the non-complying state is that of adverse criticism and delisting,[88] and delisting is contrary to the very spirit of the WHC. For instance, Oman's plan to pursue hydrocarbon exploration within the boundaries of the Arabian Oryx Sanctuary determined the deletion of the property from the World Heritage List.[89] In 2006, the Dresden Elbe Valley in Germany was delisted from the World Heritage List because of plans to build a bridge which could impact the integrity of the site.[90] In conclusion, the failure of states to protect World Heritage sites can lead to red listing, and then even to the delisting of the site, which has economic and political consequences.[91] However, there is no express means in the Convention

[83] Goodwin, 'The World Heritage Convention, the Environment, and Compliance', 174.

[84] S. Litton, 'The World Heritage "In Danger" Listing as a Taking', *NYU JIL & Politics* 44 (2011), 221 (analysing two cases in which 'it would be naive to assume that a World Heritage In Danger listing had no effect on the eventual halt of mining operations' and that 'such cases can be considered a "regulatory quasi-taking"').

[85] See D. Zacharias, 'Cologne Cathedral versus Skyscrapers: World Cultural Heritage Protection as Archetype of a Multilevel System', *Max Planck Yearbook of United Nations Law* 10 (2006), 273–366.

[86] *Ibid.*, 280. [87] Nicholson, 'The Common Heritage of Mankind and Mining', 195.

[88] *Ibid.*

[89] See 'UNESCO Removes Oman Oryx Sanctuary from Heritage List', *Reuters*, 30 June 2007.

[90] See generally von Schorlemer, 'Compliance with the UNESCO World Heritage Convention', 321–90.

[91] See E. J. Goodwin, 'The Consequences of Deleting World Heritage Sites', *King's L. J.* 21 (2010), 283–309.

of enforcing compliance by the state concerned. The Convention relies on international cooperation and goodwill for its effectiveness.

In the context of the implementation of the Convention, the World Heritage Committee has established a process of periodic reporting, a process of reactive monitoring and expert missions system. Periodic reporting requires states parties to submit a review of their management of World Heritage sites and conservation policies to the Committee every six years.[92] These reports are then discussed extensively during the meetings of the Committee. Reactive monitoring occurs with regard to sites that are under threat and/or are inscribed in the Red List.[93] The review of the state of conservation of properties on the Red List can include sending expert missions as might be determined necessary by the Committee.[94]

However, the lack of enforcement mechanisms and/or sanctions makes the World Heritage sites vulnerable to mismanagement. The lack of a dispute settlement mechanism has also determined the dispersal of cultural heritage-related disputes to other borrowed fora, determining a fragmentation of judicial and arbitral outcomes that – because of particular institutional settings with no general mandate to assess the compliance of state conduct with the WHC – may not do justice to the protection of cultural heritage.

### *3.2 Mapping contemporary heritage policy discourse*

Given that 'it is the duty of governments to ensure the protection and the preservation of the cultural heritage of mankind, as much as to promote social and economic development',[95] it may be difficult to identify the most appropriate management of cultural heritage sites. Heritage policy discourse is varied; preservation policies are not uniform and may rely on different assumptions. For instance, preservationists have long discussed whether a site is more important for reasons intrinsic to that site or because of its role in the formation of the cultural identity of a given population.[96] While the identity-focused 'populists' hold that the value of specific sites lies in their role in the formation of

[92] WHC, Articles 11(7) and 29. [93] *Operational Guidelines*, ¶¶ 169–76.
[94] *Operational Guidelines*, ¶ 190.
[95] Recommendation concerning the Preservation of Cultural Property Endangered by Public or Private Works, preamble.
[96] C. Koziol, 'Historic Preservation Ideology: A Critical Mapping of Contemporary Heritage Policy Discourse', *Preservation Education and Research* 1 (2008), 42.

cultural identity and ability to promote memory and attachment ('the heritage that people want'), essentialists focus on the value of the object itself and deem that cultural goods present an inherent value ('Heritage is heritage').[97] These positions have led to tensions and oppositions among heritage scholars as to the identification of what is worth being protected, and why and how it should be protected. Should policy-makers consider the best interests of the cultural site as the paramount consideration? Should the preferences expressed by local constitutencies be taken into account?

These two different approaches to the conservation of cultural sites are well reflected in the traditional debate between nationalists and internationalists in international cultural law.[98] While internationalists perceive cultural heritage as expressing a common human culture, wherever its place and location, nationalists perceive cultural heritage as part of the national culture.[99] Even assuming that the WHC incorporates a mixture of both approaches,[100] questions remain in those cases in which the two interests – internationalist and nationalist – diverge. Which interest should prevail in the management of cultural heritage sites: the interest of the locals or the interests of the international community? Often the two interests coincide. Both communities have an interest in the conservation of a World Heritage site. In other cases, however, such interests collide. Already in the eighteenth century Goethe aptly observed such clash of interests, noting that for centuries the candles used in religious functions had blackened the frescoes of the Sistine Chapel, and that their smoke wrapped 'the sun of art in the clouds'.[101] When interests collide, national policy-makers face the dilemma as to whether to comply with the WHC or to fulfil their mandate according to the preferences of their electors.

Different views on preservation also exist in different cultures, leading to dissonant practices. While Westerners aim to preserve the tangible aspect of historic buildings, Eastern peoples rebuild historic buildings to preserve their spiritual value. For instance, the Japanese temple of Ise is

[97] *Ibid.*

[98] See J. H. Merryman, 'Two Ways of Thinking about Cultural Property Law', *AJIL* 80 (1986), 831–53.

[99] *Ibid.*, 831–2.

[100] R. Anglin, 'The World Heritage List: Bridging the Cultural Property Nationalism-Internationalism Divide', *Yale J. L. & the Humanities* 20 (2008), 241.

[101] J. W. Goethe, *Italian Journey (1786–1788)*, transl. W. H. Auden and Elizabeth Mayer (London: Collins, 1962), p. 141, quoted by L. Casini, '*Italian Hours*: The Globalization of Cultural Property Law', *International Journal of Constitutional Law* 9 (2011), 376.

made of wood and has been preserved thanks to integral reconstruction processes which take place every twenty years.[102] These different approaches may determine different perceptions of the essential qualities of cultural property that must be protected.

As the threats to World Heritage sites are varied, the relevant state authorities need to provide a comprehensive response, striking a reasonable balance between an effective World Heritage protection, as mandated by the WHC, and other interests including economic and social development and the proprietary interests of foreign investors as mandated by the relevant investment treaties. This is necessarily a case-by-case assessment.

What are the general principles which govern the protection of cultural heritage? The WHC does not provide details on heritage protection; the establishment of management plans is left to the member states. More detail is provided by the *Recommendation concerning the Preservation of Cultural Property Endangered by Public or Private Works.*[103] While categories of economic activities which can be deemed easily and *ipso facto* to be in conflict with heritage management do exist – e.g. the construction of highways, dams, hydroelectric power, pipelines, mining etc.[104] – the impact of other economic activities on heritage sites is more difficult to ascertain. For instance, the recommendation warns that although urban expansion and renewal projects may retain scheduled monuments while removing less important structures, they risk destroying the 'historical relations and the setting of historic quarters'.[105] The recommendation also cautions against 'injudicious modifications and repair of individual historic buildings'.[106]

In other words, the conservation of heritage sites has a (relatively stable) nucleus which requires core protection. However, the outer limits of the concept of conservation are far from settled, and there may be grey areas in which heated discussion on the best management of heritage sites can take place. With regard to World Heritage sites, scholars have elaborated the concept of 'concentric regions of graduated restrictiveness to provide a margin of safety around the sites themselves'.[107] The concentric nature

[102] M. Vecco, 'A Definition of Cultural Heritage: From the Tangible to the Intangible', *Journal of Cultural Heritage* 11 (2010), 324.

[103] Recommendation concerning the Preservation of Cultural Property Endangered by Public or Private Works, adopted by the UNESCO General Conference at its 15th sess., Paris, 19 November 1968.

[104] *Ibid.*, ¶ 8(d)(e)(f) and (h). [105] *Ibid.*, ¶ 8(a). [106] *Ibid.*, ¶ 8(c).

[107] J. C. Kunich, 'Losing Nemo: The Mass Extinction Now Threatening the World's Ocean Hotspots', *Columbia J. Environmental L.* 30 (2005), 69–70.

of heritage conservation is reflected in the creation of buffer zones and the range of selected regulatory tools presenting varying degrees of shape and intensity.

Certain economic activities have been deemed to be incompatible with adequate cultural heritage protection as they could alter the physical integrity of the given site. For instance, mining or oil and gas development are activities estimated to threaten more than one-quarter of cultural heritage sites.[108] At the national level, mining at World Heritage sites has been prohibited by a number of legislations.[109] At the international level, the World Heritage Committee urged Italy to prohibit expansion of pumice extraction on the Aeolian Islands, as it could affect the values for which the site was inscribed on the World Heritage List.[110] Analogously, the World Heritage Committee expressed concern about the impact of potential mining on the Waterton-Glacier International Peace Park World Heritage site.[111]

Mining can also be prohibited in places outside the perimeter of a World Heritage site, if mining could damage the site itself by way of pollution or other noxious interferences. In scrutinizing national case law, for instance, in the UK case *Coal Contractors Limited v. Secretary of State*, which involved an application to extract coal near Hadrian's Wall World Heritage site, the Deputy Judge upheld the decision of the Secretary of State to refuse the application because insufficient weight had been given to cultural heritage protection.[112] In the *Bulankulama* case, a Sri Lankan court disallowed the mining of phosphate by a joint venture between the government and the local subsidiary of a transnational corporation in an area of extreme historical and archaeological value, the so-called 'Cultural Triangle' where several UNESCO World Heritage sites are located, including the sacred city of Anuradhapura.[113] The Court stated: 'We use the terms "money",

[108] N. Affolder, 'The Private Life of Environmental Treaties', *AJIL* 103 (2009), 510.

[109] See e.g. Kotzé and de la Harpe, 'The Good, the Bad and the Ugly', 21 (referring to South African legislation).

[110] S. Battini, 'The Procedural Side of Legal Globalization: The Case of the World Heritage Convention', *International Journal of Constitutional Law* 9 (2011), 358.

[111] Affolder, 'The Private Life of Environmental Treaties', 513.

[112] *Coal Contractors Limited v. Secretary of State for the Environment and Northumberland County Council*, High Court, Queen's Bench Division, 9 December 1993, 68 P & C R 285.

[113] *Tikiri Banda Bulankulama v. Secretary, Ministry of Industrial Development*, S.C. Application No. 884/99 (F/R), (2000) SAELR 7 (2) 1, available at www.elaw.org/node/1295.

"capital", "assets" and "wealth" interchangeably – leaving no simple means to differentiate money from real wealth. Money is a number. Real wealth is food, fertile land, buildings or other things that sustain us. Lacking language to see this difference, we accept the speculator's claim to create wealth, when they expropriate it . . .'[114]

A similar critical stance has been adopted with regard to the building of dams or other infrastructures within or in the near proximity of heritage sites. In Australia, after the Western Tasmanian Wilderness National Parks were included on the World Heritage List, the Commonwealth enacted legislation, *inter alia*, halting the Tasmanian Hydro-Electric Commission's plan to build a dam in the area.[115] Tasmania challenged this legislation, claiming that it was *ultra vires*, but the court concluded that the Commonwealth had acted within its powers. In other cases, the costs of building dams rose due to conservation efforts. For instance, in Egypt, the construction of the Aswan High Dam required the relocation of the temples of Abu Simbel and Philae Island.[116]

Moving from the core of cultural heritage protection to its periphery, conservation policies may become more nuanced and contested. In the Australian *Friends of Hinchinbrook Society Inc. v. Minister of Environment* case,[117] the applicant Society challenged the consent of the Commonwealth Minister for the Environment to the carrying out of various works associated with the building of a resort and a marina within the Great Barrier Reef World Heritage site. However, the Court found that the WHC 'does not envisage that natural or cultural heritage is to be locked away from sight and made inaccessible to the public . . . What is required in a particular case will be a balancing of the obligations of "protection" and "conservation", as well as "presentation"; each given equal weight.'[118]

In the case *Penn Central Transportation Company v. City of New York*, as New York City's Landmarks Preservation Commission refused permission to build a tower on top of the Grand Central station, the owners sued, claiming that the application of the 1965 *Landmarks Preservation Act* was an unconstitutional uncompensated taking.[119]

114 *Ibid.* 115 *Tasmanian Dam* (1983) 158 CLR 1, 218.

116 See K. Wangkeo, 'Monumental Challenges: The Lawfulness of Destroying Cultural Heritage during Peacetime', *Yale JIL* 28 (2003), 205.

117 *Friends of Hinchinbrook Society Inc. v. Minister of Environment & Others* (1997) 142 ALR 632.

118 *Ibid.* 637.

119 *Penn Central Transportation Company v. City of New York*, 438 US 104, 26 June 1978.

The claimants did not contest that the preservation of cultural heritage was a permissible governmental objective nor did they contest the appropriateness of the regulation to achieve its stated goal, rather they claimed that the airspace above the terminal was a valuable property interest that they were deprived of without compensation. The case reached the US Supreme Court which held that the regulation was not an appropriation of property and that it did not interfere with the owners' use of property, as the owners could still make a profit on the terminal.[120] That there may be controversy on the impact of conservation policies on private property interests is proven by the dissent of Justice Rehnquist who argued that the regulation decreased the value of the property producing a net gain for society; thus it would not be fair to have the entire burden of preserving Grand Central fall on its owners.[121]

In other cases, however, the relevant authorities have adopted an extensive notion of conservation, beyond the perimeter of given cultural heritage sites to include the maintenance of 'architectural or town-planning coherence',[122] for instance by imposing limits on the height of a building. In this respect, in the case of Cologne Cathedral mentioned above, the World Heritage Committee feared that the planned buildings would block the view to the same from the western areas of the city.[123] More recently, in Liverpool, a UNESCO delegation concluded that the city's waterfront would be 'irreversibly damaged' by the introduction of skyscrapers which would result in a 'serious loss of authenticity'.[124] In such cases, discussion arises as to whether the adopted conservation measures can unduly conflict with the economic interests of the relevant stakeholders. In Cologne the local authorities initially contested the legitimacy of such (expansive) interpretation of cultural heritage protection: reportedly, the Mayor declared that 'it was impossible that a city should stop all further development because it had a cathedral'[125] and that 'city planning did not fall into the Foreign Ministry's competences'.[126] In the end, however, the city of Cologne rescaled the projects.[127] Things did not go this way, however, in the case regarding the Dresden bridge; the conflict that arose was analogized to a

[120] *Ibid.* [121] *Ibid.*, Rehnquist, J., Dissenting Opinion.
[122] *Operational Guidelines*, ¶ 179.
[123] See Zacharias, 'Cologne Cathedral versus Skyscrapers', 276.
[124] H. Carter, 'English Heritage Lodge Formal Objection to Liverpool Waterfront Development', *The Guardian*, 23 February 2012.
[125] Zacharias, 'Cologne Cathedral versus Skyscrapers', 277. [126] *Ibid.*, 279.
[127] *Ibid.*, 298.

'holy war' and the federal authorities preferred to accept the deletion of Dresden from the World Heritage List, respecting the will of the local demos.[128]

Additionally, questions arise as to the legitimate boundaries of cultural heritage policies that may be adopted by host states, as an excessive zeal may undermine the authenticity and integrity of a cultural site. For instance, the Georgian government has been admonished by the World Heritage Committee for rebuilding Bagrati Cathedral, a world-renowned masterpiece of medieval Georgian architecture.[129] While architecture conservationists fear the loss of authenticity and integrity, locals seem happy to see it restored, as the cathedral is seen as a symbol of the unity of the Georgian state.[130] In the meantime, however, Bagrati has been put on the Red List and state authorities and the World Heritage Committee are discussing a more appropriate rehabilitation plan.[131]

Finally, it goes without saying that in its multifaceted and protean aspects, the governance of a World Heritage site can directly affect the rights and obligations of a number of stakeholders, including foreign investors. Construction and similar economic activities can be delayed because of archaeological excavations; some governments may have provisions for the acquisition, through purchase or expropriation, of important cultural property. In addition, an excessive heritage protection may determine an uneven burden on individual rights and economic freedoms. For instance, in an early US case, *Curtin v. Benson*, which was adjudicated soon after the creation of the Yosemite National Park (decades before its inscription on the World Heritage List), the United States Supreme Court stated that the United States could exercise 'the powers of a sovereign' over the park, but it acknowledged that 'there are limitations' upon them and such powers cannot be exercised to destroy essential uses of private property.[132] The appellant was the owner of certain lands within the Yosemite National Park. The Court found that 'A law requiring an owner in the appellant's situation to fence his land might be within such [sovereign] power [of the state]. . . A law making the trespass of his cattle on other lands a criminal offense might be within such power. Such laws might strictly be considered

[128] See generally von Schorlemer, 'Compliance with the UNESCO World Heritage Convention', 321–90.

[129] V. Gotsiridze, 'Restoration Threatens Georgian Medieval Masterpiece', *Georgian Daily*, 2 January 2012.

[130] *Ibid.* [131] *Ibid.* [132] *J.B. Curtin v. Benson*, 222 US 78 (1911), 21 October 1910.

as regulations of the use of property, – of so using it that no injury could result to others'.[133] However, the Court also found that the modalities of the exercise of such powers are not unlimited. For instance prohibiting the herding of cattle on the private property of the claimant would amount to a taking.[134]

In conclusion, World Heritage sites have local roots and a cosmopolitan soul; while the WHC expressly respects sovereign rights and territorial integrity; at the same time it shifts world heritage to a 'global legal space'.[135] Therefore, World Heritage sites are relevant to local communities and the entire global community alike including foreign investors.[136] For this reason, decisions having an impact on these sites need to take into account both local and global interests. While local interests tend to be taken into account at the national level at least in democratic systems, the WHC requires the relevant authorities to also consider the interests of the entire global community.[137] By intervening in the decision-making processes of local authorities, the World Heritage Committee represents the interests of the global community.[138] While each state party retains the right to regulate within its own territory, the WHC and investment treaties pose vertical constraints on such right, 'introducing global interests into the decision-making processes of domestic authorities'.[139] Adherence to these international regimes 'add[s] a circuit of external accountability, forcing domestic authorities to consider the interests of the wider global constituency affected by their decisions'.[140]

## 3.3 *Cultural heritage disputes*

The implementation of the WHC has raised a number of conflicts and disputes. Some disputes have concerned the territoriality of World Heritage sites. For instance, the conflict between Cambodia and Thailand over the temple of Preah Vihear, which led to a dispute before the International Court of Justice,[141] has been refuelled by the recent inscription of the Preah Vihear Temple as a World Heritage site in

133 *Ibid.*, 86. 134 *Ibid.*
135 Battini, 'The Procedural Side of Legal Globalization', 342.
136 See A. A. Ghouri, 'Positing for Balancing: Investment Treaty Rights and the Rights of Citizens', *Contemporary Asia Arbitration J.* 4 (2011), 112.
137 Battini, 'The Procedural Side of Legal Globalization', 342. 138 *Ibid.*, 363.
139 *Ibid.*, 343. 140 *Ibid.*, 364.
141 *Case Concerning the Temple of Preah Vihear* (Cambodia v. Thailand), Judgment of 15 June 1962, ICJ Reports 1962, pp. 6ff.

2008.[142] Other conflicts have surrounded the listing and/or delisting of World Heritage sites.[143] Other world heritage-related disputes have been adjudicated at both national and international levels.[144]

Much less is known about the emerging cultural heritage disputes adjudicated before investment arbitral tribunals.[145] This chapter aims to fill this gap by mapping and critically assessing the relevant arbitrations. Given the structural imbalance between the compliance mechanism provided by the WHC and the highly effective investor–state arbitration, cultural heritage disputes involving investors' rights have often been brought before arbitral tribunals. As the number of disputes with cultural elements continues to increase, it is important to reflect on the method for identifying and characterizing such disputes. To begin with, no two parties will agree that a dispute is essentially 'cultural'.[146] Indeed, the mere definition of a dispute as 'cultural' may have implications for a case. Therefore, it seems more appropriate to talk about 'disputes with a cultural component', rather than to characterize a dispute as 'cultural'. This neutral approach is based on the consideration that claims related to cultural heritage are rarely, if ever, raised in isolation from other international legal arguments. Still, the fact that cultural heritage-related claims are raised together with other claims, rather than erasing their cultural quality, simply emphasizes the need to ascertain and consider such a quality in the merits phase of the proceeding.

In general terms, cultural heritage-related investment disputes are characterized by the need to balance the legitimate interests of a state to adopt cultural policies on the one hand against the economic interests of foreign investors on the other. Several issues arise in this context.

142 ICJ, Request for Interpretation of the Judgment of 15 June 1962 in the case concerning the Temple of Preah Vihear (Cambodia v. Thailand), pending.

143 von Schorlemer, 'Compliance with the UNESCO World Heritage Convention', 321–90.

144 See, e.g. B. W. Boer, 'World Heritage Disputes in Australia', *Journal of Environmental Law and Litigation* 7 (1992), 247–79; M. Komurcu, 'Cultural Heritage Endangered by Large Dams and Its Protection under International Law', *Wisconsin ILJ* 20 (2001–2002), 233.

145 V. Vadi, 'Culture Clash? World Heritage and Investors' Rights in International Investment Law and Arbitration', *ICSID Foreign Investment Law Review* 28 (2013), 1–21.

146 For an analogous argument with regard to 'environmental disputes', see P. Sands, 'Litigating Environmental Disputes: Courts, Tribunals and the Progressive Development of International Environmental Law', in T. Ndiaye and R. Wolfrum (eds.), *Law of the Sea, Environmental Law and Settlement of Disputes: Liber Amicorum Judge Thomas Mensah* (Leiden/Boston: Martinus Nijhoff, 2007), p. 315.

While environmental concerns have been somehow integrated into investment treaties, cultural concerns receive much less attention, if any. In the vast majority of investment treaties, cultural issues are not mentioned at all. If cultural concerns are mentioned, the relevant clauses remain vague.[147] The very fact that the balancing process occurs in the context of investor–state arbitration with no mandate to adjudicate cultural entitlements could lead to the procedure being deemed structurally biased in favour of the objective of protecting foreign investments. The choice of investment arbitral tribunals to settle a given dispute may prejudge the outcome given that 'any international institution will necessarily be biased in its analysis of the dispute, depending on the specialised area which it has been designed to serve'.[148]

Turning our attention to the emerging case law, it is becoming clear that there is no such thing as a typical dispute involving cultural elements. Cultural heritage-related disputes arise in a variety of contexts, including investment in mineral exploitation, construction, tourism and other sectors. Investors may claim that certain forms of regulation constitute an indirect expropriation or regulatory taking, and that compensation is owed. If a direct expropriation has occurred, claims may concern the amount of compensation. Other claims may concern violation of fair and equitable treatment or discrimination. Although specific claims are here singled out for analysis, it is worth highlighting that they are often linked together and the respective arguments may overlap.

These disputes illustrate a potential clash between the investment liberalization objectives embedded in contemporary international investment treaties and the cultural policies of the host state. Therefore, it is important to analyse recent arbitrations that have involved elements of cultural heritage to verify whether these cases have adequately dealt with cultural values. At the normative level, not only does the WHC introduce a compelling case for the consideration of cultural heritage in policy-making and adjudication, but also creates a normative framework for good cultural governance, that is the exercise of state authority in the cultural sector according to due process and the rule of law, which includes respect for human rights and fundamental freedoms.[149] In this sense, cultural policies

[147] See section 7.8 below.

[148] B. Simma, 'Universality of International Law from the Perspective of a Practitioner', *EJIL* 20 (2009), 290.

[149] A. A. Du Plessis and C. Rautenbach, 'Legal Perspectives on the Role of Culture in Sustainable Development', *Potchefstroom Electronic L. J.* 13 (2010), 48–62.

are not to be implemented at the complete discretion of the host state, but need to be in conformity with relevant international law standards.

### 3.4 *Expropriation claims*

Several investment treaty arbitrations have dealt with the question as to whether regulation allegedly aimed at protecting cultural heritage may be deemed to be an indirect expropriation or a measure tantamount to expropriation. The case *Glamis Gold Ltd v. United States of America* involved an area of the Californian desert that the Quechan Indian tribe deemed to be a sacred place. Although the area is not listed in the World Heritage List, its cultural importance for the tribe is similar to the importance of Mecca or Jerusalem for other believers.[150] When Glamis Gold, a Canadian mining company, planned to mine gold in the area, the tribe opposed the project because it would destroy the 'Trail of Dreams', a sacred path used for performing ceremonial practices.[151] As the 2000 environmental impact study indicated that the best option was that of 'no action', the US Department of the Interior withdrew the Imperial Project from further mineral entry for twenty years to protect historic properties.[152] In 2002, however, permission for the project was granted and the State Mining and Geology Board enacted emergency regulations requiring the backfilling of all open-pit mines to recreate the approximate contours of the land prior to mining.[153]

Because the Department of the Interior had not immediately approved the project and California's regulation required the backfilling of open-pit gold mines, allegedly making the investor's mining operation uneconomical, the latter filed an investment treaty arbitration, arguing that Californian and federal measures constituted an indirect expropriation and a breach of the fair and equitable treatment standard in violation of Articles 1110 and 1105 of NAFTA, respectively. The claimant asserted that the federal and Californian actions constituted a 'continuum of facts' that deprived its property rights of their value.[154] In particular, backfilling would be uneconomic and arbitrary since it would not be rationally related to its stated purpose of protecting cultural resources.[155] The claimant pointed out that 'once you take the material out [of] the ground, if there are cultural resources on the surface, they are destroyed. Putting the dirt back in the pit actually does not protect those

[150] *Glamis Gold Ltd v. United States of America*, ICSID Award, 8 June 2009, ¶¶ 103–8.
[151] *Ibid.*, ¶ 107. [152] *Ibid.*, ¶ 152. [153] *Ibid.*, ¶ 183. [154] *Ibid.*, ¶ 358. [155] *Ibid.*, ¶ 321.

resources' but may even lead to the burial of more artifacts and cause greater environmental degradation.[156] Thus, the claimant argued that the Californian measures aimed 'to stop the Imperial Project from ever proceeding while seeking to avoid payment of compensation it knew to be required had it processed transparently and directly through eminent domain'.[157]

The Tribunal found the claimant's argument to be without merit.[158] First, it found that the Californian backfilling measures 'did not cause a sufficient economic impact to the Imperial Project to effect an expropriation of the claimant's investment'.[159] Second, the Tribunal deemed the measures to be rationally related to their stated purpose.[160] The Tribunal admitted that 'some cultural artefacts w[ould] indeed be disturbed, if not buried, in the process of excavating and backfilling', but concluded that, without such legislative measures, the landscape would be harmed by significant pits and waste piles in the near vicinity.[161] The Tribunal held that in addressing 'some, if not all, of the harms caused to Native American sacred sites by open pit mining', 'governments must compromise between the interests of competing parties'.[162] The Tribunal deemed that there was a reasonable connection between the harm and the proposed remedy and that the claimant was using too narrow a definition of artefacts: 'there are, in addition to pot shards, spirit circles, and the like, sight lines, teaching areas and view shields that must be protected and would be harmed by significant pits and waste piles in the near vicinity'.[163] Remarkably, the Tribunal also expressly referred to Article 12 of the World Heritage Convention, which requires states to protect their cultural heritage even if it is not listed in the World Heritage List. This is rather extraordinary, as cultural heritage experts have repeatedly stressed that Article 12 of the WHC is an often-neglected provision.[164]

The potential clash between heritage protection and foreign investment promotion is evident in other arbitrations. In the cases *Marion Unglaube and Reinhard Hans Unglaube v. Costa Rica*,[165] which were consolidated in early 2010,[166] the Unglaubes claimed that the Republic of Costa Rica *de facto* expropriated their respective properties

[156] *Ibid.*, ¶ 687. [157] *Ibid.*, ¶ 703. [158] *Ibid.*, ¶ 360. [159] *Ibid.*, ¶ 536.
[160] *Ibid.*, ¶ 803. [161] *Ibid.* [162] *Ibid.*, ¶ 803. [163] *Ibid.*, ¶ 805.
[164] See however P. O'Keefe, 'Case Note: Foreign Investment and the World Heritage Convention', *International Journal of Cultural Property* 3 (1994), 259–65.
[165] *Marion Unglaube and Reinhard Hans Unglaube v. Republic of Costa Rica*, ICSID Case No. ARB/09/20, Award, 16 May 2012.
[166] *Ibid.*, ¶ 8.

under the Germany–Costa Rica BIT.[167] The Unglaubes had purchased land in Playa Grande, an important beach on which female leatherback turtles lay their eggs in the Guanacaste Province of Costa Rica. Given the endangered status of these turtles, the government adopted measures to protect this nesting habitat, creating the Las Baulas National Marine Park.[168] While the government and the property owners were in agreement regarding the need for environmentally sensitive development, they differed greatly in their respective opinions as to the appropriate means for safeguarding the site.[169]

The 1995 law creating the Las Baulas National Park indicated that some private lands would be subject to expropriation and considered part of the park.[170] Preliminary steps to expropriate lands began in 2003; however, the Unglaubes challenged the measures before national courts. In its 2008 decision, the Supreme Court of Costa Rica ordered the Ministry of Environment and Energy 'either to proceed with the expropriation' of the Unglaube's property 'within a reasonable period of time, or if there were not funds available to do so, to grant the permits [. . .] to private owners to exercise their property rights'.[171] However, three years later, the government had not purchased the property nor had it granted the permits to allow the claimant to enjoy her property rights.[172] The claimants alleged that these facts among others amounted, *inter alia*, to an indirect expropriation.[173]

The Arbitral Tribunal considered at length the goal and worthiness of the regulatory measures adopted by Costa Rica, acknowledging that the properties in question were located on or close to the Playa Grande beach – 'one of the world's most important nesting sites for the highly endangered leatherback turtle'.[174] The Tribunal did not question the right of Costa Rica 'to expropriate property for a *bona fide* public purpose, pursuant to law, and in a manner which is neither arbitrary nor discriminatory'; however, it held that 'the expropriatory measure must be accompanied by compensation for the fair market value of the investment'.[175] With regard to the conduct of Costa Rica, the Tribunal found that the regulatory measures adopted by Costa Rica amounted to indirect expropriation, while dismissing all other claims of the parties. The Tribunal noted that while the regulatory measures identified land

[167] Germany–Costa Rica BIT, 13 September 1994, in force 5 November 1997, available at www.sice.oas.org/ctyindex/CRI/CRIBITs_e.asp.

[168] *Unglaubes v. Costa Rica*, ¶ 37. [169] *Ibid.*, ¶ 39. [170] *Ibid.*, ¶ 57. [171] *Ibid.*, ¶ 73.

[172] *Ibid.*, ¶ 74. [173] *Ibid.*, ¶ 97. [174] *Ibid.*, ¶ 163. [175] *Ibid.*, ¶ 205.

for expropriation, the government did not seek the necessary funds or begin the process of expropriation;[176] therefore, the Tribunal found that a *de facto* expropriation of the land had occurred and determined that compensation was due to the claimant.[177]

In *Albert J. Connolly v. Canada*, Connolly, owner of a brown-fields holding, served Canada with a notice of intent to submit a claim to arbitration in 2004, alleging breach of NAFTA Article 1110. In particular, the US investor alleged that the inclusion of its commercial marble property in the Ontario's Living Legacy Program, a natural heritage protection programme, resulted in the forfeiture of its economic interests, thereby amounting to indirect expropriation. However, no valid claim was filed and there was no arbitration on this matter.[178]

Finally, in *Renée Rose Levy and Gremcitel SA v. Republic of Peru*,[179] the Republic of Peru is facing investor–state arbitration claims under the France–Peru BIT relating to the proposed development of property in a protected historical district.[180] Reportedly, in 1995, the Peruvian municipality of Chorrillos sought tenders from private investors for the acquisition and development of oceanfront land on the periphery of Lima.[181] Ms Levy bought the land and obtained archaeological authorization from the National Institute of Culture to develop the land.[182] However, in 2007 the National Institute of Culture adopted an administrative resolution precluding any form of construction on the property, mentioning the historical value of the place.[183] According to the investor, the resolution deprived the investment of any value, thus breaching a number of investment treaty provisions.[184] As the case is still at an early phase, it is not possible to predict whether and how it will be settled.

### *3.5 Compensation claims*

Other cases involving elements of cultural heritage concerned the direct expropriation of properties owned by foreign investors. In these cases, the parties did not dispute the fact that an expropriation had taken place,

176 *Ibid.*, ¶ 211. 177 *Ibid.*, ¶ 298.

178 *Albert J. Connolly v. Canada*, Notice of Intent to Submit a Claim to Arbitration, 19 February 2004.

179 *Renée Rose Levy and Gremcitel SA v. Republic of Peru*, ICSID Case No. ARB/11/17. The case was registered on 24 June 2011.

180 L. E. Peterson and J. Bonnitcha, 'New Government in Peru Confronts Recent Arbitration Loss and New Claims by Foreign Investors in Electricity Transmission, Construction, and Port Sectors', *IAR*, 4 August 2011.

181 *Ibid.* 182 *Ibid.* 183 *Ibid.* 184 *Ibid.*

but they disagreed on the amount of compensation due to the foreign investor. In these arbitrations, the cultural and natural heritage involved in the dispute had an outstanding value and was thus included in the World Heritage List. Therefore, an interesting aspect of such arbitrations is the relevance – or irrelevance – of the World Heritage Convention.

The case of *Compañia del Desarrollo de Santa Elena SA v. Republic of Costa Rica*[185] involved a particularly beautiful natural area including over thirty kilometres of Pacific coastline, as well as numerous rivers, springs, forests and mountains in Costa Rica. In addition to its geographical and geological features, the property was home to a dazzling variety of flora and fauna, indigenous to the tropical dry forest habitat. Costa Rica directly expropriated the property of American investors to enlarge the Guanacaste Conservation Area, which was subsequently added to the World Heritage List. As the investor deemed that the compensation was not adequate, it filed a claim before the ICSID.

The ICSID Tribunal awarded compensation to the investors, based on the property's fair market value. In doing so, the Tribunal restated that international law permits the host state to expropriate foreign-owned property for a public purpose and against prompt, adequate and effective compensation. However, the legitimate public purpose of the state measure does not affect either the nature or the measure of the compensation. The Tribunal expressly noted that 'the international source of the obligation does not alter the legal character of the taking for which adequate compensation must be paid'.[186] The Tribunal famously held that:

> Expropriatory environmental measures – no matter how laudable and beneficial to society as a whole – are, in this respect, similar to any other expropriatory measures that a State may take in order to implement its policies: where property is expropriated, even for environmental purposes, whether domestic or international, the State's obligation to pay compensation remains.[187]

The award in question is often criticized because it apparently supports the *sole effect doctrine*. According to this doctrine, in order to establish that an expropriation has taken place, one has to examine the effects of such a given measure on the economic value of a given investment.[188]

[185] *Compañia del Desarrollo de Santa Elena SA v. Republic of Costa Rica*, Award, 17 February 2000, ICSID Case No ARB/96/1, 39 ILM (2000) 1317.

[186] *Compañia del Desarrollo de Santa Elena*, Award, ¶ 71. [187] *Ibid.*, ¶ 72.

[188] See e.g. B. Mostafa, 'The Sole Effects Doctrine, Police Powers and Indirect Expropriation under International Law', *Australian Int'l L. J.* 15 (2008), 267.

However, the award in question refers not to *indirect* expropriation, but to *direct* expropriation.[189] Therefore, such a ruling reflects the concept that any direct expropriation requires a public purpose and compensation to be lawful. Thus, any criticism thereof should focus on the appropriateness of the criteria used for determining the compensation to be paid.

Analogously, in *Unglaube v. Costa Rica*, when events occurred in the same Guanacaste province eleven years later, the Arbitral Tribunal held that the creation of a national park to protect endangered leatherback turtles was a legitimate goal;[190] however, the expropriation was indirect and unlawful due to the failure to pay compensation.[191] The Tribunal held that 'while there can be no question concerning the right of the government of Costa Rica to expropriate property for a *bona fide* public purpose, pursuant to law, and in a manner which is neither arbitrary nor discriminatory, the expropriatory measure must be accompanied by compensation for the fair market value of the investment'.[192] The Tribunal added: 'Assuming that compensation was properly provided for and paid, Costa Rica's legal position would have been unassailable and this dispute might never have occurred.'[193] However, the Tribunal concluded that this had not been the case, and explicitly referred to the *Santa Elena v. Costa Rica* case.[194]

In *Southern Pacific Properties (Middle East) Limited v. Arab Republic of Egypt*,[195] the result was slightly different. This case, also known as the *Pyramids case*, involved the development of a tourist village at the pyramids of Giza. During construction, artefacts of archaeological importance were unearthed. Therefore, notwithstanding the previous approval of the investment at stake, Egypt cancelled the project and the area was added to the World Heritage List.[196] The ICSID Tribunal noted that certain acts of Egyptian officials 'created expectations protected by established principles of international law' and that the listing had been requested *after* the cancellation of the project.[197] Therefore, it found

[189] B. Stern, 'In Search of the Frontiers of Indirect Expropriation', in A. Rovine (ed.), *Contemporary Issues in International Arbitration and Mediation* (Leiden/Boston: Martinus Nijhoff, 2008), pp. 29–51.

[190] *Unglaube v. Costa Rica*, Award, ¶ 210. [191] *Ibid.*, ¶ 305. [192] *Ibid.*, ¶ 205.

[193] *Ibid.*, ¶ 210. [194] *Ibid.*, ¶¶ 214–18.

[195] *Southern Pacific Properties (Middle East) Limited v. Arab Republic of Egypt* (*SPP v Egypt*), ICSID Case No. ARB/84/3, Award on the Merits, 20 May 1992, reprinted in 8 *ICSID Review–FILJ* (1993), 328.

[196] *Ibid.*, ¶ 153. [197] *Ibid.*, ¶¶ 82–3.

contractual liability and sustained the Claimant's argument that the particular public purpose of the expropriation could not change the obligation to pay fair compensation. In the Tribunal's view:

> the UNESCO Convention by itself does not justify the measures taken by the Respondent to cancel the project, nor does it exclude the Claimant's right to compensation. According to the system of the Convention . . . the choice of sites to be protected is not imposed externally, but results instead from the State's own voluntary nomination. Consequently, the date on which the Convention entered into force with respect to the Respondent is not the date on which the Respondent became obligated by the Convention to protect and conserve antiquities on the Pyramids Plateau. It was only in 1979, after the Respondent nominated 'the pyramid fields' and the World Heritage Committee accepted that nomination, that the relevant international obligations emanating from the Convention became binding on the Respondent.[198]

Cultural heritage law scholars have criticized the view that state obligations under the WHC in respect of a particular site arise only after listing,[199] relying on a different approach, one that was adopted by the High Court of Australia in *Richardson v. Forestry Commission.*[200] In addressing the question as to whether there was an obligation under Article 4 of the Convention to protect a site which had not yet been identified as world heritage, the Court stated that 'the Convention does not sustain the view that the duty to ensure protection does not arise or attach to land until the State identifies and delineates that land as part of the heritage'.[201] Analogously, in *Queensland v. Commonwealth*, the Court held that the outstanding and universal value depends on the qualities of a site rather than on its evaluation either by the state party or the World Heritage Committee.[202] Although acknowledging that such cases apply only to Australia, O'Keefe and Prott deem that their interpretation of the Convention is correct and that it should be adopted worldwide.[203]

Turning to the *SPP v. Egypt* award, although the Arbitral Tribunal interpreted the WHC as requiring the protection of World Heritage sites

198 *Ibid.*, ¶ 154.

199 P. J. O'Keefe and L. V. Prott, *Cultural Heritage Conventions and Other Instruments* (London: Institute of Art and Law, 2011).

200 *Richardson v. Forestry Commission* [1987–1988] 164 *Commonwealth Law Reports* 261.

201 *Ibid.*

202 *Queensland v. Commonwealth* [1989] 167 *Commonwealth Law Reports* 232, at 241.

203 O'Keefe and Prott, *Cultural Heritage Conventions and Other Instruments.*

only after listing, and awarded compensation to the investor, it reduced the amount of such compensation, stating that only the actual damage (*damnum emergens*) and not the loss of profit (*lucrum cessans*) could be compensated.[204] The Tribunal stated that 'sales in the areas registered with the World Heritage Committee under the UNESCO Convention would have been illegal under ... international law', and therefore '[t]he allowance of *lucrum cessans* may only involve those profits which are legitimate'.[205] Furthermore, the fact that 'the project was located in an area where the Claimants should have known there was a risk that antiquities would be discovered' was 'reflected in the method used by the Tribunal to value the claimants' loss, and particularly in the Tribunal's decision not to base compensation on profits that might have been earned after the Plateau areas were registered with UNESCO'.[206]

These cases show that states may lawfully regulate and/or expropriate private property to protect cultural heritage. This is particularly the case if the cultural heritage in question has outstanding and universal value for mankind as a whole. The issue becomes whether the amount of compensation for the economic loss suffered by the owner should be reduced vis-à-vis the public purpose of the measure.[207] While in the *Santa Elena* case, the Tribunal ultimately did not take cultural values into account, the *SPP* Tribunal adopted a more nuanced approach that has been further developed in more recent cases.[208] Furthermore, these cases show that the state's pursuit of legitimate goals such as cultural heritage protection is not unbounded; rather policy-makers and adjudicators need to achieve an appropriate equilibrium between the public interest and the protection of economic freedoms.

### 3.6 *Fair and equitable treatment*

Other arbitrations have raised claims of violation of fair and equitable treatment. The obligation of a host state to accord fair and equitable

[204] *SPP v. Egypt*, ¶ 157. [205] *Ibid.*, ¶ 190. [206] *Ibid.*, ¶ 251.

[207] Compare with *Kozacioglu v. Turkey*, in which the Grand Chamber of the ECtHR held that Turkey had violated Article 1 of Protocol No. 1 to the European Convention on Human Rights when it failed to account for the historical and architectural value of the building in its compensation for expropriation. ECtHR, Grand Chamber, *Kozacioglu v. Turkey*, Application No. 2334/03, Judgment 19 February 2009, ¶ 67.

[208] M. Hirsch, 'Interactions between Investment and Non-Investment Obligations in International Investment Law', in P. Muchlinski, F. Ortino and C. Schreuer (eds.), *The Oxford Handbook of International Investment Law* (Oxford University Press, 2008), pp. 154–81.

treatment to foreign investors has been defined as the basic norm of the international investment regime.[209] The standard of fair and equitable treatment comprises a number of different components, including procedural fairness – meant as due process in administrative and judicial proceedings – transparency, good faith and the protection of legitimate expectations.[210] In this respect, if a state makes a specific or implicit representation to a foreign investor, the investor relies on such representation in making his or her investment and the state then frustrates the expectation it previously raised, this would be considered to be a breach of the FET standard.[211] However, in assessing whether legitimate expectations exist, arbitral tribunals have to scrutinize the relevant circumstances in the respondent country at the time the investment was made 'including not only the facts surrounding the investment, but also the political, socioeconomic, cultural and historical conditions prevailing in the host state'.[212]

In the *Glamis Gold* case, the claimant contended, *inter alia*, that the review process of the Imperial Project violated the fair and equitable standard,[213] as 'numerous other projects with significant and similar cultural characteristics were approved without complete backfilling and despite severe impacts to their cultural resources'.[214] The Tribunal rejected this claim, holding that the acts of the federal government and the state of California did not violate the respondent's obligations under Article 1105 of NAFTA.[215] The Tribunal recognized that: 'It is not the role of this Tribunal or any international tribunal, to supplant its own judgment of underlying factual material and support for that of qualified domestic agency',[216] and stated that the cultural review of the claimant's plan of operations was undertaken by qualified professionals. Furthermore, California legislation was of general application.[217] The

[209] J. Salacuse, 'The Emerging Global Regime for Investment', *Harvard ILJ* 51 (2010), 453.

[210] K. Yannaca-Small, 'Fair and Equitable Treatment Standard: Recent Developments', in A. Reinisch (ed.), *Standards of Investment Protection* (Oxford University Press, 2008), pp. 111–30.

[211] See, e.g. *Grand River Enterprises Six Nations Ltd et al. v. United States of America*, Award, 12 January 2011, ¶ 140.

[212] *Suez, Sociedad General de Aguas de Barcelona SA, and Vivendi Universal SA v. Argentine Republic*, Decision on Liability, ICSID Case No. ARB/03/19, 30 July 2010, ¶ 230 (internal quotations omitted).

[213] *Glamis Gold* Award, ¶ 639. [214] *Ibid.*, ¶ 277. [215] *Ibid.*, ¶ 824. [216] *Ibid.*, ¶ 779.

[217] *Ibid.*, ¶ 765.

Tribunal concluded that the claimant's property was regulated because of the high number of cultural artefacts found there.

In *Unglaube v. Costa Rica*, the Tribunal acknowledged that the claimants had experienced delays as a result of various administrative processes but held that the claimants had not been subjected to unfair treatment, as the conduct of state authorities did not 'involve or condone arbitrariness, discriminatory behaviour, lack of due process or other characteristics which shock the conscience'.[218]

In a pending NAFTA case initiated against the Government of Canada, the Clayton family and their US corporation, Bilcon, object to the manner in which an environmental impact assessment (EIA) has been undertaken.[219] The investors proposed to mine basalt in the coastal Canadian province of Nova Scotia and build a marine terminal in order to ship the basalt down through the Bay of Fundy to New Jersey.[220] The project attracted a large amount of public discussion in Nova Scotia, and was ultimately rejected following the EIA.[221] The claimants contend that the EIA process was unusually protracted, discretionary and, ultimately, in violation of the fair and equitable treatment standard.[222]

In its Statement of Defence,[223] Canada argued that its measure had not breached Chapter 11 of NAFTA, pointing out that Digby Neck, the place where the project would be developed, is an integral part of a UNESCO biosphere reserve.[224] Biosphere reserves are internationally recognized ecosystems for the conservation and sustainable use of biological diversity, and the safeguarding of the cultural values associated with them, nominated by national governments and remaining under sovereign jurisdiction of the states where they are located. Biosphere reserves constitute innovative projects of 'ecological humanism' or 'humanist ecology' in which human beings, culture and nature are conceived holistically. Since their inception, biosphere reserves have

218 *Unglaubes v. Costa Rica*, Award, ¶ 258.

219 *William Ralph Clayton, William Richard Clayton, Douglas Clayton, Daniel Clayton and Bilcon of Delaware Inc.* v. *Government of Canada*, Notice of Arbitration, PCA Case No. 2009-04, 26 May 2008.

220 L. E. Peterson, 'Tribunal Selected to Hear NAFTA Claim between Canada and US Investors in Proposed Quarrying and Shipping Scheme', *IAR*, 10 February 2009.

221 *Ibid.*

222 *Clayton and Bilcon of Delaware Inc.* v. *Government of Canada*, Notice of Arbitration, ¶ 11.

223 *Clayton and Bilcon of Delaware Inc.* v. *Government of Canada*, Statement of Defence of the Government of Canada, 4 May 2009.

224 *Ibid.*, ¶¶ 8–10.

been governed by soft law instruments. Governments, local communities and private individuals all participate and collaborate in the management of biosphere reserves in experimenting models of sustainable development contributing to societal, cultural and economic needs of the local communities.[225] Canada maintained that 'while [the claimants] may well be disappointed with the decisions made by government officials, NAFTA does not provide "blanket protection" against such disappointment. Moreover, it is not the job of this Tribunal to second-guess these heavily fact-based and scientifically grounded decisions.'[226] At the time of writing the case is still pending, and it is uncertain how the arbitral tribunal will address these issues.

Finally, as the Tribunal held in *Glamis Gold v. USA*, 'a State may be tied to the objective expectations that it creates in order to induce investment'.[227] For instance, in *MTD v. Chile*, the Arbitral Tribunal held that Chile had breached the fair and equitable treatment standard due to the incoherent behaviour of its authorities.[228] While the Foreign Investment Commission had approved the investment plan of the investor, the Minister of Urban Development had denied the application deeming that the project was not in conformity with the zoning policy of Santiago. The Tribunal held that Chile had 'an obligation to act coherently and apply its policies consistently',[229] and that approval of an investment by the relevant authorities for a project that was against the urban policy of the government was 'a breach of the obligation to treat an investor fairly and equitably'.[230]

On the other hand, reasonable expectations cannot be unilateral.[231] Rather, claimants 'must demonstrate reliance on specific and unambiguous State conduct, through definitive, unambiguous and repeated assurances, and targeted at a specific person or identifiable group'.[232] In the situation where the host state has made no assurance or representation, and there is no stabilization clause in the contract between the investor and the host state, the state's right to regulate cannot be considered frozen or restricted.

225 See generally A. Michelot, 'Les Réserves de Biosphère du Programme sur l'Homme et la Biosphère de l'UNESCO: au delà des aires protegégées, un modèle de société durable?' in J. R. Engel, L. Westra and K. Bosselmann (eds.), *Democracy, Ecological Integrity and International Law* (Newcastle upon Tyne: Cambridge Scholars Publishing, 2010), pp. 389–408.

226 *Claytons and Bilcon v. Canada*, Counter-Memorial, 9 December 2011, ¶ 17.

227 *Glamis Gold v. USA*, Award, ¶ 766.

228 *MTD Equity Sdn Bhd and MTD Chile SA v. Republic of Chile*, ICSID Case No. ARB/01/7, Award of 25 May 2004.

229 *Ibid.*, ¶ 165. 230 *Ibid.*, ¶ 166. 231 *Unglaube v. Costa Rica*, Award, ¶ 270. 232 *Ibid.*

The protection of investors' legitimate expectations cannot mean that the host state will never be able to modify the legal framework.[233]

In *Parkerings v. Lithuania*, which related to the construction of a parking area in the city of Vilnius, the Tribunal remarked that: 'It is each State's undeniable right and privilege to exercise its sovereign legislative power . . . Save for the existence of an agreement, in the form of a *stabilization* clause or otherwise, there is nothing objectionable about the amendment brought to the regulatory framework existing at the time an investor made its investment.'[234] The Tribunal also noted that circumstances in a country in transition could not justify legitimate expectations with regard to the stability of the investment environment[235] and that legislative changes may be seen as a normal business risk (in this case due to the transition from a former Soviet Union state to candidate for EU membership). Nonetheless, this does not exempt states from a general duty of good faith and transparency.[236] *In casu*, the Tribunal admitted that: 'Even if no violation of the BIT or international law occurred, the conduct of the city of Vilnius was far from being without criticism.'[237] Therefore, the Arbitral Tribunal dismissed all the claims in their entirety, requiring each party to bear its own costs.[238]

## 3.7 *Discrimination*

A crucial element in investment disputes with elements of cultural heritage is the ascertainment of non-discrimination; the key question is whether foreign investments are being regulated because the activity in question presents certain risks to world heritage, or whether they are being regulated because they are foreign investments.[239] Discrimination

[233] *Sergei Paushok et al. v. Mongolia*, Award on Jurisdiction and Liability, 28 April 2011, ¶ 253; *Impregilo S.p.A. v. Argentina*, ICSID Case No. ARB/07/17, Award, 21 June 2011, ¶ 291.

[234] *Parkerings-Compagniet AS v. Lithuania*, ICSID Case No. ARB/05/8, Award, 11 September 2007, ¶ 332.

[235] *Ibid.*, ¶¶ 335–6.

[236] Compare the *Beyeler* case, in which the ECtHR declared that there was a violation of Article 1 of the Protocol No. 1 of the Convention, because there was an interference with the peaceful enjoyment of property – in this case, a painting by Vincent Van Gogh – and the applicable provisions of domestic law were not sufficiently accessible, precise and foreseeable. ECtHR, *Beyeler v. Italy* [2001] 33 EHRR 52, Decision 5 January 2000.

[237] *Ibid.*, ¶ 464. [238] *Ibid.*, ¶ 464.

[239] See H. Mann and K. von Moltke, 'NAFTA Chapter 11 and the Environment: Addressing the Impacts of the Investor–State Process on the Environment', IISD Working Paper (1999), 25.

and non-discrimination 'are not polar opposites in a static system',[240] as 'there may be several ways in which the notion of . . . discrimination may be understood'.[241]

It is undoubtedly difficult to spot openly discriminatory language in current environmental regulations; in most cases, regulatory measures do not openly discriminate against foreign investors, albeit some may result in *de facto* or indirect discrimination. For instance, in *Parkerings v. Republic of Lithuania*,[242] Parkerings, a Norwegian enterprise, filed a claim before an ICSID Tribunal, claiming that Lithuania breached the most favoured nation (MFN) clause as a result of allegedly preferential treatment of a Dutch competitor.[243] Parkerings had concluded an agreement with the Municipality of Vilnius (Lithuania) for the construction of parking facilities.[244] Because of technical difficulties and the growing public opposition due to the cultural impact of the investor's project on the city's Old Town – a World Heritage site – the municipality terminated the agreement and subsequently signed another contract with a Dutch company for the completion of the project. The successful contractor would not excavate under the Old Town.[245]

The Tribunal dismissed this claim, finding that Parkerings and the Dutch competitor were not in *like* circumstances.[246] The project presented by Parkerings included excavation works under the Cathedral.[247] Not only did the Tribunal pay due attention to cultural heritage matters, but it also stated that compliance with the obligations flowing from the WHC *justified* the refusal of the project,[248] holding that: 'The historical and archaeological preservation and environmental protection could be, and in this case were, a justification for the refusal of the [claimant's] project.'[249] While the Tribunal did not mention any hierarchy among different international law obligations, it concretely balanced the different norms.

In other cases, whereas the protection of a site is mandated by the World Heritage Convention or other international environmental agreement, the

[240] K. Von Moltke, *Discrimination and Non-Discrimination in Foreign Direct Investment Mining Issues* (Paris: OECD, 2002), p. 7.

[241] F. Ortino, 'Non-Discriminatory Treatment in Investment Disputes', in P. M. Dupuy, F. Francioni and E. U. Petersmann (eds.), *Human Rights in International Investment Law and Arbitration* (Oxford University Press, 2009), p. 349.

[242] *Parkerings-Compagniet AS v. Republic of Lithuania*, ICSID Case No. ARB/05/08, Award, 11 September 2007.

[243] *Ibid.*, ¶ 203. [244] *Ibid.*, ¶ 204. [245] *Ibid.*, ¶ 284. [246] *Ibid.*, ¶ 396.

[247] *Ibid.*, ¶ 392. [248] *Ibid.*, ¶ 385 and ¶¶ 381–2. [249] *Ibid.*, ¶ 392.

state maintains considerable discretion in the selection of specific protective measures. If a state adopted stringent regulations restricting the activities of a foreign investor owning an industrial plant nearby, it would be unclear whether such conduct is mandated and/or justified by international cultural law. In the case *Empresas Lucchetti v. Peru*,[250] a Chilean company owning a pasta factory constructed close to, but not within, a protected wetland, Pantanos de Villa, complained that, notwithstanding its compliance with all the environmental requirements, its licence was revoked and that the measures adopted by Peru, *inter alia*, discriminated against the foreign company and *de facto* expropriated its investment. As the Tribunal found that it lacked jurisdiction over the dispute, there was no award on the merits.

## 3.8 *New trends*

Recently, international investment law has been used to protect cultural heritage by requiring a state to respect its own cultural policies that are critical to the success of the investment. While the protection of heritage is not the actual purpose of international investment law, in some exceptional cases, the cultural interest (e.g. the construction of a tower designed by a world-renowned architect, the recovery of an ancient shipwreck, the conservation of natural heritage) can (and has) coincide(d) with the investor's interest.

For instance, a Luxembourg incorporated company threatened to file an investor–state arbitration claim against Poland due to delays in national court proceedings.[251] After having obtained the relevant construction permits, the company was in the process of building a residential complex in central Warsaw, including an iconic tower, when the project was halted due to opposition to such construction filed before national courts by neighbours.[252] As the Administrative Court in Warsaw recently reaffirmed the validity of the building permit,[253] it is likely that no claim will be filed against Poland and the construction of the tower will move forward.

[250] *Empresas Lucchetti, SA, and Lucchetti Peru, SA v. Republic of Peru*, ICSID Case No. ARB/03/4, Award, 7 February 2005.

[251] L. E. Peterson, 'Investor Warns Poland of Arbitration Unless Permit is Green-Lighted for Resumed Construction of Libeskind-Designed Tower in Warsaw', *IAR*, 28 August 2010.

[252] *Ibid.*

[253] Studio Daniel Libeskind, 'Zlota Tower Moves Forward in Warsaw', 12 January 2012, available at http://daniel-libeskind.com/news/zlota-tower-moves-forward-warsaw.

Analogously, in another dispute, an investor raised arguments related to the protection of natural heritage. A Canadian investor appears to have filed an investment treaty claim against Barbados for alleged failure to enforce its own environmental law implementing international obligations.[254] As the investor acquired wetlands and subsequently developed them into an ecotourism facility, he claimed that Barbados had failed to prevent the discharge of raw sewage into the wetlands and to investigate or prosecute polluters, thus reducing the profitability of his investment.[255] As Viñuales points out: 'Irrespective of whether this claim prospers, its interest lies in the way it has been formulated', which illustrates a novel form of interplay between international investment law and the protection of heritage.[256] More importantly, such cases may provide arguments in favour of the principle of mutual supportiveness between different treaty regimes, which can play a role in the interpretation of relevant international law instruments.[257]

A different stream of cases concerning cultural artefacts has related to the enforcement of arbitral awards. Despite the fact that cases adjudicated before national courts are outside the scope of this book, which focuses on cultural heritage in international investment law and arbitration, for the sake of accuracy it is worth briefly mentioning these cases. In 2005, a French company attempted to seize a collection of French paintings belonging to the Pushkin State Museum in Moscow which were on loan to a Swiss Gallery to enforce an arbitral award against Russia.[258] The relevant Swiss authorities rejected the claim, ruling that the paintings should be returned to Russia and emphasizing that 'in international law, national cultural treasures are public property and are not subject to confiscation'.[259]

Analogously, in Austria a creditor sought to enforce an arbitral award against certain paintings owned by the Czech Republic and loaned to the Belvedere Gallery in Vienna. In this case, the Austrian Court of Appeal

[254] *Peter A. Allard v. Government of Barbados*, UNCITRAL, Notice of Dispute, 8 September 2009, available at www.graemehall.com/legal/papers/BIT-Complaint.pdf.

[255] *Ibid.*, ¶ 16.

[256] J. Viñuales, 'Foreign Investment and the Environment in International Law: An Ambiguous Relationship', *BYIL* 80 (2010), 7.

[257] See e.g. R. Pavoni, 'Mutual Supportiveness as a Principle of Interpretation and Law-Making: A Watershed for the "WTO-and-Competing-Regimes" Debate?', *EJIL* 21 (2010), 649–79.

[258] See N. van Woudenberg, 'Immunity from Seizure: A Legal Exploration', in S. Pettersson, M. Hagedorn-Saupe, T. Jyrkkio and A. Weij (eds.), *Encouraging Collections Mobility* (Brussels, 2010), p. 186.

[259] *Ibid.*

dismissed the claim on jurisdictional grounds, recognizing the sovereign immunity of the Czech Republic.[260] Finally, the French Association of Tsarist Bondholders filed a suit in France which required that the exhibition *When Russia Spoke French: 1800–1830* be seized as collateral against a large sum the organization alleged was owed to the descendants of holders of the Tsarist Russian state bonds.[261] The claim, however, was dismissed on jurisdictional grounds.

From an investment law perspective, these cases show that immunity from execution remains the last fortress of state immunity and that the protection of cultural heritage constitutes a significant policy concern that governs national bodies' restraint to infringe the sovereignty of another state. From a cultural law perspective, as an international law scholar pinpoints, upholding sovereign immunity can favour the international exchange of art which in turn benefits the public at large.[262]

## 3.9 *Critical assessment*

As the World Heritage Convention does not have a dispute settlement mechanism, investor–state arbitration has catalysed an increasing number of cultural heritage-related disputes. Arbitrators have increasingly taken cultural concerns into consideration in deciding cases brought before them. The fact that economic standards of valuation are not the only ones that are taken into account by arbitrators is significant. From an investment law perspective, the integration of cultural concerns within international investment arbitration is a welcome move because it contributes to the harmonious development of international law. In the *Glamis Gold* case, the Tribunal accorded deference to national cultural policies, recognizing that: 'It is not the role of this Tribunal or any international tribunal to supplant its own judgment of underlying factual material and support for that of a qualified domestic agency' and that 'governments must compromise between the interests of competing parties'.[263] In *Parkerings*, the Tribunal took into account the cultural heritage elements of the case, distinguishing the two projects on the basis of their diverse cultural features. In the

[260] N. Van Woudenberg, *State Immunity and Cultural Objects on Loan* (Leiden: Martinus Nijhoff, 2012), pp. 303–4, referring to *Diag Human v. Czech Republic*, case no. 72 E 1855/11 Z-20, District Court of Vienna, 21 June 2011.

[261] C. Forrest, 'Art on Loan: The Role of Immunity in Dispute Resolution', *Transnational Dispute Management* (2013), 6.

[262] *Ibid.*, 9. [263] *Glamis Gold* Award, ¶¶ 779 and 803.

*Pyramids* case, *lucrum cessans* was not awarded because of the unlawfulness of the proposed economic activity under international (cultural) law.

However, from a cultural heritage law perspective, concerns remain with regard to the protection of cultural entitlements. While the almost universal ratification of the WHC indicates that the international community perceives the protection of world heritage as an important public interest, the Convention protects world heritage only; that is, heritage of an outstanding and universal nature that is inscribed on the World Heritage List. A monumental understanding of world heritage leaves much indigenous and rural heritage unprotected. Some of the cases mentioned demonstrate the vulnerability of indigenous and rural heritage to economic and developmental interests.

In most cases, these tribunals are activated by investors to obtain protection for their investments; certainly not for the protection of cultural heritage potentially affected by the investments themselves. At the end of the day, these cases represent an *ex post* remedy, i.e. a remedy that is available only after an investor files an investor–state claim. There may be cases in which cultural heritage concerns arise, but states prefer to ignore such concerns in favour of economic development. A number of cases are settled during the cooling off period that is required before investment arbitration. There is a risk that in such a context, the host state will scale down its cultural policies behind closed doors to avoid expensive arbitration costs. In other cases, the state may be adopting alleged cultural policies discriminating against foreign investments, but the investor may decide not to file any arbitration deeming it too expensive. Finally, and more importantly, when a tribunal is established for reasons related to the clash between the execution of an investment and cultural heritage protection, arbitrators will adjudicate the compliance of state measures with international investment law. Arbitral tribunals are tribunals of limited jurisdiction. Their mandate can be far from what would be required of a body to which significant cultural heritage authority could be entrusted.

A different concern is the limited role played by the affected communities in the context of investment arbitrations. Limited procedural participatory tools are available to the affected communities in the context of investment treaty arbitration.[264] Certainly, the affected

[264] See V. Vadi, 'When Cultures Collide: Foreign Direct Investment, Natural Resources and Indigenous Heritage in International Investment Law', *Columbia Human Rights Law Review* 42 (2011), 797–889.

communities may bring their reasons before different bodies, including domestic courts, which may block the execution of the investment to protect their heritage. Then again, if such a national decision were deemed to amount to a denial of justice or an indirect expropriation,[265] the state would face the dilemma of whether to protect its cultural heritage or to comply with relevant investment treaty provisions.

Furthermore, there is a risk of 'epistemological misappropriation', or in other words, dealing with cultural heritage in a way that is discordant with the jurisprudential developments and interpretations of other courts and tribunals. For instance, excavation will take place in the *Trail of Dreams* and backfilling does not completely avoid harm to the cultural artefacts. If digging is obviously not possible under Mecca and Jerusalem, which are both pilgrimage destinations for other believers – Jerusalem is also a World Heritage site – one may wonder why the *Trail of Dreams*, which is sacred for indigenous peoples, should receive a different treatment. Finally, what if the state had prohibited any form of economic activity? If the measures had 'destroyed' the economic viability of the investment, the outcome might have been different, regardless of what the tribunal thought about cultural heritage. Should 'economic rationality form the epistemological foundation for decision making'?[266]

The potential for conflict of norms is inherent in every legal system. As such, this should not be conceived as a sort of pathology or an anomaly in the law, but as a characteristic of the system.[267] Not only does international law not constitute an exception to this notion, but it offers a fertile ground for overlapping norms and conflicting obligations. The multitude of lawmakers and the constellation of courts and administrative bodies are elements which all contribute to the complexity of the system. As Slaughter contends, conflict may be seen as 'the motor of positive change' and the successful management of conflicts may actually strengthen the legal order.[268]

The fact that arbitral tribunals have dealt with the clash between economic interests and the protection of heritage sites is worth

[265] M. Sattorova, 'Denial of Justice Disguised? Investment Arbitration and the Protection of Investors from Judicial Misconduct', *ICLQ* 61 (2012), 223–46.

[266] M. Goodale, 'Foreword', in G. A. Sarfaty, *Values in Translation: Human Rights and the Culture of the World Bank* (Stanford, CA: Stanford University Press, 2012), p. ix.

[267] J. Pauwelyn, *Conflict of Norms in Public International Law: How WTO Law Relates to Other Rules of International Law* (Cambridge University Press, 2003), p. 12.

[268] A. M. Slaughter, *A New World Order* (Princeton N.J.: Princeton University Press, 2004), p. 209.

investigation precisely because arbitral tribunals are not courts of general jurisdiction like the International Court of Justice. In fact, one could argue that very few of the cases that were examined above apparently deal with the WHC, some being cases in which the WHC merely forms part of the factual background, and others being ones in which the WHC was not implicated in the facts, but in which the tribunal mentions it in passing. The cases in question, however, all deal with the interplay between cultural heritage protection and economic freedom. The fact that they do not seem to concentrate on the WHC is of no surprise. The fact that arbitral tribunals take the WHC into account is remarkable because other international economic institutions have not shown a similar willingness to take analogous concerns into account.[269]

International investment law is 'not a self-contained closed legal system' but has to be 'envisaged within a wider juridical context in which rules from other sources are integrated through implied incorporation methods, or by direct reference to certain supplementary rules whether of international law character or of domestic law nature'.[270] In many circumstances, international law is the law applicable to investment disputes according to the arbitral clause or the relevant treaty provision. Even in those cases where the applicable law is the law of the host state, international law permeates national legal systems, be they monist or dualist systems. Thus, when arbitrators apply national provisions that reflect international law norms, the boundaries between the international and the national planes become blurred.

Furthermore, according to the principles of systemic interpretation as restated by Article 31(3)(c) of the VCLT, together with the context, any relevant rule of international law applicable in the relationship between the parties should be taken into account. If the host state that is party to the investment treaty dispute has ratified the WHC, the relevant provisions of the WHC come into play. Because of their limited mandate, the arbitrators cannot adjudicate on the eventual breach of cultural heritage law, but may analyse the specific investment claims in the light of the relevant rules of international law applicable in the relationship between the parties, including the WHC. The consideration of international

[269] See G. A. Sarfaty, 'Why Culture Matters in International Institutions: The Marginality of Human Rights at the World Bank', *AJIL* 103 (2009), 647–83.

[270] *Asian Agricultural Products Ltd v. Sri Lanka (AAPL v. Sri Lanka)*, ICSID Case ARB/87/3, Award of 27 June 1990, 4 ICSID Reports 245 (1997), ¶ 21.

cultural law would be *incidenter tantum*.[271] Given the fact that UNESCO has an almost universal membership and that the WHC is one of its most successful conventions in terms of adhesion, this leads to the conclusion that the protection of world heritage is a general principle of law if not a norm of customary law already, and that adjudicators will have to take cultural concerns into account. If one deems cultural heritage protection to already belong to customary international law, the case for such consideration is even stronger. Finally, while arbitral tribunals have respected the cultural sovereignty of the host state, they have imposed schemes of good cultural governance, that is, governance in compliance with other norms of international law, most notably investment law. None of the competing interests have been deemed to have an absolute character.

## Conclusions

World heritage is heritage *par excellence*. It holds an incommensurable value for both present and future generations, and thus receives strengthened protection at the international level. However, as the WHC does not include a dispute settlement mechanism, cultural heritage-related investment disputes have gravitated towards a number of national, regional and international courts and tribunals. This chapter surveyed a number of heritage-related investment disputes, showing that while international investment law has not developed any institutional machinery for the protection of cultural heritage through investment dispute settlement (after all, international investment law is not intended to protect cultural heritage), in recent years, a jurisprudential trend has emerged that takes cultural heritage into consideration. Arbitral tribunals have paid increasing attention to cultural concerns and have often referred to international law principles and cases in their reasoning in order to reconcile the different interests at stake.

The magnetism of arbitral tribunals has had mixed outcomes. On the one hand, the review of substantive domestic regulations can improve good cultural governance and the transparent pursuit of legitimate

[271] For analogous reasoning in the WTO context, see F. Francioni, 'WTO Law in Context: The Integration of International Human Rights and Environmental Law in the Dispute Settlement Process', in G. Sacerdoti, A. Yanovich and J. Bohanes (eds.), *The WTO at Ten: The Contribution of the Dispute Settlement System* (Cambridge University Press, 2006).

cultural policies. On the other hand, from a cultural heritage perspective, one may wonder whether the fact that cultural heritage disputes are adjudicated before arbitral tribunals raises a sort of institutional bias. At the end of the day, such tribunals are of limited jurisdiction; they cannot adjudicate on the eventual violation of international cultural law. The mechanism is mostly triggered by foreign investors; the affected communities are represented by the host state, but have no procedural rights in the context of the proceedings.

This chapter highlighted the 'clash of cultures' between the protection of cultural heritage and the promotion of foreign investment. On the one hand, multilevel cultural governance may ensure a reinforced protection to cultural heritage. The almost universal ratification of the WHC indicates that the international community perceives the protection of world heritage as an important public interest. However, the WHC protects world heritage only, that is, heritage of outstanding and universal nature that is inscribed in the World Heritage List. A monumental understanding of world heritage leaves much indigenous and rural heritage vulnerable to economic and developmental interests.

# 4

# Underwater cultural heritage and foreign direct investment

Adparent rari nantes in gurgite vasto . . .[1]
(Rare are the swimmers in the vast sea)

## Introduction

Ancient shipwrecks contribute to our understanding of history, providing a glimpse into different epochs and societies. In recent times, the advancement of technology has made it possible to find, visit and remove artefacts from shipwrecks that have been kept remote in the abysses for centuries. The increasing capability to reach these archaeological treasures has intensified the debate on related ownership and management issues. Because of the huge investments needed to recover and rescue these shipwrecks, private actors have been particularly successful in maritime excavation. While they have recovered expenses by claiming possession rights and even selling the artefacts, the scientific community and the public at large demand the preservation of underwater cultural heritage. In dealing with the clash of these conflicting interests and philosophies, courts have struggled to settle underwater cultural heritage disputes. Given the international dimension of most of the disputes, underwater cultural heritage has become the last frontier of international legal debate.[2]

This chapter investigates the question as to whether international investment law can provide an additional layer of regulation governing underwater cultural heritage and, if so, what are the limits of such an approach. Similarly, it will also investigate whether it is possible to

[1] Virgil, *Aeneidos*, Book I, R. G. Austin (ed.) (Oxford University Press, 1984), line 118 (translated by the author).

[2] J. A. R. Nafziger, 'The Present State of Research', in *Le patrimoine culturel de l'humanité: The Cultural Heritage of Mankind* (Leiden: Martinus Nijhoff, 2008), p. 216.

reconcile private interests with the public interest of underwater cultural heritage protection within international investment law and arbitration. It is argued that international investment law can be interpreted in order to better protect underwater cultural heritage and that the preservation of underwater cultural heritage can foster economic, social and cultural development.

The argument will proceed as follows. First, this chapter defines the multifaceted concept of underwater cultural heritage and briefly describes the legal framework which disciplines it. As a 'regime complex' governs the exploration and management of underwater heritage, the fragmentation among different treaty regimes and the existence of maritime customs have led to new forms of piracy. Second, the chapter addresses the issue as to whether international investment law might provide an alternative framework. After scrutinizing whether international investment law is applicable to salvage contracts by which private actors rescue ancient shipwrecks with the state's consent, two questions arise. The first question is whether investment treaties are compatible with states' obligations to protect underwater cultural heritage. The second is whether investor–state arbitration is a suitable forum to deal with claims concerning underwater cultural heritage. In order to answer these questions, this chapter will analyse a significant case. Third, it is argued that synergy may be found between public and private actors. Also, the proposed model would show that the preservation of heritage is a key element in economic, social and cultural development.

## 4.1 *The concept of underwater cultural heritage*

Historic sunken vessels constitute the essence of underwater cultural heritage (UCH). As a distinguished archaeologist once put it: 'ships that know no frontiers on the oceans also, metaphorically, traverse the frontiers of man's achievement by virtue of the multifarious skills he has lavished upon them; they are his noblest artefacts.'[3] The concept of underwater cultural heritage is much broader though, since it can be defined as 'all traces of human existence having a cultural, historical or archaeological character which have been partially or totally underwater, periodically or continuously, for at least 100 years'.[4]

[3] See H. Frost, 'Museums from the Depths', *Museum* 137 (1983), 11.

[4] Convention on the Protection of Underwater Cultural Heritage (CPUCH), Paris, 2 November 2001, in force 2 January 2009, (2002) 41 ILM 40, Article 1(1).

Underwater cultural heritage needs protection for a series of different reasons. First, underwater cultural heritage has an intrinsic historical and archaeological value, as it allows discourse and reflection upon the past. While in some rare cases aesthetic beauty alone would justify consideration of certain archaeological remains, in other more frequent cases, it is the narrative connected to the object which makes it unique and fascinating. Not only is the existence of financial riches or works of art on board shipwrecks somehow incidental, but this may also be detrimental to the preservation of the site as it may attract looters and even acts of vandalism. Generally, sunken vessels provide unique information to assist in the reconstruction of lifestyles, trade routes, and shipbuilding that no longer exist. The knowledge unveiled by the discovery of an ancient shipwreck thus represents an authentic knowledge treasure.

More importantly, not only do ancient shipwrecks provide archaeological materials, but they also offer such materials in context. Discovering undersea heritage is like obtaining access to the secrets of a civilization in its entirety, at a certain point in time. While land sites typically present artefacts from one period mixed in with those of another due to historical stratification and disturbance of archaeological sites, finding a shipwreck on the seabed may allow archaeologists to collect a whole series of data all related to a certain society, at a certain time.[5] UCH is often very well preserved due to the low oxygen marine environment, and it presents neither alterations, nor stratifications as in the case of land archaeology, where almost everything is altered through time. What survives of the vessel and its contents still represents a unity or, in archaeological terms, a *closed group*. Therefore, underwater cultural heritage can represent a *time capsule* waiting to be unlocked.

Second, underwater cultural heritage may contribute to the formation and preservation of cultural identity and, by fostering people's sense of community, it can hold associative value.[6] In addition, it may have a spiritual dimension, as in many cases these ancient vessels represent a sort of collective burial for the sailors who lost their lives at the time of the shipwreck. As one author puts it, 'in a technical sense, many shipwrecks are in fact gravesites. For example, over 1500 perished when the

[5] R. Marx, 'The Disappearing Underwater Heritage', *Museum International* 35(1) (1983), 9.

[6] See K. Last, 'Cultural Pluralism and the Return of Cultural Heritage', in S. Tierney (ed.), *Accommodating Cultural Diversity* (Aldershot: Ashgate, 2007), p. 124.

*Titanic* sank.'[7] After the wreckage was discovered in 1985 by Dr Robert Ballard, the US Congress enacted legislation directing the Department of State to negotiate an international agreement to designate the wreck as a maritime memorial and to protect it from looting and misguided salvage.[8] Recovering a shipwreck means resolving an historical jigsaw, a collective disappearance which occurred centuries ago.

Third, a unique feature of underwater cultural heritage is its cosmopolitan character. By its very quality, underwater cultural heritage has an international nature often deriving from international and regional trade, the ships involved being wrecked at a distance from their origin or destination. It was common that vessels built in a certain country, transported cargoes from one country to another, under a third country's flag with a cosmopolitan crew. In addition, the shipwreck may be located not only in international waters but also in the territorial waters of a third country. The cosmopolitan character of underwater cultural heritage makes it a worthy object of protection by international law. As one author put it: 'the importance of cultural heritage to the international community has long been established and appreciated; not only does it manifest universally shared values, but by revealing and respecting the specific national features of different original civilizations, it also promotes understanding among nations.'[9]

### 4.2 *International law and underwater archaeology*

Despite the general consensus that archaeological remains and their treatment are a matter of public concern,[10] the existing legal framework governing underwater cultural heritage at the international law level is far from being complete and well coordinated. Due to this lack of coordination among different international norms – so typical of the incremental and non-systematic development of international law – it is not clear what the exact boundaries of the different regimes are and what role different actors

[7] See C. R. Bryant, 'The Archaeological Duty of Care: The Legal, Professional, and Cultural Struggle over Salvaging Historic Shipwrecks', *Albany Law Review* 65 (2001–2), 100 note 21.

[8] O. Varmer, '*RMS Titanic*', in R. Grenier, D. Nutley and I. Cochran (eds.), *Underwater Cultural Heritage at Risk: Managing Natural and Human Impacts* (Paris: ICOMOS, 2006), pp. 14–16.

[9] A. Strati, 'The Implications of Common Heritage Concepts on the Quest for Cultural Objects and the Dialogue between North and South', *American Society International Law Proceedings* 89 (1995), 439.

[10] J. Carman, *Against Cultural Property: Archaeology, Heritage and Ownership* (London: Duckworth, 2005), p. 45.

play. Also, such provisions are extremely vague and reflect ambiguous compromises reached in the context of separate negotiations.

The 1982 United Nations Convention on the Law of the Sea (UNCLOS),[11] which virtually governs all aspects of the law of the sea,[12] only marginally deals with underwater cultural heritage. Although the UNCLOS recognizes the obligation of states to protect archaeological and historical objects, it includes only two provisions, Articles 149 and 303, referring specifically to archaeological and historic objects and establishing an obligation to protect them.

Under Article 303 of the UNCLOS, states have the duty to protect objects of an archaeological and historical nature found at sea and shall cooperate for this purpose.[13] States can establish an archaeological zone within their contiguous zone – a band of water extending from the outer edge of the territorial sea to up to 24 nautical miles from the baseline[14] – and thus may consider the removal of any archaeological or historical object from such zone as an infringement of the Convention.[15] Notwithstanding these provisions, the content of the coastal state's rights is far from clear. In addition, Article 303 of the UNCLOS also states that the Convention does not affect the law of salvage or other admiralty rules.[16]

In parallel, Article 149 of the UNCLOS states that all objects of an archaeological and historical nature found on the seabed and ocean floor beyond the limits of national jurisdiction (the so-called Area) 'shall be preserved and disposed of for the benefit of mankind as a whole, particular regard being paid to the preferential rights of the state or country of origin, or the state of cultural origin, or the state of historical and archaeological origin'.[17]

Not only do these two provisions not define what constitutes an archaeological and historical object, but they also do not mention the measures to be taken to protect such objects. Also, there is no clarification in the UNCLOS about the regime relating to underwater cultural heritage found on the continental shelf – which extends out to the continental margin of the coastal state, but at least 200 nautical miles from the baselines of its territorial sea[18]– nor to that found in the exclusive economic zone – extending for 200 nautical miles beyond the baselines of the territorial sea

[11] United Nations Convention on the Law of the Sea, 10 December 1982, in force 16 November 2004, 1833 UNTS 397.

[12] See P. Prows, 'Though Love: The Dramatic Birth and Looming Demise of UNCLOS Property Law', *Texas ILJ* 42 (2007), 241.

[13] UNCLOS, Article 303(1). [14] UNCLOS, Article 33. [15] UNCLOS, Article 303(2).

[16] UNCLOS, Article 303(3). [17] UNCLOS, Article 149. [18] UNCLOS, Article 76.

thus including the territorial sea and the contiguous zone.[19] Thus, the Convention left room for the elaboration of a more detailed protection regime by specific international instruments.[20]

The 2001 UNESCO Convention on the Protection of the Underwater Cultural Heritage (hereinafter CPUCH)[21] aims at ensuring and strengthening the international protection of underwater cultural heritage, complementing the UNCLOS in this regard.[22] The CPUCH 'stands as a *lex specialis* for UCH and its protection, whereas UNCLOS remains an authoritative *lex generalis* for the whole law of the sea'.[23] The elaboration of the Convention reflects the increasing awareness reached within the international community of the importance of protecting underwater cultural heritage.[24] The Convention adopts a preservationist approach to underwater cultural heritage protection, requiring *in situ* preservation of the same as the preferred policy option[25] and providing a rule against the commercialization of underwater cultural heritage for trade or speculation.[26] The idea behind these provisions is to foster tourism development related to the archaeological discoveries. In fact, once the resource has been sold, particularly in a foreign state, it is no longer capable of providing any further economic benefit to the state in which it was found.

Consequently, the law of salvage and the law of finds are retained in the Convention but in an attenuated form. Under Article 4 of the CPUCH, the law of salvage or the law of finds may apply to activities

19 UNCLOS, Articles 55–75. 20 UNCLOS, Article 303(4).

21 Convention on the Protection of Underwater Cultural Heritage (CPUCH), 2 November 2001, in force 2 January 2009, (2002) 41 ILM 40.

22 For commentary see C. J. S. Forrest, 'Defining Underwater Cultural Heritage', *Journal of Nautical Archaeology* 31 (2001), 3–11; P. J. O'Keefe, *Shipwrecked Heritage: A Commentary on the UNESCO Convention on Underwater Cultural Heritage* (The Hague: T.M.C. Asser Press, 2002); R. Garabello and T. Scovazzi (eds.), *The Protection of the Underwater Cultural Heritage Before and After the 2001 UNESCO Convention* (Leiden/Boston: Martinus Nijhoff, 2003); S. Dromgoole, '2001 UNESCO Convention on the Protection of the Underwater Cultural Heritage', *International Journal of Marine and Coastal Law* 18 (2003), 59–108; D. Momtaz, 'La Convention sur la protection culturel subaquatique', in T. Malick Ndiaye and R. Wolfrum (eds.), *Law of the Sea, Environmental Law and Settlement of Disputes: Liber Amicorum Judge Thomas A. Mensa* (Leiden/Boston: Martinus Nijhoff, 2007).

23 G. Carducci, 'New Developments in the Law of the Sea: The UNESCO Convention on the Protection of Underwater Cultural Heritage', *AJIL* 96 (2002), 420.

24 G. Carducci, 'Introduction to the UNESCO Convention on the Protection of the Underwater Cultural Heritage', in R. Grenier, D. Nutley and I. Cochran (eds.), *Underwater Cultural Heritage at Risk: Managing Natural and Human Impacts* (Paris: ICOMOS, 2006), p. i.

25 CPUCH, Preamble, Article 2(5), and Rule 1 of the Annex. 26 CPUCH, Article 2(7).

relating to underwater cultural heritage to which the Convention applies only if such activities (i) are authorized by the competent authorities, (ii) are in full conformity with the Convention, and (iii) ensure that any recovery of the underwater cultural heritage achieves its maximum protection.[27] As O'Keefe highlights, 'the necessity for conformity with the Convention will restrict the applicability of salvage law'.[28]

Depending on the location of underwater cultural heritage, specific regimes for cooperation between coastal and flag states and other concerned states are applicable.[29] Certainly, in its territorial waters, a state may exercise sovereign powers, as territorial waters are assimilated to the state's territory. However, much more uncertainty arises as to the existence of such rights in other maritime zones.

The most important achievement of the Convention is represented by its Annex. Having a technical nature and having been drafted by archaeologists, the Annex benefited from unanimous support at the time of its adoption and restates the need to preserve underwater cultural heritage *in situ*, and the possibility of adopting different measures for protecting or diffusing the knowledge of underwater cultural heritage.[30] The Annex also reaffirms the idea that cultural objects should not be considered as mere commodities, considering 'the commercial exploitation of underwater cultural heritage for trade or speculation, or its irretrievable dispersal, fundamentally incompatible with the protection and proper management of underwater cultural heritage. Underwater cultural heritage shall not be traded, sold, bought or bartered as commercial goods.'[31] The Annex provides for *standards* involving an idea of reasonableness as to what is considered to be acceptable conduct under the circumstances, thus functioning as a model against which to evaluate certain behaviours. While standards are not traditionally mentioned amongst the sources of international law,[32] they complement the existing rules and have become more and more influential in shaping state conduct in international relations and eventually evolving into legal tools. As an integral part of the Convention, the Annex must be interpreted accordingly. In addition,

[27] CPUCH, Article 4.

[28] P. O'Keefe, 'Fourth Meeting of Governmental Experts to Consider the Draft Convention on the Protection of Underwater Cultural Heritage', *International Journal of Cultural Property* 11 (2002), 171.

[29] CPUCH, Articles 7–13. [30] Annex, Rule 1. [31] Annex, Rule 2.

[32] Article 38 of the Statute of the International Court of Justice. The Statute of the International Court of Justice is annexed to the Charter of the United Nations. Charter of the United Nations, 26 June 1945, in force 24 October 1946, 1 UNTS XVI.

since the Annex was drafted mainly by archaeologists and it is widely recognized as embodying professional standard guidelines, it might be replicated in national systems of law without the need to ratify the Convention.

Salvage law, which is an important component part of maritime law,[33] also regulates underwater cultural heritage. In particular, salvage law regulates *salvage*, i.e. the act of rescuing life or property from peril on water, rewarding the salvor who rescued life or property imperilled at sea. The goal of salvage law is thus to promote solidarity among mariners and ship-owners. In a seminal case, the United States Supreme Court well explained the rationale of salvage law stating that:

> Compensation as salvage is not viewed by the admiralty courts merely as pay, on the principle of *quantum meruit* . . . but as reward for perilous services, voluntarily rendered, and as an inducement to seamen and others to embark in such undertakings to save life and property. Public policy encourages the hardy and adventurous mariner to engage in these laborious and sometimes dangerous enterprises.[34]

Salvage may have a contractual or factual origin. In the first case, it is the contract that regulates the proceedings and the reward. In the second case, to have a valid claim for reward, the salvor must show that the property saved was imperilled and there was a benefit for the property. The salvor has a maritime lien on the saved property and does not need to return the property to the owner until his or her claim is satisfied. Also the salvor may file a claim *in rem* against the property to obtain a salvage award.

By way of analogy, admiralty courts – i.e. ordinary courts exercising jurisdiction and hearing disputes under the rules and procedures of admiralty law – have applied the concept of salvage to the recovery of ancient relics.[35] If a private actor rescues an ancient shipwreck, thus being considered a 'salvor', she is entitled to obtain an award granting her a reward. The reward often consists of a generous percentage of the value of the saved vessel or part of the proceeds from the sale or auctioning of recovered

[33] Maritime or admiralty law is the body of international law rules which has developed in relation to maritime commerce since the Middle Ages. While some authors consider it to be a species of private international law because it regulates the activities of private actors, other authors deem it to be a part of the *jus gentium* or the law of nations. E. Boesten, *Archaeological and/or Historic Valuable Shipwrecks in International Waters: Public International Law and what it Offers* (The Hague: T.M.C. Asser Press, 2002), p. 93.

[34] *The Blackwall*, 77 US 1 (1869) at 14.

[35] See J. A. R. Nafziger, 'The Evolving Role of Admiralty Courts in Litigation related to Historic Wreck', *Harvard ILJ* 44 (2003), 251.

treasures and artefacts. In addition, a number of salvage contracts have been signed by flag states and maritime salvors for the recovery of ancient shipwrecks. For instance, in 2002 the British relevant authorities signed a salvage contract with Odyssey, a US salvor, for the recovery of the HMS *Sussex*, which sank in 1694 in the Nine Years' War, despite the fact that the deal dismayed marine archaeologists.[36]

The 1989 International Convention on Salvage[37] allows an optional reservation to its rules, permitting states to exclude the application of the Convention 'when the property involved is maritime cultural property of prehistoric, archaeological and historic interest and is situated on the seabed'.[38] However, the reservation is limited to the application of the Convention, and 'does not [. . .] affect general admiralty law of which salvage law is a part'.[39] In conclusion, admiralty courts have applied salvage law even to historic vessels.

According to admiralty law, when no owner exists or can be determined, the party who recovers the property at sea is entitled to the application of the law of finds.[40] Under this ancient doctrine, the title to the abandoned property is given to the finder. While under salvage law, the salvor merely possesses the ship, under the law of finds, she is entitled to property. While salvage law presupposes that the shipwreck that is salvaged 'is owned by persons other than the salvor' and aims at according the salvor 'a right to compensation', the law of finds assumes that 'the property involved was never owned or was abandoned' and grants title to the property.[41]

Importantly, in the context of judicial proceedings, the salvor may invoke both salvage law and the law of finds. If the court affirms its jurisdiction, it will then focus on the specific facts of the case to verify whether the law of salvage or the law of finds applies. In order for someone to qualify as a finder, she must prove that the original owners abandoned the shipwreck.[42] The application of the law of finds to historic shipwrecks is based on the presumption that the original owner abandoned the vessel.

[36] See I. Jack, 'Who Owns What Lies Beneath?', *The Guardian*, 20 October 2007.

[37] International Convention on Salvage, 28 April 1989, in force 14 July 1996, UKTS 93 (1996).

[38] Article 30(d) of the International Convention on Salvage.

[39] Boesten, *Archaeological and/or Historic Valuable Shipwrecks in International Waters*, p. 62.

[40] The law of finds has its roots in the common law in cases such as *Pierson v. Post*. In *Pierson*, a New York Court denied a hunter's claimed right to a fox, holding that the mere pursuit of the animal did not grant title to it. Title was given to a second hunter who seized the fox. *Pierson v. Post*, 3 Cai. R. 175 (Sup. Ct. N.Y. 1805).

[41] *Hener v. United States*, 525 F. Supp. 350, 356 (S.D.N.Y. 1981). [42] *Ibid.*

However, this is extremely problematic from a cultural perspective, because salvage law and the law of finds, as they have been traditionally shaped, are not designed to deal with conservation issues. While, in the past, maritime law has dealt with underwater cultural heritage only in an accidental way, in recent times the development of sophisticated technology has increasingly allowed the rescue of ancient shipwrecks. Thus, admiralty law, which has developed in an almost autochthonous way to deal with the daily practice of commercial maritime trade, has shown its inadequacy to properly deal with the protection of underwater cultural heritage.[43] On the one hand, admiralty law provides a powerful incentive to private actors to dedicate time and money to discovering and rescuing ancient shipwrecks: 'Fame aside, the potential for overwhelming financial reward is the true engine behind the salvaging of historic shipwrecks.'[44] As salvaging ancient shipwrecks is prohibitively expensive, outside investors are often sought to fund salvage operations.[45] On the other hand, salvors lack expertise and often damage or destroy historic shipwrecks. Furthermore, as selling artefacts constitutes the primary method of capitalizing shipwrecks, commercial dealing in the artefacts implies a loss from an archaeological perspective, because after the sale the artefacts are no longer available for further study.

### *4.3 Dispute settlement mechanisms*

With regard to dispute settlement, the CPUCH provides that any dispute between two or more states parties shall be subject to negotiations in good faith or other peaceful means of dispute settlement.[46] If these negotiations fail, the dispute may be submitted to UNESCO for mediation by agreement between the states parties concerned.[47] If mediation is not undertaken or there is no settlement by mediation, the provisions relating to the settlement of disputes set out in part XV of the UNCLOS apply.[48] This is a *renvoi matériel*, as the dispute settlement mechanisms provided by the UNCLOS would apply even where this Convention was not ratified by the parties to the CPUCH.

[43] See, e.g., P. Fletcher Tomenius, P. O'Keefe and M. Williams, 'Salvor in Possession: Friend or Foe to Marine Archaeology?', *International Journal of Cultural Property* 9 (2000), 263.

[44] See Bryant, *The Archaeological Duty of Care*, 107.

[45] It is estimated that salvage operations cost more than US$30,000 per day. *Ibid.* 111.

[46] CPUCH, Article 25(1). [47] CPUCH, Article 25(2). [48] CPUCH, Article 25(3).

The Rules set forth in part XV of the UNCLOS provide for the settlement of international disputes arising out of the interpretation or application of UNCLOS.[49] For instance, state responsibility might arise in relation to Article 303(1) of the UNCLOS where a state has voluntarily destroyed underwater cultural heritage or has refused any form of cooperation with other states. The primary obligation of the conflicting parties under this regime is to resolve their dispute by peaceful means.[50] If the parties are unable to resolve their conflict, any party to the dispute that is a party to UNCLOS may submit the matter to the International Tribunal for the Law of the Sea (ITLOS),[51] or to the International Court of Justice (ICJ),[52] or to an *ad hoc* arbitral tribunal.[53] For instance, the Permanent Court of Arbitration (PCA) has acted as registry in several UNCLOS arbitrations. As one author put it: 'Although these cases were not concerned with the protection of cultural property, the procedure followed in the conduct of these proceedings should constitute a useful precedent for conduct of any future arbitration relating to cultural property either under UNCLOS or CPUCH.'[54] While forum shopping is a potential issue, it is worth recalling that both states must accept the same procedure for it to be invoked. A state might choose ITLOS where the dispute presents highly technical issues, or the ICJ where the dispute has wider implications for general international law.[55]

Dealing with claims filed by individuals, admiralty courts have applied salvage law to an overwhelming number of cases concerning underwater cultural heritage. However, these courts have rarely questioned whether salvage law is appropriate at all for historic shipwrecks. Only in recent cases has attention been paid to deep water archaeological methodology.[56] In this context, while some authors criticize admiralty law as allowing a 'first-come first-served approach'[57] others consider the recent developments in

[49] N. Klein, *Dispute Settlement in the UN Convention on the Law of the Sea* (Cambridge University Press, 2005).

[50] UNCLOS, Article 279. [51] Annex VI of the UNCLOS.

[52] The Statute of the International Court of Justice is annexed to the Charter of the United Nations. Charter of the United Nations, 26 June 1945, in force 24 October 1946, 1 UNTS XVI.

[53] UNCLOS, Article 281.

[54] B.W. Daly, 'The Potential for Arbitration of Cultural Property Disputes: Recent Developments at the Permanent Court of Arbitration', *Law and Practice of International Courts and Tribunals* 4 (2005), 273.

[55] See generally A. Boyle, 'Dispute Settlement and the Law of the Sea Convention: Problems of Fragmentation and Jurisdiction', *ICLQ* 46 (1997), 37–50.

[56] *Bemis v. RMS Lusitania*, US Federal Appellate Court 884 F. Supp. 1042.

[57] T. Scovazzi, 'The 2001 UNESCO Convention on the Protection of the Underwater

admiralty law to present a promising pattern,[58] as admiralty courts 'provide an alternative to lawlessness on the frontier of underwater cultural heritage' and constitute 'justice-administering institutions in a cosmopolitan sense'.[59]

Against this background, the existing dispute settlement mechanisms show some intrinsic limits. With regard to the dispute settlement mechanisms provided by UNCLOS and CPUCH, their main shortcoming consists in their public nature, as they concern inter-state disputes only. In other words, they do not take into account the emerging reality that private actors play a role in international relations, and a particularly important one in relation to underwater cultural heritage. With regard to admiralty courts, the fact that national courts ordinarily deal with foreign artefacts often found in international waters or even in the contiguous zones of other nations raises concerns. Issues of international comity may make these courts impartial and high-profiled. However, issues of extra-territoriality arise, with the risk that national courts unconsciously represent the hegemonic view of the maritime powers to whose jurisdiction they belong. In this sense, admiralty law has not yet developed procedural and substantive guarantees to adequately protect underwater cultural heritage.

### 4.4 *International investment law as a further layer of regulation*

The question as to whether salvage may be considered a form of investment, and salvage contracts may be protected under international investment treaties, potentially constituting another layer of international regulation governing underwater cultural heritage, was addressed in a recent arbitration which put the relationship between salvaging underwater cultural heritage and international investment law at the forefront of legal debate.[60]

In 1991, the Malaysian Government entered into a contract with Malaysian Historical Salvors (MHS), a British salvage company, to locate and salvage the cargo of the *Diana*, a vessel licensed by the East India Company which mysteriously sank in the Straits of Malacca on 5 March 1817.[61] Under the terms of the contract, which was on a *no finds-no pay* basis, all the costs of the salvage and its risks would be borne exclusively

Cultural Heritage', in B. Hoffman (ed.), *Art and Cultural Heritage: Law, Policy and Practice* (Cambridge University Press, 2006), p. 288.

[58] Bryant, 'The Archaeological Duty of Care', 97.

[59] Nafziger, 'The Evolving Role of Admiralty Courts', 256–60.

[60] *Malaysian Historical Salvors Sdn, Bhd v. Malaysia*, Award on Jurisdiction, [hereinafter *MHS* Award on Jurisdiction] ICSID Case No. ARB/05/10, 17 May 2007, ¶ 10.

[61] D. Ball, *The Diana Adventure* (Groningen: Malaysian Historical Salvors Kuala Lumpur and Kemper Printers, 1995).

by the salvage company, and artefacts directly related to Malaysian history and culture would be retained by the Government for study and exhibition in the National Museum, while the other recovered items would have been auctioned in Europe at Christie's.[62] The Malaysian Government would receive the sale proceeds, while paying a percentage of the sum to the company.[63] The salvage efforts took almost four years; when MHS found and salvaged the sunken vessel, nearly 24,000 entire pieces of Chinese blue-and-white porcelains were recovered.[64] Items which were not withheld from sale by the Malaysian authorities were auctioned in Amsterdam by Christie's for approximately US$ 2.98 million.[65]

The dispute arose with regard to the proceeds of the auction and the quantity of items which Malaysia withheld from sale. As MHS received about 40 per cent of the sale and contested the amount of the salvaged items which were withheld from sale, the company commenced arbitration proceedings against the Malaysian government in Kuala Lumpur.[66] As the award dismissed the claim, and every challenge failed,[67] the claimant filed a Request for Arbitration at the ICSID, holding that there was a violation of the UK–Malaysia Bilateral Investment Treaty.[68] In particular, the claimant argued that its performance under the contract fell within the meaning of *investment* and that, accordingly, it was protected under the BIT.[69] Substantially, the investor contended that the respondent had violated BIT provisions concerning protection of investment and expropriation.[70] For its part, the respondent objected to jurisdiction over the dispute, arguing that the contract was not an investment.[71]

This line of argument was upheld by the sole arbitrator who dismissed the claim on jurisdiction.[72] The arbitrator considered that the nature of the claimant's activities was largely similar to that of a commercial salvage contract, and that under ICSID practice and jurisprudence 'an ordinary commercial contract [could not] be considered as an *investment*'.[73]

[62] *MHS*, Award on Jurisdiction, ¶ 8. [63] *Ibid.*, ¶ 11. [64] *Ibid.*, ¶ 13. [65] *Ibid.*

[66] *Ibid.*, ¶ 14–16. [67] *Ibid.*, ¶ 16.

[68] Agreement between the Government of the United Kingdom of Great Britain and Northern Ireland and the Government of Malaysia for the Promotion and Protection of Investments, 21 May 1981, in force 21 October 1988, UKTS No. 16 (1989) (UK–Malaysia BIT).

[69] *MHS* Award on Jurisdiction, ¶ 38. [70] *Ibid.*, ¶ 40. [71] *Ibid.*, ¶ 41. [72] *Ibid.*, ¶ 112.

[73] *Ibid.*

Determining whether claimant rights conferred by a contract constitute an investment is increasingly becoming a critical threshold question in investment disputes, because a positive answer establishes the arbitral tribunal's jurisdiction.[74] While the ICSID Convention does not provide any definition of the term *investment*, such concept tends to be broad and open-ended in contemporary treaties.[75] However, the quantitative tendency towards amplifying the definition of investment in bilateral and regional treaties has not necessarily implied more clarity in its qualitative understanding.

Therefore, the clarification of the notion of investment has been in practice left to the interpretation of practitioners and arbitrators. Still, arbitral panels have not reached a conclusive definition of investment and scholars have diverging views.[76] In general terms, some authors have defined investment as 'one type of human activity in which the profit sought is economic or monetary in nature'.[77] Others have noted that it would not be realistic to attempt a definition of investment but have identified some of its features. According to these authors under Article 25(1) of the ICSID Convention an investment would require a commitment of resources, a certain duration, an element of risk and a contribution to the state's development.[78] However, the established hallmarks of investment should not be viewed as *prerequisites*, but as *characteristics*. Indeed, certain activities may deserve to be categorized as an investment notwithstanding the absence, whether qualitatively or quantitatively, of a particular hallmark of investment.[79]

Given the unusual nature of the salvage company's activities, some of the criteria were either not met, or met superficially. Thus, the sole arbitrator paid particular attention to the criterion as to whether the contract made a significant contribution to the economic development of the state. Adopting a teleological approach to the interpretation of the ICSID Convention, the

[74] See M. Sattorova, 'Defining Investment under the ICSID Convention and BITs: Of Ordinary Meaning, Telos and Beyond', *Asian JIL* 2 (2012), 267.

[75] See e.g. B. Legum, 'Defining Investment and Investor: Who is Entitled to Claim?', *Arbitration International* 22 (2006), 521–6.

[76] See R. Dolzer, 'The Notion of Investment in Recent Pratice', in S. Charnovitz, D. Steger and P. Van den Bossche (eds.), *Law in the Service of Human Dignity: Essays in Honour of Florentino Feliciano* (Cambridge University Press, 2005), p. 275.

[77] N. Rubins and S. Kinsella, *International Investment, Political Risk and Dispute Resolution* (Oxford University Press, 2005), p. 1.

[78] C. Schreuer, *The ICSID Convention: A Commentary* (Cambridge University Press, 2001), p. 140.

[79] *MHS* Award on Jurisdiction, ¶ 72.

arbitrator interpreted the word *investment* as an activity which promotes some form of positive economic development for the host state,[80] and deemed that the salvage contract only benefited the Malaysian public interest in a cultural and historical way.[81] Since the arbitrator concluded that the contract was not an investment within the meaning of Article 25(1) of the ICSID Convention, he dismissed the claim on jurisdiction.[82]

The award immediately raised a storm of criticism. While some criticized the extensive and deferential reliance on previous case law,[83] others highlighted the too narrow and conservative reading of the concept of investment,[84] emphasizing that the economic benefits of an economic activity do not have to be significant in order to qualify it as an investment.[85] Some of these criticisms were upheld by the *ad hoc* Annulment Committee which annulled the award.[86]

MHS challenged the award on the grounds that the Tribunal manifestly exceeded its powers by failing to exercise jurisdiction which it possessed over the dispute.[87] The claimant contested the overly restrictive notion of investment adopted by the Tribunal on three grounds.[88] *First*, the claimant made reference to the *travaux préparatoires* of the ICSID Convention,[89] establishing that the drafters of the ICSID Convention decided against defining the notion of investment and setting any monetary floor for this notion.[90] *Second*, the claimant challenged the elevation of the hallmarks of an investment to the level of jurisdictional conditions.[91] *Third*, the applicant contested the introduction of a further jurisdictional requirement of 'contribution to the economic development of the host state' and the quantitative assessment of such contribution.[92] The respondent countered that 'annulment is not a remedy against an incorrect decision', and that the tribunal had not manifestly exceeded its powers.[93]

80 *Ibid.*, ¶ 68. 81 *Ibid.*, ¶¶ 131–2. 82 *Ibid.*, ¶ 146.

83 C. Baltag, 'Precedent on Notion of Investment: ICSID Award in MHS v Malaysia', *TDM* 4 (2007), 5.

84 Y. Andreeva, 'The Tribunal in Malaysian Historical Salvors v Malaysia Adopts a Restrictive Interpretation of the Term "Investment"', *Journal of International Arbitration* 25 (2008), 503–8.

85 V. Vadi, 'Investing in Culture: Underwater Cultural Heritage and International Investment Law', *Vanderbilt Journal of Transnational Law* 42 (2009), 853–904.

86 *Malaysian Historical Salvors Sdn Bhd v. Government of Malaysia*, Decision on the Application for Annulment (hereinafter *MHS* Decision on the Application for Annulment) ICSID Case No. ARB/05/10, 16 April 2009.

87 *Ibid.*, ¶ 1. 88 *Ibid.*, ¶ 28. 89 *Ibid.* 90 *Ibid.* 91 *Ibid.*, ¶ 29. 92 *Ibid.*, ¶ 45.

93 *Ibid.*, ¶¶ 44–5.

The majority of the Annulment Committee established that a salvage contract is a form of investment, on the basis of the definition of investment provided by the UK–Malaysia BIT. According to Article 1 of the UK–Malaysia BIT, investment means every kind of asset including 'claims to money or to any performance under contract, having a financial value' and 'business concessions conferred by the law or under contract, including concessions to search for, cultivate, extract or exploit natural resources'.[94] The majority of the Committee noted that while the UK–Malaysia BIT did not provide any dispute settlement option other than ICSID, it endowed ICSID with an important jurisdictional reach.[95] Therefore, it concluded that the Tribunal exceeded its powers by failing to exercise jurisdiction with which it was endowed by the UK–Malaysia BIT and the ICSID Convention, and that it manifestly did so because it failed to take into account the definition of investment provided by the same BIT; it elevated certain criteria to jurisdictional requirements and it failed to take into account the *travaux préparatoires* of the ICSID Convention.[96]

However, the debate is far from over. Indeed, the third member of the Annulment Committee, Judge Mohamed Shahabuddeen, signed the decision of the *ad hoc* Committee for authentication, but issued a dissenting opinion insisting upon the need for investments to make a significant contribution to the economic development of the host state under the ICSID system.[97] In particular, he held that there are 'outer limits to an ICSID investment outside of the will of the parties'.[98] He also took the view that the annulment mechanism should not operate as a court of appeal and questioned whether the error allegedly committed by the sole arbitrator was manifest. Judge Shahabuddeen mentioned the 'titanic struggle' between different doctrinal and jurisprudential trends 'and correspondingly between capital exporting countries and capital importing ones' concerning the notion of investment.[99] This debate was also mentioned in the decision of the majority of the Annulment Committee.[100]

Arbitral panels have held different positions on the issue as to whether a *significant* contribution to the economic development of the host state is needed in order to have an investment under the ICSID Convention.

[94] UK–Malaysia BIT, Article 1.
[95] *MHS* Decision on the Application for Annulment, ¶¶ 62 and 73. [96] *Ibid.*, ¶ 80.
[97] *MHS* Decision on the Application for Annulment, dissenting opinion of Judge Mohamed Shahabuddeen, ¶ 4.
[98] *Ibid.*, ¶ 14. [99] *Ibid.*, ¶ 62.
[100] *MHS* Decision on the Application for Annulment, ¶ 17.

In the *Malaysian Historical Salvors* case, the Arbitrator concluded that the economic benefits should be significant; otherwise, 'every contract which enhances the Gross Domestic Product of an economy by any amount, however small, would qualify as an investment'.[101] Still, as the Arbitral Tribunal stated in *Mihaly*, 'the question [of] whether [or not] an expenditure constitutes an investment . . . is hardly to be governed by whether or not the expenditure is large'.[102] The claimant employed over 40 people in Malaysia, imparted valuable knowledge and know-how on the process of historical marine salvage, and raised Malaysia's profile as an attractive location for tourism.[103] In addition, the contract provided for a share of cultural items to be given to Malaysian conservation programmes. The conservation of maritime sites and cultural items is directly linked to the development of the tourism business and other economic activities.[104] In some countries tourism has replaced other sources of income.[105] The fact that the Straits of Malacca have recently been added to UNESCO's World Heritage List as a cultural site provides evidence that the Straits can be a tourist destination. In conclusion, as one of the counsel for MHS said: 'The fact that in *MHS*, the investment was relatively small and related to cultural heritage, was certainly not a ground to disqualify it as an investment.'[106]

In conclusion, salvage contracts may be deemed to be protected under international investment treaties as long as they contribute to the development of the host state. Therefore another layer of international regulation now governs underwater cultural heritage recovery and management. It is still too early to critically assess the implications of this paradigm shift. After the annulment of the award, the *Malaysian Historical Salvors* case could have moved to the substantive phase of the proceedings. However, as the salvor was short of funding, there was no

[101] Michael Hwang, quoted by D. Vis-Dunbar, 'Underwater Salvaging Firm Fails "Investment Test" in ICSID Case Against Malaysia', *ITN*, 30 June 2007, 2.

[102] *Mihaly International Corporation v. Democratic Socialist Republic of Sri Lanka*, ICSID Case No. ARB/00/2, Award, 15 March 2002, 41 ILM 862 (2002), ¶ 51.

[103] *MHS*, Award on Jurisdiction, ¶ 133.

[104] See S. A. H. B. Syed Mustapa, 'Showcasing Maritime Heritage Artefacts for the Benefit of the Tourist Industry in Malaysia', *International Journal of Nautical Archaeology* 34 (2005), 211–15.

[105] See C. C. Aniakor, 'Cultural Objects as History and National Patrimony: A Moral Challenge', *Am. Soc. Int'l L. Proc.* 89 (1995), 435.

[106] Emmanuel Gaillard, cited by L. E. Peterson, 'Majority Finds that Failure to Examine Wide Definition of Investment in UK–Malaysia BIT was Manifest Excess of Power on the Part of Earlier Arbitrator', *IAR*, 20 April 2009, 5.

award on the merits. If similar cases nonetheless arise in the future, then arbitrators will face the challenge of reconciling the protection of underwater cultural heritage and the promotion of foreign investments. Even where arbitrators were sympathetic to cultural heritage protection, they could not ignore certain limits to their mandate. The UNESCO Convention on the Protection of Underwater Cultural Heritage has been ratified by a limited number of countries.[107] In addition, the Convention does not seem likely to become part of customary international law, as it is fiercely opposed by a number of maritime powers, whose nationals practise salvage on a regular basis all around the world. Also, the arbitral tribunal would be bound to interpret the salvage contract drafted by the parties. Although admiralty law provides for a very detailed discipline which has been elaborated by admiralty courts for centuries, salvage law and the law of finds seem ambiguous with regard to undersea cultural heritage. Having been developed to save men and/or recover objects at sea, maritime customs include rules which clash with cultural heritage preservation.

However, to say that international arbitrators are entirely devoid of guidance would amount to a denial of some important developments in international law. First, the UNCLOS specifically requires states to 'protect objects of an archaeological nature found at sea' and to cooperate for this purpose.[108] Some UNCLOS provisions have already acquired customary nature, and thus are binding even on states which have not ratified it. While the relevant provisions admittedly do not affect admiralty law, they are also 'without prejudice to other international agreements and rules of international law regarding the protection of objects of an archaeological or historical nature'.[109] Second, with regard to the protection of objects of an archaeological or historical nature, international cultural law has recently become a very important part of international law.[110] There is an argument that the protection of cultural heritage might already represent a customary norm.[111] Third, the Annex to the CPUCH which includes technical standards, expressing scientific agreement by the archaeological community on

[107] So far only 41 states have ratified the Convention on the Protection of Underwater Cultural Heritage. The list is available at www.unesco.org/eri/la/convention.asp?KO=13520&language=E&order=alpha.

[108] UNCLOS, Article 303(1). [109] UNCLOS, Article 303(4).

[110] See e.g. J. A. R. Nafziger, 'The Development of International Cultural Law', *Am. Soc. Int'l L. Proc.* 100 (2006), 317.

[111] F. Francioni, 'Au-delà des traités: l'émergence d'un nouveau droit coutumier pour la protection du patrimoine culturel', *RGDIP* (2007), 19–42.

the need to protect undersea heritage, can be (and has been) implemented irrespectively of the ratification of the CPUCH. Finally, admiralty tribunals in common law countries have developed a case law which increasingly requires adequate archaeological standards, thus recognizing the need to preserve archaeological treasures.[112]

In conclusion, the interpretation of the existing legal instruments and standards may help arbitrators to properly adjudicate cases analogous to the *Malaysian Historical Salvors* case at the substantive level. Customary rules of treaty interpretation as restated by the Vienna Convention, require treaty terms to be interpreted not only according to their strict textual meaning, but also in good faith, in context and in the light of their object and purpose.[113] Moreover, terms must be interpreted taking into account any relevant rules of international law applicable in the relations between the parties.[114] This approach requires a systemic interpretation by arbitral tribunals. Investment law is part of international law, and thus it has to be consistent with the norms of the latter. Arbitrators may refer to the CPUCH, the UNCLOS and the relevant maritime customs as 'context' of the applicable law. All these instruments recognize the need to protect underwater cultural heritage.

Nevertheless, interpretation is a complex process that requires in-depth knowledge of the existing legal framework and should not result in lawmaking, which would violate the arbitration mandate. The arbitral tribunal must ascertain the goal and effect of state action. The mere presence of cultural elements in a given dispute does not imply that a state may adopt discriminatory or abusive practices. If a state fails to protect UCH, arbitrators must still respect their mandate and cannot substitute their judgment for that of the state. At the same time, arbitrators may take international law into account when reviewing state action.

### 4.5 *Critical assessment*

Historic shipwrecks are an important source of knowledge and hold a profound cultural value. According to what may be referred to as the *purist* view, commercial salvage operators should be excluded from working on historical wreck sites, and *in situ* preservation of underwater cultural heritage would be the best possible option. The purist view

[112] Nafziger, 'The Evolving Role of Admiralty Courts'. [113] VCLT, Article 31.
[114] VCLT, Article 31(3)(c).

regards UCH's archaeological and economic values as incompatible, holding that 'commercial salvage operations are fundamentally at odds with preservation'.[115] Regardless of how well they may document the site, commercial salvors usually sell a part of the cargo to recover the expenses and to make a profit. The cargo is therefore dispersed and is no longer available in its entirety for scholarly analysis.[116]

The purist view has been harshly criticized by some authors who deem it as 'a perfectionist policy' with 'an element of unrealistic romanticism',[117] only suitable to developed countries that are 'willing to commit public funds to carry out archaeological excavations, inclusive of the time consuming and costly tasks of conservation . . . of artefacts, documentation, dissemination and display'.[118] However, not only developing countries but also industrialized states may lack the will and resources necessary to recover shipwrecks. In practice, salvaging historic shipwrecks requires finding the financial resources, adopting a sophisticated methodology, and investigating the right site. Not only are most countries short of funding for such works, but at the same time they face unavailability of expertise, shortage of equipment and lack of historical documents. Furthermore, a number of authors highlight that unless salvors can recover underwater heritage, its potential addition to mankind's heritage and store of knowledge will never occur, and that 'the benefits of the quest for knowledge will only be realised if the quest is undertaken'.[119]

Therefore, according to what may be referred to as the *mercantilist view*, salvage contracts represent useful joint ventures, by which investors assume financial risks, while receiving consistent benefit shares in the revenue provided by the auction of the salvaged items. Several arguments support the mercantilist view. First, commercial salvage operators have been extremely successful in locating and rescuing underwater cultural heritage. Second, as the risk of losing UCH is relatively high

115 C. Forrest, 'Has the Application of Salvage Law to Underwater Cultural Heritage Become a Thing of the Past?', *Journal of Maritime Law and Commerce* 34 (2003), 318.

116 See generally, O. Varmer, 'The Case Against the "Salvage" of the Cultural Heritage', *Journal of Maritime Law and Commerce* 30 (1999), 279.

117 D. Luxford, 'Finders Keepers Losers Weepers – Myth or Reality? An Australian Perspective on Historic Shipwrecks', in B. Hoffmann (ed.), *Art and Cultural Heritage: Law, Policy and Practice* (Cambridge University Press, 2006), p. 307.

118 M. Flecker, 'The Ethics, Politics, and Realities of Maritime Archaeology in Southeast Asia', *International Journal of Nautical Archaeology* 31 (2002), 13.

119 F. Booth, 'The Collision of Property Rights and Cultural Heritage; the Salvors' and Insurers' Viewpoints', in Hoffmann (ed.), *Art and Cultural Heritage: Law, Policy and Practice*, p. 299.

because of natural and human factors, commercial salvage operators represent a means of recovering UCH before it is damaged. With regard to human factors, UCH may be threatened both by legitimate activities and by unauthorized appropriation. Construction work and exploitation of living and non-living resources are legitimate activities that may incidentally affect UCH by altering the shore or the seabed. Also the unauthorized commercial exploitation of underwater cultural heritage puts it in danger. Often local divers recover artefacts, without a licence and without any archaeology expertise, and sell archaeological finds directly to antique dealers. In this context, valuable archaeological and historical information is lost forever. Salvage operators could help stop such damage and loss of UCH.

Can the mercantilist view be reconciled with the purist view? From an economic perspective, the preservation of historic assets has the potential to generate powerful heritage industry, tourism and related business. These revenues could constitute a means for *project financing*, that is the financing of long-term investment projects based upon a complex financial structure where project debt and equity are used to finance the project, and debt is repaid using the cash-flow generated by operation of the project. If the salvor were given the possibility to co-participate in the management of cultural heritage after its recovery and in exploiting subsequent revenues for a given amount of time, this might constitute the necessary warranty for obtaining equity financing. Economists and lawyers might help policy-makers to envisage concession-agreement-like contracts between countries and investors. If the primary objective of the salvage company is to make a profit, profits can come from entertainment markets in which salvors would retain media rights and copyright on derivative products such as movies or books.[120] More importantly, the host state would benefit from this as well, as it would not have to finance salvage operations and would have any finds properly salvaged and stored in appropriate museums. Crucially, after a certain number of years, the host state's rights would re-expand to full management. In conclusion, sale is not the only available option to recover the costs and expenses of salvaging historic shipwrecks.

Exhibitions of the artefacts themselves may represent a suitable cultural and economic option for the host state. Not only do museums have cultural and social functions as they are institutions in the service

[120] See e.g. J. S. Stern, 'Smart Salvage: Extending Traditional Maritime Law to Include Intellectual Property Rights in Historic Shipwrecks', *Fordham L. Rev.* 68 (2000), 2489.

of society and important forums for dialogue and critical thinking, but they can be profitable. The case in point is well illustrated by the example set by the salvage company in the case of the *Titanic*. In 1994, after conducting numerous expeditions recovering artefacts from the *Titanic* wreck, the salvage company went on city tours to display them to the public. The huge success of the RMS *Titanic* exhibitions bears testimony to the potential profitability of a salvage operation without the sale of recovered artefacts. Remarkably, the company decided not to do much future shipwreck salvage work, 'preferring above-water cash-paying customers to chasing high risk dreams of underwater riches'.[121]

Similarly, states have financed the creation of maritime museums. Actually, there are more than 800 nautical museums in the world mainly due to private-public partnership.[122] No longer the exclusive reserve of particularly erudite visitors,[123] today museums carry out diverse functions that range from research and documentation, to exhibition and education, attracting a large number of visitors.[124] Akin to maritime museums on land, underwater museums presuppose the conservation *in situ* of the wrecks and may be a suitable option in areas which present transparent waters and are not particularly deep. Initiatives to publish archaeological results and books should be welcomed as they are capable of reaching a wide audience. Finally, the digital environment provides an unparalleled opportunity to communicate information to the public about this form of heritage.

## Conclusions

Ancient shipwrecks are an invaluable source of knowledge and hold a profound historic and cultural value. From a cultural perspective, underwater cultural heritage represents an 'integral part of the cultural heritage of humanity and a particularly important element in the history of peoples

[121] P. Hodson, 'How to Invest in Sunken Treasures; Salvage Stocks Offer High Returns, but Big Risks', *National Post*, 31 May 2007.

[122] See F. Serafini, *Musei navali e collezioni marittime nel mondo* (Milano: Gribaudo, 2005).

[123] O. Genin, 'Les musées maritimes, gardiens d'un patrimoine mondial', *Museum International* 48 (1996), 5.

[124] Y. Herreman, 'The Role of Museums Today: Tourism and Cultural Heritage', in B. Hoffmann (ed.), *Art and Cultural Heritage* (Cambridge University Press, 2006), pp. 419–26.

and their relations with each other concerning their common heritage'.[125] Thus conservation of unique assets provides cultural and societal benefits. From a historical perspective the discovery of underwater heritage offers us the possibility of unveiling often neglected episodes of the past. From an economic perspective, the management of underwater cultural heritage may constitute an engine for growth and sustainable development, catalysing tourism and related economic activities. From a legal perspective, a complex regulatory matrix governs UCH.

At a preliminary phase, with regard to the discovery and recovery of undersea heritage, public-private partnerships should be carefully envisaged. Since archaeologists do not have funds to discover and excavate sites, archaeological remains may be irremediably lost through illegal excavation and trade or because of natural events. Therefore, incentives to recover artefacts in a legitimate way need to be established. The approach proposed in this book would allocate the management of cultural goods to private actors and the states or, eventually, to joint ventures between them. In this context, international investment law may constitute a useful legal framework. This sensible approach is based on the assumption that an incentive-based system may be coupled with a preservation policy; by enhancing the synergy between private and public actors underwater cultural heritage can be preserved for the benefit of present and future generations.

This chapter has questioned whether international investment law might provide an alternative framework in order to reconcile private interests with the public interest of underwater cultural heritage protection in international law. After scrutinizing whether investment law is applicable to salvage contracts by which private actors rescue ancient shipwrecks with the state's consent, two questions arise. The first question is whether investment treaties are compatible with states' obligations to protect underwater cultural heritage. The second is whether investor–state arbitration is a suitable forum to deal with claims concerning underwater cultural heritage. In order to answer these questions, this contribution has analysed the *Malaysian Historical Salvors* case. While the *MHS* award on jurisdiction did not categorize salvage as a form of investment, the Annulment Committee, on the other hand, did qualify salvage as such. As the case did not move to the substantive level, it remains to be seen, should similar cases arise in the future, how the competent arbitral tribunal will deal with the challenge of reconciling the

[125] CPUCH, *Preamble*.

promotion of foreign investment with underwater cultural heritage conservation.

The *Malaysian Historical Salvors* case may have crucial implications for the cultural policies of maritime states. If salvage contracts with foreign companies are considered to be investments; they are not regulated merely by national law, but they are also governed by international investment law, which is a subset of public international law. In this regard, if a dispute arises out of the implementation of a salvage contract, foreign investors may claim that state regulations on the protection of underwater cultural heritage amount to a violation of investment treaty standards. Arbitrators will then face the challenge of reconciling cultural heritage protection and the promotion of foreign investments.

# 5

# Cultural diversity, intangible heritage and foreign direct investment

*Exegi monumentum aere perennius*
*regalique situ pyramidum altius,*
*quod non imber edax, non Aquilo impotens*
*possit diruere aut innumerabilis*
*annorum series et fuga temporum.*
*Non omnis moriar multaque pars mei*
*vitabit Libitinam . . .*[1]

## Introduction

While economic globalization has brought cultures and people into closer contact than ever before[2] since trade and foreign direct investment facilitate constant exchanges and interaction between cultures, asymmetry in flows and exchanges of cultural goods at the global level can jeopardize cultural diversity, leading to cultural homogenization.[3] Admittedly, the enhanced interaction between cultures creates a series of opportunities. Global flows of culture are as significant as global flows of capital;[4] not only because in the new economy 'the competitive advantage of nations' lies in the creativity of their peoples,[5] and the

[1] Horace, *Odes*, Book III, Ode 30 ('I built a monument more permanent than bronze/and much higher than the Pyramids,/which the corroding rain and furious north wind/ cannot destroy, nor the long/lapse of immemorial time. I shall not die completely, /and a great part of me will escape the goddess of funerals . . .' (author's translation)).

[2] Globalization refers to both the worldwide process of liberalizing state controls on the international movement of goods, services and capital and the social, economic and political consequences of liberalization. See S. Sassen, *Globalization and its Discontents: Essays on the New Mobility of People and Money* (New York: New Press, 1998).

[3] UNDP, *Human Development Report 2004, Cultural Liberty in Today's Diverse World* (New York: UNDP, 2004), p. 10.

[4] R. Coombe, 'Legal Claims to Culture in and against the Market: Neoliberalism and the Global Proliferation of Meaningful Difference', *Law, Culture and the Humanities* 1 (2005), 37.

[5] *Ibid.*, 42.

growing international trade and investment in cultural products constitute an important part of the global economy,[6] but also because culture is not a static concept, but a dynamic force resulting from a process of exposure to other cultures. By leading to more choice for consumers, trade and foreign direct investment may enhance cultural diversity and media pluralism, thus facilitating the constant exchanges and interaction between cultures. The free flow of ideas across borders promotes cultural dialogue and fosters individual freedom against authoritarian thought-control.[7]

However, the exchange volume should not be confused with the promotion of cultural diversity. In particular, the economic principle of the comparative advantage, which is the theoretical basis of the current regulation of international trade and the delocalization of economic activities worldwide, requires that countries specialize in the sectors in which they are most efficient. Some countries have an absolute advantage in the production of cultural goods such as movies because of economies of scale. Therefore, the products of powerful cultural industries tend to crowd out the products of smaller producers. The current asymmetry in flows and exchanges of cultural goods at the global level jeopardizes cultural diversity possibly leading to cultural homogenization and ultimately to 'cultural hegemony'.[8] According to critical theorists Theodor Adorno and Max Horkheimer, cultural industries producing standardized cultural goods can manipulate the masses into passivity and constitute a form of social domination.[9] When cultural exchanges take place, 'a country is actually "importing" or "exporting" culture, because a significant component of culture is embodied in . . . the cultural products . . . Transactions in these goods and services are

[6] See S. Peng, 'International Trade in "Cultural Products": UNESCO's Commitment to Promoting Cultural Diversity and Its Relations with the WTO', *Int'l Trade and Business L. Rev.* 11 (2008), 220.

[7] *Ibid.*

[8] Cultural hegemony is a sociological concept, originated by the philosopher Antonio Gramsci. In its original meaning, cultural hegemony indicates that a society can be ruled or dominated by one of its social classes that is able to impose on other groups, through everyday practices and shared beliefs, their views until they are internalized. A. Gramsci, *Quaderni del carcere* (Torino: Einaudi, 1948–1951). In this chapter this term indicates the predominance of a certain national culture over other competing cultures.

[9] T.W. Adorno and M. Horkheimer, *Dialektik der Aufklärung* (Amsterdam: Querido Verlag, 1947); *Dialectic of Enlightenment*, trans. E. Jephcott (Stanford: Stanford University Press, 2002).

thus an expression, if not an expansion, of the cultural identity of the exporting country'.[10]

One might object that cultural goods are just another type of commodities: cultural considerations should not affect the marketplace of ideas.[11] If some states are better at producing cultural goods, 'the invisible hand' should regulate the demand and supply of such goods. Others see cultural concerns as a 'smokescreen for economic self-interest, casting the issue as one of free trade v. protectionism',[12] and perceive 'attempts by governments to come between consumers and their living room screens' as 'paternalistic, bordering on outright censorship'.[13]

However, the idea that cultural goods have a double nature – i.e. economic and cultural – and thus deserve special consideration by policy-makers, has increasingly gained prominence at the theoretical and normative levels.[14] At the theoretical level, arguments are made that cultural goods do not have a mere monetary value; rather, they 'convey ideas, symbols and lifestyles and are an intrinsic part of the identity of the community which produces them'.[15] Such goods can have a powerful cultural impact, influencing human behaviour and cultural identity.[16]

At the normative level, the adoption of a number of international instruments evidences a growing international support for the cultural diversity of states.[17] Such instruments promote a 'dialogic understanding of culture' as a process rather than as outcome, seeking a balance between the internal production of cultural goods and external influences.[18] As Pager puts it: 'while culture need not be hermetically sealed from external influences, retaining a degree of autonomy allows each country to define its own narrative'.[19] Seeking a middle ground between cultural autarchy and external hegemony would enable the preservation

[10] Peng, 'International Trade in "Cultural Products"', 220.

[11] E. A. Posner, 'The International Protection of Cultural Property: Some Skeptical Observations', *Chicago JIL* 8 (2007), 213.

[12] S. A. Pager, 'Beyond Culture v. Commerce: Decentralizing Cultural Protection to Promote Diversity Through Trade', *Northwestern JIL & Business* 31 (2011), 66.

[13] *Ibid.*, 70.

[14] See generally M. Braun and L. Parker, 'Trade in Culture: Consumable Product or Cherished Articulation of a Nation's Soul?' *Denver J. of Int'l Law and Policy* 22 (1993), 155–91.

[15] UNDP, *Human Development Report* 2004, p. 97. [16] *Ibid.*

[17] See section 5.2 below. [18] Pager, 'Beyond Culture v. Commerce', 71. [19] *Ibid.*

of 'space for each culture to evolve on its own terms' and the realization of diversity through trade.[20]

The *clash of cultures* between economic globalization and cultural diversity raises a number of questions and has been scrutinized from several perspectives.[21] While economists have used economics lenses to read this interplay,[22] international law scholars have focused on the well-known *trade v. culture* debate.[23] However, the parallel interplay between cultural diversity and foreign direct investment in international investment law and arbitration has received scarce, if any, attention. As international investment law and international cultural law have traditionally been considered two separate branches of public international law, there is a general lack of literature concerning the linkage in international investment law and arbitration between cultural diversity and intangible heritage on the one hand, and foreign investments on the other.[24]

This chapter addresses this lacuna, questioning whether international investment law and arbitration can hinder the regulatory autonomy of the host state in the cultural domain. Can governments promote a *Leitkultur* (leading culture) within the borders of the state and require foreigners to respect it? If so, what are the boundaries between legitimate cultural policies and unlawful treatment of foreign investors that is banned by international investment law? Is investor–state arbitration a suitable mechanism to adjudicate cultural diversity-related disputes?

This chapter will proceed as follows. *First*, the multifaceted concept of cultural diversity will be defined and the relevant UNESCO convention will be sketched out. *Second*, the concept of intangible cultural heritage will be introduced. While the two concepts – cultural diversity on the one hand and intangible cultural heritage on the other – are distinct, their protection presents some overlapping, as intangible cultural heritage is a

[20] *Ibid.*, 127.

[21] See e.g. T. Voon, 'UNESCO and the WTO: A Clash of Cultures?', *ICLQ* 55 (2006), 635 and M. Hahn, 'A Clash of Cultures? The UNESCO Diversity Convention and International Trade Law', *JIEL* 9 (2006), 515–52.

[22] See e.g. K. Acheson and C. Maule, 'Convention on Cultural Diversity', *Journal of Cultural Economics* 28 (2004), 243–56.

[23] The literature is extensive. See e.g. H. Schneider and P. Van den Bossche (eds.), *Protection of Cultural Diversity from a European and International Perspective* (Antwerp: Intersentia, 2008); L. Mayer-Robitaille, *Le statut juridique des biens et services culturels dans les accords commerciaux internationaux* (Paris: L'Harmattan, 2008).

[24] See, however, V. Vadi, 'Cultural Diversity Disputes and the Judicial Function in International Investment Law', *Syracuse JIL and Commerce* 39 (2011), 89–136.

mainspring of cultural diversity. *Third*, the conflict areas between international investment law and international cultural law protecting cultural diversity and intangible heritage will be scrutinized through the analysis of some relevant case studies. Finally, some conclusions will be drawn.

## 5.1 Cultural diversity

Cultural diversity can be defined as 'the manifold ways in which the culture of groups and societies finds expression', and 'is made manifest not only through the varied ways in which the cultural heritage of humanity is expressed ... but also through diverse modes of artistic creation, production, dissemination, distribution and enjoyment, whatever the means and technologies used'.[25] Cultural diversity is thus an inclusive concept comprised of two interrelated components: culture and diversity. In order to understand what cultural diversity means, it is necessary to explore both components.[26]

As mentioned in Chapter 1, three different meanings of culture can be identified: (1) culture in its material sense, as the product of a given cultural process; (2) culture in its immaterial sense as a process of artistic or scientific creation; and (3) culture in its anthropological sense, that is, culture as a way of life.[27] Cultural diversity draws upon the third meaning of culture, whereby culture is holistically meant as 'the set[s] of distinctive spiritual, material, intellectual and emotional features of society' which encompass in addition to art and literature lifestyles, ways of living together, value systems, traditions and beliefs.[28] As culture is not a static concept but a fluid and dynamic force which changes over time, it is by nature diverse. Thus, diversity is inextricable from culture.

In the past decade, cultural diversity has increasingly been linked to cultural rights. While the existence of a right to cultural diversity as

[25] UNESCO Convention on the Protection and Promotion of the Diversity of Cultural Expressions (CCD), Paris, 20 October 2005, in force 18 March 2007, 2440 UNTS 311, Article 4(1). On the Convention, see section 5.2 below.

[26] M. Burri Nenova, 'Cultural Diversity as a Concept of Global Law: Origins, Evolution and Prospects', *Diversity* 4 (2010), 1059–75.

[27] A. Eide, 'Cultural Rights as Individual Human Rights', in A. Eide, C. Krause and A. Rosas (eds.), *Economic, Social and Cultural Rights. A Textbook* (Dordrecht: Martinus Nijhoff Publishers, 1995), p. 230.

[28] Universal Declaration on Cultural Diversity, November 2001, ILM 41 (2002), preamble.

an autonomous human right is contested,[29] cultural diversity has increasingly been linked to the right to participate in the cultural life of the community and to enjoy the arts, as enshrined in Article 27 of the Universal Declaration of Human Rights[30] and Article 15 of the International Covenant on Economic, Social and Cultural Rights (ICESCR).[31] The mutually reinforcing link 'between respect for cultural diversity and the cultural rights of all' has been affirmed at the UN level,[32] and the same UNESCO that preferred a cultural policy approach in the past has started to make express reference to cultural rights.[33]

A human rights-based approach to cultural diversity puts people and human values at the centre of the concept of cultural diversity, entailing 'an epistemological reversal of the perspective from a state-oriented approach, which sees the nation as a whole under the mantle of sovereignty, to a bottom-up approach, which places the community or group that creates and maintains the heritage to be safeguarded at its centre'.[34] Linking cultural diversity to human rights can help promote the democratization of cultural governance and 'avoid the marginalization and exclusion of, and discrimination against, specific sectors of society'.[35] A human rights approach to cultural diversity also entails that the protection of cultural diversity is not unbounded.[36]

Instead, a cultural policy approach to cultural diversity focuses on the state's cultural policies rather than on individual cultural entitlements and investigates the best way to govern cultural resources. In this context, UNESCO's commitment to protect cultural diversity has reinforced the cultural sovereignty of states and their top-down capacity to regulate

[29] See Y. Donders, *Towards a Right to Cultural Identity?* (Antwerp: Intersentia, 2002), p. 327.

[30] Universal Declaration of Human Rights (UDHR) GA Res. 217(III) UNGAOR, 3rd sess., UN Doc A/810 (1948) 10 December 1948.

[31] International Covenant on Economic, Social and Cultural Rights (ICESCR) UNGA Res. 2200 (XXI) 16 December 1966, in force 3 January 1976, 993 UNTS 3.

[32] UNGA Resolution, *Human Rights and Cultural Diversity*, A/RES/60/167, 7 March 2006.

[33] Universal Declaration on Cultural Diversity, Article 5.

[34] F. Francioni, 'Culture, Heritage and Human Rights: An Introduction', in F. Francioni and M. Scheinin (eds.), *Cultural Human Rights* (Leiden/Boston: Martinus Nijhoff Publishers, 2008), p. 15.

[35] UNGA Resolution, *Human Rights and Cultural Diversity*, A/RES/60/167, 7 March 2006, ¶ 12.

[36] CCD, Article 2(1) and Convention for the Safeguarding of the Intangible Cultural Heritage (CSICH), Paris, 17 October 2003, in force 20 April 2006, 2368 UNTS 3.

individuals in the cultural domain,[37] diffusing the idea that cultural diversity is the common heritage of mankind[38] and thus ascribing an international relevance to it. Respect for the diversity of cultures, dialogue and cooperation are deemed to be among the best guarantees of international peace and security.[39] The wide diffusion of culture is deemed to be indispensable to the dignity of man and to constitute a 'sacred duty' which all nations must fulfil in a spirit of mutual assistance.[40] UNESCO instruments also clarify that cultural policies must comply with the relevant human rights treaties.

This chapter focuses on the common nucleus of these approaches, adopting a *cultural policy* approach rather than a *cultural rights* approach; the focus is on the states' cultural policies rather than on individual cultural entitlements. The selected lens does not imply a value judgement on which is the best approach; it simply draws on the consideration that claims before investment tribunals are based on the regulatory behaviour of states. At the same time, it is uncontroversial that the content of the cultural policy approach, which deems cultural policies to be a traditional component of state sovereignty, partially overlaps with the cultural rights approach, which entails both individual rights and the state's duty to respect, protect and fulfil these rights. In this manner, the analysis assumes a more general character and concerns even those states that have signed but not ratified the ICESCR.[41]

## 5.2 *The Convention on Cultural Diversity*

The 2005 UNESCO Convention on the Protection and Promotion of the Diversity of Cultural Expressions, often referred to as the Convention on Cultural Diversity (CCD),[42] reaffirms 'the sovereign rights of States to

[37] J. Morijn, 'The Place of Cultural Rights in the WTO System', in F. Francioni and M. Scheinin (eds.), *Cultural Human Rights* (Leiden/Boston: Martinus Nijhoff Publishers, 2008), p. 292.

[38] Universal Declaration on Cultural Diversity, Article 1.

[39] Constitution of the United Nations Educational, Scientific, and Cultural Organization (UNESCO Constitution), London, 16 November 1945, in force 4 November 1946, UNTS 275 (1945), preamble.

[40] *Ibid.*

[41] Most notably, the United States signed but never ratified the ICESCR. See P. Alston, 'U.S. Ratification of the Covenant on Economic, Social and Cultural Rights: The Need for an Entirely New Strategy', *AJIL* 84 (1990), 375.

[42] Convention on the Protection of the Diversity of Cultural Contents and Artistic Expressions (CCD), Paris, 20 October 2005, in force 17 March 2007, 2440 UNTS 311.

maintain, adopt and implement policies and measures that they deem appropriate for the protection and promotion of the diversity of cultural expressions on their territory'.[43] At the root of this Convention was the need to establish a legal counterweight to trade agreements, safeguarding the state power to encourage its national audio-visual sector – a sector with high economic value – against the general applicability of free trade.[44] Having failed to overcome the resistance by the United States against the inclusion of a cultural exception into the law of the World Trade Organization and the proposed Multilateral Agreement on Investment, the EU and other actors, most notably Canada, 'abandoned their defensive approach and opted for a proactive stance'.[45] The adoption by acclamation of the UNESCO Universal Declaration on Cultural Diversity in 2001 constituted evidence of growing momentum and international support for such an approach.[46]

During the negotiations the positions were polarized.[47] As the US rejoined UNESCO in 2003, some inferred this move to be due to 'the alarming prospects of a legally binding instrument on cultural diversity to be negotiated in a forum in which the United States had no formal input'.[48] Whatever the reasons for the rejoining, as Kelsey points out: 'The US delegation made constant and vigorous interventions throughout the drafting process ... even though the US was unlikely ever to ratify the instrument.'[49] When the Convention was finalized, the US protested that decisions by voting had undermined the spirit of *consensus* that normally characterized UNESCO decision-making; more substantially, it objected that the Convention was not about *culture* but about *trade*, and thus exceeded the mandate of

[43] CCD, Article 1.

[44] J. Wouters and M. Vidal, 'International Normative Action for Cultural Diversity: The Contribution of UNESCO', in M.-C. Foblets, J.-F. Gaudreault-Desbiens and A. Dundes Renteln (eds.), *Cultural Diversity and the Law: State Responses from around the World* (Bruxelles: Bruylant, 2010), p. 781.

[45] See A. Herold, 'EU External Policy in the Audio Visual Field: From "Cultural Exception" to "Cultural Diversity"', *ERA Forum* 6(1) (2006), 93–108.

[46] Coombe, 'Legal Claims to Culture in and Against the Market', 41.

[47] See generally Y. Donders, 'The History of the UNESCO Convention on the Protection and Promotion of the Diversity of Cultural Expressions', in H. Schneider and P. van den Bossche (eds.), *Protection of Cultural Diversity from an International and European Perspective* (Antwerpen: Intersentia, 2008), pp. 1–30.

[48] M. Burri, 'Cultural Diversity as a Concept of Global Law: Origins, Evolution and Prospects', *Diversity* 2 (2010), 1064.

[49] J. Kelsey, *Serving Whose Interests? The Political Economy of Trade in Services Agreements* (Abingdon: Routledge, 2008), p. 248.

UNESCO.[50] The United States voted against its adoption in the UNESCO General Conference in 2005.

However, despite the opposition of the United States, the CCD was generally perceived as a desirable political and legal outcome. While some countries, most notably the EU and Canada, aimed at creating a counterweight to free trade discourse, the CCD has gone beyond this limited goal giving cultural diversity a place on the international political agenda, and conceiving culture as a key component of sustainable development.[51] International cultural law mirrors international economic law with regard to the study of the same phenomenon – that is globalization and culture. In this respect, while international economic law encapsulates economic discourses about culture, the CCD includes cultural discourses about economic globalization and its impact on cultural diversity. Accordingly, 'cultural goods' are deemed to have a double nature embodying both commercial and cultural values.[52]

Not only does this Convention introduce a compelling case or argumentative framework for the consideration of cultural diversity in policy making and adjudication but it also creates a normative framework for *good cultural governance*.[53] Cultural governance expresses the need to regulate human activities and their effects on cultural diversity (including, for example, cultural practices and cultural goods and services) by means of processes mandated by law so as to protect the cultural interests of present and future generations.[54] Cultural governance entails a number of 'legislative, executive and administrative functions, instruments and ancillary processes that could be used by governments . . . to organize and regulate culturally relevant activities'.[55] *Good cultural governance* refers to the exercise of state authority according to due process and the rule of law, which includes the respect for human rights and fundamental freedoms.[56]

In this sense, the CCD is not to be implemented at the entire discretion of the parties. The proclaimed cultural aim of a particular measure does not automatically justify it. On the contrary, the Convention requires

[50] *Ibid.*, p. 251.

[51] J. Musitelli, 'L'invention de la diversité culturelle', *Annuaire Français de droit international* 51 (2005), 515.

[52] CCD, Article 4(4).

[53] On 'cultural governance', see A. A. Du Plessis and C. Rautenbach, 'Legal Perspectives on the Role of Culture in Sustainable Development', 13 *Potchefstroom Electronic L. J.* 13 (2010), 48–62.

[54] *Ibid.*, 46. [55] *Ibid.*, 46. [56] *Ibid.*, 62.

respect for human rights and fundamental freedoms, such as freedom of expression, information and communication. The preamble of the CCD recalls that cultural diversity flourishes within a framework of democracy, and reaffirms that 'freedom of thought, expression and information, as well as diversity of the media, enable cultural expressions to flourish within societies'.[57] Article 2.1 of the CCD expressly affirms that 'cultural diversity can be protected and promoted only if human rights and fundamental freedoms, such as freedom of expression, information and communication ... are guaranteed', and adds that the provisions of the Convention cannot be invoked to breach 'human rights and fundamental freedoms as enshrined in the Universal Declaration of Human Rights, or guaranteed by international law, or to limit the scope thereof'.[58] The Convention also emphasizes the importance of protecting the cultures of minorities and indigenous peoples.[59]

More importantly, cultural diversity should not be used as a pretext for establishing a monoculture, as such an interpretation would defeat some of the very objectives of the Convention. The objectives set forth by Article 1 of the Convention include: (1) the creation 'of the conditions for cultures to flourish and to freely interact in a mutually beneficial manner';[60] (2) the encouragement of 'dialogue among cultures' to 'ensur[e] wider and balanced cultural exchanges in the world in favour of intercultural respect and a culture of peace';[61] and (3) the promotion of cultural interaction to 'build bridges among people'.[62] Openness to other cultures is expressly included among the guiding principles of the Convention[63] and 'access to a rich and diversified range of cultural expressions from all over the world' is deemed to constitute an important element for enhancing cultural diversity.[64]

Anthropologists have highlighted the 'complex tectonics of cultures and civilizations' on the one hand, and the 'porosity of cultural boundaries' on the other,[65] emphasizing that in order not to perish, cultures need to maintain a level of equilibrium between permeability and impermeability.[66] In sum, cultural diversity should be interpreted so as to maintain a balance

[57] CCD Preamble, ¶¶ 4, 11, and 12. [58] CCD Article 2(1).
[59] CCD Preamble, ¶¶ 8–15, and Article 2(3). [60] CCD Article 1(b).
[61] CCD Article 1(c). [62] CCD Article 1(d). [63] CCD Article 2, principle 8.
[64] CCD Article 2, principle 7.
[65] UNESCO World Report, *Investing in Cultural Diversity and Intercultural Dialogue* (Paris: UNESCO, 2009), p. 39.
[66] S. Labadi, 'Introduction: Investing in Cultural Diversity', *International Social Science Journal* 61 (2010), 8 (internal citation omitted).

between the protection of local cultures and openness to other cultures. The regulation of cultural diversity has been compared to 'tightrope walking, requiring continual adjustment to preserve the elusive point of balance',[67] providing space for osmosis and conceptual fluidity between cultural inputs and outputs, and recognizing the individual freedom to choose from a broad spectrum of cultural goods.

While international economic law presents clear-cut rules, the CCD has been criticized for the vagueness and soft wording of its provisions, which could lead adjudicators to perceive them as having a programmatic character.[68] The Convention is not meant to unify, let alone impose, specific regulations to be translated into national law;[69] rather it establishes common principles and objectives, 'leaving the question of how to reach them to the states parties' discretion and best efforts'.[70] The *Operational Guidelines* approved by the Conference of the Parties in 2009 do not add much specificity to the Convention.[71]

The fact that the Convention presents dispositive norms does not imply that these norms are not binding. On the one hand, the principles of good faith and the *pacta sunt servanda* rule are universally recognized.[72] On the other hand, the selection of the appropriate cultural policies in fact depends on the specific needs of the state, to be assessed on a case-by-case basis. In order to comply with the CCD the contracting parties can adopt policies which diverge from the policies adopted by other states. For instance, while state Alpha can impose minimum quotas for the transmission of domestic music in order to protect national culture, state Beta can reduce these quotas in order to enhance access to cultural products.[73] Therefore, states have the faculty to adopt

[67] A. Pratt, 'Cultural Industries and Public Policy – An Oxymoron?', *International Journal of Cultural Policy* 11 (2005), 35.

[68] Kelsey, *Serving Whose Interests?*, p. 252.

[69] J. Chan-Tibergien, 'Cultural Diversity as Resistance to Neoliberal Globalization: The Emergence of a Global Movement and Convention', *Review of Education* 52 (2006), 94.

[70] T. Kono and S. Wrbka, 'General Report', in T. Kono (ed.), *The Impact of Uniform Laws on the Protection of Cultural Heritage and the Preservation of Cultural Heritage in the 21st Century* (Leiden/Boston: Martinus Nijhoff, 2010), p. 104.

[71] UNESCO CCD Conference of the Parties, *Article 7, 8 and 17 of the Convention on the Protection and Promotion of the Diversity of Cultural Expressions, Measures to Promote and Protect Cultural Expressions, Operational Guidelines* (2009), Article 7, principles 1.3 and 1.1.

[72] See Vienna Convention on the Law of Treaties (VCLT), 23 May 1969, in force 27 January 1980, 1155 UNTS 331, preamble.

[73] See A. Dahrendorf, 'Trade Meets Culture: The Legal Relationship between WTO Rules and the UNESCO Convention on the Protection and Promotion of the Diversity of Cultural Expressions', Maastricht Faculty of Law Working Papers, 2006/11.

the cultural policies they deem appropriate to protect and promote cultural diversity in response to their specific needs, provided that these measures are taken in a manner consistent with the provision of the CCD – i.e. in respect of the objectives of the CCD and existing treaties, as well as of human rights and fundamental freedoms.

The Convention does not modify rights and obligations under other treaties,[74] but requires parties to perform their obligations under the CCD – and all other treaties to which they are parties – in good faith. Article 20 of the CCD puts forward the principle of mutual supportiveness, complementarity and non-subordination with other conventions,[75] stating that the parties shall foster mutual supportiveness between the CCD and the other treaties to which they are parties, and requiring them to take into account the obligations and relevant provisions of the CCD when interpreting and applying the other treaties. Although it is unclear how this principle can be applied to concrete situations and this clause has been criticized as a chimera or a Pyrrhic victory,[76] it should not be dismissed by adjudicators as a mere agreement to disagree. The provision is included in a binding treaty which requires 'taking into account' the provisions of the CCD when interpreting other treaties.

The fact that the CCD does not set out a hierarchical relation between international cultural law and international economic law merely reflects the paradigm shift of contemporary international relations from a pyramidal model of international organization to a network system[77] or spaghetti bowl.[78] As it is difficult to articulate the interaction of different legal paradigms at the normative level, this articulation was left to the adjudicative branch.[79]

Like most UNESCO instruments, the CCD does not provide for a compulsory dispute settlement mechanism but requires mandatory negotiations.[80] If the parties cannot reach an agreement by negotiation,

[74] CCD Article 20(2). [75] CCD Article 20.

[76] See S. Regourd, 'Le projet de Convention UNESCO sur la diversité culturelle: vers une victoire à la Pyrrhus', *Légipresse* 226 (2005), 116.

[77] M. Van Den Kerchov and F. Ost, *De la Pyramide au réseau? Pour une théorie dialectique du droit* (Bruxelles: Publications des facultés universitaires Saint-Louis, 2002), p. 597.

[78] J. Bhagwati, 'U.S. Trade Policy: The Infatuation with Free Trade Agreements', in J. Bhagwati and A. O. Krueger (eds.), *The Dangerous Drift to Preferential Trade Agreements* (Washington D.C.: AEI Press, 1995).

[79] J. Gerkrath, 'Libre-échange et diversité culturelle: de l'antagonisme à la conciliation?', *Légicom* 36 (2006), 31.

[80] CCD Article 25(1).

they 'may jointly seek the good offices of, or request mediation by a third party'.[81] If these procedures fail, the parties may have recourse to conciliation.[82] The parties are then under an obligation to consider in good faith the proposal for the resolution of the dispute made by the Conciliation Commission established on an *ad hoc* basis.[83] The Conciliation Commission is composed of five members, two appointed by each party and a president chosen jointly by those members.[84] Taking a decision by majority vote, the Commission renders a proposal for the resolution of the dispute.[85] The only obligation of the parties is to 'consider in good faith the proposal made by the conciliation commission'.[86] The conciliation procedure is compulsory for all parties, except those who have expressed a reservation at the time of ratification.[87] Every four years the parties submit a report to UNESCO, including the measures they have adopted to protect and promote the diversity of cultural expressions within their territory and at the international level.[88] Given the structural imbalance between the vague and non-binding dispute settlement mechanisms provided by the CCD and the highly effective and sophisticated dispute settlement mechanism available under international investment law, cultural diversity-related disputes involving investors' rights have been brought before arbitral tribunals. These disputes will be examined in Section 5.4.

## 5.3 *Intangible cultural heritage*

Intangible cultural heritage (ICH) indicates the cultural processes, skills and beliefs leading to the creation of cultural heritage and the immaterial heritage such as music, dances, rituals, and other forms of expressions resulting therefrom.[89] The three essential components of ICH are: (1) a community (subject); (2) a manifestation of such heritage (object); and (3) a cultural space (space).[90]

While processes of globalization create the conditions for renewed dialogue among communities, they can jeopardize the transmission and

[81] CCD Article 25(2). [82] CCD Article 25(3). [83] CCD Article 25(3).
[84] Annex on Conciliation Procedure of the Convention, Article 1. [85] *Ibid.*, Article 5.
[86] *Ibid.*, Article 5. [87] CCD Article 25(4). [88] CCD Article 9.
[89] L. Lixinski, 'Selecting Heritage: The Interplay of Art, Politics and Identity', *EJIL* 22 (2011), 83.
[90] T. Scovazzi, 'The Definition of Intangible Cultural Heritage', in S. Borelli and F. Lenzerini (eds.), *Cultural Heritage, Cultural Rights, Cultural Diversity* (Leiden/Boston: Martinus Nijhoff, 2012), p. 180.

diffusion of intangible cultural heritage.[91] For instance, linguists believe that half the languages in the world will be extinct by the end of the century.[92] Languages – such as English or Swahili – are a 'vehicle of intangible cultural heritage';[93] not only does the use of a particular language help functional communication, but it also expresses 'the worldviews, values and belief systems inherent in a given culture'.[94] The extinction of a language results in the loss of unique cultural knowledge embodied in it for centuries. Analogously, given the increasingly dominant and global Western mass culture, certain types of local music are disappearing.[95] As intangible cultural heritage is an important factor in maintaining cultural diversity in the face of growing globalization, its safeguarding is perceived as 'a common concern'.[96]

Among the various regimes regulating ICH, the UNESCO Convention for the Safeguarding of the Intangible Cultural Heritage (CSICH)[97] constitutes the central legal framework for protecting such heritage. The CSICH is expressly meant to safeguard intangible cultural heritage, and to raise awareness of its importance at local, national, and international levels, providing for international cooperation and assistance.[98] In this context, 'safeguarding' means not only measures aimed at the identification and protection of intangible cultural heritage, but also measures aimed at ensuring its viability – including its promotion, enhancement and transmission, particularly through education – as well as the revitalization of its various aspects.[99]

The CSICH constitutes a major achievement, a useful counterbalance to international economic instruments governing aspects of intangible cultural heritage.[100] Furthermore, within international cultural law, the CSICH constitutes a 'counterpoint to the WHC', acknowledging cultural

91 CSICH, preamble.
92 'The Languages of Extinction: The World's Endangered Tongues', *The Independent*, 19 September 2007.
93 CSICH Article 2.
94 UNESCO, *Investing in Cultural Diversity and Intercultural Dialogue* (Paris: UNESCO, 2009), p. 73.
95 G. McKay, *Yankee Go Home (and Take Me with You): Americanization and Popular Culture* (Sheffield: Sheffield Academic Press, 1997).
96 CSICH, preamble.
97 UNESCO Convention for the Safeguarding of the Intangible Cultural Heritage (CSICH), Paris, 17 October 2003, in force 20 April 2006, 2368 UNTS 1.
98 CSICH, Article 1. 99 CSICH, Article 2(3).
100 See e.g. Agreement on Trade-Related Aspects of Intellectual Property Rights, 15 April 1994, Marrakesh Agreement establishing the World Trade Organization, Annex 1C, 33 ILM 1997 (1994) (TRIPS Agreement).

manifestations of indigenous peoples and Asian, African and South American countries.[101]

The protection of intangible cultural heritage has significant human rights implications, complementing and reinforcing cultural rights, freedom of religion, self-determination and the rights of indigenous peoples among others. The preamble of the CSICH expressly refers to the UDHR and the two human rights covenants. Furthermore, only ICH that is in accordance with internationally recognized human rights receives protection under the CSICH.[102]

The CSICH adopts two listing mechanisms: (1) the List of Representative Intangible Heritage of Mankind, which requires states to determine which heritage should be inventoried and protected;[103] and (2) the List of Intangible Cultural Heritage in Need of Urgent Safeguarding, composed of intangible heritage elements that require urgent measures to be kept alive.[104] Importantly, the states parties are committed to 'ensure the widest possible participation of communities, groups and, where appropriate, individuals that create, maintain and transmit [ICH], and to involve them actively in its management'.[105]

However, the CSICH also presents a few drawbacks. *First*, although the importance of intangible cultural heritage to communities and individuals is included in the preamble of the CSICH, the text of the treaty betrays the continuing predominance of states in the governance of intangible cultural heritage. States – not individuals or communities – select the intangible heritage to be listed and protected. Therefore, the intangible heritage of minorities and of indigenous peoples may not be adequately represented in the lists. In parallel, the Convention's focus on state sovereignty has broader implications on the potential politicization of the safeguarding of given intangible heritage. For instance, some argue that by inscribing Tibetan folklore in the list, 'the Chinese government actually asserts control over the [given] cultural manifestations'.[106] The fact that listing is proposed by states can suggest, as Coombe and Turcotte argue, that the CSICH constitutes 'a new regime of power' imposed on the local communities and indigenous peoples; local communities and indigenous peoples may neither desire nor

[101] R. J. Coombe and J. F. Turcotte, 'Indigenous Cultural Heritage in Development and Trade: Perspectives from the Dynamics of Cultural Heritage Law and Policy', in C. Beat Graber, K. Kuprecht and J. C. Lai (eds.), *International Trade in Indigenous Cultural Heritage* (Cheltenham: Edward Elgar, 2012), p. 30.

[102] CSICH, Article 2(1). [103] CSICH, Article 16. [104] CSICH, Article 17.

[105] CSICH, Article 15. [106] Lixinski, 'Selecting Heritage', 96.

approve the fact that their culture be 'targeted in new regimes . . . that do not necessarily accord with their own values and aspirations'.[107]

*Second*, the listing mechanism may create the misleading perception of a hierarchy of cultures while this should not be the case. In fact, with regard to intangible cultural heritage, the notion of representative cultural heritage overcomes that of exceptional cultural heritage.[108]

*Third*, the CSICH does not deal with the relationship between intangible cultural heritage and intellectual property, which is governed by other international law instruments.[109] This is a major gap, as misappropriation of indigenous heritage has taken place increasingly, and international knowledge governance in its current shape – mainly in the form of intellectual property rights – has not been designed to address the specific needs of indigenous peoples.[110] In fact, there is a number of aporias between the protection of intangible cultural heritage and international knowledge governance. Intellectual property rights emphasize an individualistic notion of property, while indigenous intangible heritage is based on communal notion of custodianship.[111] The condition of originality does not suit large parts of intangible cultural heritage, which is an incremental form of knowledge transmitted from generation to generation.[112] The protection of several types of intellectual property rights tends to be limited in time, and this does not match the potentially perpetual cultural relevance of the given heritage.[113]

*Fourth*, the fixation requirement which requires that cultural expression be fixed in a material support is not necessarily consistent with indigenous heritage, which is essentially oral.[114] Although certain types of intellectual property – for instance, geographical indications – 'lend themselves to the goals of safeguarding ICH better than others . . . because they can be

[107] Coombe and Turcotte, 'Indigenous Cultural Heritage in Development and Trade', p. 32.

[108] T. Scovazzi, 'La Convention pour la Sauvegarde du Patrimoine Culturel Immateriel', in J. R. Engel, L. Westra and K. Bosselmann (eds.), *Democracy, Ecological Integrity and International Law* (Newcastle upon Tyne: Cambridge Scholars Press, 2010), p. 415.

[109] CSICH, Article 3(b).

[110] See e.g. P. K. Yu, 'Cultural Relics, Intellectual Property, and Intangible Heritage', *Temple Law Rev.* 81 (2008), 433.

[111] D. E. Long, 'The Impact of Foreign Investment on Indigenous Culture: An Intellectual Property Perspective', *North Carolina JIL and Commercial Regulation* 23 (1998), 246.

[112] Scovazzi, 'La Convention pour la Sauvegarde du Patrimoine Culturel Immateriel', p. 418.

[113] *Ibid.* [114] *Ibid.*

collectively held and managed,[115] intellectual property presupposes the commodification of culture, which local communities and indigenous peoples may oppose.

Finally, the Convention sets out a policy-oriented system of protection of intangible cultural heritage rather than a legal one.[116] In fact, most provisions of the CSICH 'simply affirm that states parties shall endeavour to take appropriate measures for [the] safeguarding [of intangible cultural heritage]',[117] and 'appear to establish soft and weak obligations'.[118]

### *5.4 The tension between cultural diversity, intangible heritage and economic globalization*

As the number of investment disputes with elements of cultural diversity and ICH continues to grow, it is important to reflect on the method employed for identifying and characterizing such disputes. No two parties will at the outset agree that a dispute is essentially 'cultural'. Therefore, it seems more appropriate to talk about 'disputes which have a cultural component' rather than to characterize a dispute as 'cultural'. Indeed, the mere definition of a dispute as a 'cultural dispute' may have implications for a case. This neutral approach is based on the consideration that claims involving cultural diversity or intangible heritage are rarely, if ever, raised in isolation from other international legal arguments.

While most of the following disputes relate to cultural diversity, disputes involving aspects of intangible cultural heritage have begun to emerge; and other disputes may arise in a number of additional areas. Consider the following three different hypothetical scenarios. The first concerns food cultural practices. Undeniably, food 'constitutes a basic element of the culture of a people or of a community',[119] and even

115 Coombe and Turcotte, 'Indigenous Cultural Heritage in Development and Trade', p. 28.

116 Lixinski, 'Selecting Heritage', 94.

117 F. Lenzerini, 'Intangible Cultural Heritage: The Living Culture of Peoples', *EJIL* 22 (2011), 111.

118 S. Urbinati, 'The Role of Communities, Groups and Individuals under the Convention for the Safeguarding of the Intangible Cultural Heritage', in S. Borelli and F. Lenzerini (eds.), *Cultural Heritage, Cultural Rights, Cultural Diversity* (Leiden/Boston: Martinus Nijhoff, 2012), p. 208.

119 M.C. Maffei, 'Food as a Cultural Choice: A Human Rights to Be Protected?', in S. Borelli and F. Lenzerini (eds.), *Cultural Heritage, Cultural Rights, Cultural Diversity* (Leiden/Boston: Martinus Nijhoff, 2012), p. 83.

human rights instruments refer to 'the need to take into account, as far as possible, cultural values attached to, *inter alia*, food and food consumption'.[120] In 2010 three types of diets were inserted in the Representative List, namely: the *Gastronomic Meal of the French* (France), the *Traditional Mexican Cuisine* (Mexico) and the *Mediterranean Diet* (Spain, Greece, Italy and Morocco).[121] All of these diets encompass more than just food bringing people together, strengthening social ties and expressing community identity.

A number of Italian towns prohibit fast foods in their historical centres for cultural reasons, in order to protect their respective diets, ways of life, and architectural heritage.[122] The Italian Constitutional Court rejected the claims of affected companies which contended that such measures violated economic freedom.[123] The Court held that the protection of cultural heritage is a constitutional value protected under the Italian Constitution[124] and that the given measures did not infringe economic freedom but merely regulated and allowed the relevant economic activities in other areas of the same towns.[125] Analogous zoning measures have been adopted by a number of towns in the US for a range of different reasons. For instance, since 1996, the City of Calistoga, in California, has banned fast foods in order 'to preserve the unique and historic character of Calistoga's downtown commercial district'.[126] Analogously, the City of Concord, Massachusetts, bans both 'fast food restaurants' and 'drive-in' services 'to preserve and enhance the development of the natural, scenic and aesthetic qualities of the community'.[127] Other towns in the US have banned fast food

[120] General Comment No. 21, Right of Everyone to Take Part in Cultural Life (Article 15(1)(a) of the International Covenant on Economic, Social and Cultural Rights), UN doc. E/C.12/GC/21, 21 December 2009, ¶ 16(e).

[121] Scovazzi, 'The Definition of Intangible Heritage', 185.

[122] M. N. De Luca, 'La Consulta Boccia i Fast Food: "Fuori dai Centri Storici"', *La Repubblica*, 31 July 1992.

[123] Corte Costituzionale, sentenza 388, 21 July 1992, available at www.giurcost.org/decisioni/1992/0388s-92.html.

[124] *Ibid.*, ¶ 4 (referring to Article 9 of the Costituzione della Repubblica Italiana, 22 December 1947, in force 1 January 1948, *Gazzetta Ufficiale della Repubblica Italiana* 298 (1947)).

[125] *Ibid.*, ¶ 6.

[126] Section 17.22.020(D)(2) of the Calistoga Municipal Code, Calistoga, California.

[127] Section 4.7.1 of the Town of Concord Zoning Bylaw, Town of Concord, Massachusetts.

restaurants for public health reasons, to prevent the diffusion of obesity.[128]

These measures raise a number of questions. Should not everyone have the right to freely select the food of their choice? Can states limit individual freedom in order to protect public health or cultural heritage? Would restrictions on foreign foods be based on genuine cultural and/or public health reasons? Aren't these measures reducing cultural diversity?[129] Would they be consistent with foreign investors' economic interests? From a cultural perspective, culinary practices are dynamic and evolve through time; if Italians had blocked the importation of tomatoes from the Americas in the sixteenth century, pizza would not be in the Mediterranean diet.[130] At the same time, there may be legitimate concerns about the conservation of traditional food practices for public health reasons or in order to protect the aesthetic qualities of city centres. From an investment law perspective, one may wonder whether 'economic and commercial interests . . . prevail over the cultural ones'.[131] At the same time the comparative survey of analogous bans in other countries show that these measures may be rationally related and reasonably proportionate to their legitimate objectives.

Conversely, foreign investors could file claims against the host state for eventually failing to protect their economic interests by not protecting its intangible cultural heritage. For instance, the European Commission recently considered a US request to drop a ban on import into Europe of American wines bearing the label *château*, a term used mainly on wines from Burgundy in eastern France. However, French wine producers contended that American competitors should not be allowed to sell *château*-type wine in the EU, as their production standards differ from the French ones. In France, wine labelled *château* is entirely made from grapes grown on a *terroir* – a specific area of land – giving it a unique character and flavour.[132] According to French winemakers, the *château* label is a guarantee of quality and an expression of

128 M. Ashe, D. Jernigan, R. Kline, and R. Galaz, 'Land Use Planning and the Control of Alcohol, Tobacco, Firearms, and Fast Food Restaurants', *American Journal of Public Health* 93 (2003), 1404–8.

129 M. C. Maffei, 'Culinary Traditions as Cultural Intangible Heritage and Expressions of Cultural Diversity', in S. Borelli and F. Lenzerini (eds.), *Cultural Heritage, Cultural Rights, Cultural Diversity* (Leiden/Boston: Martinus Nijhoff, 2012), pp. 245–6.

130 *Ibid.*, p. 248. 131 *Ibid.*, p. 237.

132 D. Lauter, 'French Winemakers concerned over "Chateau" Change', *The Telegraph*, 16 September 2012.

intangible heritage.[133] Instead, American wines are made with a mixture of grapes purchased from different growers as the American labelling system 'traditionally highlights grape variety, rather than where the fruit was grown'.[134] Given the fact that foreign investors from Britain, Japan and China have long invested in Burgundy,[135] if France were to decline to support the claims of its winemakers, would foreign investors file an investment treaty claim for failure to protect their investments?[136]

The term *château* constitutes a geographical indication, i.e. an indication which identifies a good as originating in a given territory, 'where a given quality, reputation or other characteristic of the good is essentially attributable to its geographical origin'.[137] Geographical indications are a type of intellectual property protected by a number of international law instruments, including the Agreement on Trade-Related Aspects of Intellectual Property Rights (TRIPS Agreement)[138] and international investment treaties.[139] Intellectual property scholars have highlighted the 'potential for [geographical indications] to act as a bulwark against the neoliberal excesses of globalisation, as well as the continuing significance of place-based communities'.[140]

The second hypothetical scenario relates to indigenous intangible heritage. Traditional medicine is the sum of the knowledge, skills, and practices based on the theories, beliefs, and experiences indigenous to different cultures used in the maintenance of health.[141] Indigenous peoples generally view traditional medicine as emanating from a spiritual base and may oppose the commodification of their intangible

133 E. Cody, '"Chateau" isn't made in America, French Vintners Say', *Washington Post*, 24 September 2012.

134 *Ibid.* 135 *Ibid.*

136 For this hypothetical scenario, see S. Lester, 'Trade and Investment in French Chateau Wine', *International Economic Law and Policy Blog*, 26 September 2012.

137 Agreement on Trade-Related Aspects of Intellectual Property Rights, 15 April 1994, Marrakesh Agreement Establishing the World Trade Organization, Annex 1C, 1869 UNTS 299, 33 ILM 1197 (1994) (hereinafter TRIPS Agreement). TRIPS Agreement, Article 22.

138 See generally D. Gangjee, *Relocating the Law of Geographical Indications* (Cambridge University Press, 2012).

139 See e.g. US 2012 Model BIT, Article 1, para. 16(f).

140 D. Gangjee, 'Geographical Indications and Cultural Heritage', *WIPO Journal* 4 (2012), 92.

141 V. Vadi, 'Intangible Heritage, Traditional Medicine and Knowledge Governance', *Journal of Intellectual Property Law and Practice* 2 (2007), 682.

heritage.[142] In fact, this form of intangible cultural heritage is vulnerable in a globalizing world where major pharmaceutical companies aim at 'transform[ing] indigenous culture into a deculturized and marketable commodity'.[143] On the other hand, while traditional medicinal knowledge plays an important role in treating illnesses in developing countries, where it helps meet some of the primary health care needs, it can also have a fundamental role in industrialized countries, serving as the basis for further research and development of new medicines.[144] It is estimated that 'today almost 5000 medicines worldwide are derived from plants grown in indigenous areas'.[145] The commercialization of intangible cultural heritage is not prohibited under the CSICH, although it does require that such processes remain under the control of the communities concerned. Other international law instruments, including the United Nations Declaration on the Rights of Indigenous Peoples,[146] the Convention on Biological Diversity (CBD)[147] and the Nagoya Protocol (NP)[148] require the prior informed consent of the relevant communities and benefit sharing.[149]

Imagine that a multinational company buys land in a developing country, rich in biodiversity and traditional medical knowledge, to develop a pharmaceutical business. If the host state adopted regulation to protect traditional medicines and the relevant biological resources, requiring benefit sharing and the prior informed consent of the relevant indigenous communities, could the company file a claim before an investor-arbitral tribunal claiming that the regulation amounts to indirect expropriation? How can the host state reconcile the economic

[142] D. E. Long, 'The Impact of Foreign Investment on Indigenous Culture: An Intellectual Property Perspective', *N.C. JIL & Com. Reg.* 23 (1997–1998), 232.

[143] *Ibid.*, 244.

[144] Vadi, 'Intangible Heritage, Traditional Medicine and Knowledge Governance'.

[145] G. K. Foster, 'Foreign Investment and Indigenous Peoples: Options for Promoting Equilibrium between Economic Development and Indigenous Rights', *Michigan JIL* 33 (2012), 688.

[146] United Nations Declaration on the Rights of Indigenous Peoples (UNDRIP), GA Res. 61/295, UN Doc A/RES/61/295, 13 September 2007, 46 ILM 1013 (2007).

[147] Convention on Biological Diversity (CBD), Rio de Janeiro, 5 June 1992, in force 29 December 1993, 31 ILM 818 (1992).

[148] Nagoya Protocol on Access to Genetic Resources and the Fair and Equitable Sharing of Benefits from their Utilization to the Convention on Biological Diversity (NP), Nagoya, 29 October 2010, not in force yet, available at www.cbd.int/abs/doc/protocol/nagoya-protocol-en.pdf.

[149] UNDRIP, Articles 19 and 32; CBD, preamble, Articles 1, 8(j), 15(7); NP, preamble, Articles 4–6, 8, 10, 12–17, 20–22, 24.

interests of the foreign company, with the need to protect the rights and intangible heritage of indigenous peoples?

The third (less) hypothetical scenario relates to music and language. That music and language can be instruments of power in addition to being vehicles of cultural heritage, is well known.[150] Since the emergence of the nation state, governments have attempted to direct and influence the uses of languages, 'strengthening and standardizing specific dialects as national languages',[151] and encouraging linguistic homogeneity.[152] Languages of power were promoted at the expense of other languages spoken within the state boundaries in a process of symbolic domination.[153] International and regional instruments today protect the linguistic rights of persons belonging to minorities,[154] and measures to protect languages are implicit in a number of human rights treaties.[155] The Executive Board of UNESCO is considering the feasibility of a new standard-setting instrument on languages, debating 'the issue of whether it should be focused on the safeguarding of linguistic diversity generally, or on the protection of the linguistic rights of certain vulnerable groups'.[156] Certainly, UNESCO promotes linguistic diversity, as an

[150] P. Bourdieu, *Language and Symbolic Power* (Cambridge: Polity Press, 1991); J. Street, 'Music, Market and Manifestos', *International Journal of Cultural Policy* 19(3) (2013), 281–97.

[151] M. Nic Craith, 'Linguistic Heritage and Language Rights in Europe', in M. Langfield, W. Logan and M. Nic Craith (eds.), *Cultural Diversity, Heritage and Human Rights* (Abingdon: Routledge, 2010), p. 47.

[152] *Ibid.* [153] *Ibid.*, p. 48.

[154] See UNGA, Declaration on the Rights of Persons Belonging to National or Ethnic, Religious and Linguistic Minorities, resolution 47/135 of 18 December 1992, 32 ILM 911 (1993); European Charter for Regional or Minority Languages, adopted in 1992, CETS 148.

[155] In *Ballantyne v. Canada*, the applicants contended that the language law of Quebec which prohibited the use of English in advertising violated their right of freedom of expression, violated their minority rights, and discriminated against them. The Committee found a violation of the right of freedom of expression but dismissed the other claims. UN Human Rights Committee, *Ballantyne, Davidson, McIntyre v. Canada*, UN doc. CCPR/C/47/D/359/1989, 385/1989/rev. 1, 5 May 1993 (holding that Canadian English speakers could not be considered a linguistic minority in Quebec for purposes of Article 27 of the International Covenant on Civil and Political Rights because English is the majority language of Canada (*Ibid.*, ¶ 11(2)), deeming that 'A State may choose one or more official languages, but it may not exclude, outside the spheres of public life, the freedom to express oneself in a language of one's choice' (*Ibid.*, ¶ 11(4)).

[156] UNESCO, *Investing in Cultural Diversity and Intercultural Dialogue* (Paris: UNESCO, 2009), p. 79.

expression of cultural diversity and a vehicle of intangible cultural heritage.[157]

Despite these regulatory efforts, the question of language remains contentious in a number of countries. For instance, since most East European countries gained their independence after the fall of the Soviet Union, they have limited newspapers and broadcasts in non-national languages in order to reverse the effects of historical Russianization.[158] These countries now face an additional challenge – the challenge of contemporary patterns of linguistic erosion due to economic globalization. In fact, globalization is 'characterized by the dominance of a few so-called international languages over the rest.'[159] Can foreign broadcasters challenge national policies allegedly aimed to protect national language and music?

In general terms, investment disputes with cultural elements are characterized by the need to balance the legitimate interests of a state to adopt cultural policies, and the economic interests of foreign investors. Turning our attention to the emerging arbitrations, it is becoming clear that there is no such thing as a typical dispute involving cultural diversity or intangible cultural heritage. The analysed disputes operate *across the board*, arising in relation to investment in the media and other sectors.[160] For instance, certain claims may concern the violation of the fair and equitable treatment; other claims relate to alleged discrimination. Although certain specific claims are hereby singled out for analysis, it is worth highlighting that they are often linked together with other issues and the respective arguments may overlap.

## 5.5 *Fair and equitable treatment*

The 'fair and equitable treatment' (FET) clause provides an absolute standard of treatment that is detached from the host country's law and whose exact content is determined by reference to the concrete

157 CCD, Article 6(2)(b) and preamble ('*Recalling* that linguistic diversity is a fundamental element of cultural diversity'), CSICH, Article 2(2)(a) (mentioning 'language as a vehicle of the intangible cultural heritage').

158 UNDP, *Cultural Liberty in Today's Diverse World*, Human Development Report 2004 (New York: UNDP, 2004), p. 65.

159 UNESCO, *Investing in Cultural Diversity*, p. 85.

160 L. E. Peterson, 'International Investment Law and Media Disputes: A Complement to WTO Law', *Columbia FDI Perspectives* 17, 27 January 2010, 1–3.

circumstances of application.[161] This clause is almost ubiquitous in recent investment litigation. Indeed, as Dolzer points out, the purpose of the FET clause is to fill gaps which may be left by more specific standards in order to obtain the level of investor protection intended by the treaties.[162] The standard traditionally includes transparency, non-discrimination, non-arbitrariness and good faith.[163] Some BITs expressly state that such standard includes the obligation not to deny justice in adjudicatory proceedings.[164]

The *Lemire* case[165] involved several claims related to the fair and equitable treatment standard. After having made the investment in Gala Radio, a radio company in Ukraine, a US investor, Mr Lemire, planned to increase the size and audience of his radio company and participated in several tenders for the awarding of broadcasting licences.[166] Although Gala Radio 'presented more than 200 applications for all types of frequencies, [it] was only able to secure a single license (in a small village in rural Ukraine)'.[167] The claimant argued that the Ukrainian legal procedure for the allocation of frequencies was in itself unfair and inequitable, and was applied in an arbitrary and discriminatory fashion.[168] As the Ukrainian *Law on Television and Broadcasting* required the National Council to take into account the objective of freedom of speech, the claimant argued that: 'Since [the competitor] already had a radio network, *pluralism could arguably be better served if the new channel was awarded to a different company*' [emphasis added].[169]

161 See UNCTAD, WIR 1996 *Investment Trade and International Policy Agreements* (New York and Geneva: UN, 1996), p. 182.
162 R. Dolzer, 'Fair and Equitable Treatment: A Key Standard in Investment Treaties', *International Lawyer* 39 (2005), 87–106.
163 See R. H. Kreindler, 'Fair and Equitable Treatment: A Comparative International Law Approach', *TDM* 3 (2006), 7.
164 See e.g. Treaty between the United States of America and the Government of [Country] Concerning the Encouragement and Reciprocal Protection of Investment (2012 US Model BIT Article 5(2)(a)), available at www.state.gov/documents/organization/117601.pdf.
165 *Joseph Charles Lemire v. Ukraine*, Decision on Jurisdiction and Liability, ICSID Case No. ARB/06/18, 14 January 2010 and *Joseph Charles Lemire v. Ukraine*, Award, ICSID Case No. ARB/06/18, 28 March 2011. On 27 July 2011, the ICSID Secretary-General registered an application for the institution of annulment proceedings. At the time of writing, the decision on annulment is not public; reportedly the Annulment Commitee found no errors in the Tribunal's analysis.
166 *Lemire v. Ukraine*, Decision on Jurisdiction and Liability, ¶ 420. 167 *Ibid.*
168 *Ibid.*, ¶ 42. 169 *Ibid.*, ¶ 354.

Although the Arbitral Tribunal did not comment on media pluralism, it acknowledged that 'informational channels . . . are politically more sensitive because they are important elements for the formation of public opinion'[170] and that the presence of Gala Radio 'as an independent broadcaster . . . would reinforce freedom of speech'.[171] The Tribunal found that the legal and administrative procedures for the issuance of radio frequencies presented some shortcomings which could facilitate arbitrary decision-making and 'resulted in an arbitrary advantage to local investors with greater political clout'.[172] These shortcomings involved, *inter alia*, the absence of clearly established criteria for the evaluation of the tenders, the absence of reasoning concerning National Council decisions, and the lack of transparency with regard to who were the ultimate owners of radio companies.[173] Since the National Council did not reason or explain its decisions, it was impossible to verify whether Gala's applications were rejected because its programming concept was worse than that of its competitors.[174] However, if Gala was an 'average radio station' as the respondent admitted, the Arbitral Tribunal inferred it 'should have had an average success rate in its tenders'; while the record showed that 'it had a success rate which was much below average'.[175] While the Tribunal acknowledged that Gala Radio was not a 'large company', it recognized that 'throughout its lifetime, Gala Radio ha[d] been a reasonably successful broadcaster'[176] and 'had won a number of awards for the quality of its broadcasting'.[177]

Therefore, the Tribunal analysed each particular tender. With regard to the first tender under consideration, the Tribunal found that politically motivated interference with independent and impartial decision-making violated the FET standard.[178] Other tenders were similarly held to be arbitrary and discriminatory because foreign and national companies were treated differently in similar cases.[179] In response to the dissenting opinion of one of the arbitrators,[180] the majority of the Arbitral Tribunal clarified that 'not every violation of domestic law necessarily translates into an arbitrary or discriminatory measure

170 *Lemire v. Ukraine*, Award, ¶ 60. 171 *Ibid.*, ¶ 179. 172 *Ibid.*, ¶ 64.
173 *Lemire v. Ukraine*, Decision on Jurisdiction and Liability, ¶¶ 315–16.
174 *Ibid.*, ¶ 420. 175 *Ibid.*, ¶¶ 315–16. 176 *Lemire v. Ukraine*, Award, ¶ 206.
177 *Ibid.*, ¶ 207. 178 *Lemire v. Ukraine*, Decision on Jurisdiction and Liability, ¶ 356.
179 *Ibid.*, ¶ 369 and ¶¶ 384–5.
180 *Joseph Charles Lemire v. Ukraine*, Dissenting Opinion, ICSID Case No. ARB/06/18, 1 March 2011. While Dr Voss signed the first decision, he did not sign the award; his dissenting opinion refers to both decision and award.

under international law and a violation of the FET Standard', holding that 'for this to happen, it is necessary that the state incur in a blatant disregard for applicable tender rules, distorting fair competition among tender participants'.[181] The Tribunal concluded that in the instant case, Ukraine 'acted in blatant disregard of applicable tender rules'.[182]

The case *Pey Casado v. Chile* concerned the closure of the newspaper *Clarìn*, owned by Mr Victor Pey Casado during the past Pinochet regime. In 1973, when President Allende was overthrown in a putsch led by General Pinochet, 'military troops occupied the physical premises of "El Clarín"' and 'the property thereafter remained under complete control by the military'.[183] Soon after these events, Mr Pey left the country and came back in 1989 after the return of democracy.[184] In 1997 Mr Pey filed an investor–state arbitration under the Spain–Chile BIT.[185] In 1998 Chile enacted a law to compensate those persons who had been expropriated during the military regime.[186] However, due to a number of other shortcomings in the procedure, the Tribunal concluded that Chile had committed a denial of justice and had breached the fair and equitable treatment standard under the Spain–Chile BIT.[187] A recent annulment proceeding has annulled the part of the award dealing with damages.[188] Although a detailed analysis of this case would go beyond the scope of this book, this arbitration is significant because it shows the linkage between foreign investment and media pluralism.

## 5.6 *Discrimination*

A crucial element in disputes with cultural elements is the ascertainment of non-discrimination. The non-discrimination principle is typically reflected in the provisions of national treatment (NT) and most-favoured nation (MFN) treatment.[189] These two standards do not

[181] *Lemire v. Ukraine*, Award, ¶ 43. [182] *Ibid.*

[183] *Víctor Pey Casado and President Allende Foundation v. Republic of Chile*, ICSID Case No. ARB/98/2, Decision on the Application for Annulment of the Republic of Chile, 18 December 2012, ¶ 23.

[184] *Ibid.* [185] *Ibid.* [186] *Ibid.*

[187] *Pey Casado v. Chile*, ICSID Case No. ARB/98/2, Award, 8 May 2008, ¶¶ 659, 674.

[188] *Víctor Pey Casado and President Allende Foundation v. Republic of Chile*, ICSID Case No. ARB/98/2, Decision on the Application for Annulment of the Republic of Chile, ¶ 354.

[189] See F. Ortino, 'Non-Discriminatory Treatment in Investment Disputes', in P.-M. Dupuy, F. Francioni and E.-U. Petersmann (eds.), *Human Rights in International Investment Law and Arbitration* (Oxford University Press, 2009), pp. 344–66.

guarantee a specific level of protection but are *relative* standards that require a state to treat a foreign investor in the same way that a domestic investor or an investor from another country would be treated. The basic purpose of the MFN and NT clauses is to avoid discrimination and to guarantee equality of opportunities for foreign investors in the host state. Discrimination can be direct or indirect. Direct discrimination indicates openly discriminatory language in regulations. Indirect discrimination occurs when the use of apparently neutral criteria affect a particular group of people.

Difficulties arise in ascertaining discrimination in the cultural sector: while states 'could have legitimate reasons for imposing cultural policy measures that involve *de jure* or *de facto* discrimination' against foreign investors, 'it may be extremely difficult to differentiate between protectionist and nonprotectionist motives' for adopting allegedly cultural regulation.[190] As Voon highlights, identifying the true motive for a governmental measure may be problematic not only because such measure may be determined by a number of factors, but also because the true reasons may diverge from the official narratives.[191] In order to detect discrimination, Voon suggests the use of criteria such as those of efficiency and/or effectiveness and trade restrictiveness of the given regulatory measure.[192] Craufurd Smith analogously argues that proportionality 'could guide the application of [cultural policy] measures and serve to prevent more blatant forms of protectionism'.[193] The concept of proportionality allows adjudicators reviewing state measures to weigh the extent to which legitimate policy objectives are pursued against the interference with the claimant's interests, in the light of the array of alternative tools available for the pursuit of those state interests. Therefore, such principle can allow arbitral tribunals 'to bar governments from forcing some people alone to bear public burdens which, in all fairness and justice, should be borne by the public as a whole'.[194] Such concept has been elaborated by the *Tecmed* Tribunal, which took the

[190] T. Voon, 'State Support for Audiovisual Products in the World Trade Organization: Protectionism or Cultural Policy?', *International Journal of Cultural Property* 13 (2006), 142–3.

[191] *Ibid.*, 144. [192] *Ibid.*, 144–5.

[193] R. Craufurd Smith, 'The UNESCO Convention on the Protection and Promotion of Cultural Expressions: Building a New World Information and Communication Order?', *International Journal of Communications* 1 (2007), 40–1.

[194] V. Lowe, 'Regulation or Expropriation?', *Current Legal Problems* 55 (2002), 462 (internal citation omitted).

view that in considering 'whether such actions or measures are proportional to the public interest presumably protected thereby and to the protection legally granted to investments, taking into account the significance of such impact plays a key role in deciding the proportionality'.[195] However, in the absence of treaty provisions or textual hooks in this regard, it may be difficult for arbitrators to evaluate a given policy measure in the light of the proposed criteria: investment treaty disputes touch on issues that can go to the heart of a state's public policies, and arbitrators are not cultural policy experts.

Furthermore, cultural policies may present internal tensions. Even in admitting that a cultural policy has a legitimate objective, there is an array of different tools available in order to achieve such an objective. For instance, in order to sustain linguistic diversity, states may give support to expression, creation and dissemination in the greatest possible number of languages.[196] On the other hand, in order to protect a certain language in danger of extinction, states might restrict the dissemination of other languages. Liberals may find the latter type of top-down cultural policies inadequate to foster cultural phenomena, and deeply detrimental to individual freedom. They contend that: 'Dying cultures should be preserved, but in museums and archives, not by forcing them upon people for whom they may be obsolete.'[197] Against this background, international economic law scholars call for a 're-valuation of the policy tools for the attainment of cultural diversity' suggesting that some cultural policy measures 'may in fact be counterproductive to a thriving cultural environment'.[198]

Turning now to the available arbitrations, in the *Lemire* case, Mr Lemire challenged the fact that a tender for a radio channel required it to broadcast in Ukrainian only. Mr Lemire argued that the 100 per cent Ukrainian language content requirement favoured national vis-à-vis foreign investors. It was no surprise that the foreign investor who was participating in the bidding process was not awarded the licence. The Arbitral Tribunal dismissed the arguments in support of *cultural freedom* brought by Mr Lemire that 'we should allow the audience to

[195] *Tecnicas Medioambientales Tecmed SA v. United Mexican States*, ICSID Case No. ARB (AF)/00/2, at ¶ 122.

[196] Universal Declaration on Cultural Diversity, Annex II, ¶¶ 5–6.

[197] See e.g. V. Popovski, 'Cultural Diversity and Freedom of Expression', in P. Meerts (ed.), *Culture and International Law* (The Hague: Hague Academic Press, 2008), p. 62.

[198] M. Burri-Nenova, 'Trade and Culture in International Law: Paths to (Re)conciliation', *JWT* 44 (2010), 79.

determine what it wants' and that 'since Ukraine is seeking the status of a country with a market economy, it should not introduce Ukrainian culture by force'.[199] Instead, the Arbitral Tribunal held that this condition of the bidding process 'was a legitimate decision, based on a public interest choice to extend the use of Ukrainian in the media', arguably contributing to the preservation and diffusion of Ukrainian culture.[200]

In the *UPS* case,[201] United Parcel Service of America (UPS), a US company providing courier and package delivery services both throughout Canada and worldwide,[202] claimed that Canada's Publications Assistance Program (PAP) – a policy designed to promote the wider distribution of Canadian periodicals – was discriminatory to foreign investors.[203] Such policy 'provide[d] financial assistance to the Canadian magazine industry but only on the condition that any magazines benefitting from the financial assistance [we]re distributed through Canada Post [an institution of the Government of Canada], and not through companies such as UPS Canada'.[204] The investor did not challenge the cultural policy measure *per se* (i.e. the financial assistance to the Canadian Magazine industry *inter alia* by providing postal subsidies to publications) because such measure arguably felt within the cultural exception clause set out in Article 2106 and Annex 2106 of the North American Free Trade Agreement (NAFTA).[205] Rather, the investor challenged the design and implementation of the cultural policy.[206] According to UPS, the preferential treatment received by Canada Post 'ha[d] nothing to do with protecting cultural industries and so f[elt] outside the scope of the cultural industries exception'.[207] UPS maintained that the cultural industries exception 'applie[d] only to cultural industries themselves, not to their delivery mechanism, and that there [wa]s no connection between the program's objective and Canada Post's involvement'.[208]

Canada objected that the PAP felt under the cultural industries exception set out in Article 2106 and Annex 2106 of NAFTA, constituting

[199] *Lemire v. Ukraine*, Decision on Jurisdiction and Liability, ¶ 407 (internal citations omitted).
[200] *Ibid.*
[201] *United Parcel Service of America Inc. v. Government of Canada*, Award on the Merits, 24 May 2007, 46 ILM 922 (2007).
[202] *Ibid.*, ¶ 8. [203] *Ibid.*, ¶¶ 156–160. [204] *Ibid.*, ¶ 80.
[205] North American Free Trade Agreement (NAFTA), 17 December 1992, in force 1 January 1994 (1993) 32 ILM 289.
[206] *United Parcel Service of America Inc. v. Government of Canada*, Award on the Merits.
[207] *Ibid.*, ¶ 157. [208] *Ibid.*, ¶ 159.

one component of a broader Canadian cultural policy.[209] According to Canada, such cultural policy had 'two main purposes: (1) to connect Canadians to each other through the provision of accessible Canadian cultural products; and (2) to sustain and develop the Canadian publishing industry'.[210] Against this background, Canada also added that in any case Canada was not breaching the national treatment standard as Canada Post and UPS were not in 'like circumstances'.[211] According to Canada, Canada Post had played an essential role in the cultural life of Canadians, 'through its provision of an accessible, effective system of national communication' to all addresses in Canada (the so-called 'universal service obligation').[212] In so doing, Canada Post has assisted in the formation 'of a literate, educated and aware citizenry, providing inexpensive, reliable and timely delivery of newspapers, books and information'.[213] Accordingly, Canada deemed that 'delivery through Canada Post [wa]s the best and most effective means of meeting its policy objectives',[214] which '[we]re not governed solely by commercial considerations'.[215]

The Tribunal upheld Canada's argument that PAP was exempted from review under NAFTA by virtue of the cultural industries exception which removed from the scope of the NAFTA any measure adopted or maintained '*with respect to* cultural industries'.[216] The Tribunal noted that the language of the cultural exception is intentionally broad and that 'it was clearly understood by the Parties ... that a Party's ability to pursue its domestic cultural policies would be virtually unimpaired by these trade and investment instruments'.[217]

The Tribunal acknowledged that not every measure that refers on its face to some cultural objective would fall within the cultural exception clause; there is indeed a 'point in which the cultural connection is sufficiently tangential that a tribunal could say this is outside the cultural exemption'.[218] However, it deemed that the involvement of Canada Post was 'rationally and intrinsically connected to assisting the Canadian publishing industry'[219] and 'strengthening Canada's cultural identity', as delivery through Canada Post was 'the best and most effective way' to meet such policy objective.[220]

Finally, the Tribunal concluded that the PAP did not breach the national treatment provision of NAFTA Chapter Eleven because it

[209] *Ibid.*, ¶ 137. [210] *Ibid.*, ¶ 146–9. [211] *Ibid.*, ¶ 138. [212] *Ibid.*, ¶ 140.
[213] *Ibid.*, ¶ 57. [214] *Ibid.*, ¶ 155. [215] *Ibid.*, ¶ 161. [216] *Ibid.*, ¶ 167.
[217] *Ibid.*, ¶ 162. [218] *Ibid.*, ¶ 167. [219] *Ibid.*, ¶ 168. [220] *Ibid.*, ¶ 166.

considered that UPS Canada and Canada Post were not 'in like circumstances'.[221] As the Canadian market for publications was characterized by a high percentage of home-delivered subscription sales as opposed to newsstand sales, the PAP aimed to achieve the widest possible distribution of Canadian publications at affordable prices throughout the country. While Canada Post was capable of delivering to individual readers across the country, UPS Canada had a different delivery capacity.[222] It is worth noting that in his separate statement, Dean Ronald Cass dissented with the majority in that he found that the way of implementing the PAP ended up subsidizing Canada Post's mail and package delivery services and should not fall within the cultural industries exception.[223]

The approach adopted by the Arbitral Tribunal sensibly differs from the approach adopted by the World Trade Organization panels and Appellate Body in an analogous dispute, *Canada–Periodicals*,[224] which concerned the restriction of the commercialization and the imposition of high taxes on split-run magazines marketed in Canada, i.e. magazines having substantially the same content as a foreign publication, but containing advertisements aimed at the Canadian market. The Canadian government prohibited the import of split-run periodicals that contained advertisement directed at the Canadian market that did not appear in the home country edition of that periodical, arguing that such publications threatened to supplant Canadian culture. The Parliament also imposed a tax on split-run periodicals equal to 80 per cent of the value of all the advertising revenue earned by the edition. The US challenged the Canadian measure before a WTO panel, arguing that the Canadian ban violated the prohibition on import bans under Article XI of the General Agreement on Tariffs and Trade (GATT)[225] and that the tax violated the national treatment provision under Article III of the GATT. The US also argued that the application of favourable postage rates to certain Canadian periodicals was inconsistent with GATT Article III.

221 *Ibid.*, ¶ 173. 222 *Ibid.*, ¶¶ 175–6.

223 *UPS v. Canada*, Separate Statement of Dean Ronald A. Cass, ¶ 147.

224 WTO Panel Report, *Canada–Certain Measures Concerning Periodicals*, WT/DS31/R, 15 March 1997; WTO Appellate Body Report, *Canada–Certain Measures Concerning Periodicals*, WT/DS31/AB/R, 30 June 1997.

225 General Agreement on Tariffs and Trade 1994 (GATT 1994), 15 April 1994, Marrakesh Agreement Establishing the World Trade Organization, Annex 1A, 33 ILM 1153 (1994).

Canada responded, *first*, that the dispute concerned access to advertising services and should be subject to the General Agreement on Trade in Services (GATS). Under GATS, Canada did not make any commitment to grant national treatment to advertising services. *Second*, Canada argued that even if the GATT did apply, split-run magazines are not like products as their intellectual content make them different. As one author puts it: 'at its heart, this disagreement mirrored an underlying value difference between the United States and Canada; in the view of the United States, there was no essential difference between cultural commodities like magazines or books and other commodities like automotive parts'.[226] In the view of Canada, cultural products had a specificity that distinguished them from ordinary items of trade.

The Panel found that both GATT and GATS were applicable and accepted the US view that split-run periodicals were like Canadian magazines, and thus deemed that the Canadian measures were not consistent with the GATT. The Panel emphasized that 'despite the Canadian claim that the purpose of the legislation is to promote publications of original Canadian content, this definition essentially relies on factors external to the Canadian market – whether the same editorial content is included in a foreign edition and whether the periodical carries different advertisements in foreign editions'.[227] In an *obiter dictum* the Panel concluded that 'the ability of a Member to take measures to protect its cultural identity was not an issue in the present case'.[228] The Appellate Body (AB) voided the Panel's finding that split-run periodicals and domestic periodicals were like products; rather it deemed them to be directly competitive or substitutable products. In conclusion, however, the AB concurred with the Panel that the tax afforded protection to domestic products in violation of GATT Article III. Finally, the application of favourable postage rates to certain Canadian periodicals was found to be inconsistent with GATT Article III.

That there are analogies between the *UPS* arbitration and the *Canada–Periodicals* case is also shown by the fact that the investor made reference to the Panel report, mentioning, *inter alia*, its finding that the application of higher rates to foreign products 'clearly affected the sale, transportation and distribution of imported periodicals' violating the national treatment provision under GATT Article III:4.[229]

[226] J. R. Paul, 'Cultural Resistance to Global Governance', *Michigan JIL* 22 (2000–2001), 48.

[227] WTO Panel Report, *Canada–Certain Measures Concerning Periodicals*, ¶ 5.24.

[228] *Ibid.*, ¶ 5.45. [229] *UPS v. Canada*, Award on the Merits, ¶ 52.

Although the Arbitral Tribunal deemed that the analysis of the WTO Panel report in the *Canada–Periodicals* case was not in point, it is important to highlight that there are two major divergences between the approaches adopted by the different international economic fora. First, the NAFTA expressly provides for a cultural exemption, while the WTO *acquis*, for historical reasons, only has an exception concerning 'the protection of national treasures of artistic, historic or archaeological value', referring to the need to prevent the illicit traffic of art works and a provision on movies.[230] Second, the very text of the non-discrimination provisions in investment agreements is less defined than the analogous trade law provisions.[231]

The textual differences give rise to a number of questions: is it possible to 'borrow' or to refer to the WTO case law? Can one import the requirement of least restrictive measures to assess the legitimacy of state measures in the pursuit of legitimate goals? Can we adopt a reasonableness test to evaluate state conduct? UPS referred to such reasonableness arguing that there was no need to have the PAP benefits go to a single firm, and that two or more firms together could achieve nationwide coverage.[232] UPS also called for a 'least restrictive means test – one that would require any government program to be tailored so that it discriminates as little as possible between national investors or investments and other parties' investors or investments'.[233] However, arbitral tribunals have been reluctant to adopt an overly critical examination of governmental policy choices.[234]

This has not been the case at the WTO. More recently, in *China–Publications and Audiovisual Entertainment Products*,[235] the US alleged that various Chinese restrictions on the importation and distribution of US films, sound recordings and publications violated provisions of the GATT, GATS and the Accession Protocol. The challenged measures included prohibiting foreign-owned enterprises from

230 GATT Article XX and Article IV respectively.

231 For instance, with regard to national treatment, compare GATT Article III with NAFTA Article 1102.

232 See *UPS v. Canada*, Separate Statement of Dean Ronald A. Cass, ¶ 99.

233 *Ibid.*, ¶ 113. 234 *Ibid.*, ¶ 125.

235 WTO Panel Report, *China–Measures Affecting Trading Rights and Distribution Services for Certain Publications and Audiovisual Entertainment Products (China–Publications and Audiovisual Products* Panel Report), WT/DS363/R adopted 12 August 2009; WTO Appellate Body Report, *China–Measures Affecting Trading Rights and Distribution Services for Certain Publications and Audiovisual Products* (*China–Publications and Audiovisual Products* AB Report), WT/DS363/AB/R, adopted 21 December 2009.

importing the relevant products, requiring publication import entities to be subject to an approval system pursuant to a state plan, and granting trading rights in a discretionary manner. The Panel held that restrictions on the distribution of publications violated Articles XVI and XVII of GATS and the national treatment requirement under GATT and found a number of Chinese measures inconsistent with the Accession Protocol. The Panel's report was upheld by the Appellate Body, despite China's request to consider the specific dual nature of cultural goods and services.[236]

The Panel noted China's reference to the Declaration on Cultural Diversity and stated that since China had not invoked the Declaration as a defence to its breaches of trading rights commitments, but had referred to the Declaration 'as support for the general proposition that the importation of products of the type at issue in this case could, depending on their content, have a negative impact on public morals in China', 'it had no difficulty in accepting this general proposition'.[237] The Panel admitted the applicability of Article XX(a) and noted that since the content of public morals 'can vary in time and space, depending upon a range of factors, including prevailing social, cultural, ethical and religious values', members 'should be given some scope to define and apply for themselves [this concept] in their respective territories, according to their own systems and scales of values' [internal citations omitted].[238] However, the Panel found that, because there was at least one other reasonably available alternative, China had not demonstrated that the adopted measures were 'necessary'.[239] This holding was confirmed by the AB.

Two competing epistemic perspectives emerge from the available case law: while WTO adjudicators have tended to adopt a rather strict trade-oriented approach, arbitral tribunals have adopted a more flexible approach. If one analyses the rhetorical structure of WTO bodies, it is evident that the cultural claim has never been addressed explicitly. In the *Canada–Periodicals* case, the Panel incidentally dismissed the cultural arguments put forward by Canada holding that 'the ability of a Member to take measures to protect its cultural identity was not an issue in the present case'.[240] More importantly, cultural arguments were not

[236] *China–Measures Affecting Trading Rights and Distribution Services for Certain Publications and Audiovisual Products*, Appellate Body Report, ¶ 25.
[237] *China–Publications and Audiovisual Products*, Panel Report, footnote 538.
[238] *Ibid.*, ¶ 7.759. [239] *Ibid.*, ¶ 7.913.
[240] WTO Panel Report, *Canada–Certain Measures Concerning Periodicals*, ¶ 5.45.

discussed autonomously but were 'encoded in the determination of what is a like, directly competitive or substitutable product', translating a claim about cultural sovereignty 'into a more technocratic argument about the common characteristics of different products'.[241] The *China–Publications and Audiovisual Entertainment Products* case, albeit adjudicated after the inception of the CCD, does not significantly change the argumentative framework of both Panel and AB. The Panel did not make reference to the CCD in its *ratio decidendi*, and noted China's reference to the Declaration on Cultural Diversity only incidentally. The focus of both Panel and AB was the question as to whether given regulatory measures were authentically cultural or a disguised restriction to trade. In sum, 'economic factors drive the WTO analysis', and 'in the cultural arena, the prism will be focused on economic values only'.[242] International economic law scholars have found ways to ratify this approach.[243] When referring to Article 20, reference is made to Article 20(2) of the CCD instead of referring to this provision in a holistic fashion.[244] Instead, as Pauwelyn puts it, Article 20 CCD 'goes both ways'.[245] By contrast, within the investor–state arbitration mechanism, one may identify underlying processes that lead to a different consideration of cultural concerns.

### 5.7 *Performance requirements*

Performance requirements are host state regulatory measures that impose certain obligations on investors to act in ways considered beneficial for the host economy. The most common requirements relate to local content, joint ventures, technology transfer and employment of nationals. Performance requirements aim to ensure that FDI in the host state will contribute to domestic development. From an economic perspective, however, the case for the imposition of performance requirements upon foreign investors remains controversial; and a number of BITs prohibit a broad range of these measures.

[241] Paul, 'Cultural Resistance to Global Governance', 51.
[242] H. Loeb, 'Telecommunications and Culture: Transborder Freedom of Information or Cultural Identity?', *Canada–US Law Journal* 303 (2000), 308–9.
[243] M. Burri-Nenova, 'Trade v Culture in the Digital Environment: An Old Conflict in Need of a New Definition', *JIEL* 12 (2008), 29.
[244] *Ibid.*
[245] J. Pauwelyn, 'The UNESCO Convention on Cultural Diversity, and the WTO: Diversity in International Law-Making?', *ASIL Insights*, 15 November 2005.

In *Lemire v. Ukraine*, the Ukrainian Law on Television and Radio Broadcasting required that at least 50 per cent of the general broadcasting of each radio company should be comprised of music produced in Ukraine including any music where the author, the composer and/or the performer was Ukrainian.[246] The claimant argued that the 50 per cent local music requirement implied a violation of Article II.6 of the US–Ukraine BIT, namely of the prohibition to 'impose performance requirements . . . which specify that goods and services must be purchased locally, or which impose any other similar requirements'.[247] In the claimant's opinion, the abnormally high level of the requirement caused significant damages, because its programme concept was based 100 per cent on hits.[248] As there were too few music hits in Ukrainian music, it had to continuously replay the same few Ukrainian songs.[249] Thus, the claimant alleged a loss of advertising revenue.[250]

In the opinion of the respondent, however, local music requirements were justified on 'public policy grounds'[251] due to 'the State's legitimate right to organize broadcasting'.[252] In the Annex to the BIT both states reserved the right to make or maintain limited exceptions to the national treatment principle with regard to radio broadcasting stations.[253] More importantly, Ukraine claimed that:

> In all jurisdictions, radio and TV are special sectors subject to specific regulations. There are two reasons for this: first, radio frequencies are by technical nature scarce assets, and consequently the law must articulate systems for allocating licenses to prospective bidders; but there is also a second reason: when regulating private activity in the media sector, states can, and frequently do, take into consideration a number of legitimate policy issues: thus media companies can be subject to specific regulation and supervision in order to guarantee transparency, political and linguistic pluralism, protection of children or minorities and other similar factors.[254]

The Arbitral Tribunal upheld Ukraine's line of argument. In a preliminary fashion, it considered that the local music requirement applied to all broadcasters in Ukraine.[255] Then, it affirmed:

> As a sovereign state, Ukraine has the *inherent right to regulate its affairs* and adopt laws in order *to protect the common good of its people*, as

[246] *Lemire v. Ukraine*, Decision on Jurisdiction and Liability, ¶ 227.
[247] US–Ukraine BIT, Article II.6.
[248] *Lemire v. Ukraine*, Decision on Jurisdiction and Liability, ¶ 499. [249] *Ibid.*, ¶ 503.
[250] *Ibid.*, ¶ 499. [251] *Ibid.*, ¶ 218. [252] *Ibid.*, ¶ 227. [253] *Ibid.*, ¶ 242.
[254] *Ibid.*, ¶ 241. [255] *Ibid.*, ¶ 501.

> defined by its Parliament and Government. The prerogative extends to promulgating regulations which define the State's own *cultural policy. The promotion of domestic music may validly reflect a State policy to preserve and strengthen cultural inheritance and national identity.* The 'high measure of deference that international law generally extends to the right of domestic authorities to regulate matters within their own borders'[256] is reinforced in cases when *the purpose of the legislation affects deeply felt cultural or linguistic traits of the community.* (Emphasis added)[257]

The Arbitral Tribunal inquired about international society's prevailing ideas about ways to protect national culture, acknowledging that 'the desire to protect national culture is not unique to Ukraine', and taking into account the fact that 'a number of other countries impose similar requirements'.[258] For instance, France requires that radio stations broadcast a minimum of 40 per cent of French music, and Portugal has a 25–40 per cent Portuguese music quota.[259] Therefore, the Tribunal held that such requirement could not be deemed to be 'unfair' or 'inequitable'.[260]

The Tribunal then asked whether the prohibition of performance requirements was applicable to a cultural restriction like the 50 per cent Ukrainian music requirement. To answer to this question, the Tribunal interpreted Article II.6 of the BIT adopting two different interpretation criteria: textual interpretation and teleological interpretation.[261] Looking at the ordinary meaning of Article II.6 of the BIT, this provision clearly prohibited local law requirements that 'goods or services ... must be purchased locally'.[262] While the Ukrainian law did not specify that radio stations should purchase local goods, *de facto* Ukrainian music was produced and commercialized locally.[263] With regard to the object and purpose of Article II.6 of the BIT, the Arbitral Tribunal held that it was 'trade-related: to avoid that states impose local content requirements as a protection of local industries against competing imports'.[264] Since the objective of the local law was 'not to protect local industries and restrict imports, but rather to promote Ukraine's cultural inheritance' it was deemed to be 'compatible with Article II.6 of the BIT'.[265]

[256] *S.D. Myers v. Canada*, UNCITRAL, First Partial Award, 13 November 2000, ¶ 263.
[257] *Lemire v. Ukraine*, Decision on Jurisdiction and Liability, ¶ 505.
[258] *Ibid.*, ¶ 506 (internal citations omitted). [259] *Ibid.* [260] *Ibid.*, ¶ 507.
[261] *Ibid.*, ¶ 508. [262] *Ibid.*, ¶ 509. [263] *Ibid.*, ¶ 509. [264] *Ibid.*, ¶ 510. [265] *Ibid.*, ¶ 510.

## 5.8 *Compensation*

While it is well settled that a wrong committed by a state against an investor must always give rise to the right to compensation for the economic harm sustained, the quantification of damages is more problematic. In *Lemire v. Ukraine*, the claimant contended that the calculation of damages should place him 'in the position he should have been in, had there not been a breach by the respondent',[266] and also asked for moral damages alleging that 'the constant rejections [of his bids] ... eroded his image'.[267] On the other hand, Ukraine argued that it would be 'inherently speculative' for arbitrators to award compensation to one of several unsuccessful bidders in a public tender process.[268] For his part, the dissenting arbitrator cautioned that awarding compensation to losing tender bidders could determine 'incalculable liability avalanches'[269] and referred to municipal systems which 'provid[e] only for recovery of the costs incurred in relation to the tender (*damnum emergens*), but not for recovery of loss of profits (*lucrum cessans*)'.[270]

In its final award, the *Lemire* Tribunal addressed two issues: (1) the quantification of damages; and (2) the merit of awarding moral damages.[271] With regard to the quantification of damages, the Tribunal referred to the classic *Chorzow factory* case,[272] in which the PCIJ held that reparation 'must, so far as possible wipe out all the consequences of the illegal act and re-establish the situation which would, in all probability, have existed if that act had not been committed'.[273] The Arbitral Tribunal stated that 'the aim of compensation is the elimination of all negative consequences of the wrongful act, through the payment to the injured party of an amount sufficient to cover any financially assessable damage including loss of profits insofar as it is established'.[274] Therefore, the Tribunal established the compensation by comparing the value of Gala Radio at the time of the hearing with

[266] *Joseph Charles Lemire v. Ukraine*, Award, ICSID Case No. ARB/06/18, 28 March 2011, ¶ 123.

[267] *Ibid.*, ¶ 315.

[268] L. E. Peterson, 'Majority Awards Damages for Lost Tenders', *IAR*, 11 April 2011, 4.

[269] *Joseph Charles Lemire v. Ukraine*, Dissenting Opinion, ICSID Case No. ARB/06/18, 1 March 2011, p. vii.

[270] *Ibid.* [271] *Lemire v. Ukraine*, Award, ¶ 117.

[272] *Case Concerning Certain German Interests in Polish Upper Silesia* (*Germany v. Poland*), Merits, 1928, PCIJ, Series A, No. 17, p. 21 *et seq.*

[273] *Lemire v. Ukraine*, Award, ¶ 149. [274] *Ibid.*, ¶ 151 (internal citation omitted).

'what Gala would be worth, if no violation of the BIT had taken place'.[275] The Tribunal admitted that 'valuation is not an exact science'[276] and that the calculation of damages 'inevitably requires a certain amount of conjecture'; however, it held that such difficulty in calculation 'cannot ... deprive an investor, who has suffered injury, from his fundamental right to see his losses redressed'.[277] The Discounted Cash Flow (DCF) methodology was adopted to establish the damage and calculated losses at US$8.7 million.[278]

With regard to moral damages, the Tribunal acknowledged that 'moral damages could only be awarded in exceptional circumstances'.[279] Referring to a number of cases, including the *Lusitania* cases,[280] the *Desert Line Projects v. Yemen*,[281] and *Siag/Vecchi v. Egypt*,[282] the Tribunal concluded that: 'as a general rule moral damages are not available to a party injured by the wrongful acts of a state, but can be awarded in exceptional cases provided that the state actions imply physical threat, illegal detention or other analogous situations ... [and that] the state's actions cause a deterioration of health, stress, anxiety, [or] other mental suffering ... and both cause and effect are grave or substantial'.[283] The Tribunal concluded that in the instant case, 'the gravity required under the standard [wa]s not present'.[284]

## 5.9 *Critical assessment*

Since the interplay between the protection of cultural diversity and intangible heritage on the one hand and the promotion of FDI on the other is not clearly spelled out in the text of treaties, with some remarkable exceptions,[285] there is no sort of pre-established harmony between the two objectives. In this fragmented landscape where arbitral tribunals seem to have the last word on important themes at the crossroads between culture and economics, the role of arbitrators is of fundamental importance.

275 *Ibid.*, ¶ 83. 276 *Ibid.*, ¶ 248. 277 *Ibid.*, ¶ 249. 278 *Ibid.*, ¶ 254.

279 *Ibid.*, ¶ 311.

280 Mixed Claims Commission (United States and Germany), *Lusitania* cases, (1 November 1923–30 October 1930), UN RIAA vol. vii.

281 *Desert Line Projects LLC v. Republic of Yemen*, ICSID Case No. ARB/05/17, Award, 6 February 2008.

282 *Waguih Elie George Siag and Clorinda Vecchi v. Arab Republic of Egypt*, ICSID Case No. ARB/05/15, Award, 1 June 2009.

283 *Lemire v. Ukraine*, Award, ¶ 333. 284 *Ibid.*, ¶ 339. 285 See Chapter 7 below.

The survey of the relevant investor–state arbitrations shows that international investment law has not yet developed any institutional machinery for the protection of cultural diversity and intangible heritage through investment dispute settlement. However, one may identify underlying processes of investment treaty arbitration that lead to a construction of unity and coherence in international law. As the Arbitral Tribunal in *Asian Agricultural Products Ltd. v. Sri Lanka* put it,[286] bilateral investment treaties are 'not a self-contained closed legal system' but have to be 'envisaged within a wider juridical context in which rules from other sources are integrated through implied incorporation methods, or by direct reference to certain supplementary rules whether of international law character or of domestic law nature'.[287]

In *Lemire v. Ukraine*, the Arbitral Tribunal acknowledged that, according to the treaty preamble, the main purpose of the BIT was the promotion of foreign investment instrumental to the pursuit of economic development.[288] Accordingly, the Tribunal recognized that 'the object and purpose of the Treaty is not to protect foreign investments *per se*, but as an aid to the development of the domestic economy', and developmental objectives require that the treatment of foreign investors be balanced against the legitimate right of the host state 'to pass legislation and adopt measures for the protection of what as a sovereign it perceives to be its public interest'.[289]

The Tribunal reaffirmed full respect for Ukraine's cultural sovereignty, stating that 'It certainly is not the task of this Arbitral Tribunal, constituted under the ICSID Convention, to review or second-guess the rules which the representatives of the Ukrainian people have promulgated',[290] and acknowledging that 'in all jurisdictions, Radio and TV are special sectors subject to specific regulation' as states regulate media companies, *inter alia*, 'to guarantee transparency, political and linguistic pluralism . . . and other similar factors'.[291] According to the *Lemire* Tribunal, the inherent right to regulate 'extends to promulgating regulations which define the State's own cultural policy' and 'the "high measure of deference that international law generally extends to the right of domestic authorities to regulate matters within their own borders" is

[286] *Asian Agricultural Products Ltd v. Sri Lanka (AAPL v. Sri Lanka)*, ICSID Case ARB/87/3, Award, 27 June 1990, 4 ICSID Reports 245 (1997).

[287] *Ibid.*, ¶ 21.

[288] *Lemire v. Ukraine*, Decision on Jurisdiction and Liability, ¶¶ 272–3.

[289] *Ibid.*, ¶ 273. [290] *Ibid.*, ¶ 240. [291] *Ibid.*

reinforced in cases when the purpose of the legislation affects deeply felt cultural or linguistic traits of the community.'[292]

While acknowledging state cultural concerns, arbitral tribunals have imposed schemes of *good governance*, requiring respect for investment treaty provisions that prohibit discrimination and requiring fair and equitable treatment. While not every breach of local administrative law and practice amounts to a violation of investment treaty provisions, relevant violations will undergo the scrutiny of arbitral tribunals.[293] Such an assessment is in line with good cultural governance as demanded by the relevant UNESCO instruments: as Germann points out, 'unrestricted state sovereignty may be detrimental to the very cause of cultural diversity'.[294] In this sense, the delimitation of state sovereignty in cultural matters can 'contribute to a better check and balance between the promotion of the cultural identity and the cultural diversity in any given state'.[295]

To ascertain whether Ukraine had violated certain guarantees offered to foreign investors under the relevant BITs in adopting the domestic content requirement rule, the Arbitral Tribunal adopted a *comparative approach* holding that 'a rule cannot be said to be unfair, inadequate, inequitable or discriminatory when it has been adopted by many countries around the world'.[296] This comparative approach may clearly play a positive role in building coherence at the international law level. Comparative surveys may help adjudicators to reach results in harmony with what may have achieved the status of general principles of international law or even customary law. More importantly, the Tribunal was not driven by a cost-benefit analysis or a review of the efficiency of the national measure; rather it was interested in the 'normality' of such measure – i.e. assessing whether it was a regulatory choice divergent from the canons commonly accepted by the international community. The fact that economic standards of valuation are not the only ones that are taken into consideration by arbitral tribunals seems to be distinctive.

[292] *Ibid.*, ¶ 505 (internal citation omitted).

[293] See C. N. Brower and S. W. Schill, 'Is Arbitration a Threat or a Boon to the Legitimacy of International Investment Law?', *Chicago JIL* 9 (2008–2009), 476.

[294] C. Germann, 'Towards a Global Cultural Contract to Counter Trade-Related Cultural Discrimination', in N. Obuljen and J. Smiers (eds.), *UNESCO's Convention on the Protection and the Promotion of the Diversity of Cultural Expressions: Making it Work* (Zagreb: Institute for International Relations, 2006), p. 290.

[295] *Ibid.*, p. 291.

[296] *Lemire v. Ukraine*, Decision on Jurisdiction and Liability, ¶ 506.

## Conclusions

Economic globalization has brought cultures and people into closer contact with one another than ever before. By leading to more choices for people, trade and foreign direct investment may enhance cultural diversity and media pluralism, thus facilitating free speech, the free flow of ideas, and constant exchanges and interaction between cultures. However, the enhanced interaction between cultures can endanger cultural diversity and intangible cultural heritage. Due to economies of scale, the current asymmetry in flows and exchanges of cultural goods at the global level can lead to cultural homogenization. At the same time, foreign direct investments can affect the cultural policies of the host state.

Because the CCD and the CSICH do not include compulsory dispute settlement mechanisms, cultural diversity and intangible heritage-related disputes have gravitated towards investment treaty tribunals. The magnetism of investment treaty tribunals has been a mixed blessing. On the one hand, the review of substantive domestic regulations can improve good cultural governance and the transparent pursuit of legitimate cultural policies. Arbitral tribunals have paid increasing attention to cultural concerns, often referring to international law principles in their reasoning in order to reconcile the different interests at stake. These results open up new lines of enquiry that can enrich international investment law scholarship. On the other hand, it may be questioned whether these tribunals constitute the best available fora for settling this kind of dispute. Investment treaty tribunals are tribunals of limited jurisdiction and have no mandate to adjudicate on the conformity of a given state measure with international cultural law.

International investment treaties are not closed legal system but have to be contextualized within international law. In many circumstances, international law is the law applicable to investment disputes according to an applicable arbitral clause or other relevant treaty provision. Even in those cases where the applicable law is the law of the host state, international law permeates national legal systems. Furthermore, according to the principle of systemic interpretation as restated by Article 31(3)(c) of the Vienna Convention on the Law of Treaties, together with the context, any relevant rule of international law applicable in the relationship between the parties should be taken into account.

If the states, parties to the dispute, have ratified the CCD or the CSICH, these conventions may become relevant. Arbitral tribunals are not courts of general jurisdiction, and cannot adjudicate on the eventual breach of international cultural law, but may analyse the specific investment claims in the light of the relevant rules of international law applicable in the relationship between the parties. The consideration of international cultural law would be *incidenter tantum* and cursory. Given the fact that UNESCO has an almost universal membership and that the CCD and the CSICH are widely ratified, this leads to the conclusion that arbitrators will have to take cultural concerns into account. If one deems that cultural diversity protection already belongs to customary international law or to general principles of law, the case for such consideration is even stronger.

In conclusion, as the interest in the legitimate exercise of authority and the maintenance of juridical values is of utmost importance in the international community, the fact that economic standards of valuation are not the only ones that are taken into consideration by arbitral tribunals is distinctive. Inward-looking approaches, that is, non-consideration of broader cultural concerns, may weaken the perceived legitimacy of adjudicative bodies. While investor–state arbitration deals with an area at the crossroads between economics and law, the legal dimension of these disputes cannot be neglected or dismissed in favour of purely economic considerations.

6

# When cultures collide: Foreign direct investment, natural resources and indigenous heritage in international investment law

What thou lovest well remains . . .
What thou lov'st well is thy true heritage

Ezra Pound, *Pisan Cantos* LXXXI

## Introduction

Indigenous cultural heritage plays an essntial role in the building of the identity of indigenous peoples and its protection thus has profound significance for the realization of their human rights. Although the recognition of indigenous peoples' rights and cultural heritage has gained some momentum in international law since the adoption of the United Nations Declaration on the Rights of Indigenous Peoples (UNDRIP),[1] states have interpreted the right to develop 'on their own terms' in order to prosper 'as they see fit',[2] emphasizing productivity and economic development.[3] Conceptualizing economic progress as 'a process of successive upgrading', economists have highlighted the pressures on societies to adopt a productive economic culture and the 'growing convergence around the productivity paradigm'.[4]

Because policymakers tend to favour growth, regardless of actual or potential infringement of culture entitlements, 'existing laws frequently

[1] United Nations Declaration on the Rights of Indigenous Peoples, G.A. Res. 61/295, UN Doc. A/RES/61/295, 13 September 2007, 46 ILM 1013 (2007) (hereinafter UNDRIP).

[2] K. Bosselmann, 'Introduction to State Sovereignty, Indigenous Governance and International Law', in J. R. Engel, L. Westra and K. Bosselmann (eds.), *Democracy, Ecological Integrity and International Law* (Newcastle Upon Tyne: Cambridge Scholars Press, 2010), p. 116.

[3] M. E. Porter, 'Attitudes, Values, Beliefs, and the Microeconomics of Prosperity', in S. P. Huntington and L. E. Harrison (eds.), *Culture Matters: How Values Shape Human Progress* (New York: Basic Books, 2000), p. 27.

[4] *Ibid.*, at p. 20.

fail to strike a balance between economic development' and indigenous peoples' rights.[5] As a consequence, indigenous peoples suffer the consequences of a regime that favours, for example, mining, over indigenous culture. Many of the estimated 370 million indigenous peoples around the world have lost, or are under the threat of losing, their ancestral lands, due to the exploitation of natural resources.

While the clash between economic development and indigenous peoples' rights is by no means new,[6] this chapter approaches this well-known theme from a new perspective by focusing on international investment law and arbitration. It explores the way in which international investment treaties and arbitral tribunals have dealt with indigenous heritage. This research is timely as in the past decade there has been a boom of investor–state arbitrations with elements of indigenous heritage. While the traditional focus of investment lawyers has been the analysis of the relevant investment law provisions, little, if any, research has focused on the interactions between indigenous heritage and economic interests in international investment law and arbitration. Only recently have legal commentaries begun to analyse and critically assess the substantive interplay between different international law regimes in investment treaty law and arbitration.[7] Among these pioneering works, however, specific focus on the linkage between the promotion of foreign direct investment and the protection of indigenous heritage is missing.[8] This chapter aims to fill this lacuna in contemporary legal studies.

The key questions are whether international investment law has embraced a pure *international economic culture* or whether it is open to encapsulate non-economic or cultural concerns in its *modus operandi*. Until recently, international investment law had developed only limited tools for the protection of cultural heritage through investment dispute

[5] L. Barrera-Hernández, 'Indigenous Peoples, Human Rights and Natural Resource Development: Chile's Mapuche Peoples and the Right to Water', *Ann. Surv. Int'l & Comp. L.* 11 (2005), 1.

[6] The literature is extensive. See, e.g., L. Westra, *Environmental Justice and the Rights of Indigenous Peoples: International and Domestic Perspectives* (London: Earthscan, 2008), pp. 17–21. For earlier works, see generally W. M. Reisman, 'Protecting Indigenous Rights in International Adjudication', *AJIL* 89 (1995), 350; D. E. Cycon, 'When Worlds Collide: Law, Development, and Indigenous Peoples', *New England L. Rev.* 25 (1991), 761.

[7] See generally, P. M. Dupuy, F. Francioni and E. U. Petersmann (eds.), *Human Rights in International Investment Law and Arbitration* (Oxford University Press, 2009).

[8] See, however, V. Vadi, 'When Cultures Collide: Foreign Direct Investment, Natural Resources and Indigenous Heritage in International Investment Law', *Columbia Human Rights Law Review* 42 (2011), 797–889.

settlement. While recent arbitral awards have shown an increasing awareness of the need to protect cultural heritage within investment disputes, and arbitrators have increasingly considered non-investment related values in the context of such investment disputes,[9] questions remain as to the adequacy of investor–state arbitration to deal with indigenous cultural heritage. Indigenous peoples' rights have played only a marginal role in the context of investor–state arbitration; affected indigenous peoples have virtually no legal standing in these procedures and have made use of only limited participatory procedures.

The argument of this chapter will proceed as follows. First, the notion of indigenous cultural heritage is analysed. Second, the international norms protecting indigenous cultural heritage will be scrutinized. As the evolution of *opinio juris* and state practice has led many to conclude that 'some indigenous rights have attained the status of customary international law . . . binding states regardless of whether they have ratified the relevant treaties',[10] this chapter addresses the question as to whether a norm of customary international law requires the protection of indigenous cultural heritage. Third, relevant case studies will be analysed and critically assessed. Finally, some conclusions will follow. It is argued that cultural entitlements are a significant component of indigenous peoples' rights. Although the UNDRIP contributes significantly to current discourse on indigenous heritage, the collision between international investment law and indigenous entitlements risks jeopardizing indigenous rights, thus making the case for strengthening the current regime protecting indigenous heritage. In particular, the participation of indigenous peoples in the decisions which affect them and their heritage is crucial.

## 6.1 *The notion of indigenous cultural heritage*

Indigenous cultural heritage comprises 'all objects, sites and knowledge, the nature of use of which has been transmitted from generation to generation, and which is regarded as pertaining to a particular people or its territory'.[11] The concept of indigenous cultural heritage includes

9 V. Vadi, 'Fragmentation or Cohesion? Investment versus Cultural Protection Rules', *JWIT* 10 (2009), 593–6.

10 S. Wiessner, 'The Rights and Status of Indigenous Peoples: A Global Comparative and International Legal Analysis', *Harvard Human Rights Journal* 12 (1999), 127.

11 Special Rapporteur, Sub-Commission on Prevention of Discrimination and Protection of Minorities, *Principles and Guidelines for the Protection of the Heritage of Indigenous Peoples*, ¶ 11, UN Doc. E/CN.4/Sub.2/1994/31 (8 July 1994) (by Erica-Irene Daes).

both tangible and intangible elements and contributes to cultural diversity. In order to understand it properly one needs to clarify the notion of indigeneity, and the concept of cultural heritage.

Literally, indigeneity indicates the quality of being indigenous, born in a land or belonging to the region.[12] Although indigeneity is 'a term of art in the politics and philosophy of cultural rights and the rights of First Peoples',[13] no single definition of indigenous peoples exists at the international law level. While the UNDRIP does not define indigeneity, two notions of indigeneity are found in the International Labour Organization (ILO) Convention 169 and in the Martinéz-Cobo Report. The ILO Convention 169 regards peoples as indigenous on account of their descent from the populations that inhabited a country at the time of conquest or colonization who retain some or all of their social, economic, cultural and political institutions.[14] Self-identification of a group as indigenous or tribal is regarded as the fundamental criterion.[15] The Martinéz-Cobo Report to the UN Sub-Commission on the Prevention of Discrimination of Minorities (hereinafter Martinéz-Cobo Report),[16] provides a slightly different definition, identifying indigenous peoples as those who 'having a historical continuity with pre-invasion and pre-colonial societies that developed on their territories, consider themselves distinct from other sectors of society now prevailing in those territories or parts of them'.[17]

Analytically, the notion of indigeneity presents both objective and subjective elements. The objective elements of indigeneity are made up of a historical link with a certain territory and a characteristic social structure. With regard to the historical link with a certain territory, while the ILO Convention 169 refers to descent from the populations that inhabited a country at the time of conquest or colonization; the

[12] J. Waldron, 'Indigeneity? First People and Last Occupancy', *New Zealand Journal of Public and Int'l Law* 1 (2003), 56.

[13] *Ibid.*, 57.

[14] See International Labour Organization Convention 169 Concerning Indigenous and Tribal Peoples in Independent Countries, 27 June 1989, 1650 UNTS 384 (hereinafter ILO Convention 169), Article 1.

[15] ILO Convention 169, Article 1(2).

[16] Special Rapporteur on the Rights of Indigenous People, *Study of the Problem of Discrimination Against Indigenous Populations*, Sub-Comm'n on Prevention of Discrimination and Protection of Minorities, UN Econ. and Soc. Council, UN Doc. E/CN.4/Sub.2/1986/7/Add.4 (1987) (by José R. Martínez-Cobo) (hereinafter Martinéz-Cobo Report).

[17] *Ibid.*, ¶ 379.

Martinéz-Cobo Report refers to 'a historical continuity with pre-invasion and pre-colonial societies that developed on their territories'.[18] With regard to the peculiar social structure, the ILO Convention 169 refers to peoples that 'retain some or all of their social, economic, cultural and political institutions'.[19] Similarly, the Martinéz-Cobo Report mentions specific 'cultural patterns, social institutions and legal systems'.[20]

The subjective element of indigeneity is characterized by the way indigenous peoples define and consider themselves, i.e. the self-identification of a group as indigenous or tribal. The Martinéz-Cobo Report mentions the fact that indigenous peoples 'consider themselves distinct from other sectors of society'[21] and 'are determined to preserve, develop and transmit to future generations their ancestral territories, and their ethnic identity, as the basis of their continued existence as peoples'.[22] The UNDRIP states that '[i]ndigenous peoples have the right to determine their own identity or membership in accordance with their customs and traditions'.[23]

Indigenous cultural heritage includes both material manifestations, such as burial sites and rock and cave paintings, and immaterial elements, including traditional knowledge and cultural expressions, oral traditions, literature, designs, and visual and performing arts.[24] However, for indigenous peoples the distinction between these two categories of cultural heritage is artificial: 'They see the land and the sea, all of the sites they contain and the knowledge and the laws associated with those sites as a single entity that must be protected as a whole.'[25] Because of this holistic approach of indigenous peoples, a UN study insists that 'all elements of heritage should be managed and protected as a single, interrelated and integrated whole'.[26]

Some scholars contend that emphasizing the cultural entitlements of indigenous peoples can reduce their political rights and dilute their

[18] *Ibid.* [19] ILO Convention 169, Article 1(1)(b). [20] Martinéz-Cobo Report, ¶ 379.

[21] *Ibid.* [22] *Ibid.* [23] UNDRIP, Article 33.

[24] C. O'Faircheallaigh, 'Negotiating Cultural Heritage? Aboriginal Mining Company Agreements in Australia', *Development and Change* 39 (2003), 27.

[25] *Ibid.*

[26] Special Rapporteur, Sub-Commission on Prevention of Discrimination and Protection of Minorities, *Study on the Protection of the Cultural and Intellectual Property of Indigenous Peoples*, ¶ 31, UN Doc. E/CN.4/Sub.2/1993/28 (28 July 1993) (by Erica-Irene Daes).

claims to self-determination.[27] According to these authors, over-emphasizing culture risks undermining self-determination.[28]

Yet, understanding and protecting indigenous identity and cultural heritage is complementary to other approaches. Indigenous sovereignty is deeply rooted in cultural identity:[29] 'to the degree that a nation loses its sense of cultural identity, to that degree it suffers a loss of sovereignty'.[30] While according to the classical Westphalian system of international law, indigenous governance did not fit into the form of nation states,[31] sovereignty in our times is seen 'in variable terms, as a basket of attributes and corresponding rights and duties'.[32] Accordingly, indigenous peoples have the 'inherent powers' of a 'sovereignty which has never been extinguished'.[33] As Lenzerini highlights, 'a principle has emerged requiring states to recognize a given degree of sovereignty in favour of [indigenous] peoples'.[34] Such parallel sovereignty includes the right of indigenous peoples, *inter alia*, to live in their traditional lands, the right to enjoy their own culture, the right to self-determination and the right to participate in decisions which may affect them.[35]

Cultural entitlements and self-determination are deeply connected and occur along the same spectrum of human rights.[36] The UNDRIP recognizes the right of indigenous peoples to self-determination, encompassing the right to freely determine 'their political status

[27] See generally C. Cutler, 'The Globalization of International Law, Indigenous Identity, and the "New Constitutionalism"', in W. Coleman (ed.), *Property, Territory, Globalization: Struggles over Autonomy* (Vancouver: University of British Columbia Press, 2010).

[28] K. Engle, *The Elusive Promise of Indigenous Development: Rights, Culture, Strategy* (Durham, NC: Duke University Press, 2010), p. 4.

[29] W. Coffey and R. Tsosie, 'Rethinking the Tribal Sovereignty Doctrine: Cultural Sovereignty and the Collective Future of Indian Nations', *Stanford L. & Policy Rev.* 12 (2001), 210.

[30] V. Deloria Jr., 'Self-Determination and the Concept of Sovereignty', in J. R. Wunder (ed.), *Native American Sovereignty* (New York: Garland, 1996), p. 118.

[31] M. V. Cabrera Ormaza, 'Re-thinking the Role of Indigenous Peoples in International Law: New Developments in International Environmental Law and Development Cooperation', *Goettingen JIL* 4 (2012), 248.

[32] F. Lenzerini, 'Sovereignty Revisited: International Law and Parallel Sovereignty of Indigenous Peoples', *Texas ILJ* 42 (2006), 159.

[33] *United States v. Wheeler*, 435 US 313, 322 (1978).

[34] Lenzerini, 'Sovereignty Revisited', 186. [35] *Ibid.*, 188.

[36] A. F. Vrdoljak, 'Self-Determination and Cultural Rights', in F. Francioni and M. Scheinin (eds.), *Cultural Human Rights* (Leiden/Boston: Martinus Nijhoff Publishers, 2008), pp. 41–78.

and freely pursue their economic, social and cultural development'.[37] As stated by the Supreme Court of Canada, 'the international law right to self-determination ... generates, at best, a right to external self-determination ... where a definable group is denied meaningful access to government to pursue their political, economic, social and cultural development'.[38]

In any case, while traditionally indigenous peoples were not viewed as 'legal unit[s] of international law',[39] as '[i]nternational law knew no other legal subjects than the state',[40] due to the failures of national law to address indigenous peoples' rights adequately, international law has increasingly regulated indigenous peoples' affairs in the past five decades, reaffirming their rights and various entitlements.[41] There has been a paradigm shift in international law; and some authors now consider indigenous peoples to be 'legal subjects under international law'.[42]

## *6.2 The protection of indigenous cultural heritage in international law*

A complex framework governs indigenous cultural heritage at the international law level. In particular, five streams of international law instruments protecting indigenous cultural heritage can be identified: (1) the UNDRIP; (2) human rights instruments of general application (i.e. not exclusively or specifically focused on indigenous peoples); (3) labour and environmental law instruments; (4) UNESCO instruments protecting cultural heritage and cultural diversity; and (5) certain World Bank policies. Whether some of these norms have been crystallized in customary international law is also discussed, since customary law is binding upon states irrespective of consent.

[37] UNDRIP, Article 3. [38] *Reference re Secession of Quebec* [1998] SCR at 286, 287.

[39] *Cayuga Indians (Great Britain) v. United States*, 6 RIAA 173 (1926) 176 (stating that an Indian tribe 'is not a legal unit of international law').

[40] E.-I. Daes, 'Indigenous Peoples' Rights to their Natural Resources', in A. Constantinides and N. Zaikos (eds.), *The Diversity of International Law* (Leiden/Boston: Martinus Nijhoff, 2009).

[41] S. Wiessner, 'Indigenous Self-Determination, Culture, and Land: A Reassessment in Light of the 2007 UN Declaration on the Rights of Indigenous Peoples', in E. Pulitano (ed.), *Indigenous Rights in the Age of the UN Declaration* (Cambridge University Press, 2012), pp. 31–63.

[42] See R. L. Barsch, 'Indigenous Peoples in the 1990s: From Object to Subject of International Law', *Harvard Human Rights Journal* 7 (1994), 33.

Indigenous culture is a key theme of the UNDRIP,[43] which constitutes 'a milestone of re-empowerment' of indigenous peoples.[44] Many articles of the UNDRIP are devoted to different aspects of indigenous culture; and the word 'culture' appears no less than thirty times in its text.[45] Not only does the UNDRIP recognize the importance of indigenous peoples' culture for the realization of a number of indigenous peoples' rights, but it also acknowledges its essential contribution to the 'diversity and richness of civilization and cultures which constitute the common heritage of mankind'.[46] The UNDRIP states that indigenous peoples have 'the right to maintain, protect, and have access in privacy to their religious and cultural sites'[47] and the right 'to designate and retain their own names for communities, places and persons'.[48] The Declaration also recognizes the right of indigenous peoples to practise their cultural traditions[49] and maintain their distinctive spiritual and material relationship with the land which they have traditionally owned, occupied or otherwise used.[50] For indigenous peoples, land is the basis not only of economic livelihood, but also the source of spiritual and cultural identity.[51] While this landmark instrument is currently not binding *per se*, this may change in the future to the extent that its provisions reflect customary international law.[52]

In general terms, human rights provisions requiring the protection of cultural rights also require the protection of indigenous cultural heritage.[53] For instance, Article 27 of the International Covenant on Civil and Political Rights (ICCPR) provides: 'In those states in which ethnic, religious or linguistic minorities exist, persons belonging to such minorities shall not be denied the right, in community with the other members of their

[43] See S. Wiessner, 'The Cultural Rights of Indigenous Peoples: Achievements and Continuing Challenges', *EJIL* 22 (2011), 139.

[44] Wiessner, 'Indigenous Self-Determination, Culture, and Land', 31.

[45] See Y. Donders, 'The UN Declaration on the Rights of Indigenous Peoples: A Victory for Cultural Autonomy?', in I. Boerefijn and J. Goldschmidt (eds.), *Changing Perceptions of Sovereignty and Human Rights* (Antwerp/Oxford/Portland: Intersentia, 2008), p. 99.

[46] UNDRIP, preamble. [47] UNDRIP, Article 12(1). [48] UNDRIP, Article 13(1).

[49] UNDRIP, Article 11. [50] UNDRIP, preamble and Articles 8, 11.

[51] J. Gilbert, 'Custodians of the Land: Indigenous Peoples, Human Rights and Cultural Integrity', in M. Langfield, W. Logan and M. Craith (eds.), *Cultural Diversity, Heritage and Human Rights* (Abingdon: Routledge, 2010), p. 31.

[52] M. Barelli, 'The Role of Soft Law in the International Legal System: The Case of the United Nations Declaration on the Rights of Indigenous Peoples', *ICLQ* 58 (2009), 957 at 983.

[53] See, e.g., Francioni, 'Culture, Heritage and Human Rights: An Introduction', in F. Francioni and M. Scheinin (eds.), *Cultural Human Rights* (Leiden/Boston: Martinus Nijhoff Publishers, 2008), pp. 6–7.

group, to enjoy their own culture, to profess and practise their own religion, or to use their own language.'[54] The Human Rights Committee has 'advance[d] a broad interpretation of the international norm of cultural integrity in the context of indigenous peoples, understanding that norm to encompass all aspects of indigenous culture including rights to lands and resources'.[55] In the *Lubikon Lake Band* case, the failure of the Canadian government to adequately address the Band's need for a stable land base, in combination with the granting of large-scale concessions for the exploitation of timber, gas, and oil in the Band's traditional territory, was found to amount to a violation of Article 27 of the ICCPR.[56] These activities effectively destroyed the Band's traditional hunting and trapping grounds, thus threatening the Band's way of life and culture.[57] In *Länsman v. Finland*,[58] several reindeer breeders of Sami ethnic origin, contended that mining 'would disturb their reindeer herding activities and the complex system of reindeer fences determined by the natural environment' and observed that 'the site of the quarry, mount Etelä-Riutusvaara, [wa]s a sacred place of the old Sami religion'.[59] Thus, they claimed that these extractive activities 'violate[d] their rights under Article 27 of the Covenant, in particular their right to enjoy their own culture, which has traditionally been and remains essentially based on reindeer husbandry'.[60] While limited quarrying on the slopes of a mountain was not deemed to jeopardize the applicant's cultural rights, it was held that if mining activities were approved on a large scale, they could give rise to a violation of Article 27 of the ICCPR.[61] At the regional level, the Inter-American Court of Human Rights has expanded the notion of property to include cultural entitlements recognizing the linkage between indigenous land rights and the cultural survival of indigenous peoples.[62]

[54] ICCPR Article 1.

[55] UN Human Rights Council, Special Rapporteur on the Situation of Human Rights and Fundamental Freedoms of Indigenous People, Promotion and Protection of All Human Rights, Civil, Political, Economic, Social and Cultural Rights, including the Right to Development, UN Doc. A/HRC/9/9 (11 August 2008), available at www.un.org/ga/search/view_doc.asp?symbol=A/HRC/9/9 (hereinafter Anaya, Promotion and Protection), ¶ 22.

[56] *Chief Bernard Ominayak and the Lubicon Lake Band v. Canada*, Human Rights Comm., No. 511/1992, ¶ 33, UN Doc. CCPR/C/38/D/167/1984 (26 March 1990).

[57] *Ibid.*, ¶¶ 3.5, 12, 23.2, 27.4.

[58] *Ilmari Länsman v. Finland*, Human Rights Comm., No. 511/1992, ¶ 9.6, UN Doc. CCPR/C/52/D/511/1992, 14 October 1993.

[59] *Ibid.*, ¶¶ 2.5 and 2.6. [60] *Ibid.*, ¶ 3.1. [61] *Ibid.*, ¶ 9.8.

[62] *Mayagna (Sumo) Awas Tingni Community v. Nicaragua*, Judgment of 31 January 2001, Inter-Am. Ct H.R. (ser. C) No. 79 (2001). See generally I. Madariaga Cuneo, 'The Rights

A number of international labour and environmental law instruments refer to indigenous peoples' culture. For instance, the ILO Convention 169 concerning Indigenous and Tribal Peoples in Independent Countries, recognizes 'the aspirations of [indigenous] peoples to exercise control over their own institutions [and] ways of life . . . and to maintain and develop their identities, languages and religions, within the framework of the state in which they live'.[63] The Convention also requires that the cultural values and practices of indigenous peoples be recognized and protected.[64] The Rio Declaration on Environment and Development provides, *inter alia*, that '[s]tates should recognize and duly support th[e] identity, culture and interests [of indigenous peoples] and enable their effective participation in the achievement of sustainable development'.[65] Agenda 21[66] exhorts governments to protect indigenous lands from activities that indigenous peoples consider to be culturally inappropriate,[67] and to recognize that 'traditional and direct dependence on renewable resources and ecosystems, including sustainable harvesting, continues to be essential to the cultural, economic and physical well-being of indigenous peoples and their communities'.[68] The Convention on Biological Diversity also refers to 'traditional cultural practices'.[69]

Several UNESCO instruments protect elements of indigenous cultural heritage. Although some indigenous cultural sites are deemed to have outstanding universal value and have been included in the World Heritage List, the fact that indigenous cultural heritage does not correspond to the Western monumental vision of beauty, or is not publicly disclosed, can (and has) prevent(ed) the categorization of a number of indigenous cultural sites as world heritage.

An opportunity for better representation of indigenous heritage in the World Heritage List came in 1992 when the World Heritage Committee first introduced the concept of cultural landscapes as an autonomous category to justify the inscription of properties on the World Heritage List. The adoption of this category aimed at overcoming the traditional

of Indigenous Peoples and the Inter-American Human Rights System', *Arizona J. Int'l & Comp. L.* 22 (2005), 53.

63 ILO Convention 169, preamble. 64 *Ibid.*, Article 5.

65 *Rio Declaration on Environment and Development*, Principle 22.

66 UN Conference on Env't and Dev., *Report of the United Nations Conference on Environment and Development: Agenda 21*, UN Doc. A/CONF.151/26/Rev.1 (Vol. I) Annex 2 (12 August 1992) (hereinafter *Agenda 21*).

67 *Agenda 21*, Article 26(3)(a)(ii). 68 *Ibid.* Article 26(3)(a)(iv).

69 Convention on Biological Diversity, Rio de Janeiro, 5 June 1992, in force 29 December 1993, 31 ILM 818 (1992), Article 10(c).

dichotomy between nature and culture, thus promoting an integrated approach to the safeguard of world heritage.[70] A cultural landscape is a geographic area which represents the combined work of man and nature.[71] By adopting this new category, the Committee aimed to achieve a greater balance in the World Heritage List, by including cultural expressions of under-represented regions and cultures of the world. The concept of cultural landscape goes beyond the appreciation of mere natural or monumental beauty to include intangible values. By placing emphasis on humanity being *within* the environment, rather than disconnected from it, the protection of cultural landscapes can be particularly appropriate in protecting indigenous cultural heritage. Landscape is central to indigenous peoples' cultures. For indigenous peoples, land is the basis not only of economic livelihood, but also the source of spiritual and cultural identity.[72]

However, the WHC's listing approach generally protects only those sites expressly designated by the Member States and selected by the World Heritage Committee. By solely empowering the nation-state to select sites for inscription, the listing process does little to protect the cultural heritage of minorities and indigenous peoples.[73] Furthemore, a number of indigenous cultural heritage sites have been inscribed in the List without consultations with the tribes which inhabit the land or without involving them in the management phase. The African Commission on Human and Peoples' Rights recently noted that 'there are numerous World Heritage sites in Africa that have been inscribed without the free, prior and informed consent of the indigenous peoples in whose territories they are located' and the management frameworks of such sites 'are not consistent with the principles of the UN Declaration on the Rights of Indigenous Peoples'. Therefore, the African Commission on Human and Peoples' Rights urged 'the World Heritage Committee and UNESCO to

> review and revise current procedures and Operational Guidelines, in consultation and cooperation with the UN Permanent Forum on Indigenous Issues and indigenous peoples, in order to ensure that the implementation of the World Heritage Convention is consistent with the

[70] K. Whitby-Last, 'Article 1 Cultural Landscapes', in F. Francioni (ed.), *The 1972 World Heritage Convention* (Oxford University Press, 2008), pp. 51–62.

[71] C. O. Sauer, 'The Morphology of Landscape', *University of California Publications in Geography* 2 (1925), 19–54.

[72] Gilbert, 'Custodians of the Land', p. 31.

[73] R. Anglin, 'The World Heritage List: Bridging the Cultural Property Nationalism-Internationalism Divide', *Yale J. L. & the Humanities* 20 (2008), 271.

> UN Declaration on the Rights of Indigenous Peoples and that indigenous peoples' rights, and human rights generally, are respected, protected and fulfilled in World Heritage areas.[74]

In 2011, a few indigenous groups petitioned the United Nations Permanent Forum on Indigenous Issues, pointing out that three sites to be considered for inscription in the World Heritage List were of interest to indigenous peoples, yet the relevant communities had not been meaningfully involved in the process.[75]

Of more concern, some tribes have been evicted from the inscribed sites as well.[76] As anthropologists put it, the traditional notion of conservation privileges physical authenticity, disembeds World Heritage sites from their habitual and everyday context and deprives them of their intangible dimensions ('heritagization of culture').[77] For instance, the African Commission on Human and Peoples' Rights recommended the restitution of land belonging to the Kenyan Endorois tribe after its eviction in the 1970s from a World Heritage site.[78] The Endorois community claimed that the governmental measures had denied them access to grazing land and cultural and religious sites, thus violating, *inter alia*, their rights to property and culture under the African Charter.[79] The African Commission's Decision on the Merits upheld all of the Endorois' claims and included the recommendation that Kenya should 'restitute Endorois ancestral land', and 'ensure that the Endorois community has unrestricted access to Lake Bogoria and surrounding sites for religious and cultural rites and for grazing their cattle'.[80] The Commission acknowledged that 'the right to preserve

[74] African Commission on Human and Peoples' Rights ACHPR/Res.197 (L)2011: Resolution on the protection of indigenous peoples' rights in the context of the World Heritage Convention and the designation of Lake Bogoria as a World Heritage site, 5 November 2011, available at www.achpr.org/sessions/50th/resolutions/197/ (last visited on 14 January 2013).

[75] T. te Heuheu, M. Kawharu, R. A. Tuheiava, 'World Heritage and Indigeneity', *World Heritage* 62 (2012), 13.

[76] L. Lankarani, 'La notion de dispersion en droit international des patrimoines culturels (immaterial, naturel et mondial)', *Journal de droit international* 2 (2011), 298.

[77] C. de Cesari, 'World Heritage and Mosaic Universalism', *Journal of Social Archaeology* 10 (2010), 307.

[78] Decision on Communication 276/2003, *Centre for Minority Rights Development (Kenya) and Minority Rights Group International on behalf of Endorois Welfare Council v. Kenya* (Endorois Decision), Decision of the African Commission on Human and Peoples' Rights, adopted at the 46th Ordinary Session held 11–25 November 2009 in Banjul, The Gambia.

[79] African [Banjul] Charter on Human and Peoples' Rights, 27 June 1981, in force 21 October 1986, 21 ILM 58 (1982).

[80] Endorois Decision, p. 80.

one's identity through identification with ancestral lands, cultural patterns, social institutions and religious systems' lies at 'the heart of indigenous rights'.[81] Finally, there is a pressing concern that the designation of certain reserves and the presence of mineral resources on traditional lands might affect indigenous land claims, traditional hunting and fishing within the reserve's boundaries. For instance, the San tribe was evicted from the Central Kalahari Game Reserve, which is a World Heritage site, after diamond exploration began in the park.[82]

The protection of indigenous cultural heritage as world heritage should include respect for the lifestyle of its inhabitants. However, the WHC is a conservative instrument since it 'predates many of the advances in participatory processes articulated in more recent instruments such as the Aarhus Convention'.[83] In this sense, the UN Expert Mechanism on the Rights of Indigenous Peoples, has called on UNESCO and the World Heritage Committee to establish 'robust procedures and mechanisms to ensure [that] indigenous peoples are adequately consulted and involved in the management and protection of World Heritage sites and that their free, prior and informed consent is obtained when their territories are being nominated and inscribed as World Heritage sites'.[84] While the *Operational Guidelines* indicate that the 'participation of local people in the nomination process is essential to enable them to have a shared responsibility with the State Party in the maintenance of the property',[85] they include only a vague reference to the lifestyle of the inhabitants of World Heritage sites: 'Human activities, including those of traditional societies and local communities, often occur in natural areas. These activities may be consistent with the Outstanding Universal Value of the area where they are ecologically sustainable.'[86]

Furthermore, powerful economic interests may endanger indigenous heritage sites.[87] The controversy which surrounded the listing of the

[81] Endorois Decision, ¶ 157.

[82] B. Bearak, 'For Some Bushmen, a Homeland Worth the Fight', *New York Times*, 4 November 2010.

[83] N. Affolder, 'Mining and the World Heritage Convention: Democratic Legitimacy and Treaty Compliance', *Pace Environmental L. Rev.* 24 (2007), 47.

[84] Expert Mechanism Advice No. 2 (2011) Indigenous Peoples and the Right to Participate in Decision Making, ¶ 38, available at www.ohchr.org/Documents/Issues/IPeoples/EMRIP/Advice2_Oct2011.pdf (last visited 13 April 2013).

[85] 2012 *Operational Guidelines*, ¶ 123. [86] *Ibid.*, ¶ 90.

[87] V. Vadi, 'The Protection of Cultural Landscapes and Indigenous Heritage in International Investment Law', in L. Westra, C. Soskolne and D. Spady (eds.), *Human Health and Ecological Integrity: Ethics, Law and Human Rights* (Earthscan: London, 2012), pp. 250–61.

Kakadu National Park in Australia erupted because a section of the park included a uranium mine within its boundaries.[88] Investors attempted to block the listing of this part of the park, filing a suit at the local court, and were opposed by non-governmental organizations and the Mirrar Aboriginal people, who wanted to block the mining as it was having an irreversible impact on Aboriginal cultural heritage.[89] In response to international pressure, the federal government decided not to permit mining in the zone and to include the entire park on the World Heritage List.[90]

Other UNESCO Conventions protecting indigenous cultural heritage are the UNESCO Convention for the Safeguarding of the Intangible Cultural Heritage (CSICH)[91] and the Convention on the Protection and Promotion of the Diversity of Cultural Expressions (CCD).[92] The former protects intangible cultural heritage meant as 'the practices, representations, expressions, knowledge, skills – as well as the instruments, objects, artefacts and cultural spaces associated therewith – that communities, groups and, in some cases, individuals recognize as part of their cultural heritage'.[93] The CSICH acknowledges the dynamic nature of intangible cultural heritage as heritage 'transmitted from generation to generation . . . constantly recreated by communities and groups in response to their environment' and protects only that heritage which respects human rights.[94] In parallel, the CCD recognizes 'the importance of traditional knowledge as a source of intangible and material wealth, and in particular the knowledge systems of indigenous peoples, and its positive contribution to sustainable development, as well as the need for its adequate protection and promotion'.[95] Both conventions are of particular significance for the protection of indigenous peoples' cultural identity.[96]

Finally, even the World Bank has recognized how the lack of adequate protection of indigenous land may affect such peoples' physical and cultural integrity, acknowledging that 'indigenous peoples require special attention, as they are particularly vulnerable to negative effects caused by

[88] UNESCO World Heritage Comm., *Report on the Mission to Kakadu National Park, Australia 26 October to 1 November 1986*, 1, WCH-98/CONF. 203/INF.18 (29 November 1998), available at http://unesdoc.unesco.org/images/0011/001175/117512e.pdf (hereinafter Report on the Mission to Kakadu).

[89] *Ibid.*, p. 1. [90] *Ibid.*, pp. 2–4.

[91] Convention for the Safeguarding of the Intangible Cultural Heritage (CSICH), 17 October 2003, in force 20 April 2006. 2368 UNTS 3.

[92] Convention on the Protection and Promotion of the Diversity of Cultural Expressions (CCD), Paris, 20 October 2005, in force 18 March 2007, 2440 UNTS 311.

[93] CSICH, Article 2(1). [94] *Ibid.* [95] CCD, preamble. [96] See Chapter 5 above.

Bank-funded activities'.[97] In this sense, it has adopted a number of policy statements in the attempt to provide safeguards for indigenous peoples. For instance both Operational Directive 4.20 on Indigenous Peoples and its successor Operational Policy 4.10 on Indigenous Peoples recognize the need 'to ensure that the development process fully respects the dignity, human rights, economies and cultures of indigenous peoples'.[98] Notwithstanding the adoption of these instruments, 'internal reviews as well as frequent complaints by indigenous peoples repeatedly demonstrate that compliance failure rates are far beyond acceptable'.[99]

In the light of the existing plethora of international law instruments, some authors have argued that an emerging norm of customary law requires states to protect cultural heritage.[100] With regard to indigenous cultural heritage, the evolution of *opinio juris* and state practice has led many to conclude that customary international law already includes a norm recognizing, *inter alia*, that indigenous peoples are entitled to maintain and develop their distinct cultural identity, their spirituality, their language, and their traditional ways of life.[101] As Anaya puts it, 'significant international legal developments provide evidence that customary international law has accepted the right of cultural self-determination for indigenous peoples and the consequent autonomous control necessary to achieve that'.[102]

Whether a norm of international law of *jus cogens* status requires the protection of indigenous cultural heritage is a matter of debate.[103]

[97] F. MacKay, 'Universal Rights or a Universe unto Itself? Indigenous Peoples' Human Rights and the World Bank's Draft Operational Policy 4.10 on Indigenous Peoples', *American University Int'l L. Rev.* 17 (2002), 538.

[98] See World Bank, 'Operational Directive 4.20 on Indigenous Peoples', in *The World Bank Operational Manual*, ¶ 6 (1991); World Bank, 'Operational Policy 4.10 on Indigenous Peoples' (as revised in April 2013), ¶ 1.

[99] See F. MacKay, 'The Draft World Bank Operational Policy 4.10 on Indigenous Peoples: Progress or More of the Same?', *Arizona J. Int'l & Comp. Law* 22 (2005), 66.

[100] See F. Francioni, 'Au-delà des traités: l'émergence d'un nouveau droit coutumier pour la protection du patrimoine culturel', *RGDIP* (2007), 19–42.

[101] See Wiessner, 'The Rights and Status of Indigenous Peoples', 127.

[102] J. Anaya, *Indigenous Peoples in International Law* (Oxford University Press, 1996), pp. 242–3. For a more restrictive approach, see A. Xanthaki, 'Indigenous Rights in International Law over the Last 10 Years and Future Developments', *Melbourne JIL* 10 (2009), 36 (noting that 'viewing the Declaration or substantial parts of it as customary international law may be rather premature').

[103] See e.g. C. P. Cline, Note, 'Pursuing Native American Rights in International Law Venues: A Jus Cogens Strategy after *Lyng v. Northwest Indian Cemetery Protective Association*', *Hastings Law Journal* 42 (1991), 591.

Considering the strict linkage between the protection of indigenous cultural heritage and human dignity, not only does the systematic violation of indigenous peoples' cultural identity violate their right to self-determination – defined as the right of peoples to 'freely determine their political status and freely pursue their economic, social and cultural development'[104] – but it can ultimately lead to the cultural genocide of an indigenous group. Far from being a superfluous element, culture constitutes the *conditio sine qua non* of the existence of indigenous peoples and the meaningful exercise of self-determination which is an *erga omnes* obligation,[105] if not a 'peremptory norm of general international law'.[106] While cultural entitlements and the right to self-determination are conceptually different, cultural entitlements promote self-determination by enabling indigenous people to freely pursue their economic, social and cultural development.[107]

## *6.3 When cultures collide*

Many of the estimated 370 million indigenous peoples around the world have lost, or are under the imminent threat of losing, their ancestral lands, because of the exploitation of natural resources.[108] The development of natural resources is steadily increasing, in or very close to traditional indigenous areas.[109] While development analysts point to extractive projects as anti-poverty measures and international economic organizations similarly advocate for foreign direct investment as a major catalyst for development,[110] rising investment in the extractive

104 ICCPR, Article 1(1) and ICESCR, Article 1(1).

105 See e.g. *Case Concerning East Timor (Portugal v. Australia)*, Judgment, 30 June 1995, 1995 ICJ Reports 90, ¶ 29; *Legal Consequences of the Construction of a Wall in the Occupied Palestinian Territory*, Advisory Opinion, 9 July 2004, ICJ Reports 2044, 136, ¶¶ 155–8.

106 E. J. Criddle and E. Fox-Decent, 'A Fiduciary Theory of Jus Cogens', *Yale JIL* 34 (2009), 374.

107 See A. F. Vrdoljak, 'Self-Determination and Cultural Rights', in F. Francioni and M. Scheinin (eds.), *Cultural Human Rights* (Leiden/Boston: Martinus Nijhoff Publishers, 2008), p. 53.

108 N. Pillay, Statement by the United Nations High Commissioner for Human Rights, United Nations, New York, 9 August 2011, available at www.ohchr.org/en/NewsEvents/Pages/DisplayNews.aspx?NewsID=11284&LangID=E.

109 See e.g. K. M. Gast, 'Environmental Justice and Indigenous Peoples in the United States: An International Human Rights Analysis', *Transnat'l L. & Contemp. Probs.* 14 (2004), 255.

110 See e.g. OECD, *Foreign Direct Investment for Development: Maximising Benefits, Minimising Costs* (Paris: OECD, 2002), 3.

industries can have a devastating impact on the livelihood of indigenous peoples and their culture.[111] As one author puts it, 'for the most part, the peoples in the areas where the resources are located tend to bear a disproportionate share of the negative impacts of development through reduced access to resources and direct exposure to pollution and environmental degradation'.[112] This phenomenon has been acutely perceived by groups of indigenous peoples who filed claims for protecting their entitlements before national courts and tribunals[113] and human rights bodies at the regional[114] and international level.[115] This case law and the relevant literature are extensive; what is less known is the emerging number of arbitral awards dealing with elements of indigenous cultural heritage. Given the impact that foreign direct investments can have on indigenous peoples' culture, scrutiny and critical assessment of these awards is of the utmost relevance.

To date several investment arbitrations have involved indigenous cultural heritage. While it is not possible to examine all of these awards in the context of this chapter, a selection of case studies will be analysed and critically assessed. Although this case law is not homogeneous, it can be scrutinized according to the taxonomy of the claims brought by foreign investors, including, inter alia: (1) expropriation; (2) lack of fair and equitable treatment; (3) discrimination; and (4) lack of full protection and security.

## 6.4 *Expropriation claims*

Several investment treaty arbitrations have dealt with the question of whether regulation allegedly aimed at protecting indigenous cultural heritage may be deemed to be an indirect expropriation or a measure tantamount to expropriation. As mentioned in Chapter 3, the *Glamis*

[111] M. Satterwhite and D. Hurwitz, 'The Right of Indigenous Peoples to Meaningful Consent in Extractive Industry Projects', *Arizona J. Int'l & Comp. L.* 22 (2005), 3–4.

[112] Barrera-Hernández, 'Indigenous Peoples, Human Rights and Natural Resource Development', 6.

[113] See e.g. T. Chapman, 'Corroboree Shield: A Comparative Historical Analysis of (the Lack of) International, National and State Level Indigenous Cultural Heritage Protection', *Macquarie J. Int'l & Comp. Envtl. L.* 5 (2008), 81.

[114] See e.g. O. Kreimer, 'Collective Rights of Indigenous Peoples in the Inter-American Human Rights System, Organization of American States', *Proceedings of the American Society of International Law at its Annual Meeting* 94 (2000), 315–16.

[115] See e.g. L. Westra, *Environmental Justice and the Rights of Indigenous Peoples* (London: Earthscan, 2008), p. 71.

*Gold* case involved a mining project within the California Desert Conservation Area which included a number of cultural and religious sites of the Native American Quechan Tribe.[116] The area was heavily used by pre-contact Native Americans as a travel route, and more recently, the Quechan used to walk a sacred path, the 'Trail of Dreams', while performing ceremonial practices.[117] Although the area was not listed on the World Heritage List, its cultural importance for the tribe was similar to the importance of Mecca or Jerusalem for other believers.[118] When Glamis Gold, a Canadian mining company, planned the Imperial Project to mine gold on this federal land, the Department of the Interior withdrew the project from further mineral entry for twenty years to protect historic properties.[119] In 2002, however, permission for the project was granted and regulations required the backfilling of all open-pit mines to re-create the approximate contours of the land prior to mining.[120]

In response to the federal and state actions, the claimant filed its Notice of Arbitration, arguing that state and federal measures constituted an indirect expropriation in violation of Article 1110 of the North American Free Trade Agreement (NAFTA).[121] According to the claimant, the expropriation began with the federal government's unlawful refusal to approve the claimant's plan of operations and continued with the backfilling requirement.[122] In particular, backfilling would be uneconomical and arbitrary since it would not be rationally related to its stated purpose of protecting cultural resources.[123] The claimant pointed out that excavation can destroy existing cultural resources and that backfilling does not protect those artefacts but may lead to the burial of more items and cause greater environmental degradation.[124] Thus, the claimant argued that the California measures amounted to an indirect expropriation.[125]

In its statement, the United States argued that mining is a highly regulated industry and that any reasonable investor should have reasonably anticipated the extension of those regulations.[126] The respondent

[116] *Glamis Gold Ltd v. United States of America* Award (*Glamis Gold*, Award), 8 June 2009, ¶¶ 100–1. While Chapter 3 provided a brief analysis of the *Glamis Gold* case with regard to its reference to the World Heritage Convention, this chapter considers this case in the light of its relevance for indigenous heritage.

[117] *Ibid.*, ¶ 107. [118] *Ibid.*, ¶¶ 103–8. [119] *Ibid.*, ¶ 152. [120] *Ibid.*, ¶ 183.

[121] North American Free Trade Agreement (NAFTA), 17 December 1992, in force 1 January 1994 (1993) 32 ILM 289.

[122] *Glamis Gold*, Award, ¶ 321. [123] *Ibid.*, ¶ 687. [124] *Ibid.* [125] *Ibid.*, ¶ 703.

[126] *Ibid.*, ¶ 729.

relied on the fact that, while other states had completely prohibited the use of all open-pit mining, the Californian legislation did not impede the excavation and mineral exploitation of the zone: it required backfilling to restore the landscape to the way it was before the mining operations.[127] The respondent also stressed that in this case the legislature was attempting 'to reconcile competing interests by addressing the threat to Native American sites in the [California Desert Conservation Area] while recognizing mining companies' rights to mine there'.[128] On the one hand, the California measures effectively limited the waste piles that would have obstructed the view from the geoglyph of the Running Man to the Indian Pass.[129] On the other hand, the company could still use its property. According to the United States, it would not be disproportionate for a state to require mining operators to internalize the costs of the environmental damage caused by their own activities.[130]

The Arbitral Tribunal found the claimant's expropriation argument to be without merit.[131] In order to distinguish a non-compensable regulation and a compensable expropriation, the Tribunal established a two-tier test, according to which it ascertained: (1) the extent to which the measures interfered with reasonable and investment-backed expectations of a stable regulatory framework; and (2) the purpose and the character of the governmental actions taken.[132] First, the Tribunal found that the California backfilling measures 'did not cause a sufficient economic impact to the Imperial Project to effect an expropriation of [the] Claimant's investment'.[133] Second, the Tribunal deemed the measures to be rationally related to their stated purpose.[134] The Tribunal admitted that 'some cultural artifacts will indeed be disturbed, if not buried, in the process of excavating and backfilling',[135] but concluded that, without such legislative measures, the landscape would be harmed by significant pits and waste piles in the near vicinity.[136]

In *Grand River v. United States*, the claim of expropriation was brought by a foreign company made up of indigenous peoples against the host state.[137] A Canadian company engaged in exporting tobacco in the United States argued that its investment had been harmed by the US Master Settlement Agreement (MSA), a settlement between forty-six states and tobacco companies which requires the contribution of funds

[127] *Ibid.* [128] *Ibid.*, ¶ 726. [129] *Ibid.*, ¶ 720. [130] *Ibid.*, ¶ 722. [131] *Ibid.*, ¶ 360.
[132] *Ibid.*, ¶ 356. [133] *Ibid.*, ¶ 536. [134] *Ibid.*, ¶ 803. [135] *Ibid.*, ¶ 805. [136] *Ibid.*
[137] *Grand River Enterprises Six Nations Ltd et al. v. United States of America*, Award, 12 January 2011 [*Grand River*, Award].

from tobacco companies as compensation for the states' costs of treating tobacco-related illnesses.[138] In exchange for such payments, the US states dropped all lawsuits against the tobacco industry.[139] The claimants argued that such regulation amounted, *inter alia*, to indirect expropriation, in violation of NAFTA Article 1110.[140]

The Arbitral Tribunal rejected the expropriation claim. While one of the claimants had argued that the disputed measures were inconsistent with his reasonable investment-backed expectations not to be subject to such measures because of his status as a member of one of the First Nations in North America,[141] the Arbitral Tribunal declined to 'decide whether or not [Mr Montour] [wa]s correct on the underlying domestic legal proposition of immunity from the state regulation'.[142] Rather, the Tribunal considered that: 'Ordinarily, reasonable or legitimate expectations of the kind protected by NAFTA are those that arise through targeted representations or assurances made explicitly or implicitly by a state party.'[143] As 'trade in tobacco products has historically been the subject of close and extensive regulation by U.S. States', the Tribunal held that the investor should have known this circumstance and could not have reasonable expectations to carry on a large-scale tobacco distribution business without encountering state regulation.[144] Relying on previous NAFTA cases, the Tribunal also stated that NAFTA Article 1110 requires 'a complete or very substantial deprivation of owners' rights' to constitute a taking.[145] As the claimant's business had remained 'profitable', the Tribunal concluded that there was no expropriation.[146]

## 6.5 *Fair and equitable treatment*

Other cases have related to the fair and equitable treatment (FET) standard. This standard requires that foreign investors be accorded 'treatment in accordance with international law, including fair and equitable treatment and full protection and security'.[147] As mentioned above, in the *Grand River* case, a Canadian company engaged in exporting tobacco in the United States argued that its investment had been harmed by the US Master Settlement Agreements and that the United States had breached, *inter alia*, the FET standard.[148] As the individual claimants were members of the Six Nations of Native Americans, they argued that:

[138] *Ibid.*, ¶¶ 8–9. [139] *Ibid.*, ¶ 8. [140] *Ibid.*, ¶ 126. [141] *Ibid.*, ¶ 128.
[142] *Ibid.*, ¶ 139. [143] *Ibid.*, ¶ 141. [144] *Ibid.*, ¶ 144–5. [145] *Ibid.*, ¶ 148.
[146] *Ibid.*, ¶¶ 153–5. [147] See e.g. NAFTA Article 1105.
[148] *Grand River*, Award, ¶¶ 125 and 173.

> This arbitration is not about health protection or promotion. It is not about state rights to regulate in the interests of the public good . . . This arbitration concerns and arises out of the Respondent's discrimination against a group of aboriginal investors, their traditions, businesses and livelihoods, and the expropriation of their markets, all in violation of their rights under international law.[149]

According to the claimants, Article 1105 of the NAFTA required respect of international law, including indigenous peoples' rights.[150] They contended that a number of international law instruments illustrated the crystallization of customary international law with respect to the protection of the rights of indigenous peoples,[151] requiring states, *inter alia*, to actively consult with indigenous peoples before taking regulatory action that would substantially affect their interests.[152]

The Tribunal, with the exception of one member, believed that state legal officers 'acted less than optimally' in developing the proposed regulatory measures and considered that 'the First Nations or tribal governments, particularly those in the United States whose regulatory authority is or may be implicated by application of the MSA, should have been included in these discussions'.[153]

With regard to the right of indigenous peoples to be consulted before the adoption of regulatory measures potentially affecting them, the Tribunal stated:

> It may well be, as the Claimants urged, that there does exist a principle of customary international law requiring governmental authorities to consult indigenous peoples on governmental policies or actions . . . as pointed out by the claimants, the duty of states to consult with indigenous peoples is featured in the UN Declaration on the Rights of Indigenous Peoples, particularly in its Article 19 as well as in several other articles.[154]

Nonetheless, as the Tribunal noted that 'the notion of specialized procedural rights protecting some investors, but not others, cannot readily be reconciled with the idea of a minimum customary standard of treatment due to all investments',[155] it held that 'whatever unfair treatment was rendered to [the claimant] or his business enterprise, it did not rise to the level of an infraction of the fair and equitable treatment'.[156] As a matter

[149] *Grand River Enter. Six Nations, Ltd. v. United States of America*, Statement of Claimants' Claims Arising Directly Out of the Adoption and Implementation of the Allocable Share Amendments, 6 November 2006, at 1.
[150] *Grand River*, Award, ¶ 180. [151] *Ibid.*, ¶ 182. [152] *Ibid.* [153] *Ibid.*, ¶ 128.
[154] *Ibid.*, ¶ 210. [155] *Ibid.*, ¶ 213. [156] *Ibid.*, ¶ 187.

of applicable law, the Tribunal stated that 'the customary standard of protection of alien investors' investments does not incorporate other legal protections that may be provided [for] investors or classes of investors under other sources of law'.[157] As a matter of interpretation, the Arbitral Tribunal took into account other rules of international law as required by customary norms of treaty interpretation, but reaffirmed it was a 'tribunal of limited jurisdiction' with 'no mandate to decide claims based on treaties other than NAFTA'.[158]

In *Glamis Gold*, the claimant contended, *inter alia*, that the review process of its project violated the FET standard,[159] as 'numerous other projects with significant and similar cultural characteristics were approved ... without complete backfilling and despite severe impacts to their cultural resources'.[160] The Tribunal, however, noted that other properties did not present such a significant amount of archaeological items of cultural significance. Because the contested legislation was of general application and did not target the claimant's investment,[161] the Tribunal concluded that the acts of the federal government and the State of California did not violate the respondent's obligations under Article 1105 of NAFTA.[162] The Tribunal noted that the cultural review of the claimant's plan of operations was undertaken by qualified professionals, who provided reasoned, substantiated opinions and were not biased. Finally, it held that 'it is not the role of this Tribunal, or any international tribunal, to supplant its own judgment of underlying factual material and support for that of a qualified domestic agency'.[163]

## 6.6 *Discrimination*

The ascertainment of non-discrimination against the foreign investor is a crucial element in investment disputes with elements of cultural heritage. In *John Andre v. Canada*, a US-based businessman lodged a notice of intent to arbitrate, alleging losses arising from legislative measures affecting his caribou-hunting outfitter in Northern Canada.[164] The claimant used to have 360 caribou hunting licences (called 'caribou quota tags') and organized hunting camps for tourists and hunters who would travel from locations outside Canada to the aboriginal land in Canada's North West

[157] *Ibid.*, ¶ 219. [158] *Ibid.*, ¶ 71. [159] *Glamis Gold*, Award, ¶ 639. [160] *Ibid.*, ¶ 645.
[161] *Ibid.*, ¶ 765. [162] *Ibid.*, ¶ 824. [163] *Ibid.*, ¶ 779.
[164] *John R. Andre v. Government of Canada*, Notice of Intent to Submit Claim to Arbitration Pursuant to Chapter Eleven of the North American Free Trade Agreement, 19 March 2010, ¶ 8.

Territories (NWT).[165] In 2007, the government of NWT decided to grant only seventy-five caribou quota tags per outfitter.[166] Outfitters with commitments to clients would be required to buy caribou quota tags from their competitors.[167] The claimant complained that the relevant authorities cut the number of hunting licences in a discriminatory manner.[168] As many of the local outfitters only used seventy-five to one hundred caribou quota tags or less per year, the claimant alleged that the government developed a strategy to minimize the negative effect on local outfitters and maximize the negative effects on the investor.[169] The investor thus claimed to have been discriminated against on the basis of his US nationality.[170]

The press has subsequently reported that while the ban initially also included the aboriginal caribou hunt, the NWT government and the Tlicho aboriginal government jointly agreed to keep a total hunting ban only for non-aboriginal hunters and commercial hunting outfitters.[171] In other words, while the sporting hunt of caribou remains cancelled, the aboriginal subsistence hunt will be permitted.[172]

This differential treatment may be justified under human rights law. The autumn hunt allows the indigenous tribes to preserve their traditional culture and to rely on caribou meat in the winter. In fact, the subsistence activities of indigenous peoples are an integral part of their culture.[173] In this regard, the Human Rights Committee, observed that:

> culture manifests itself in many forms, including a particular way of life associated with the use of land resources, especially in the case of indigenous peoples. That right may include such traditional activities as fishing or hunting ... The enjoyment of those rights may require positive legal measures of protection and measures to ensure the effective participation of members of minority communities in decisions that affect them ... The protection of these rights is directed to ensure the survival and continued development of the cultural, religious and social identity of the minorities concerned, thus enriching the fabric of society as a whole.[174]

165 *Ibid.*, ¶ 12. 166 *Ibid.*, ¶ 51. 167 *Ibid.* 168 *Ibid.*, ¶ 35. 169 *Ibid.*, ¶ 51.
170 *Ibid.*, ¶ 35.
171 'New Plan for Canadian Bathurst Caribou Herd Management', *Eye on the Arctic*, 2 June 2010.
172 'Debate over N.W.T. Caribou Hunting Goes Public', *CBC News*, 9 February 2010.
173 United Nations Economic and Social Council, Human Rights Committee, *General Comment No. 23: The Rights of Minorities* (Art. 27), UN Doc. CCPR/C/21/Rev.1/Add.5, 8 April 1994, ¶¶ 7, 9.
174 *Ibid.*

A number of cases at the international, regional, and national levels provide evidence of the recognition of indigenous peoples' cultural rights in this sense. In the *Kitok* case, the Human Rights Committee stated that reindeer husbandry, as a traditional livelihood of the indigenous Sami people, is an activity protected under Article 27 of the ICCPR.[175] In *Jouni Lansman v. Finland*, the Committee found that reindeer herding fits into the definition of cultural activities.[176]

More recently, at the regional level, the Canadian Inuit filed a lawsuit before the Court of Justice of the European Union (CJEU) to overturn a European Union (EU) regulation[177] banning the import of seal products into the EU.[178] The regulation expressly recognizes the hunt as an element of the cultural identity of the members of the Inuit society and exempts the Inuit from the ban.[179] Since the Inuit people did not export seal products themselves, but exported them via non-indigenous exporters, they alleged that the derogation in their favour would remain an 'empty box'.[180] Although the Court rejected the claim as inadmissible;[181] the case was interesting as it showed that indigenous peoples may perceive aboriginal exemptions as inadequate to sustain cultural practices. The dispute is now pending before the WTO dispute settlement mechanism.[182]

At the national level, in 1999, the High Court of Australia dismissed a charge against a member of an aboriginal tribe who had caught two young crocodiles in Queensland using a traditional harpoon.[183] Although the appellant did not have a hunting permit, the Court concluded that he was exempted from the obligation of obtaining a permit, since his act was based on a traditional aboriginal custom which deems catching young crocodiles of high spiritual significance.[184] The US case

175 *Ivan Kitok v. Sweden* (Communication No. 197/1985), UN Human Rights Committee, UN Doc. CCPR/C/33/D/197/1985, 27 July 1988, ¶ 4.2.

176 *Jouni Lansman v. Finland* (Communication No. 671/1995), UN Human Rights Committee, ¶ 10.2, UN Doc. CCPR/C/58/D/671/1995, 22 November 1996.

177 Council Regulation 1007/2009, 2009 O.J. (L 286) 36 (EC).

178 CJEU, *Inuit Tapiriit Kanatami and others v. Parliament and Council*, Case T 18/10 R, Order of the General Court, 6 September 2011, available at http://eur-lex.europa.eu/LexUriServ/LexUriServ.do?uri=CELEX:62010TO0018(04):EN:HTML.

179 Council Regulation 1007/2009, preamble, para. 14.

180 *Inuit Tapiriit Kanatami and others v. Parliament and Council*, Order of the General Court, ¶ 103.

181 *Ibid*, ¶ 94.

182 *European Communities–Certain Measures Prohibiting the Importation and Marketing of Seal Products*, Request for the Establishment of a Panel, by Canada, 14 February 2011, WT/DS369/2, available at www.worldtradelaw.net/pr/ds369-2(pr).pdf.

183 *Yanner v. Eaton* (1999) 166 ALR 258, 301 (Austl.). 184 *Ibid.*, 277.

of the Makah people, who obtained permission to hunt whales, also bears testimony to competing cultural and environmental interests in the aboriginal hunting debate.[185]

Finally, aboriginal exemptions are a common feature of international environmental treaties which protect certain species. Such derogations aim to 'accommodate the needs of traditional subsistence users of such species',[186] thus protecting traditional hunting practices linked to the cultural heritage of the communities concerned. For instance, the 1957 Convention on Conservation of North Pacific Fur Seals describes the aboriginal hunting practices that are exempted by the application of the Convention.[187] Analogously, the 1946 International Convention for the Regulation of Whaling retains aboriginal rights to subsistence whaling, permitting the taking of various whales by aborigines but stipulating that 'the meat and products of such whales are to be used exclusively for local consumption by the aborigines'.[188]

However, questions remain as to whether such positive measures can be considered to be compatible with international investment law. In particular, it is uncertain whether the Arbitral Tribunal will consider the indigenous exception as a legal *acquis*. On the one hand, the preservation of reindeer is a legitimate policy objective; on the other, human rights considerations justify the aboriginal exemption as the hunt is part of the culture of indigenous peoples and supports their subsistence. The case study analysed here, still pending at the time of writing, highlights several different clashes: the clash between international investment law and domestic regulatory autonomy; the clash between an international economic culture and a local indigenous culture; and the clash between the conservation of endangered species and traditional cultural practices. It remains to be seen how the Arbitral Tribunal will deal with these complex issues.

## *6.7 Full protection and security*

Most international investment treaties contain clauses requiring 'full protection and security' for foreign direct investment. Traditionally, the primary

185 See D. Wagner, 'Competing Cultural Interests in the Whaling Debate: An Exception to the Universality of the Right to Culture', *Transnat'l L. & Contemp. Probs.* 14 (2004), 831.

186 Convention on Conservation of Migratory Species, 23 June 1979, 19 ILM 11, Article 3(5).

187 Interim Convention on Conservation of North Pacific Fur Seals, 9 February 1957, 314 UNTS 105, Article 7.

188 International Convention for the Regulation of Whaling, 2 December 1946, 161 UNTS 72, Article III(13)(b).

objective of the standard has been to protect the investor against the various types of physical violence and adverse effects which may stem from actions of the host state and its organs, or from third parties.[189] In *Burlington v. Ecuador*, the claimant sought, *inter alia*, to hold Ecuador liable for failing to provide physical protection and security for the company's hydrocarbon concession in Blocks 23 and 24 of the Amazonian rain forest.[190] Burlington complained, *inter alia*, that the opposition of indigenous communities to oil development had impeded its business and that Ecuador's purported failure to provide physical security violated the standard of full protection and security under the US–Ecuador BIT.[191]

In its decision on jurisdiction, the Arbitral Tribunal dismissed this specific claim on jurisdictional grounds, stressing the importance of states being put on notice of disputes so that they have the opportunity to remedy a possible breach and thereby avoid arbitration proceedings.[192] Because Burlington failed to give clear notice to Ecuador of its claims for denial of full protection and security, arbitrators ruled that the treaty's mandatory six-month waiting period before arbitration can be initiated, had not run. As a result the claim was declared inadmissible.[193]

## 6.8 *Critical assessment*

Without protection of indigenous cultural heritage all of the other claims of indigenous peoples lose strength. In fact, the protection of the cultural identity of indigenous peoples is at the heart of indigenous peoples' rights and the *raison d'être* of the UNDRIP.[194] According to Stamatopoulou, 'one can find the cultural rights angle in each article of the Declaration'.[195] The increasing interplay between international investment law and other areas of law, including international cultural law and indigenous peoples' rights, serves as a laboratory of confrontation between different values,

[189] R. Dolzer and C. Schreuer, *Principles of International Investment Law* (Oxford University Press, 2008), p. 149.

[190] *Burlington Resources, Inc. v. Republic of Ecuador*, ICSID Case No. ARB/08/5, Decision on Jurisdiction, 2 June 2010 (hereinafter *Burlington Resources*, Decision on Jurisdiction), ¶¶ 27–37.

[191] *Ibid.*, ¶¶ 26 and 53. [192] *Ibid.*, ¶ 315. [193] *Ibid.*, ¶¶ 317 and 336.

[194] F. Francioni, 'The Human Dimension of International Cultural Heritage Law: An Introduction', *EJIL* 22 (2011), 15.

[195] E. Stamatopoulou, 'Taking Cultural Rights Seriously: The Vision of the UN Declaration on the Rights of Indigenous Peoples', in S. Allen and A. Xanthaki (eds.), *Reflections on the UN Declaration on the Rights of Indigenous Peoples* (Oxford: Hart Publishing, 2011), p. 392.

allowing one to shift the discussion about fragmentation from a static to a dynamic and contextual perspective focusing on the interests protected by both bodies of law.

At the procedural level, investor–state arbitration distinguishes between two types of non-state actors: (1) the investor engaged in foreign direct investment; and (2) the affected communities, including indigenous peoples impacted by the investment.[196] While foreign investors have direct access to investor–state arbitration under the relevant BIT, the affected indigenous peoples do not have direct access to these fora; rather their arguments need to be espoused by their governments. While indigenous peoples can (and have) present(ed) *amicus curiae* briefs reflecting their interests, the investment tribunals are not legally obliged to consider such briefs, rather they have the faculty to do so should they deem it appropriate. As Professor Caron puts it, 'the question of whether the state adequately represents the investor-impacted community in a particular proceeding is ultimately a contextual question and depends on the state and community in question'.[197] One may wonder whether indigenous peoples need additional procedural guarantees, due to their special status under international law. Only recently has investment arbitration started to respond positively to requests by public interest groups to make *amicus curiae* submissions.[198] In doing so, some tribunals have decided that the advantages of public debate outweigh the disadvantage of any additional costs and procedural complexity. Furthermore, some arbitral institutions have adopted policies concerning transparency and openness that facilitate public scrutiny. For instance, in *Glamis Gold*, the parties agreed to make the hearing open to the public.[199] The hearing was also broadcast live at the World Bank.[200]

More substantively, international economic fora are tribunals of limited jurisdiction and cannot adjudicate on eventual infringements of indigenous peoples' rights. In the *Glamis Gold* case, the rights of the foreign company and the protection of indigenous cultural heritage were jointly considered, and the Arbitral Tribunal ascertained to what

[196] N. Gal-Or, 'The Investor and Civil Society as Twin Global Citizens: Proposing a New Interpretation in the Legitimacy Debate', *Suffolk Transnational Law Review* 32 (2008–2009), 271–301.

[197] D. D. Caron, 'Investor State Arbitration: Strategic and Tactical Perspectives on Legitimacy', *Suffolk Transnat'l L. Rev.* 32 (2009), 520.

[198] See e.g. C. Knahr, 'Transparency, Third Party Participation and Access to Documents in International Investment Arbitration', *Arbitration International* 23 (2007), 327.

[199] *Glamis Gold*, Award, ¶¶ 102, 121.

[200] ICSID, 'Glamis Gold v. United States of America, Hearings on the Merits', Press release, 13 August 2007.

degree the limitation of the rights of the foreign company was justified by the protection of indigenous cultural heritage.[201] Implicitly, the Arbitral Tribunal deemed that protection of indigenous cultural heritage did not affect the core of investors' rights, but legitimately restricted the periphery of such rights. From an international investment law perspective, the award has to be welcomed as the Arbitral Tribunal 'took an especially sensitive approach in reviewing a state's decision to restrict property rights as a means of protecting non-investment interests'.[202]

From a cultural heritage perspective, however, one may wonder whether the result is fully satisfying. While digging may destroy indigenous cultural artefacts, backfilling may not preserve the sacred value of certain landscapes. If excavation is obviously not possible under Mecca and Jerusalem, which are both pilgrimage destinations for other believers – Jerusalem is also a World Heritage site – one may wonder why the 'Trail of Dreams' which is sacred for indigenous peoples should receive a different treatment.

In the *Grand River* case, the Tribunal referred to the duty of prior consultation with indigenous peoples before the adoption of regulatory measures that may affect them.[203] This is significant as it shows that arbitral tribunals are open to consider non-investment concerns within international investment law while fully respecting their arbitral mandate which requires them to adjudicate only on possible breaches of international investment law. On the other hand, the *Grand River* case also shows that it is primarily the responsibility of states to respect indigenous peoples' entitlements, including their right to participate in the decision-making processes that can affect them.

The duty to consult indigenous peoples as an underpinning principle of indigenous peoples' rights has been recognized by the Inter-American Court of Human Rights and the African Commission on Human and Peoples' Rights.[204] In addition, a number of international law instruments require states to consult indigenous peoples and obtain their consent before undertaking developmental activities which may affect

[201] *Glamis Gold*, Award, ¶ 804.
[202] S. Schill, 'Glamis Gold v. United States', *AJIL* 104 (2010), 257.
[203] *Grand River*, Award, ¶ 210.
[204] According to the IACtHR, the duty to consult is 'a general principle of international law'. *Kichwa Indigenous Community of Sarayaku v. Ecuador*, IACtHR (ser. C) No. 245, 27 June 2012, ¶ 164.

their traditional lands,[205] or before accessing their traditional knowledge.[206] Developers who obtain the consent of local communities may gain a competitive advantage due to the stability of the project. Banks and project developers conceive participatory frameworks as a way to mitigate the security and development of the project. On the other hand, the UNDRIP and a number of human rights instruments frame free, prior and informed consent (FPIC) as a part of indigenous peoples' rights to self-determination. These diverging approaches fuel the debate as to whether indigenous peoples' right to participation in decisions affecting them extends to veto power. When cultural integrity is at stake, such right of indigenous peoples to be consulted becomes veto power.[207] For instance, the Inter-American Court of Human Rights held that with regard to 'large-scale . . . investment projects that would have a major impact' within the territories of indigenous peoples, 'the State has a duty, not only to consult with [indigenous peoples], but also to obtain their free, prior and informed consent, according to their customs and traditions'.[208]

The fact that arbitrators have taken non-investment values into account is significant and praiseworthy, as it shows a trend towards the unity of international law. Nonetheless, the existing case law also pinpoints the sophistication of international investment law and arbitration vis-à-vis other branches of international law and, albeit indirectly,

[205] UNDRIP, Articles 19, 32.2; ILO Convention No. 169 Concerning Indigenous and Tribal Peoples in Independent Countries, 1650 UNTS 383, 27 June 1989, Article 6(1)(a); World Bank Operational Directive 4.10 on Indigenous Peoples (2005), ¶ 1; International Finance Corporation Policy and Performance Standards on Social and Environmental Sustainability (2012) Performance Standard 7.

[206] Nagoya Protocol on Access to Genetic Resources and the Fair and Equitable Sharing of Benefits from their Utilization to the Convention on Biological Diversity, Nagoya, 29 October 2010, Article 7.

[207] International Financial Corporation, Performance Standard 7, ¶¶ 11–2 (requiring the free prior and informed consent of indigenous peoples). General Comment No. 21, 'Right of everyone to take part in cultural life (art. 15, para. 1 (a), of the International Covenant on Economic, Social and Cultural Rights)', UN Doc. E/C.12/GC/21 of 21 December 2009, ¶ 55(e) (States 'should obtain [the] free and informed prior consent [of indigenous peoples] when the preservation of their cultural resources, especially those associated with their way of life and cultural expression, are at risk'). UNDRIP Article 10 ('No relocation shall take place without the free, prior and informed consent of the indigenous peoples concerned').

[208] IACtHR, *Saramaka People v. Suriname*, Judgment of 28 November 2007, ¶ 134; IACtHR, *Mary and Carrie Dann v. United States*, Case No. 11.140, Report No. 75/02, ¶ 131 (2003); *Centre for Minority Rights Development (Kenya) and Minority Rights Group International on behalf of Endorois Welfare Council v. Kenya*, 276/2003, ¶ 291.

highlights the gaps of other branches of international law (e.g. the lack of an institutional dispute settlement mechanism for cultural heritage-related disputes, or the lack of consultation mechanisms with indigenous peoples for matters which can affect their interests). Furthermore, there is a risk of 'epistemological misappropriation', i.e. that arbitrators develop lines of arguments concerning the protection of indigenous cultural heritage which are divergent from mainstream international cultural law and human rights law, diluting the protection of cultural heritage and indigenous peoples' rights vis-à-vis economic development needs.[209]

The fact that some arbitrators have been former judges of the International Court of Justice, UN experts, and are distinguished professors of international law may facilitate the dialogue between international investment law and international law. For instance, in the *Grand River* case, Professor James Anaya – the UN Special Rapporteur on the Rights of Indigenous Peoples – acted as arbitrator. However, given the fact that the composition of arbitral tribunals varies, it is not possible to give a general answer to the question as to whether all of the arbitrators have the expertise to fully appreciate non-investment concerns.

In conclusion, there seems to be an attempt by arbitral tribunals to be responsive to broader societal concerns and to allow conceptual fluidity between international investment law and public international law protecting indigenous heritage. Nonetheless, international investment law and arbitration may not structurally be the forum best equipped to adequately protect indigenous cultural entitlements due to the limited participatory tools granted to indigenous peoples and the limited mandate of arbitral tribunals which can only adjudicate on investment treaty claims.

## Conclusions

The interplay between the promotion of foreign direct investment on the one hand and the protection of indigenous cultural heritage on the other in international investment law and arbitration is an almost unexplored field. The case studies presented here provide a snapshot of the clash of cultures between international economic governance and indigenous

[209] P. Alston, 'Resisting the Merger and Acquisition of Human Rights by Trade Law: A Reply to Petersmann', *EJIL* 13 (2002), 815–44 (cautioning against 'embracing the human rights agenda from within the citadel of international economic law', *ibid.*, at 815–16).

heritage. They also highlight a fundamental clash between local and global dimensions of regulation. Indigenous heritage is local, it belongs to specific places; economic governance has an international character. At the same time, indigenous heritage also belongs to the international discourse; in this sense, the UNDRIP and other international law instruments have recognized the importance of indigenous culture, highlighting the fundamental linkage between cultural identity and the human rights of indigenous peoples.

This chapter has investigated the impact of foreign direct investment on indigenous cultural heritage scrutinizing and critically assessing the relevant investment treaty arbitrations. Such arbitrations show that indigenous cultural heritage can be endangered by FDI and that while investor–state arbitration depoliticizes international disputes, it may not be the most suitable forum for the settlement of disputes involving indigenous cultural entitlements. Being tribunals of limited jurisdiction, arbitral tribunals cannot adjudicate on state violations of indigenous peoples' entitlements. In parallel, the fact that such disputes are adjudicated before investment treaty tribunals may ultimately pinpoint the sophistication of international investment law and arbitration vis-à-vis international cultural law and – albeit indirectly – some failures of the latter. International cultural law maintains the centrality of the state as the right-holder and primary bearer of international obligations. The fact that international cultural law remains defined by state interests has implications for the identification of the type of cultural heritage to be protected and the way such heritage is governed.

At the procedural level, arbitration rules of procedure are not sufficiently developed to adequately protect indigenous peoples' rights. The participation of indigenous peoples as *amici curiae* at arbitral proceedings is not automatically granted, and arbitral proceedings involving cultural heritage have not always been open to the public. Only recently has investment arbitration started to respond positively to the requests by public interest groups to make *amicus curiae* submissions and adopt policies concerning transparency and openness that facilitate public scrutiny.

At the substantive level, the fact that arbitrators have taken non-investment values into account is remarkable, as it shows a trend towards the unity of international law. There seems to be an attempt by arbitral tribunals to be responsive to broader societal concerns and to allow conceptual fluidity between international investment law and international cultural law protecting indigenous heritage. The fact that some arbitrators have been former judges of the International Court of

Justice, UN experts, and are professors of international law can facilitate the dialogue between international investment law and international law. However, international investment law and arbitration may not structurally be the most suitable forum to adequately protect indigenous cultural entitlements due to the limited jurisdiction of arbitral tribunals. Furthermore, there is a risk of arbitrators interpreting and applying international cultural law restrictively, developing lines of arguments divergent from mainstream international law.

In conclusion, while FDI can represent a potentially positive force for development, state policy and practice concerning economic activities must be mindful of its implications for the culture of indigenous peoples. Some places should be off limits to development as we know it.

# PART III

# Investing in culture

# Investing in culture

> The reconciliation of the irreconcilable, the merger of antitheses, the synthesis of opposites, these are the great problems of law.[1]

## Introduction

This book scrutinizes the interplay between international investment law and international cultural law as a case study of the interaction between international investment law and general international law, shifting the discussion about fragmentation in international law from a static to a dynamic and contextual perspective. Part I focused on the definition and connection of the two fields of study. Part II analysed and critically assessed the relevant investment treaty arbitrations. Part III offers insights about how international investment law should be interpreted and applied to foster its humanization and the unity of international law.

[1] B. Cardozo, *The Paradoxes of Legal Science* (New York: Columbia University Press, 1928), p. 4.

# 7

# Investing in culture

## Introduction

In recent years international cultural law and international investment law have increasingly intersected. The disparity between the two fields of law has made their interaction particularly uneven. International cultural law has only emerged after the Second World War in a piecemeal fashion, through a series of international conventions and the formation of customs. This branch of law lacks a dispute settlement mechanism. By contrast, international investment law constitutes a well-developed part of public international law and presents a sophisticated dispute settlement mechanism.

Are investment treaties compatible with states' obligations to protect cultural heritage? At the substantive level, investment treaties provide extensive protection of investors' rights in order to encourage foreign direct investment. At the procedural level, investment treaties offer investors direct access to an international arbitral tribunal. Thus, a potential tension exists when a state adopts cultural policies interfering with foreign investments. Foreign investors can (and have) directly challenge(d) national measures allegedly aimed at protecting cultural heritage before arbitral tribunals, seeking compensation for the impact of such regulation on their business.

Far from being self-contained regimes,[1] international cultural law and international investment law have increasingly intersected. While these areas of international law reflect the increasing specialization of this area of the law, and the progressive 'legalisation of world politics',[2] they are

[1] The term 'self-contained regime' was first used by the PCIJ in the *Wimbledon* case to determine the relationship between conflicting treaty provisions, *Case of the SS Wimbledon (United Kingdom, France, Italy and Japan v. Germany)* PCIJ Reports Series A No. 1 at 23–24. The ICJ used the expression in a different context. *Diplomatic and Consular Staff in Teheran Case (United States v. Iran)* 1980 ICJ Reports 40, at ¶ 86.

[2] M. Prost, *The Concept of Unity in Public International Law* (Oxford: Hart Publishing, 2012), p. 4.

not separate from international law; rather they maintain continuity with their matrix. There seems to be osmosis and reciprocal conceptual fluidity between international law and its sub-systems.

On the one hand, the contained systems are contributing to the development of the container system. Investment treaty arbitration plays an active role in the development of the substantive and procedural content of international law. The contributions of this process include the emergence of investors' direct claims before international arbitral tribunals, which has contributed to the increasing obsolescence of diplomatic protection; the clarification of rules relating to treaty interpretation; and the same interpretation of treaty and customary norms relating to the protection of aliens to mention a few.

More interestingly, through their constant interactions, international investment law and international cultural law are continuously contributing to the development of international law itself. Arbitral tribunals are building an ongoing dialogue and borrowing of concepts between international investment law and international cultural law, contributing to the current debate on the unity or fragmentation of international law, and supporting the argument that international law, albeit decentralized, is not an anarchic amalgam of different norms, rather it has a structure similar to a system.[3] Arguably, these developments have implications for some of the assumptions on which international law has traditionally been based. On the other hand, the container system is contributing to the development of the contained systems, and arbitral tribunals constantly refer to international law cases and principles in their awards.

To say that there is *continuity* between international law on the one hand, and international investment law and international cultural law on the other, does not imply a sort of *pre-established harmony* between the system and its sub-systems. Rather, in considering the fluidity of the international legal order and its vitality,[4] it is up to the interpreters to act as cartographers of international law and to find the appropriate

[3] The notion of legal system or legal order was famously articulated by Santi Romano. For Romano, the legal system was not only a set of norms, but it was the unit comprising these rules and a specific social constituency. As international law governs the relations of a social body, namely the international community, international law is a legal system. S. Romano, *L'ordinamento giuridico*, 2nd edn (Firenze: Sansoni, 1946). Because distinct sets of rules of international law are not applied to distinct social entities, 'they cannot give rise to different independent legal systems'. O. Casanovas, *Unity and Pluralism in Public International Law* (The Hague: Martinus Nijhoff Publishers, 2001), p. 67.

[4] B. Conforti, 'Unité et Fragmentation du droit international: Glissez, mortels, n'appuyez pas!', *RGDIP* 111 (2007), 5–18.

equilibrium within the system. The unity of international law is a dynamic concept, presenting inherent tensions. International law is a legal matrix where different kinds of regulation based on different epistemological roots are crossed and may clash.

Against this background, this chapter explores the number of policy options that may help policy-makers and adjudicators to reconcile the different interests at stake. The chapter is divided into two parts. The first part explores the mechanisms that *de lege lata* can help relevant stakeholders to settle disputes with cultural elements, and focuses on negotiation, applicable law, treaty interpretation, standards of review and reconciliation of norms. The second part of the chapter explores the mechanisms that *de lege ferenda* can prevent such disputes and is divided into two sub-sections dealing with cultural exceptions and cultural impact assessments respectively. The conclusions will then sum up the key findings of the study.

## A. *De lege lata*

### 7.1 Negotiating cultural disputes

Disputes involving cultural heritage often raise complex political, social and ethical issues.[5] While 'adjudication is not designed to address extra-legal issues' which are deemed non-justiciable,[6] alternative dispute resolution (ADR) methods (that is, alternative to judicial settlement) can be suited to resolve complex disputes involving political, social, cultural and ethical interests.

BITs typically include a three to six month 'cooling-off period' for consultation and negotiation before a claim may be brought.[7] The period runs from the date when the dispute arose or when the host state was formally notified by the investor. The practical purpose of the 'cooling off period' is twofold. On the one hand, the host state is granted the right to be informed about the dispute and 'an opportunity to redress the

[5] J. A. R. Nafziger, R. K. Paterson, and A. Dundes Renteln, *Cultural Law: International, Comparative and Indigenous* (Cambridge University Press, 2010), p. 605.

[6] A. Spain, 'Integration Matters: Rethinking the Architecture of International Dispute Resolution', *University of Pennsylvania JIL* 32 (2010–2011), 16.

[7] See, for instance, US–Ecuador BIT, Article VI. Treaty between the United States of America and the Republic of Ecuador Concerning the Encouragement and Reciprocal Protection of Investment, 27 August 1993, in force 11 May 1997.

problem' before the eventual arbitration.[8] On the other hand, the cooling-off period can facilitate settlement before positions become entrenched.[9] While the obligation to negotiate is an obligation of means, not of results,[10] failure to observe a treaty's cooling-off period results in a tribunal declining jurisdiction. Negotiations can take place even after the cooling-off period; although complete statistics are not available due to confidentiality, it is estimated that almost one-third of ICSID cases and almost two-thirds of ICC cases are settled by negotiation.[11]

Negotiation is based on cooperative and interest-based approaches. In abstract terms, it creates a situation where the parties cooperate to reach a satisfactory result. Agreement can often be reached if both parties look at their underlying interests. Negotiation may also produce more successful outcomes than the adversarial 'winner takes all' approach.[12]

Negotiation has proven to be a strategic tool to enhance cultural heritage protection while allowing economic activities. For instance, when the Yellowstone National Park, which is a World Heritage site, was added to the Danger List in 1995, due to the proposed development of a gold and copper mine three miles outside the Park boundary, negotiation allowed the US government to eliminate the threat to the Park, while creatively swapping the investor's property rights.[13]

Similarly, in Germany, after strenuous litigation before national courts, the local community was able to negotiate the relocation of a fortified ancient church as part of an investment deal.[14] By the end of 2008 the complete town of Heuersdorf in Saxony had to make way for a lignite mine, to fuel a nearby power plant.[15] Although the local inhabitants could not save their village, they saved the 750-year-old

[8] *Burlington Resources Inc. v. Republic of Ecuador*, ICSID Case No. ARB/08/5, Decision on Jurisdiction of 2 June 2010, ¶ 31.

[9] *Murphy Exploration and Production Company International v. Republic of Ecuador*, ICSID Case No. ARB/08/4, Award on Jurisdiction, 15 December 2010, at ¶¶ 151 and 154.

[10] *Ibid.*, ¶ 135.

[11] J. Salacuse, 'The Emerging Global Regime for Investment', *Harvard ILJ* (2010), 459.

[12] R. Fisher and W. Ury, *Getting to Yes: Negotiating Agreement Without Giving In* (New York: Penguin Books, 1983).

[13] D. L. Gebert, 'Sovereignty Under the World Heritage Convention: A Questionable Basis for Limiting Federal Land Designation Pursuant to International Agreements', *Southern California Interdisciplinary Law Journal* 7 (1998–1999), 428.

[14] 'A Holy Journey: Church Moved to Make Way to Coal Mine', *Spiegel Online*, 24 October 2007.

[15] Constitutional Court of Saxony, Judgment of 25 November 2005, Vf. 119-VIII-09. Retrieved from: www.justiz.sachsen.de/esaver/internet/2004_119_VIII/2004_119_VIII.pdf

*Emmauskirche* (Emmaus Church) which was relocated to the nearby town of Borna. The US mining company had the chance to exploit its investment, albeit ultimately agreeing to pay the transplantation costs.[16]

The images of the church's journey have definitely crossed boundaries, capturing the imagination of thousands of people and making headlines worldwide.[17] While some heritage scholars contend that cultural heritage should be preserved in its original environment, others, more pragmatically, accept the possibility of relocation for the sake of pre-eminent public interests. To the former inhabitants of Heuersdorf, the Emmaus Church epitomizes the eight-centuries-old history of their small village, and reminds them of their lost *Heimat* (home). For the locals, the Emmaus Church symbolizes the numerous German towns and churches that have given way to mineral exploitation during the past decades. For foreigners, such an event exemplifies the apparent resilience of cultural heritage vis-à-vis powerful economic imperatives.

Conciliation and mediation may also play a useful role in cultural heritage-related disputes. Where the degree of animosity between the parties is so great that direct negotiations are unlikely to lead to a dispute settlement, the intervention of a third party to reconcile the parties may be very practical.[18] In this sense, a number of institutions provide the institutional and procedural framework for conciliation, including UNCITRAL, the International Chamber of Commerce and the ICSID, although conciliation has been used sparingly.[19]

Mediation of foreign investment disputes is also possible.[20] Mediation involves the good offices of a neutral third party which facilitates communication between the discussants.[21] Like negotiation, mediation is guided by the goal of finding a win-win situation for all parties through a process that focuses on the interests of the parties rather than on their positions, and searches for creative alternatives to solve the dispute. The Multilateral Investment Guarantee Agency (MIGA), a member of the

16 'A Holy Journey'.

17 See V. Vadi, *Culture Clash: Investors' Rights v. Cultural Heritage in International Investment Law & Arbitration*, SIEL Working Paper, June 2012, 18.

18 J. Collier and V. Lowe, *The Settlement of Disputes in International Law* (Oxford University Press, 2000), p. 27.

19 C. Schreuer, *The ICSID Convention: A Commentary* (Cambridge University Press, 2001), p. 416.

20 S. Schwebel, 'Is Mediation of Foreign Disputes Plausible?', in S. Schwebel, *Justice in International Law* (Cambridge University Press, 2011), pp. 318–22.

21 J. Salacuse, 'Is There a Better Way? Alternative Methods of Treaty Based, Investor-State Dispute Resolution', *Fordham ILJ* 31 (2007–2008), 161.

World Bank Group, has been mediating disputes between investors on the one hand and host states on the other to help resolve investment claims resulting from state measures.[22]

In illustrating the merits of mediation, Professor Scott Rau exemplified the diplomatic method of dispute settlement with the parable of two children, each of whom wants a single orange.[23] Three possible solutions come to mind. The first solution entails allocating the orange to the child with 'greater rights' to the orange. This is the strictly legal approach that would be the outcome of the arbitration. The second solution is to divide the orange in two parts and award half of the orange to each child. The third solution investigates the reasons why the children want the orange. After verifying that one wants the pulp of the orange for orange juice, and the other wants the orange peel for preparing a cake, the third solution proposes the appealing compromise of allocating the pulp to one child, while awarding the skin to the other. The satisfaction of both parties is maximized, as the settlement constitutes a more-than-zero-sum game. As the mediator does not have the authority to make a binding decision and does not follow a fixed procedure, she may promote flexible and dynamic dialogue. Furthermore, mediation might involve the participation of other stakeholders.[24]

ADR methods present a number of intrinsic advantages. First, they usually achieve results in a short time frame. Second, they are not required to deal with the past: they ask the parties to look at their future and reshape their duties and responsibilities towards each other. Third, foreign investors participate in the decision-making process that will ultimately affect them, becoming aware of local interests. In these proceedings all the different interests concerned are disclosed and discussed. Experience shows that agreements entered into through a voluntary process stand out for their durability. The underlying reason is that the parties strongly identify with the achieved result which is perceived as fair. Finally, the confidentiality characterizing ADR mechanisms allows the parties to focus on the underlying interests of a given dispute.

22 V. Vadi, 'Converging Divergences: The Rise of Chinese Outward Foreign Investment and Its Implications for International (Investment) Law', *Yearbook of International Investment Law* (2011–2012), 716.

23 A. S. Rau, 'Mediation in Art-Related Disputes', in Q. Byrne-Sutton and F. Geisinger-Mariéthoz (eds.), *Resolution Methods for Art Related Disputes* (Zurich: Schultess Verlag, 1999), p. 157.

24 A. Crocker Chester *et al.*, *Herding Cats: Multiparty Mediation in a Complex World* (Washington D.C.: United States Institute of Peace, 1999).

However, ADR methods also present a number of limits. First, the confidential nature of these methods makes documenting their use and lessons learned difficult.[25] Second, the parties to a given investment dispute may be 'disinclined to subject disputes between them' to ADR mechanisms 'primarily because bureaucracies, governmental and corporate, may be reluctant to assume responsibility for accepting the provisions of a mediated settlement which afford them less than their publicly voiced demands'.[26] Third, while ADR methods can be useful in those situations where both contracting parties have equal or similar bargaining power, such methods do not seem to be advisable when there are power asymmetries. This is particularly the case when the cultural heritage in question is associated with indigenous peoples and minorities, for such groups have often been disregarded by the relevant state authorities in the race to attract foreign investment.[27] Without adequate safeguards, ADR may fail to address power imbalances. Furthermore, in prioritizing the interests of the parties present, there is a concern that ADR methods cannot adequately ensure that the disputes are settled 'in conformity with the principles of justice and international law' including 'universal respect for, and observance of, human rights and fundamental freedoms for all'.[28]

Next, from a political science perspective, the spectre of a potential dispute with a powerful investor can exert a chilling effect on government's decisions to regulate in the public interest. For instance, in 2002, a group of mainly foreign-owned mining companies threatened to commence international arbitration against the government of Indonesia in response to its ban on open-pit mining in protected forests.[29] Six months later, the Ministry of Forestry agreed to change the forest designation from *protected* to *production* forests.[30] In this problematic context, a legal approach is very much needed.

In conclusion, ADR can be cheaper and less time-consuming, preserving the relations between the investor and the host state.[31] For instance, Professor Salacuse reports that in the *Pyramids* case, the state authorities

[25] Spain, 'Integration Matters', 23.
[26] Schwebel, 'Is Mediation of Foreign Disputes Plausible?'.
[27] See C. Rodríguez-Garavito, 'Ethnicity.gov: Global Governance, Indigenous Peoples, and the Right to Prior Consultation in Social Minefields', *Indiana J. Global Legal Studies* 18 (2011), 299.
[28] Vienna Convention on the Law of Treaties (VCLT), 23 May 1969, in force 27 January 1980, 1155 UNTS 331, preamble.
[29] See S. Grass, Note, 'Inordinate Chill: BITs, Non-NAFTA MITs and Host-State Regulatory Freedom: An Indonesian Case Study', *Michigan JIL* 24 (2003), 894.
[30] *Ibid.* [31] Salacuse, 'Is There a Better Way?', 176.

ended up paying higher damages after they refused a tentative settlement.[32] Such methods can provide more flexibility than arbitration in enabling the consideration of legal, cultural, economic and ethical questions raised by cultural heritage-related disputes. Creative solutions can include land swaps and/or rerouting of investment projects.

However, when assessing the merit of ADR mechanisms, several factors require delicate assessment. ADR mechanisms should not be meant as a tool for diluting the host state's obligations under international law or as a delaying tactic. In some cases, it may be better to have recourse to arbitration because its outcome can contribute to the development of international (investment) law and can inhibit further spurious claims on the part of the investor, or illegal misconduct on the part of the state.[33] Finally, ADR mechanisms are not suitable when there is uneven bargaining power between the parties.

## 7.2 Corporate responsibility to respect cultural heritage

The idea of corporate responsibility under international law is relatively recent,[34] but has increasingly become influential and gained momentum since the inception of the *Protect, Respect and Remedy Framework for Business and Human Rights*, initiated by Professor Ruggie, the Special Representative of the Secretary-General on the issue of human rights and transnational corporations and other business enterprises, and unanimously adopted by the UN Human Rights Council in 2008.[35] The UN Framework has three pillars: first, states have the duty to protect against human rights abuses by third parties – including business – through appropriate policies. Second, businesses have the responsibility to respect human rights, that is, to avoid infringing the rights of others and to address adverse impacts. As Ruggie puts it: 'To respect rights essentially means not to infringe the rights of others – put simply, to do no harm. Because companies can affect virtually all internationally recognized rights, they should consider the

[32] *Ibid.* [33] *Ibid.*, 179.

[34] R. De Vietri, 'Incorporating Humanity and the Global Economy: The Law of International Investment and Human Rights', *International Trade and Business Law Review* 15 (2012), 216–17.

[35] J. Ruggie, *Protect, Respect and Remedy: A Framework for Business and Human Rights*, Report of the Special Representative of the Secretary General on the Issue of Human Rights and Transnational Corporations and Other Business Enterprises (Protect, Respect and Remedy Framework Report), 7 April 2008, A/HRC/8/5 (2008).

responsibility to respect in relation to all such rights.'[36] In particular, companies should exercise due diligence, 'not only ensur[ing] compliance with national laws'[37] but also doing no harm, taking positive steps[38] and adopting a human rights policy.[39] Third, affected parties should have access to effective remedies.[40] As Ruggie has correctly pointed out, 'markets work optimally only if they are embedded within rules, customs and institutions'.[41] The corporate responsibility to respect human rights is recognized in a few soft law instruments including the OECD Guidelines for Multinational Enterprises[42] and the UN Guiding Principles of Business and Human Rights.[43]

Of particular interest are the OECD Guidelines for Multinational Enterprises – non-binding recommendations providing principles and standards for responsible business conduct for multinational corporations operating in or from countries which have adhered to the OECD Declaration on International Investment and Multinational Enterprises.[44] The National Contact Points (NCPs) constitute their implementation mechanism: they aim to encourage observance of the Guidelines in a given national context and to promote awareness of these soft law norms by the companies and other interested parties. NCPs also deal with the so-called 'specific instances', i.e. complaints, providing a mediation and conciliation platform for resolving issues that may arise with the implementation of the Guidelines. Some NCPs are based in a relevant government department; others are independent structures comprising government officials, trade unions, employer unions and sometimes NGOs.

NCPs have mediated a number of cases dealing with indigenous cultural heritage providing an alternative way to settle emerging disputes between local communities and foreign investors, and facilitating dialogue and communication between the parties.[45] Companies may voluntarily decide to comply with the recommendation of the NCP in order to maintain reputation. In this sense, NCPs provide a fast and

[36] *Ibid.*, ¶ 24. [37] *Ibid.*, ¶ 25. [38] *Ibid.*, ¶ 55. [39] *Ibid.*, ¶ 60. [40] *Ibid.*, ¶ 4.

[41] *Ibid.*, ¶ 2.

[42] OECD Guidelines for Multinational Enterprises, available at www.oecd.org/daf/inv/mne/48004323.pdf.

[43] Guiding Principles on Business and Human Rights: Implementing the United Nations 'Protect, Respect and Remedy' Framework, 21 March 2011, A/HRC/17/31. The Human Rights Council endorsed the Guiding Principles in its resolution 17/4 *Human Rights and Transnational Corporations and Other Business Enterprises* of 6 July 2011. A/HRC/RES/17/4.

[44] 1976 *OECD Declaration on International Investment and Multinational Enterprises*, available on the OECD website.

[45] See e.g. OECD, *Quarterly Case Update*, November 2010, 2–8.

inexpensive direct avenue for local communities affected by the activities of foreign companies. However, in cases in which the companies did not adhere to the recommendation of the NCPs, national courts and human rights courts remain available avenues.

Recently, a growing number of companies have committed themselves to respect for cultural law, and to abiding by a 'cultural heritage duty of care'.[46] Some have even recognized World Heritage sites as territories off-limits to mining and similar economic activities.[47] For instance, the International Council on Mining and Metals (ICMM) – an organization bringing together a number of mining and metals companies as well as national and regional mining associations – released its Position Statement on Mining and Protected Areas, according to which its companies undertook 'not to explore or mine in World Heritage properties' and to ensure that 'existing operations in World Heritage properties as well as existing and future operations adjacent to World Heritage properties, are not incompatible with the outstanding universal value for which these properties are listed, and do not put the integrity of these properties at risk'.[48] Furthemore, the Sustainable Development Framework elaborated by the ICMM requires signatory companies to 'respect the culture and heritage of local communities, including indigenous peoples'.[49]

In parallel, bank and insurance companies are increasingly refraining from financing extractive industries in World Heritage sites.[50] The International Finance Corporation (IFC)[51] Performance Standard 8, which applies to companies seeking loans from the IFC, provides comprehensive guidelines for best practice in cultural heritage management, 'regardless of whether or not it has been legally protected or previously disturbed'.[52] Performance Standard 8 requires IFC clients to 'compl[y]

[46] See N. A. Bainton, C. Ballard, K. Gillespie and N. Hall, 'Stepping Stones across the Lihir Islands: Developing Cultural Heritage Management in the Context of Gold-Mining Operation', *International Journal of Cultural Property* 18 (2011), 88 (internal references omitted).

[47] N. Affolder, 'The Private Life of Environmental Treaties', *AJIL* 103 (2009), 510.

[48] International Council on Mining and Metals (ICMM), Position Statement: Mining and Protected Areas, Commitment, 20 August 2003, at www.icmm.com/document/43.

[49] ICMM, Sustainable Development Framework, principle 3 available at www.icmm.com/our-work/sustainable-development-framework/10-principles.

[50] Affolder, 'The Private Life of Environmental Treaties', 519.

[51] IFC Articles of Agreement, 25 May 1955, 264 UNTS 118.

[52] 2012 IFC Performance Standards, available at www1.ifc.org/wps/wcm/connect/c8f524004a73daeca09afdf998895a12/IFC_Performance_Standards.pdf?MOD=AJPERES, Performance Standard 8(5).

with applicable law on the protection of cultural heritage, including national law implementing the host country's obligations under the Convention Concerning the Protection of the World Cultural and Natural Heritage', and to 'identify and protect cultural heritage by ensuring that internationally recognized practices for the protection . . . of cultural heritage are implemented'.[53] Emphasis is put on consultation with affected communities.[54] In parallel, Performance Standard 7, which applies to indigenous peoples,[55] states that:

> where a project may significantly impact on critical cultural heritage that is essential to the identity and/or cultural, ceremonial, or spiritual aspects of Indigenous Peoples' lives, priority will be given to the avoidance of such impacts. Where significant project impacts on critical cultural heritage are unavoidable, the client will obtain the [free prior informed consent] of the Affected Communities of Indigenous Peoples.[56]

In addition, the same standard also clarifies that 'clients must comply with applicable national law, including those laws implementing host country obligations under international law'.[57] As Hoffman highlights, by including high standards of heritage conservation in the lending documents, the lender stimulates companies to conform to conservation standards.[58] However, the impact of these standards has been limited 'in part because [the relevant bodies] sometimes fail to apply their own standards and in part because these bodies do not always enforce them once applied'.[59]

Firm-specific policies have been adopted as well. Compliance with cultural entitlements can build positive relations with local communities, contributing to the security of the investment, and the reputation of the investor. Affolder highlights that the WHC is being internalized by companies as a standard for appropriate conduct, noting that 'of the twenty largest mining companies, eleven now recognize World Heritage sites as no-go areas'.[60] Multinational companies have also paid

[53] *Ibid.*, ¶ 6. [54] *Ibid.*, ¶ 9. [55] IFC Performance Standard 7. [56] *Ibid.*, ¶ 16.

[57] *Ibid.*, footnote 1.

[58] B. Hoffman, 'A Consideration of Cultural and Natural Heritage Guidelines Applicable to Infrastructure Projects, Mining Operations, and Their Financing', in B. Hoffman (ed.), *Art and Cultural Heritage: Law, Policy and Practice* (Cambridge University Press, 2009), p. 243.

[59] G. K. Foster, 'Foreign Investment and Indigenous Peoples: Options for Promoting Equilibrium between Economic Development and Indigenous Rights', *Michigan JIL* 33 (2012), 663; G. A. Sarfaty, 'The World Bank and the Internalization of Indigenous Rights Norms', *Yale Law Journal* 114 (2005), 1802.

[60] Affolder, 'The Private Life of Environmental Treaties', 515–16.

increasing attention to the cultural concerns of the host state. For instance, when a Chinese corporation leased land and planned to develop an iron mine on the site of Wilgie Mia in Australia, concerns arose with regard to the protection of indigenous cultural heritage.[61] Wilgie Mia is of great cultural significance to indigenous Australians who extract red ochre from the site to use it in ceremonies, healing practices and pictographic rock art.[62] Desert cultures believe red ochre to be the blood of ancestral beings.[63] Perhaps aware of the potential for damaging publicity, a chief operating officer of the company stated that the company will not mine 'some sites of very strong significance' and that it 'cannot afford to get this wrong'.[64] It remains to be seen whether and how Wilgie Mia and its significance for Aborigines will be conserved as the project moves forward.

In Sicily, notwithstanding obligations under the World Heritage Convention to protect and preserve the Noto Valley site – a fine example of Baroque architectural style – local authorities granted a Texan investor, Panther Oil, a concession to drill gas in the Valley.[65] The Noto Valley is characterized by a number of 'stunning Baroque church[es], honey-colored or pale white' which were rebuilt 'in the wake of a devastating earthquake in 1693'.[66] Considered to be 'a defiant answer to nature's wrath, an ambitious affirmation of wealth and faith',[67] the site remains in permanent danger of earthquakes and Etna's eruptions. Against this background, drilling is risky in that it could cause an environmental collapse.[68] Because a regional administrative court had confirmed the permission to drill in the area, the Italian government declared its willingness to override Sicily's autonomy and to stop the project. This intervention was not needed, however, as Panther Oil decided to reduce the number of wells planned in the region and to avoid the Val di Noto.[69] In conclusion, multinational companies have

[61] G. Lloyd, 'Wilgie Mia Mine Site Will Test China's Iron Will', *The Australian*, 4 January 2011.

[62] *Ibid.*

[63] P. Cleary, 'Heritage Status for WA Ochre Mine Site', *The Australian*, 8 March 2011.

[64] S. Sackur, 'Australian Resources Key to Booming China', BBC News, 12 April 2011.

[65] T. J. Puleo, 'Baroque Disruptions in Val di Noto', *Geographical Review* 100 (2010), 476–93.

[66] C. Bohlen, 'Joyous Design Defies Nature in Sicily', *International Herald Tribune*, 1–2 June 2013, at 23.

[67] *Ibid.* [68] S. Aloisi, 'Gas War Rages in Sicilian Baroque Valley', *Reuters*, 7 June 2007.

[69] 'Sicilian Valley Wins Battle against Gas Wells', *Reuters*, 17 June 2007.

paid increasing attention to the cultural concerns of the host state. However, the number of such initiatives is still too limited.

## 7.3 The applicable law in investor–state arbitration

Investment disputes are to be resolved on the basis of law, unless the parties have expressly agreed otherwise.[70] Several BITs contain a composite choice of law clause, typically including treaty rules, host state law and customary international law. For instance, the 2012 US Model BIT[71] provides that in certain cases, 'the tribunal shall decide the issues in dispute in accordance with this Treaty and applicable rules of international law'.[72] Article 1131 of NAFTA similarly states that: 'A Tribunal established under this Section shall decide the issues in dispute in accordance with this Agreement and applicable rules of international law.'[73] For cases brought before ICSID, the ICSID Convention provides that a tribunal will apply the law selected by the parties or, in the absence of such a choice, the law of the host country and such principles of international law as are applicable.[74]

Such clauses do not extend the jurisdiction of the arbitral tribunals. Arbitral tribunals are of limited jurisdiction, and cannot adjudicate on claims based on different treaty regimes. If they did so, their award would be *ultra vires* or *extra fines mandati* and could be challenged under Article V of the New York Convention,[75] or, if the case were to be adjudicated at the ICSID, under Article 52(1)(c) of the ICSID Convention on the grounds that it had 'manifestly exceeded its powers'.[76] In *Grand River*, the Arbitral Tribunal affirmed: 'This is a Tribunal of limited jurisdiction; it has no mandate to decide claims based on treaties other than NAFTA.'[77] The Arbitral Tribunal expressly quoted the warning of the *Methanex* Tribunal: 'interpreting Article 1131(1) [of the NAFTA] to create a jurisdiction extending beyond Section A of Chapter 11 would indeed be to transform it ... into an unqualified and

[70] O. Spiermann, 'Applicable Law', in P. Muchlinski, F. Ortino and C. Schreuer (eds.), *The Oxford Handbook of International Investment Law* (Oxford University Press, 2008), p. 92.

[71] Treaty Between the Government of the United States of America and the Government of [Country] Concerning the Encouragement and Reciprocal Protection of Investment.

[72] *Ibid.*, Article 30(1). [73] NAFTA, Article 1131(1).

[74] ICSID Convention, Article 42. [75] New York Convention, Article V.

[76] ICSID Convention, Article 52(1)(c). [77] *Grand River v. United States*, Award, ¶ 71.

comprehensive jurisdictional regime, in which there would be no limit *ratione materiae* to the jurisdiction of a tribunal established under Chapter 11'.[78]

If the jurisdictional mandate of an arbitral tribunal is clearly limited, why have treaty-makers inserted clauses referring to 'applicable rules of international law'? Persuasively, eminent authors have argued that international law should always apply, as either national law is consistent with it, or if it is not, then international law supersedes national law.[79] When the constitution of the host state opts for monism granting primacy to public international law, the latter permeates the law applicable to the contract. Even in states which adopt the dualist theory and require international law norms to be 'translated' into national ones, arbitrators apply norms of international law when they apply the national norms which convey them. As Professor Kreindler points out, 'Thus, even where the parties have not agreed, directly or indirectly, to the application of international law "rules" or "principles", international law may already be internally applicable as part of the domestic law chosen by the parties.'[80]

In the case *Maffezini v. Spain*, the choice of law clause in the Argentina–Spain BIT[81] expressly mentioned the applicability of the law of the host state.[82] In this case, an Argentine investor complained, *inter alia*, that the Spanish authorities had pressured the company to make the investment before the Environmental Impact Assessment (EIA) process was finalized and before its implications were known. Therefore, according to the claimant, the Spanish authorities would have been responsible for the additional costs resulting from the EIA.

[78] *Ibid.*, citing *Methanex Corp. v. United States*, UNCITRAL NAFTA Tribunal, Final Award on Jurisdiction and Merits, 3 August 2005, Part II, Chapter B, ¶ 5. See also *Biloune and Marine Drive Complex v. Ghana*, UNCITRAL ad hoc Tribunal, Award on Jurisdiction and Liability, 27 October 1989, 95 ILR 184, 203.

[79] See e.g. P. M. Dupuy, 'Unification Rather than Fragmentation of International Law? The Case of International Investment Law and Human Rights Law', in P. M. Dupuy, F. Francioni and E. U. Petersmann (eds.), *Human Rights in International Investment Law and Arbitration* (Oxford University Press, 2009), p. 25.

[80] R. H. Kreindler, 'The Law Applicable to International Investment Disputes', in N. Horn (ed.), *Arbitrating Foreign Investment Disputes* (The Hague: Kluwer Law International, 2004), pp. 413–14.

[81] Argentina–Spain BIT, 3 October 1991, in force 28 September 1992, available at the UNCTAD website.

[82] *Emilio Agustin Maffezini v. Kingdom of Spain*, ICSID Case No. ARB/97/7, Decision on Jurisdiction, 25 January 2000, ¶ 19.

Spain replied that the investor should be aware of the EIA requirement under Spanish and European Law, and in fact was aware of such requirement. The Arbitral Tribunal dismissed the claims concerning the EIA: 'the environmental impact assessment procedure is basic for adequate protection of the environment and the application of appropriate environmental measures. This is true not only under Spanish and EEC Law, but also increasingly so under international law.'[83]

If the host state that is party to the investment treaty dispute has ratified a relevant UNESCO Convention, the pertinent provisions of the given UNESCO Convention would become relevant. In the *Glamis Gold* case, the fact that the US is a party to the WHC was of relevance; the arbitrators took the WHC into account when considering the protection that the US afforded to indigenous cultural heritage, citing Article 12 of the WHC which refers to the protection of cultural heritage sites that are not listed on the World Heritage List. The Tribunal pointed out: 'The Convention makes special note that the fact of a site's non-inclusion on the register does not signify its failure to possess "outstanding universal value".'[84] The *Parkerings* Tribunal also referred to the WHC, to which Lithuania was a party, in order to establish whether there was any likeness between the two competing projects.[85] With regard to customary international law, the *Grand River* Tribunal could not 'avoid noting the strong international policy and standards articulated in numerous written instruments and interpretative decisions that favour state action to promote ... [the] rights and interests of indigenous peoples'.[86]

If the relevant treaty provision directs the arbitral tribunal to apply domestic law, some scholars have pointed out that a state could bring a counterclaim against an investor for breach of the domestic (cultural) law.[87] As Kryvoi puts it, 'obligations of investors arise not from the express language of treaties, but out of applicable law'.[88] Analogously, if a given investment treaty protects only investments

[83] *Ibid.*, ¶ 67. [84] *Glamis Gold v. United States*, Award, footnote 194.

[85] *Parkerings-Compagniet AS v. Republic of Lithuania*, Award, ICSID Case No. ARB/05/8, 11 September 2007, ¶ 392.

[86] *Grand River v. United States*, Award, ¶ 186.

[87] See H. E. Veenstra-Kjos, 'Counter-Claims by Host States in Investment Dispute Arbitration "without Privity"', in P. Kahn and T. Waelde (eds.), *New Aspects of International Investment Law* (Leiden: Martinus Nijhoff Publishers, 2007), chapter 14.

[88] Y. Kryvoi, 'Counterclaims in Investor-State Arbitration', *Minnesota JIL* 21 (2012), 219.

made 'in accordance with the laws' of the host state, where the operation of an investment occurs in breach of the host state's cultural laws, the host state could use this circumstance as a substantive defence.[89]

What seems clear is that cultural claims need to be substantiated: the *Grand River* Tribunal affirmed that it was 'respectful of the cultural patterns that inform business relations among First Nation peoples' and did not question that 'the written or unwritten laws of indigenous peoples could be the basis for establishing an enterprise for the purposes of NAFTA'.[90] However, it required evidence of this law: 'mere assertions of the existence of Seneca law and custom, just as mere assertions of other forms of law are not enough'.[91] Similarly, when the Arbitral Tribunal discussed the question as to whether a norm of customary international law exists which requires governmental authorities to consult indigenous peoples on governmental policies significantly affecting them, it recalled the number of international law instruments mentioned by the claimants which feature such a norm.[92]

## 7.4 *Ordre public culturel*

Some norms belonging to international cultural law may present a peremptory character and thus be applicable in the context of investment disputes. Transnational public policy (or *ordre public international*) aims at maintaining the integrity of the fundamental norms of international law and must always apply.[93] The UK House of Lords in 1853 described *public policy* as 'that principle of law which holds that no subject can lawfully do that which has a tendency to be injurious to the public or against the public good'.[94] In positive terms, public policy reflects the fundamental principles of a given society.[95] *Transnational public policy* refers to those principles that receive an international consensus as to universal standards and accepted norms of conduct

[89] J. Vinuales, 'Foreign Investment and the Environment in International Law: An Ambiguous Relationship', *British YIL* 80 (2010), 244–332.
[90] *Grand River*, Award, ¶ 103. [91] *Grand River*, Award, ¶ 103. [92] *Ibid.*, ¶ 210.
[93] A. Orakhelashvili, *Peremptory Norms in International Law* (Oxford University Press, 2006), p. 492.
[94] *Egerton v. Brownlow* (1853) 4 HLC 1.
[95] M. Hunter and G. Conde e Silva, 'Transnational Public Policy and Its Application in Investment Arbitrations', *JWIT* 4 (2003), 367.

that must always apply,[96] and to fundamental laws with a higher status than the ordinary rules of international law (*jus cogens*).[97]

The Vienna Convention on the Law of Treaties defines *jus cogens* as 'a norm accepted and recognized by the international community of states as a whole as a norm from which no derogation is permitted and which can be modified only by a subsequent norm of general international law having the same character'.[98] While this provision sets a legal framework on how peremptory norms work, it does not specify which norms belong to *jus cogens*.[99] In fact, some authors contend that *jus cogens* is not a scientific reality[100] and that 'the sheer ephemerality of *jus cogens* is an asset, enabling any writer to christen any ordinary norm of his or her choice as a new *jus cogens* norm, thereby in one stroke investing it with magical power'.[101] In this vein, Koskenniemi contends that '[*jus cogens* and obligations *erga omnes*] have no clear reference in this world ... Instead of meaning, they invoke a nostalgia for having such a meaning'.[102]

However, the concept of *jus cogens* is positive law.[103] Generally accepted examples are the prohibition of: the use of force, slavery, torture, piracy, genocide etc.[104] Given the legal uncertainty surrounding this concept, it is up to international adjudicating bodies to decipher the complex tapestry of international law in determining its meaning. For instance, in its *Congo v. Rwanda* judgment, the ICJ affirmed that *jus cogens* is part of international law and that the prohibition of genocide belongs to this category of norms.[105] A year

[96] A. Sheppard, 'Public Policy and the Enforcement of Arbitral Awards: Should There Be a Global Standard?', *TDM* (2004), 1.

[97] P. Lalive, 'Ordre public transnational (ou réellement international) et arbitrage international', *Revue de l'Arbitrage* (1986), 329–73.

[98] VCLT, Article 53.

[99] A. Bianchi, 'Human Rights and the Magic of *Jus Cogens*', *EJIL* 19 (2008), 491 (internal citation omitted).

[100] See M. W. Janis, 'Jus Cogens: An Artful Not a Scientific Reality', *Connecticut JIL* 3 (1987–1988), 370.

[101] A. D'Amato, 'It's a Bird, It's a Plane, It's Jus Cogens!', *Connecticut JIL* 6 (1990–1991), 1.

[102] M. Koskenniemi, 'International Law in Europe: Between Tradition and Renewal', *EJIL* 16 (2005), 113.

[103] P. -M. Dupuy, 'Some Reflections on Contemporary International Law and the Appeal to Universal Values: A Response to Martti Koskenniemi', *EJIL* 16 (2005), 136.

[104] E. J. Criddle and E. Fox-Decent, 'A Fiduciary Theory of Jus Cogens', *Yale JIL* 34 (2009), 331.

[105] ICJ, *Armed Activities on the Territory of the Congo* (*Congo v. Rwanda*) Judgment of 3 February 2006, ¶ 64.

later, the Court restated its recognition of *jus cogens* in the *Genocide* case.[106]

One may wonder whether some elements of international cultural law have the character of *jus cogens* or whether they may acquire it, because of the dynamic character of *jus cogens* norms. In fact, new peremptory norms may arise and may modify the existing norms.[107] Although *jus cogens* does not yet include the protection of every aspect of cultural heritage, it is dynamic and can expand to include the prohibition of cultural genocide. Cultural genocide is a term that lawyer Raphael Lemkin proposed in 1933 as a component to genocide.[108] Some authors have looked at 'cultural genocide as a potential precursor to physical genocide';[109] others have considered it as 'wanton acts of cultural annihilation in the wake of, even independently from, genocide'.[110] The drafters of the 1948 Genocide Convention[111] considered using the term, but decided against it.[112] The International Law Commission followed this approach, stating that: 'As clearly shown by the preparatory work for the Convention . . . the destruction in question is the material destruction of a group either by physical or by biological means, not the destruction of the national, linguistic, religious, cultural or other identity of a particular group.'[113] A 1994 draft of the United Nations Declaration on the Rights of Indigenous Peoples (UNDRIP) used the phrase 'cultural genocide', but the term was dropped in the final text of the UNDRIP.[114] Nonetheless, the

[106] ICJ, *Application of the Convention on the Prevention and Punishment of the Crime of Genocide* (Bosnia and Herzegovina v. Serbia and Montenegro), Judgment of 26 February 2007, ICJ Reports (2007), p. 43, ¶ 161.

[107] VCLT Articles 64 and 53.

[108] See A. Dirk Moses, 'Raphael Lemkin, Culture, and the Concept of Genocide', in D. Bloxham and A. Dirk Moses (eds.), *The Oxford Handbook of Genocide Studies* (Oxford University Press, 2010), p. 39.

[109] See R. van Krieken, 'Cultural Genocide Reconsidered', *Australian Indigenous Law Review* 12 (2008), 77.

[110] D. Conversi, 'Genocide, Ethnic Cleansing and Nationalism', in G. Delanty and K. Kumar (eds.), *The Sage Handbook of Nations and Nationalism* (London: Sage Publications, 2006), p. 326.

[111] Convention on Prevention and Punishment of the Crime of Genocide, 9 December 1948, 78 UNTS 277.

[112] See *ICTY Prosecutor v. Krstic*, Case No. IT-98–33-T, Judgment, 2 August 2001, ¶ 576.

[113] International Law Commission, Report of the International Law Commission on the work of its Forty-eighth Session, *Yearbook of the International Law Commission 1996*, Vol. II, Part Two, pp. 45–6, ¶ 12.

[114] See Moses, 'Raphael Lemkin, Culture, and the Concept of Genocide', p. 39.

UNDRIP substantially prohibits such genocide, recognizing that 'indigenous peoples and individuals have the right not to be subjected to forced assimilation or destruction of their culture'.[115] The same article also identifies some circumstances that can lead to the destruction of indigenous peoples' culture,[116] requiring the state to:

> provide effective mechanisms for prevention of, and redress for:
> (a) Any action which has the aim or effect of depriving them of their integrity as distinct peoples, or of their cultural values or ethnic identities;
> (b) Any action which has the aim or effect of dispossessing them of their lands, territories or resources; [and]
> (c) Any form of forced population transfer which has the aim or effect of violating or undermining any of their rights [. . .][117]

In the *Genocide* case, Bosnia and Herzegovina alleged, *inter alia*, that the Serbian forces' attempt 'to eradicate all traces of the culture of the protected group through the destruction of historical, religious and cultural property', amounted to a form of genocide under the Genocide Convention.[118] The Court considered that there was 'conclusive evidence of the deliberate destruction of the cultural and religious heritage of the protected group'.[119] However, in the Court's view, the destruction of historical, cultural and religious heritage 'd[id] not fall within the categories of acts of genocide set out in Article II of the [Genocide] Convention'.[120] Quoting the *Krstic* case,[121] the Court endorsed the statement that 'where there is physical or biological destruction there are often simultaneous attacks on the cultural and religious property and symbols of the targeted group as well, attacks which may legitimately be considered as evidence of an intent to physically destroy the group'.[122] When determining the exact content of the notion of persecution, the ICTY has included the attempts to erase religious and education institutions of a certain community from the landscape of a given zone.[123] Furthermore, the systematic destruction of

[115] UNDRIP, Article 8(1). [116] *Ibid.*, Article 8(2). [117] *Ibid.*
[118] *Case Concerning Application of the Convention on the Prevention and Punishment of the Crime of Genocide* (*Bosnia and Herzegovina v. Serbia and Montenegro*) (Genocide case), Judgment of 26 February 2007, ICJ Reports (2007) p. 43, at ¶ 320.
[119] *Ibid.*, ¶ 344. [120] *Ibid.*
[121] *ICTY Prosecutor v. Krstic*, IT-98-33-T, Judgment, 2 August 2001, ¶ 580. [122] *Ibid.*
[123] *ICTY Prosecutor v. Kordic & Cerkez*, Case No. IT-95-14/2-T, Judgment, 26 February 2001, ¶ 207.

cultural heritage has been accepted as evidence of the *mens rea* that is the *dolus specificus* of the crime of genocide.[124]

International criminal tribunals have acknowledged the duty to protect cultural heritage as an *erga omnes* obligation under international law. In the *Strugar* and *Jokic* cases, the ICTY found military leaders guilty of violations of the laws or customs of war, for the destruction or wilful damage done to historic monuments during the Balkan war. In determining the sentences, the Tribunal was conscious of the serious attack to the Old Town of Dubrovnik that is inscribed in the World Heritage List.[125]

Courts have highlighted the existence of *ordre publique culturel*.[126] For instance, the Swiss Supreme Court has recognized the existence of an international public order in the field of cultural property in cases concerning the restitution of cultural goods.[127] The regulatory framework protecting such goods against looting is deemed to express the international public order:

> Lorsque, comme l'espèce, la demande porte sur la restitution d'un bien culturel, le juge de l'entraide doit veiller à prendre en compte l'intérêt public international ... lié à la protection de ces biens. Ces normes, qui relèvent d'une commune inspiration, constituent autant d'expressions d'un ordre public international en vigueur ou en formation ... ces normes, qui concrétisent l'impératif d'une lutte internationale efficace contre le trafic de biens culturels.[128]

[124] See *Prosecutor v. Krstic*, Case No. IT-98-33-T, Judgment, ICTY, 2 August 2001, ¶ 580.

[125] *Prosecutor v. Pavle Strugar*, Judgment of the Trial Chamber, 31 January 2005; *Prosecutor v. Miodrag Jokic*, Trial Chamber Judgment, 18 March 2004, Appeals Chamber Judgment, 30 August 2005.

[126] V. Mainetti, 'Le principe du patrimoine culturel de l'humanité: de la république des arts à un ordre public international', in *Alberico Gentili: La salvaguardia dei beni culturali nel diritto internazionale: atti del convegno Dodicesima Giornata Gentiliana* (Milano: Giuffré, 2008), pp. 581–601.

[127] See P. Lalive, 'Réflexions sur un ordre public culturel', in E. Wyler and A. Papaux (eds.), *L'extranéité ou le dépassement de l'ordre juridique étatique* (Paris: Pédone, 1999), p. 155.

[128] Bundesgericht (Federal Supreme Court) 1 April 1997, 123 Arrets du Tribunal Federal Suisse (ATF) II 134 (Switz.) (author's translation): 'When, as in this case, the request is for the return of a cultural object, the judge must be careful to take into account the interest of the international community ... tied to the protection of cultural property. These provisions are based on a common inspiration and constitute the expression of an international public order which is in force or in the process of developing. These norms concretize the imperative of an international struggle against the traffic in cultural property.'

Courts have considered contracts violating foreign regulations prohibiting the export of national treasures as null and void.[129] For instance, the German Bundesgerichtshof (Supreme Court) has recognized that an insurance contract subject to German law was null and void because it related to the illegal export of cultural goods from Nigeria.[130] In *Soleimany v. Soleimany*, the Court of Appeal in the UK ultimately refused enforcement of an award on a contract based on smuggled goods because of public policy grounds.[131]

International public policy demands that international arbitrators apply it as part of the applicable law.[132] Public policy has been forcefully asserted in a series of international arbitrations. For example, in the *Maria Luz* arbitration, the Czar of Russia, sitting as the sole arbitrator, drew upon public policy in declaring that Japan 'had not breached the general rules of the Law of the Nations' in freeing the slaves carried on the Peruvian vessel *Maria Luz* and denying the subsequent demands for indemnity of the Peruvian citizens.[133] In *Aminoil*, the Arbitral Tribunal maintained the existence of *jus cogens*, albeit excluding that the invoked norm had peremptory character. In particular, the Arbitral Tribunal stated that permanent sovereignty over natural resources did not prohibit the possibility of states to subscribe to stabilization clauses. In fact, stabilization clauses aim to ensure that the contract will not be unilaterally changed or terminated by the host state through legislation or administrative action.[134] Adopting a more subtle solution, in *Texaco* the Arbitral Tribunal did not deny the *jus cogens* nature of permanent sovereignty, but stated that the contested contract between the host state and the foreign investor was the exercise of sovereignty over natural resources.[135] In an ICC arbitration, Mr Lagergreen, acting as a sole arbitrator, stated that 'it cannot be contested that there exists a general

[129] M.-A. Renold, 'An Important Swiss Decision Relating to the International Transfer of Cultural Goods: The Swiss Supreme Court's Decision on the Giant Antique Mogul Gold Coins', *Int'l J. of Cultural Prop.* 13 (2006), 365.

[130] *Ibid.*, 368. [131] *Soleimany v. Soleimany* [1999] QB 785 (CA).

[132] See J. Lew, L. Mistelis and S. Kröll, *Comparative International Commercial Arbitration* (The Hague: Kluwer Law, 2003), pp. 93–4.

[133] *Maria Luz* Arbitration, award rendered by the Czar of Russia, 17–19 March 1875. See M. Rubino-Sammartano, *International Arbitration Law and Practice*, 2nd edn (The Hague/Boston: Kluwer Law International, 2001), pp. 534–5.

[134] See *Government of Kuwait v. American Independent Oil Co (Kuwait v. Aminoil)*, 66 ILR 1984, 587–8, ¶ 90.2.

[135] *Texaco Overseas Petroleum et al. v. Libya*, 53 ILR 482, ¶ 78.

principle of law recognized by civilised nations that contracts which seriously violate *bonos mores* or international public policy are invalid or at least unenforceable and that they cannot be sanctioned by courts or arbitrators.'[136]

Similarly, in *World Duty Free Company Limited v. The Republic of Kenya*,[137] the ICSID Tribunal referred to international public policy and did not allow claims based on bribes or on contracts obtained by corruption.[138] The Tribunal stated that 'in light of domestic laws and international conventions relating to corruption, and in light of decisions taken in the matter by courts and international tribunals, this tribunal is convinced that bribery is contrary to the international public policy of most, if not all states. Thus, claims based on contracts of corruption or on contracts obtained by corruption cannot be upheld by this Arbitral Tribunal'.[139] According to the Tribunal, transnational public policy 'protects not the litigating parties but the public'.[140] In *Inceysa v. El Salvador*, the Tribunal concluded that it did not have jurisdiction over the claim brought before it by the investor, as the respondent had not consented to the protection of investments procured by fraud, forgery or corruption.[141] In the case *Plama v. Bulgaria*, the Arbitral Tribunal assessed the legality of the investment under both national and international law.[142] After finding the claimant in violation of Bulgarian and international law, the Tribunal did not grant the investor the substantive protections under the Energy Charter Treaty.[143] In *Phoenix Action Ltd v. the Czech Republic*, an ICSID Tribunal held that 'nobody would suggest that ICSID protection should be granted to investments made in violation of the most fundamental rules of protection of human rights'.[144] Adopting a similar view, in the *Methanex* case, an ICSID Tribunal asserted that 'as a matter of international constitutional law, a tribunal has an independent duty to apply imperative principles of law or jus cogens and not to give effect to

136 ICC International Court of Arbitration, Case No. 1110 of 1963, *Y.B. Comm. Arb.* 47, 61.

137 *World Duty Free v. Republic of Kenya*, ICSID Case No. ARB/00/7, Award, 4 October 2006.

138 *Ibid.*, ¶ 157. 139 *Ibid.* 140 *Ibid.*, ¶ 181.

141 *Inceysa Vallisoletana SL v. Republic of El Salvador*, ICSID Case No. ARB/03/26, Award, 2 August 2006, ¶¶ 263–4.

142 See R. Moloo and A. Khachaturian, 'The Compliance with the Law Requirement in International Investment Law', *Fordham Int'l L. J.* 34 (2010–2011), 1484.

143 *Plama Consortium Ltd v. Republic of Bulgaria*, ICSID Case No. ARB/03/24, Award, 27 August 2008.

144 *Phoenix Action Ltd v. Czech Republic*, Case No. ARB/06/5, Award of 15 April 2009, ¶ 78.

the parties' choice of law that are inconsistent with such principles'.[145] In other cases, as Professor Martin Hunter points out, although arbitrators 'would claim that they have never applied transnational public policy principles in formulating their awards', they have applied public policy principles, in particular with regard to environmental goods.[146]

Public policy is a flexible and dynamic concept that can be used as a corrective mechanism or as a tool to balance complex and often conflicting goals.[147] Therefore, commentators have highlighted that '[a]ny tribunal owes an obligation to the international community to apply international public policy' and that 'nothing can acquit a tribunal of its mandate to apply public policy'.[148] In other words, according to eminent authors, arbitrators 'have the right – and even the obligation – to themselves raise the issue of whether disputed contracts or legal provisions before them satisfy the requirements of international public policy'.[149] Kreindler also highlights that 'the arbitrator need not apply the agreed or determined governing law if doing so would cause him to violate international public policy'.[150] Finally, Lew *et al.* emphasize that 'To the extent that human rights protection constitutes a core part of international or national public policy, human rights aspects must be considered by the tribunal.'[151]

As to the content of transnational public policy, arbitral tribunals have stressed: 'Tribunals must be very cautious ... and must check the objective existence of a particular transnational public policy rule in identifying it through international conventions, comparative law and arbitral awards.'[152] In any case, arbitrators are bound to apply relevant peremptory norms of international law whether or not they were pleaded by the parties. The question is not whether to add new claims to those articulated by the parties, but to determine which law is applicable to the

145 *Methanex v. United States of America*, UNCITRAL (NAFTA), Final Award of the Tribunal on Jurisdiction and Merits, 3 August 2005 Part IV, ch. C, ¶ 24.

146 M. Hunter and G. Conde e Silva, 'Transnational Public Policy and its Application in Investment Arbitrations', *JWIT* 4 (2003), 372.

147 *Ibid.*, 374.

148 See E. Gaillard and J. Savage, *Fouchard, Gaillard, Goldmann on International Commercial Arbitration* (The Hague: Kluwer Law International, 1999), p. 861.

149 *Ibid.*

150 R. H. Kreindler, 'Approaches to the Application of Transnational Public Policy by Arbitrators', *JWIT* 4 (2003), 244.

151 Lew, Mistelis and Kroell, *Comparative International Commercial Arbitration*, pp. 93–4.

152 *World Duty Free v. Republic of Kenya*, Award, ¶ 141.

dispute.[153] The principle of *nec ultra petita* concerns the arguments raised by the parties but does not infringe or supersede the mandatory rules eventually applicable to the dispute. Arbitrations do not take place in a vacuum; rather they contribute to the development of international law and must be in conformity with its basic rules.

## 7.5 Treaty interpretation

Investment treaties are creatures of international law to be construed in accordance with customary norms of treaty interpretation, as set out in Articles 31, 32 and 33 of the Vienna Convention on the Law of Treaties (VCLT).[154] These norms guide parties and arbitrators to interpret the text of treaties, and contemporary arbitral jurisprudence is replete with references to Articles 31–33 VCLT.[155] Article 31 of the VCLT includes the principle of good faith in interpreting treaty provisions, and provides that the intentions of the parties are revealed through the ordinary meaning of the terms of the treaty, in their context, and in light of the object and purpose of the treaty. Article 32 of the VCLT provides that

> recourse may be had to supplementary means of interpretation, including the preparatory work of the treaty and the circumstances of its conclusion, in order to confirm the meaning resulting from the application of Article 31, or to determine the meaning when the interpretation according to Article 31:
> (a) leaves the meaning ambiguous or obscure; or
> (b) leads to a result which is manifestly absurd or unreasonable.

Article 33 of the VCLT deals with interpretation of treaties authenticated in two or more languages and may be useful when interpreting investment treaties, which are generally written in the languages of the contracting parties.

Although Article 31 of the VCLT uses mandatory terms, it does not clarify how much weight should be given to each of its elements.[156] All of the relevant approaches – textual, contextual, and purposive or teleological – are not set in a hierarchical order; rather they need to be

[153] See, e.g., G. Cordero Moss, 'Is the Arbitral Tribunal Bound by the Parties' Factual and Legal Pleadings?', *Stockholm Int'l Arb. Rev.* 3 (2006), 12.

[154] Vienna Convention on the Law of Treaties (VCLT), 23 May 1969, in force 27 January 1980, 1155 UNTS 331.

[155] See, e.g., *Siemens A.G. v. Argentine Republic*, Decision on Jurisdiction, 3 August 2004, 44 ILM 138 (2005), ¶ 80.

[156] M. Waibel, 'Demystifying the Art of Interpretation', *EJIL* 22 (2011), 574.

balanced in a single combined interpretative process. Therefore, the use of the customary norms of treaty interpretation as restated by the VCLT does not lead to any univocal results or 'irrebuttable interpretation';[157] rather it leaves the interpreter with 'considerable flexibility',[158] providing 'principles of logic and order which both constrain and empower the interpreter'.[159]

As the overwhelming majority of investment treaties does not address the interplay between cultural heritage protection and the promotion of FDI, purposive and contextual interpretation criteria are of fundamental importance. The purposive or teleological interpretation of treaties is based on the analysis of the object and purpose of the treaty, which are usually included in preambles. While most BIT preambles are unidimensional, emphasizing the need to foster FDI, a number of more recent preambles state that investment promotion must be consistent with certain policy goals, including public health, safety and sustainable development.[160] Certainly, if the preamble of a given treaty includes reference to sustainable development, which encapsulates a cultural dimension as seen above in Chapter 2, it will be possible for an arbitral tribunal to take cultural concerns into account. Even where the preamble makes no reference to sustainable development, authors caution against a one-sided interpretation of the purpose of bilateral investment treaties as merely aiming at protecting and promoting foreign direct investment *per se*.[161] One-sided approaches risk repoliticizing investment disputes 'and, in the long-run, losing support among states parties'.[162] As Berman pinpoints: 'it would surely be wrong to take too narrow a view of "object and purpose", for example, by claiming that the object and purpose of investment treaties is to protect the investor . . . Deducing the object and purpose is specific to the particular treaty under discussion, and does not admit general postulates.'[163] As the *Amco* Tribunal held: 'the [ICSID] Convention is aimed to protect, to the same extent and with the same

[157] R. Gardiner, *Treaty Interpretation* (Oxford University Press, 2008), p. 9.

[158] Waibel, 'Demystifying the Art of Interpretation', 575.

[159] I. Van Damme, *Treaty Interpretation by the WTO Appellate Body* (Oxford University Press, 2009), p. 38.

[160] A. Newcombe and L. Paradell, *Law and Practice of Investment Treaties* (Aalphen aan den Rijn: Wolters Kluwer, 2009), p. 123.

[161] M. Waibel, 'International Investment Law and Treaty Interpretation', in R. Hoffman and C. Tams (eds.), *International Investment Law and General International Law: From Clinical Isolation to Systemic Integration* (Baden Baden: Nomos, 2011), p. 40.

[162] *Ibid.*

[163] F. Berman, 'Evolution or Revolution?', in C. Brown and K. Miles (eds.), *Evolution in Investment Treaty Law and Arbitration* (Cambridge University Press, 2011), p. 668.

vigour, the investor and the host state, not forgetting that to protect investment is to protect the general interest of development and of developing countries'.[164] Most IIAs aim to stimulate foreign investment; however, as the *Lemire* Tribunal pointed out,

> this main purpose is not sought in the abstract; [rather] it is inserted in a wider context, the economic development for both signatory countries. Economic development is an objective which must benefit all . . . Thus, the object and purpose of the Treaty is not to protect foreign investments *per se*, but as an aid to the development of the domestic economy. And local development requires that the preferential treatment of foreigners be balanced against the legitimate right of [the host state] to pass legislation and adopt measures for the protection of what as a sovereign it perceives to be its public interest.[165]

Analogously, in the *UPS* case, Canada referred to the preambular language of NAFTA to preserve the flexibility of the parties to safeguard public welfare to enlighten the interpretation of the relevant investment provisions with cultural concerns.

Pursuant to Article 31(3)(c) of the Vienna Convention, the treaty interpreter shall take into account 'any relevant rules of international law applicable in the relations between the parties'.[166] Pursuant to Article 31 (3)(c): 'Every treaty provision must be read not only in its own context, but in the wider context of general international law, whether conventional or customary.'[167] Therefore, this provision properly expresses the principle of 'systemic integration' within the international legal system, indicating that treaty regimes are themselves creatures of international law.[168]

The expression 'any relevant rules of international law applicable in the relations between the parties', indicates 'all sources of international law, including custom, general principles and, where applicable, other treaties'.[169] As aptly noted by Sands, for a rule of international law to be taken into account in interpreting a treaty, it must be: (1) relevant

[164] *Amco Asia Corp. v. Republic of Indonesia*, ICSID Case No. ARB/81/01, Award on Jurisdiction, 24 September 1985, 1 ICSID Reports 389 (1993) ¶ 23.

[165] *Joseph Charles Lemire v. Ukraine*, ICSID Case No. ARB/06/18, Decision on Jurisdiction and Liability, 21 January 2010, ¶ 273.

[166] VCLT, Article 31(3)(c).

[167] I. Sinclair, *The Vienna Convention on the Law of Treaties* (Manchester: Manchester University Press, 1984), p. 139.

[168] C. McLachlan, 'The Principles of Systemic Integration and Article 31(3)(c) of the Vienna Convention', *ICLQ* 54 (2005), 280.

[169] J. P. Gaffney, 'Going to Pieces without Falling Apart: Waelde's Defence of "Specialisation" in the Interpretation of Investment Treaties', in J. Werner and

i.e. related to the treaty norm being interpreted; and (2) applicable, i.e. legally binding.[170] As Sands points out: 'the treaty being interpretated retains a primary role', while the rule of international law which is relevant and applicable between the parties 'must be taken into account'.[171] International law does not define what taking into account means; Sands highlights that 'the formulation is stronger than "take into consideration" but weaker than "apply"'.[172] One may wonder whether 'taking into account' is analogous to 'drawing inspiration', a formulation that appears in Article 60 of the African Charter, enabling the Commission to draw inspiration from international law on human rights as well as 'from the provisions of various instruments adopted within the Specialized Agencies of the United Nations of which the parties to the . . . Charter are Members'.[173]

The principle of systemic integration operates so as to apply a presumption that the investment law system is to be interpreted consistently with general international law. Such presumption has both positive and negative dimensions: on the one hand, the parties are to refer to public international law for all questions which are not resolved by the treaty; on the other hand, the parties should not act inconsistently with general international law.[174] Systemic thinking contributes to the unity of international law. As the Arbitral Tribunal put it in *AAPL v. Sri Lanka*,[175] BITs are 'not a self-contained closed legal system' but have to be 'envisaged within a wider juridical context in which rules from other sources are integrated through implied incorporation methods, or by direct reference to certain supplementary rules whether of international law character or of domestic law nature'.[176] Furthermore, as investment treaties typically enshrine investors' rights in 'general, open-textured language', 'practical considerations may impel the interpreter to seek guidance from general international law'.[177]

A. Hyder Ali (eds.), *A Liber Amicorum: Thomas Wälde: Law Beyond Conventional Thought* (London: CMP, 2009), p. 57.

170 P. Sands, 'Treaty, Custom and the Cross-Fertilization of International Law', *Yale Human Rights & Development Law Journal* 1 (1998), 102.

171 *Ibid.* 172 *Ibid.*, at 103.

173 African Charter on Human Rights and Peoples' Rights, 21 ILM 58, Article 60.

174 McLachlan, 'The Principles of Systemic Integration', 311.

175 *Asian Agricultural Products Ltd v. Republic of Sri Lanka (AAPL v. Sri Lanka)*, ICSID Case No. ARB/87/3, Award, 27 June 1990, 4 ICSID Rep. 245 (1997).

176 *Ibid.*, ¶ 21.

177 C. McLachlan, L. Shore and M. Weiniger, *International Investment Arbitration: Substantive Principles* (Oxford University Press, 2008), p. 16.

Treaty interpretation cannot be invoked to displace the applicable law.[178] While some argue that little difference exists between the interpretation of a given treaty and its application, these are different, albeit interrelated, processes. While treaty interpretation aims at 'discovering the proper meaning of treaty terms through various interpreting methods'; treaty application aims at 'identifying the source of law and applying it'.[179] As Radi puts it, 'Article 31(3)(c) of the VCLT broadens the normative horizons of a judge – not her competence'.[180] Furthermore, states have agreed on specific dispute settlement mechanisms in the various fields of international law; 'such intentions would be frustrated if a procedure created for one branch were to be extended to another branch where it has for quite particular reasons not been chosen before.'[181] Because of their limited mandate, the arbitrators cannot adjudicate on the eventual breach of international cultural law. Arbitral tribunals are not allowed to decide whether a certain governmental measure is in conformity with an agreement of public international law outside international investment law. They are only permitted to decide whether the measure at issue violates international investment law.

However, while being aware of their limited jurisdiction and their specific mandate to interpret the instruments under which they are set up, arbitral tribunals have recognized that the rules which they have the jurisdiction to apply and interpret are not detached from international law. Public international law, including international cultural law, is relevant in the interpretation of international investment law. Arbitrators may analyse the specific investment claims in the light of the relevant rules of international law applicable in the relationship between the parties. For instance, in the case *Micula and others v. Romania*, the Arbitral Tribunal considered Article 15 of the Universal Declaration of Human

[178] *Case Concerning Oil Platforms* (Iran v. United States), Judgment, 6 November 2003, ICJ Reports 2003, 161, Separate Opinion by Judge Higgins, ¶ 49.

[179] C.-F. Lo, 'The Difference between Treaty Interpretation and Treaty Application and the Possibility to Account for Non-WTO Treaties during WTO Treaty Interpretation', *Indiana Int'l & Comp. L. Rev.* 22 (2012), 9.

[180] Y. Radi, 'Realizing Human Rights in Investment Treaty Arbitration: A Perspective from Within the International Investment Law Toolbox', *North Carolina JIL & Commercial Regulation* 37 (2011–2012), 1125.

[181] T. W. Wälde, 'Interpreting Investment Treaties: Experiences and Examples', in C. Binder, U. Kriebaum, A. Reinisch and S. Wittich (eds.), *International Investment Law for the 21st Century: Essays in Honour of Christoph Schreuer* (Oxford University Press, 2009), p. 774.

Rights (UDHR)[182] in the process of interpreting a BIT's nationality requirements by referring to Article 31(3)(c).[183] In the case *Saluka Investments v. Czech Republic*, the Arbitral Tribunal took into account the customary international law principle 'that a deprivation can be justified if it results from the exercise of regulatory actions aimed at the maintenance of public order' by referring to Article 31(3)(c).[184]

The relevant rules of international law applicable in the relationship between the parties may include international cultural law. This consideration of international cultural law would be *incidenter tantum*, on a cursory basis or as *obiter dicta*. Given the fact that UNESCO has an almost universal membership, and that some of its conventions are very successful in terms of adhesion, this leads to the conclusion that adjudicators should take cultural concerns into account. If one deems that some elements of cultural heritage protection already belong to customary international law,[185] or are general principles of law, the case for such consideration is even stronger. If the applicable law is the law of the host state, and the host state has ratified certain UNESCO conventions, then the relevant provisions of these instruments would become relevant.

For instance, reference to the relevant UNESCO conventions may be made to clarify the meaning of investment treaty provisions including the fair and equitable treatment standard and the reasonableness criterion. In particular, when ascertaining the legitimate expectations of foreign investors, arbitral tribunals should take into account the host state's obligations under international law. The expectations of foreign investors cannot be legitimate if they disregard the host state's obligations under international cultural law. Conversely, foreign investors have legitimate expectations that measures adopted by the host state should comply with the relevant international law treaties. Therefore, national measures allegedly protecting cultural values but which infringe

[182] Universal Declaration of Human Rights (UDHR), GA Res. 217 (III) UNGAOR 3rd Sess. UN Doc. A/810 (1948) 10 December 1948.

[183] *Micula and Others v. Romania*, Decision on Jurisdiction and Admissibility, ICSID Case No. ARB/05/20, 24 September 2008, ¶¶ 86–8.

[184] *Saluka Investments BV v. Czech Republic*, Partial Award, PCA UNCITRAL, 17 March 2006, at ¶¶ 254–5.

[185] See F. Francioni, 'La protezione internazionale dei beni culturali: un diritto consuetudinario in formazione?', in P. Benvenuti and R. Sapienza (eds.), *La tutela internazionale dei beni culturali nei conflitti armati* (Milano: Giuffré, 2007), p. 12. *Contra*, see C. Forrest, *International Law and the Protection of Cultural Heritage* (Abingdon: Routledge, 2010), p. 52.

human rights may be in violation of both international cultural law and international investment law, and would constitute, *inter alia*, grounds for an investment treaty claim.

In parallel, the host state's obligations under international cultural law may help in establishing the lawfulness of particular expropriatory measures, such obligations constituting evidence of the legitimate objectives of such measures. In *SPP v. Egypt*, the Arbitral Tribunal took Egypt's international obligations into account to ascertain the legitimacy of its actions: 'Clearly, as a matter of international law, the Respondent was entitled to cancel a tourist development project situated in its own territory for the purpose of protecting antiquities. This prerogative is an unquestionable attribute of sovereignty. The decision to cancel the project constituted a lawful exercise of the right of eminent domain.'[186] In other cases, the host state's obligations under international cultural law may help arbitrators distinguish a legitimate regulation from an indirect expropriation. For instance, in *Glamis Gold v. United States*, the backfilling requirement was deemed to constitute a feature of a legitimate regulation rather than an indirect expropriation.

In addition, the obligations of the host state under international cultural law may help arbitrators to determine whether a given investment is comparable to another one or not, for the purpose of establishing a violation of the non-discrimination principle under the relevant investment treaty. For instance, in *Parkerings v. Lithuania*, the Arbitral Tribunal deemed that 'the City of Vilnius did have legitimate grounds to distinguish between the two projects . . . especially in terms of historical and archaeological preservation'.[187]

Article 31(3)(c) also allows space for dynamic or evolutive treaty interpretation. As the content of international law changes and develops continuously, and international investment treaties can be considered as living instruments, any approach to interpretation should include a means of dealing with this dynamism: 'terms and concepts used in investment law should reflect the progress of law'.[188] An adjudicator's interpretation cannot remain unaffected by subsequent developments of law and 'an international instrument has to be interpreted and applied

[186] *Southern Pacific Properties (Middle East) Ltd v. Arab Republic of Egypt*, ICSID Case No. ARB/84/3, Award on the Merits, 20 May 1992, ¶ 158.

[187] *Parkerings-Compagniet AS v. Republic of Lithuania*, ICSID Case No. ARB/05/8 Award, 11 September 2007, ¶ 396.

[188] Wälde, 'Interpreting Investment Treaties', p. 774.

within the framework of the entire legal system prevailing at the time of interpretation'.[189] Analogously, in the *Shrimp–Turtle* case, the WTO Appellate Body interpreted the term 'exhaustible natural resources' in Article XX(g) of the GATT as to include living natural resources 'in the light of contemporary concerns of the community of nations about the protection and conservation of the environment'.[190] Similarly, international public policy may gradually be interpreted so as to include the notions of human dignity, human rights and some elements of cultural heritage.

Arbitral tribunals, however, have often adopted a reductionist or minimalist vision of the arbitral mandate. Such tribunals have rarely addressed law external to investment law, as these norms are rarely invoked by investors in investment arbitrations.[191] Even when non-investment norms are invoked, the arbitral tribunals have either dismissed them on jurisdictional grounds or failed to address them at all.[192] Even when host states have relied on human rights considerations to justify measures with adverse effects on investments, arguing that their measures were in furtherance of certain international human rights commitments, they have met only little success.[193] As Reiner and Schreuer point out: 'These awards seem to indicate the tribunals' reluctance to take up matters concerning human rights, preferring to dismiss the issues raised, on a procedural basis, rather than dealing with the substantive arguments themselves.'[194] The unwillingness of arbitral tribunals to consider law which is external to that of investment law may weaken the perceived legitimacy of investor–state arbitration. As seen above, international customary norms of treaty interpretations require systematic interpretation.

[189] ICJ, *Legal Consequences for States of the Continued Presence of South Africa in Namibia (South-West Africa) Notwithstanding Security Council Resolution 276 (1970)*, Advisory Opinion of 21 June 1971, ICJ Reports 1971, 31.

[190] AB Report, *United States–Import Prohibition of Certain Shrimp and Shrimp Products*, WT/DS58/AB/R, 12 October 1998, ¶ 152.

[191] See C. Reiner and C. Schreuer, 'Human Rights and International Investment Arbitration', in P.-M. Dupuy, F. Francioni and E.-U. Petersmann (eds.), *Human Rights in International Investment Law and Arbitration* (Oxford University Press, 2009), p. 82.

[192] See, e.g., *Biloune and Marine Drive Complex Ltd v. Ghana Investments Centre and the Government of Ghana*, Award on Jurisdiction and Liability, 95 ILR 184 (UNCITRAL ad hoc Tribunal 1989). See also *Patrick Mitchell v. Dem. Rep. Congo*, ICSID Case No. ARB/99/7, Decision on the Application for Annulment of the Award, 1 November 2006, ¶ 48.

[193] *CMS Gas Transmission Co. v. Argentine Republic*, ICSID Case No. ARB/01/8, Award, ¶ 114, 12 May 2005, 44 ILM 1205, 1217 (2005).

[194] Reiner and Schreuer, 'Human Rights and International Investment Arbitration', p. 90.

## 7.6 The standards of review

In the clash of cultures between investment protection and the pursuit of cultural objectives by the host state, the standards of review, i.e. the degree of deference given by arbitral tribunals in reviewing a given decision of the relevant authorities, play a fundamental role as they influence the outcome of the proceedings. Appropriate standards of review can enhance the legitimacy of investment treaty arbitration and 'may mitigate some elements of the frequently asserted "legitimacy crisis" of, and "backlash" against, investment arbitration'.[195] The standards of review can range from full deference, where the determinations of the decision makers are not questioned, to *de novo* review, which amounts to a new trial, where the reviewing body reprocesses and re-evaluates the evidence, and takes the decision anew.[196] Given the fact that most (if not all) BITs do not explicitly define which standards of review are to be adopted by arbitral tribunals, defining the appropriate standards of review has been left to adjudicators.

Given its hybrid features, investment treaty law and arbitration has been analogized to different legal systems. First, given the fact that under most investment treaties, states have waived their sovereign immunity, and have agreed to give arbitrators a comprehensive jurisdiction over what are essentially regulatory disputes, such an investment review has been compared to a sort of administrative review. Van Harten and Loughlin claim that investment arbitration can be analogized to domestic administrative review since investment disputes arise from the exercise of public authority by the state and arbitral tribunals are given the power to review such an exercise of public authority.[197] Second, because of the procedural rules which govern it, investor–state arbitration has been analogized to commercial arbitration. Arbitrators are selected by the parties and/or an appointing institution and the hearings are held *in camera*. Third, arbitral tribunals have been analogized to other public international law tribunals because their jurisdiction is based on international treaties.

[195] A. Von Staden, 'Deference or no Deference, that is the Question: Legitimacy and Standards of Review in Investor-State Arbitration', *ITN* 4 (2012), 3.

[196] S. Schill, 'Deference in Investment Treaty Arbitration: Re-conceptualizing the Standard of Review through Comparative Public Law', SIEL Working Paper No 33/2012, 6.

[197] G. Van Harten and M. Loughlin, 'Investment Treaty Arbitration as a Species of Global Administrative Law', *EJIL* 17 (2007), 121–50.

Depending on the selected perspective, the outcomes of a given dispute can be different. If one adopts a private international law paradigm, according to which, investment arbitration is analogous to commercial arbitration, the principle of equality of the parties requires that no deference whatsoever be paid to the state.[198] On the other hand, if one adopts a comparative public law approach, which deems investment treaty arbitration 'an internationalized discipline of public law',[199] then the standard of review allows for qualified deference, due to its connection with the separation of powers doctrine.[200] In this context, the standard of review reflects 'the allocation of authority between a legal system's primary decision-makers and its adjudicators and shapes the balance of power within a legal system'.[201] Under this model, the state is divided into three branches – executive, legislative and judiciary – each with separate powers and areas of responsibility so that no single branch has more power than the others.

Similarly, if one adopts a public international law paradigm, according to which, investment arbitration is akin to other international fora, a qualified level of deference does play a role. For instance, in the trade law context, one can identify a 'middle level of review that d[oes] not amount to either *de novo* review ... or total deference'.[202] Analogously, the ECtHR has developed the *margin of appreciation doctrine*, which grants states a space for manoeuvring in fulfilling their international law obligations due to their social, cultural and historic features[203] and 'their direct and continuous contact with the vital forces of their countries'.[204] In particular, states have a margin of manoeuvre in determining what is in the general interest and how to pursue it, eventually restricting

[198] A. Roberts, 'Clash of Paradigms: Actors and Analogies Shaping the Investment Treaty System', *AJIL* 106 (2013), p. 32.

[199] S. Schill, 'Enhancing International Investment Law's Legitimacy: Conceptual and Methodological Foundations of a New Public Law Approach', *Virginia JIL* 52 (2011–2012), 59.

[200] Schill, 'Deference in Investment Treaty Arbitration', 4.

[201] C. Henckels, 'Proportionality and the Standard of Review in Fair and Equitable Treatment Claims: Balancing Stability and Consistency with the Public Interest', SIEL Working Paper No. 27/2012, 9.

[202] Roberts, 'Clash of Paradigms', 36.

[203] *Handyside v. United Kingdom* (5493/72) [1976] ECHR 5 (7 December 1976), ¶ 48. For commentary, see E. Benvenisti, 'Margin of Appreciation, Consensus and Universal Standards', *NYU JIL & Politics* 31 (1999), 843; Y. Shany, 'Towards a General Margin of Appreciation Doctrine in International Law?', *EJIL* 16 (2005), 907.

[204] ECtHR, *Wingrove v. United Kingdom*, 25 November 1996, Reports of Judgments and Decisions, 1996-V, ¶ 58.

individual entitlements. Such a doctrine is coupled with a comparative assessment: when the Court finds that the practice of the majority of European states goes against a given restrictive measure, it narrows the margin of appreciation, and obliges the states to abolish such measures.[205] Instead, where the Court has found that 'there is little common ground amongst the member States of the Council of Europe and . . . the law appears to be in a transitional stage, a wide margin of appreciation must be left to the authorities of each state'.[206] Such doctrine grants qualified deference to governmental regulations and reduces the risk of arbitral tribunals second-guessing democratic authorities.

With regard to public policy-related disputes, public law approaches – whether international or comparative – seem preferable due to the implications that such disputes may have on the public weal. Accordingly, in adjudicating such disputes, arbitrators should adopt a 'qualified deference'.[207] Like other international adjudicative bodies,[208] arbitral tribunals are not to undertake a *de novo* review of the evidence once brought before the national authorities, merely repeating the fact-finding conducted by the latter. It is not appropriate for arbitral tribunals to 'second-guess the correctness of the science-based decision-making of highly specialized national regulatory agencies'.[209] For instance, in the *Glamis Gold* case, the Arbitral Tribunal adopted a high standard of review, according deference to the federal and state legislative measures. The Arbitral Tribunal recognized that: 'It is not the role of this Tribunal or any international tribunal, to supplant its own judgment of underlying factual material and support for that of a qualified domestic agency'[210] and that 'governments must compromise between the interests of competing parties'.[211]

On the other hand, arbitral tribunals, as other international tribunals, should not be deterred from scrutinizing the given national measures

[205] E. Brems, 'Accommodating Diversity in International Human Rights: Legal Techniques', in P. Meerts (ed.), *Culture and International Law* (Hague Academic Press, 2008), p. 68.

[206] ECtHR, *Fretté v. France* (36515/97) [2002] ECHR 156, 26 February 2002, ¶ 41.

[207] M. Orellana, 'Science, Risk and Uncertainty: Public Health Measures and Investment Disciplines', in P. Kahn and T. Wälde (eds.), *New Aspects of International Investment Law* (Leiden: Martinus Nijhoff, 2007), p. 723 (referring to public health-related disputes).

[208] See, e.g., DSU, Article 11.

[209] *Chemtura Corporation (formerly Crompton Corporation) v. Canada*, Award, PCA-NAFTA Chapter 11 Arbitration, 2 August 2010 (*Chemtura* award), ¶ 134.

[210] *Glamis Gold* Award, ¶ 779. [211] *Ibid.*, ¶ 803.

and their compliance with the host state investment law obligations. Thus, arbitral tribunals should not pay uncritical deference to national measures, simply accepting determinations of the relevant national authorities as final. Rather, they should objectively assess whether the competent authorities complied with their international investment law obligations in making their determinations.

The arbitral tribunal will evaluate the relevance and probative force of the evidence, and interpret the relevant applicable law for the purpose of determining whether the host country has met its obligations under the BIT.[212] Thus, it will be important for the states to show that their regulations are aimed at achieving legitimate public goals and that they follow due process of law.[213] As an arbitral tribunal held: '"public interest" requires some genuine interest of the public. If mere reference to "public interest" can magically put such interest in existence and therefore satisfy this requirement, then this requirement would be rendered meaningless since the Tribunal can imagine no situation where this requirement would not have been met.'[214]

Similarly, Wälde and Kolo point out that acts of protectionism or mistreatment of foreign investors are often 'camouflaged in the much more palatable clothes of sacred environmental causes' and caution against 'not so holy alliances between protectionist interest and environmental idealism'.[215] In this sense, investment treaty arbitration 'can be seen as a desirable constraint over the domestic political process' and 'a step towards good governance in international economic relations'.[216] In addition, in a system of global cultural governance in which decision-making processes tend to be elitist and opaque, and rely on epistemic

[212] PCIJ, *Certain German Interests in the Upper Silesia* (Germany v. Poland), Judgment of 25 August 1925, [1926] PCIJ Rep., Series A, No. 7, p. 19.

[213] Questions remain as to the possibility of arbitral tribunals appointing neutral experts and/or seeking information from relevant international organizations.

[214] *ADC Affiliate Limited and ADC & ADMC Management Limited v. Republic of Hungary*, ICSID Case ARB/03/16, Award 2 October 2006, ¶ 432. Compare with ECtHR, *Former King of Greece and Others v. Greece*, Application No. 25701/94, 23 November 2000, ¶ 88 (in which the ECtHR noted that the government had not adduced evidence to support the claim that the property in question was expropriated with the purpose of protecting forests and archaeological sites, and that the passage of twenty years from the transition to the Republic and the expropriation raised doubts as to the real intentions behind the measures).

[215] T. Wälde and A. Kolo, 'Environmental Regulation, Investment Protection and "Regulatory Taking" in International Law', *ICLQ* 50 (2001), 820.

[216] *Ibid.*, 846.

communities of experts, investment treaty arbitration can introduce a bottom-up mechanism of checks and balances.

## 7.7 Conflict and reconciliation of norms in investor–state arbitration

International law offers a fertile ground for overlapping norms and conflicting obligations. The multitude of lawmakers and the constellation of courts, tribunals and administrative bodies contribute to making international law a vibrant legal system accommodating new fields and actors. At the same time, the chaotic and incremental nature of international law facilitates the potential for a conflict of norms. Although conflict has been traditionally perceived in a negative fashion – as a source of separation or a struggle for definite dominance – the potential for conflict of norms is inherent in every legal system.[217] Provided that conflict is successfully managed, it can foster positive change and strengthen the legal order.[218] Reconciling seemingly opposing interests, as expressed in norms, increases the legitimacy and the strength of the legal system.

The act of reconciling conflicts, or of perceiving them as compatible entails a complex interpretative process. When the domestic law is the law applicable to the dispute, apart from the compulsory application of transnational public policy norms, arbitrators will have to apply the relevant internal norms which are generally structured in a precise hierarchical order. On the other hand, if international law is the applicable law, a subsequent question which arises is whether norms belonging to different international law subsystems are truly comparable.

According to some authors, the difference in nature between different branches of law means that they operate on different levels and are thus not amenable to *balancing*.[219] Therefore, only human rights courts should be empowered to adjudicate on highly sensitive issues involving cultural rights. However, one may wonder whether a holistic approach might be preferred. Not only would such an approach bring coherence to

[217] J. Pauwelyn, *Conflict of Norms in Public International Law* (Cambridge University Press, 2003), p. 12.

[218] A. M. Slaughter, *A New World Order* (Princeton N.J.: Princeton University Press, 2004), p. 209.

[219] I. Tudor-Knoll, 'The Fair and Equitable Treatment Standard and Human Rights Norms', in Dupuy *et al.*, *Human Rights in International Investment Law and Arbitration*, p. 338.

international law, but it would also favour the 'humanization' of the same.[220] Considering international public law as a 'universe of inter-connected islands' may have a positive impact on economic globalization, spurring and bringing together economic, social and cultural development.[221]

While it is not possible to contest the importance of protecting aliens in international law, it is important to keep in mind that property rights guarantees do not provide absolute protection but may be limited for legitimate reasons. Even if we accept the assumption that property rights are human rights, the very idea of granting these rights makes it necessary to limit their exercise in situations where such exercise would collide with the rights and protected interests of others. For instance, according to the European Convention on Human Rights, the right to property can be limited to the extent necessary 'to control the use of property in accordance with the general interest or to secure the payment of taxes or other contributions or penalties'.[222] Owners do not only have rights, but also obligations.[223] This is particularly true with regard to the protection of cultural heritage.

In case of conflict in the implementation of state obligations concerning cultural heritage and investor rights, arbitrators will be called on to balance these interests, through a procedure similar to that established and consolidated by human rights bodies and national constitutional courts. There may be both apparent conflicts and conflicts in the applicable law. Apparent conflicts indicate those conflicts that are avoidable according to the time-tested criterion of presumption of conformity in the cumulative application of different legal regimes. It is important to consider that 'in many instances, what may seem like a conflict' may prove not to be such, rather, 'only a divergence which can be streamlined by means of . . . treaty interpretation'.[224] Pursuant to the process of treaty interpretation and other legal techniques, many apparent conflicts can be resolved or even prevented. The attempt to prove the compatibility of two norms – when there is at least one way of

[220] T. Meron, *The Humanization of International Law* (Leiden: Martinus Nijhoff, 2006).

[221] J. Pauwelyn, 'Bridging Fragmentation and Unity, International Law as a Universe of Inter-connected Islands', *Michigan JIL* 25 (2004), 903.

[222] Article 1(2) Protocol No. 1 to the European Convention on Human Rights.

[223] J. W. Singer, 'The Ownership Society and Takings of Property: Castles, Investments, and Just Obligations', *Harvard Environmental Law Review* 30 (2006), 309.

[224] Pauwelyn, *Conflict of Norms in Public International Law*, p. 6.

complying with all their requirements – has been defined as the 'reconciliation' of norms.[225]

However, other conflicts may have a genuine nature. Genuine or material conflicts of norms include two species of conflicts: inherent normative conflict and conflict in the application of the relevant norm. When a norm constitutes, in and of itself, breach of another norm, there is an inherent normative conflict. A conflict in the application of norms arises when a party to two treaties cannot simultaneously comply with its obligations under both treaties; compliance with one norm entails non-compliance with the other.[226]

With regard to the relationship between the protection of cultural heritage and the promotion of FDI, inherent normative conflicts, albeit theoretically conceivable, will rarely if ever appear in practice. Instead, both apparent conflicts and conflicts in the applicable law have often arisen in the context of investor–state arbitration. Indeed, it may be argued that conflicts in the application of norms arise because conflict prevention and management of apparent conflicts have not been attempted or have failed. Thus, both kinds of conflicts deserve scrutiny and theoretical effort is needed in order to reconcile the relevant interests.

### B. *De lege ferenda*

Having analysed the *ex post* approach to cultural issues in the context of arbitral proceedings, it can be questioned whether an *ex ante* or legislative approach to cultural heritage protection can be envisaged.[227] In this sense, the inclusion of cultural exceptions and cultural impact assessment in investment treaties and contracts respectively will be considered.

## 7.8 Cultural exceptions

Inserting cultural concerns in the text of investment agreements may reinforce the regulatory autonomy of the states parties in the cultural sector. For instance, including cultural concerns or the notion of sustainable development in the preamble of investment treaties can

[225] S. A. Sadat-Akhavi, *Methods of Resolving Conflicts between Treaties, Methods of Resolving Conflicts between Treaties* (Leiden: Brill, 2003), p. 33.

[226] W. Jenks, 'The Conflict of Law-Making Treaties', *BYIL* 30 (1953), 426.

[227] See B. Choudhury, 'Exception Provisions as a Gateway to Incorporating Human Rights Issues into International Investment Agreements', SIEL Working Paper No. 2010/13 (2010), 8–13.

empower state authorities and adjudicators to take into account such concerns in their policies and awards respectively. Cultural exceptions can also provide the states with the flexibility to adopt measures derogating from treaty substantive obligations in certain circumstances without incurring liability under international law.[228]

During the negotiations of the Multilateral Agreement on Investment (MAI) under the aegis of the Organization for Economic Co-operation and Development,[229] France and Canada applied for an exception in the area of culture for the protection of national cultural goods. Such a clause would have enabled all parties to follow cultural policies to protect cultural diversity and enterprises dealing with cultural activities. However, since the MAI was perceived as a one-sided instrument, unilaterally prepared by OECD countries to ensure higher standards of protection and legal security for foreign investors, the negotiations of this instrument failed in 1998 because of the opposition of civil society and, since then, countries have adopted different approaches to the issue.

For instance, the Trans-Pacific Strategic Economic Partnership Agreement, which establishes a free trade area between Brunei Darussalam, Chile, Singapore and New Zealand (hereinafter Trans-Pacific SEP), contains an exception to protect items or specific sites of historical or archaeological value.[230] The Trans-Pacific SEP recognizes the need to promote cultural policies aimed at protecting the cultural heritage of the countries involved, both in its tangible dimension (archaeological and historical sites) as well as in its intangible one (creative arts).[231]

Analogously, the China–New Zealand Free Trade Agreement expressly provides, *inter alia*, that:

> For the purposes of this Agreement, subject to the requirement that such measures are not applied in a manner which would constitute a means of arbitrary or unjustifiable discrimination between the Parties where like conditions prevail, or a disguised restriction on trade in goods or services

[228] See generally A. Newcombe, 'General Exceptions in International Investment Agreements', in M. C. Cordonnier Segger, M. W. Gehring and A. Newcombe (eds.), *Sustainable Development in World Investment Law* (The Hague: Kluwer, 2011), p. 355.

[229] OECD Multilateral Agreement on Investment, Consolidated Text and Commentary, Draft DAFFE/MAI/NM(97)2.

[230] The Trans-Pacific Strategic Economic Partnership Agreement, Brunei-Chile-Sing.-N.Z., 18 July 2005, available at www.mfat.govt.nz/downloads/trade-agreement/transpacific/main-agreement.pdf (hereinafter Trans-Pacific SEP).

[231] *Ibid.*, Article 19(1)(3).

> or investment, nothing in this Agreement shall be construed to prevent the adoption or enforcement by a Party of measures necessary to protect national works or specific sites of historical or archaeological value, or to support creative arts of national value.[232]

Similarly, in the Annex of the US–Lithuania BIT, Lithuania reserved 'the right to make or maintain limited exceptions to national treatment' with regard to, *inter alia*, national parks, biosphere reserves, 'monuments of nature, history, archaeology and culture as well as the surrounding protective areas', and the land of the Curonian Spit[233] – a landscape of sand dunes that is a World Heritage site.

With regard to indigenous peoples, the Trans-Pacific SEP expressly states that New Zealand can provide more favourable treatment to the Maori in fulfilment of its obligations under the Treaty of Waitangi,[234] 'provided that such measures are not used as a means of arbitrary or unjustified discrimination against persons of the other Parties or as a disguised restriction on trade in goods and services'.[235] In light of the constitutional concerns and fundamental issues raised by the implementation of the Treaty of Waitangi, which is considered to be New Zealand's founding document, the parties' inclusion of an *ad hoc* cultural exception excluding New Zealand's efforts to comply with the Treaty's requirements from the dispute settlement provisions of the Trans-Pacific SEP represents a sensible approach.[236] It remains to be seen whether such an approach will be maintained in the Trans-Pacific Partnership Agreement (TPPA), the free trade agreement (FTA) currently under negotiation between New Zealand and other countries, including the United States.

Analogously, the Energy Charter Treaty[237] allows the contracting parties to adopt or enforce:

> any measures . . . designed to benefit Investors who are aboriginal people or socially or economically disadvantaged individuals or groups or their

[232] China–New Zealand Free Trade Agreement, Article 200(3), in force 1 October 2008. The text is available at www.chinafta.govt.nz.

[233] Treaty between the Government of the United States of America and the Government of the Republic of Lithuania for the Encouragement and Reciprocal Protection of Investment, signed on 14 January 1998, Annex, para 3, available at www.sice.oas.org/Investment/BITSbyCountry/BITs/US_Lithuania_e.asp (accessed on 3 April 2013).

[234] Treaty of Waitangi (United Kingdom–New Zealand), 6 February 1840, available at www.nzhistory.net.nz/politics/treaty/read-the-treaty/english-text.

[235] Trans-Pacific SEP, Article 19(5)(1). [236] *Ibid.*, Article 19(5)(2).

[237] Energy Charter Treaty (ECT), 34 ILM 360 (1995).

> Investments, provided that such measure a) has no significant impact on that Contracting Party's economy; and b) does not discriminate between Investors of any other Contracting Party and Investors of that Contracting Party not included among those for whom the measure is intended, provided that no such measure shall constitute a disguised restriction on Economic Activity in the Energy Sector, or arbitrary or unjustifiable discrimination between Contracting Parties or between Investors or other interested persons of Contracting Parties.[238]

Canada's new model Foreign Investment Protection Agreement (FIPA) does not include such an exception in its text, but includes preferential treatment for aboriginals in its annex.[239] Malaysia has similarly excluded measures designed to promote economic empowerment of the Bumiputras ethnic group from the scope of BITs.[240]

With regard to FTAs, two different approaches have emerged in negotiations. The first approach is adopted by Canada and the European Union in their FTAs which typically contain some form of positive cultural exception.[241] The second approach, embodied in the FTAs negotiated by the United States, is the negative list approach in which all services are covered in an agreement, except those that are specifically carved out by the parties.

Since the adoption of the 2007 *European Agenda for Culture in a Globalising World*,[242] 'a new strategic framework for culture in the EU's external relations has emerged. Culture is increasingly perceived as a strategic factor of political, social and economic development.'[243] As a party to the UNESCO Convention on the Protection and Promotion of the Diversity of Cultural Expressions (CCD), the EU is committed to taking full account of the specific nature of cultural activities, goods and services in its external relations. The objective is twofold: on the one

[238] ECT, Article 24.

[239] IISD, 'Clarification on Aboriginals and Canada's Investment Treaties', *Investment Law and Policy Weekly News Bulletin*, 11 June 2004.

[240] M. Sornarajah, *The International Law on Foreign Investment* (Cambridge University Press, 2004), pp. 120–1, pp. 366–7.

[241] See L. Richieri Anania, 'Cultural Diversity and Regional Trade Agreements: The European Union Experience with Culture Cooperation Frameworks', SIEL Working Paper (July 2012).

[242] The *European Agenda for Culture in a Globalizing World* was endorsed by the Council of the European Union in November 2007. Council of the European Union, Resolution of 16 November 2007 on a European Agenda for Culture, 2007/C 287/01, OJEU, 29 November 2011.

[243] *Ibid.*

hand, the EU aims to promote an understanding of European cultures throughout the world. Thus, the protection, preservation and promotion of cultural heritage, both tangible and intangible is reaffirmed.[244] On the other, it aims to contribute to the vitality of the European economy of culture and to promote 'external cultural policies that encourage dynamism and balance in the exchange of cultural goods and services with third countries'.[245]

Recent EU economic partnership agreements (EPAs) have incorporated cultural concerns in the context of trade and FDI. For instance, the Cariforum–EU EPA includes a Protocol on Cultural Cooperation which aims to promote cultural diversity and cooperation for the development of cultural industries and the protection of cultural heritage sites and historic monuments.[246] A specific provision of the EPA addresses the relationship between intellectual property, biodiversity, traditional knowledge and folklore.[247]

Before the accession of some Eastern European countries to the European Union, the European Commission had expressed concerns about the compatibility of their earlier BITs with European standards on European content in broadcasting. Notwithstanding the EU Commission's initial pressures for the abrogation of these BITs, an understanding was reached with the United States and prospective member states. The memorandum 'expressed the US intent to amend the US BITs in order to eliminate incompatibilities between certain BIT obligations and EU law'.[248] For instance, the Amending Protocol to the US–Poland BIT provides a specific exemption with regard to performance requirements, *inter alia*, 'in the audio-visual sector that relate to the production, distribution and exploitation of audio-visual works, that implement quotas, or that require the purchase or use of goods produced or services provided in countries of the Council of Europe or, with respect to goods produced or services provided, a particular level or percentage of content

244 Council of the European Union, Council Conclusions on the Promotion of Cultural Diversity and Intercultural Dialogue in the External Relations of the Union and its Member States, Brussels, 20 November 2008 at p. 4. http://ec.europa.eu/culture/documents/icd_external_relations_en.doc.pdf.

245 *Ibid.*

246 Protocol III on Cultural Cooperation to the Cariforum EPA available at http://ec.europa.eu/culture/our-policy-development/doc/cultural_cooperation_protocol.pdf.

247 Cariforum EU EPA, Article 150.

248 Letter of Transmittal by George W. Bush to the Senate of the United States, 12 March 2004, available at http://tcc.export.gov/%5C%5C/static/TGA.Poland_protocol.pdf.

from a source in countries of the Council of Europe'.[249] The same provision appears in the amending protocols to the US BITs with other EU Member States, notably the Czech Republic, Estonia, Latvia, Lithuania, the Slovak Republic, Bulgaria and Romania.[250]

In parallel, Canada has always adopted a firm stance with regard to the protection of its cultural sector, elaborating a specific exemption related to cultural goods in its trade agreements. According to Article 2005 of the Canada–United States Free Trade Agreement (CUSFTA),[251] the predecessor of NAFTA, cultural industries are exempt from the provisions of the Agreement, except as specifically provided for.[252] NAFTA similarly provides for such an *exception culturelle*, making reference to the relevant CUSFTA provisions with regard to cultural industries.[253] As one of the Canadian negotiators noted, the capacity to protect cultural industries, which is 'considered to be vital to Canadian identity', led Canada to insist on a cultural exception in both the FTA and NAFTA.[254] Analogously, the Canada–Israel FTA states that 'measures affecting cultural industries are exempt from the provisions of this Agreement, except as specifically provided in Article 2.1' which relates to tariff elimination.[255]

In contrast, the United States 'has used FTA negotiations essentially to achieve cultural liberalization',[256] using a 'negative list' approach whereby all services and investments not specifically excluded from the agreements are covered by liberalization commitments. Such an approach can constrain the ability of states to adopt cultural policies. For instance, during the

[249] Additional Protocol between the United States of America and the Republic of Poland to the Treaty between the United States of America and the Republic of Poland concerning Business and Economic Relations of 21 March, 1990, signed in Brussels on 12 January 2004, Article 1(b). The text of the Additional Protocol is available at http://tcc.export.gov/%5C%5C/static/TGA.Poland_protocol.pdf.

[250] See L. E. Peterson, 'Bush Administration Sets Process in Motion to Amend BITs with Eastern and Central Europe', *Investment Law & Policy Weekly News Bulletin*, 16 February 2004, 7–8.

[251] Canada–United States Free Trade Agreement (CUSFTA) entered into force on 1 January 1989, 27 ILM (1988) 281 ff.

[252] CUSFTA, Article 2005. [253] NAFTA, Article 2106.

[254] T. A. McDonald, 'Canada, the FTA and NAFTA: A View from the Negotiating Table', *London Journal of Canadian Studies* 14 (1998/1999), 64.

[255] Free Trade Agreement Between the Government of Canada and the Government of the State of Israel (Canada–Israel FTA), in force 1 January 1997, available at www.international.gc.ca/trade-agreements-accords-commerciaux/agr-acc/israel/index.aspx?view=d.

[256] G. Gagné, 'Free Trade and Cultural Policies: Evidence from Three US Agreements', *JWT* 45 (2011), 1269.

negotiations of the Australia–United States Free Trade Agreement (AUSFTA),[257] notwithstanding the United States' requests to increase foreign market access, Australia insisted that local content requirements in audiovisual and broadcasting media were necessary to preserve Australian culture. The 'non-conforming measures' are now listed in Annex 1 of the AUSFTA.[258] However, any modification of such measures must not diminish their conformity to liberalization principles.[259] Analogously, in the US–Chile FTA, while Chile retained the right to employ a screen quota,[260] regulatory measures embodying cultural policies 'are subject to significant restraint'.[261] The US–Singapore FTA similarly contains a carve-out provision with regard to national content broadcasting and distribution and publication of printed media.[262] Notwithstanding such carve-out provisions, a negative list approach tends to promote the liberalization of the market of the cultural goods and services.[263]

The merit of introducing a cultural clause in BITs is further demonstrated by the case *United Parcel Service of America, Inc. v. Government of Canada*,[264] which involved debate over the applicability of the cultural industries clause in a NAFTA claim. United Parcel Service of America (UPS), a US company providing courier and package delivery services both throughout Canada and worldwide, claimed that Canada's Publications Assistance Program (PAP) – a policy designed to promote the wider distribution of Canadian periodicals – was discriminatory to foreign investors[265] as it 'provide[d] financial assistance to the Canadian magazine industry but only on the condition that any magazines benefitting from the financial assistance [we]re distributed through Canada

257 Australia–US Free Trade Agreement (AUSFTA) in force 1 January 2005. The text of Annex 1 is available at www.dfat.gov.au/trade/negotiations/us_fta/final-text/non-conforming_measures/Annex_I_combined.rtf.

258 See AUSFTA, Annex 1, p. 14.

259 Gagné, 'Free Trade and Cultural Policies', 1271.

260 United States–Chile Free Trade Agreement, in force 1 January 2004. The text of the FTA is available at www.ustr.gov/trade-agreements/free-trade-agreements/chile-fta/final-text, Annex I.

261 Gagné, 'Free Trade and Cultural Policies', 1275.

262 See US–Singapore FTA, Annex 8A. US–Singapore FTA, in force 1 January 2004. The text of the FTA is available at www.ustr.gov/trade-agreements/free-trade-agreements/singapore-fta/final-text.

263 L. Mayer-Robitaille, 'L'impact des accords de libre-échange américains sur le statut juridique des biens et services culturels', *Annuaire Français de Droit International* (2004), 727.

264 *United Parcel Service of America Inc. v. Government of Canada*, Award on the Merits, 24 May 2007, 46 ILM 922 (2007).

265 *Ibid.*, ¶¶ 156–60.

an institution of the Government of Canada], and not through nies such as UPS Canada'.[266] The Tribunal upheld Canada's ument that PAP was exempted from review under NAFTA by virtue of the cultural industries exception.[267]

It is more often the case that the lack of careful drafting in investment treaties can undermine the regulatory power of the host state to adopt and implement affirmative actions aimed at promoting economic, cultural, and social opportunities for disadvantaged groups, because such programmes may run foul of the bans on discrimination and performance requirements included in investment treaties. The idea that affirmative action can be needed for achieving substantive equality (equality in fact) among communities was first formulated by the Permanent Court of International Justice (PCIJ) in its Advisory Opinions on *German Settlers in Poland*[268] and *Greek Minority Schools in Albania* respectively,[269] and has been further developed by human rights bodies.[270] In the words of the PCIJ: 'Equality in law precludes discrimination of any kind; whereas equality in fact may involve the necessity of different treatment in order to attain a result which establishes an equilibrium between different situations.'[271] More recently, affirmative action has been considered to be required by the principle of equality 'to diminish or eliminate conditions which cause or help to perpetuate discrimination', and to be 'a case of legitimate differentiation'.[272]

Affirmative action may be needed to protect the cultural expressions of minorities or indigenous peoples, or those cultural expressions which are at risk of extinction or which need urgent protection. For instance, the Convention on Cultural Diversity (CCD) expressly entitles states parties to adopt measures to protect cultural expressions 'at risk of extinction, under serious threat, or otherwise in need of urgent safeguarding'.[273] According to Kolliopoulos, this provision implies that such special conditions would enable the state to adopt special measures

[266] *Ibid.*, ¶ 80. [267] NAFTA, Annex 2106.

[268] PCIJ, *Settlers of German Origin in Poland*, Advisory Opinion 6, 10 September 1923, 1923 PCIJ. (ser. B) No. 6.

[269] PCIJ, *Minority Schools in Albania*, Advisory Opinion 26, PCIJ, Ser. A.B., No. 64, 1935.

[270] See A. Yupsanis, 'The Concept and Categories of Cultural Rights in International Law: Their Broad Sense and the Relevant Clauses of the Human Rights Treaties', *Syracuse JIL & Commerce* 37 (2009–2010), 241.

[271] PCIJ, *Minority Schools in Albania*, p. 19.

[272] Human Rights' Committee, General Comment 18(37), UN Doc. A/45/40 Vol. I (1990) Annex VI sub A pp. 173–5, ¶ 10.

[273] CCD, Article 8.

beyond the cultural policies usually adopted by that state, and that this would not amount to a positive discrimination against other cultural communities in its territory.[274]

Turning now to investment law developments, a recent case tested the compatibility between affirmative measures adopted by the host state and its international investment law obligations. When South Africa adopted an ambitious social and economic programme to advance the standing of historically disadvantaged persons, in the aftermath of the apartheid regime, such programme generated much controversy among domestic and foreign investors and was challenged before an international arbitral tribunal.[275] The Mineral and Petroleum Resources Development Act (MPRDA) vests all mineral and petroleum rights with the South African government and requires that companies apply for a right to convert their former property rights into 'new order' rights, that is, licences for mineral exploitation from the South African government.[276] Companies are also required to sell 26 per cent of their shareholding to disadvantaged individuals.[277]

Holding large investments in the natural stone business in South Africa, the investors claimed that the MPRDA extinguished their property rights thus amounting to indirect expropriation in breach of the relevant provisions in the Italy–South Africa BIT and the Luxembourg–South Africa BIT.[278] They also alleged that they were denied fair and equitable treatment because of affirmative action requirements for the hiring of historically disadvantaged managers.[279] South Africa contended that the MPRDA aimed at countering 'negative social effects caused by apartheid',[280] and that it did not amount to indirect expropriation or a breach of the fair and equitable treatment.[281]

Although the case was settled, and what is publicly available does not give a clear picture of how it would have been adjudicated by the Arbitral Tribunal, this case shows the merit of introducing a specific clause or exception in the context of investment treaties in order to create a shield

[274] A. Kolliopoulos, 'La Convention de l'UNESCO sur la protection et la promotion de la diversité des expressions culturelles', *Annuaire Français de droit international* 51 (2005), 498.

[275] *Piero Foresti, Laura De Carli and Others v. Republic of South Africa*, ICSID Case No. ARB (AF)/07/1, Award, 4 August 2010, available at http://icsid.worldbank.org/ICSID/FrontServlet?requestType=CasesRH&actionVal=showDoc&docId=DC1651_En&caseId=C90 (hereinafter *Foresti* Award).

[276] *Ibid.*, ¶ 59. [277] *Ibid.*, ¶ 56. [278] *Ibid.*, ¶¶ 58–9. [279] *Ibid.*, ¶ 78. [280] *Ibid.*, ¶ 69.

[281] *Ibid.*, ¶¶ 74–5 and 78.

for policies of particular cultural or social relevance in accordance with human rights law. As a matter of dispute avoidance, the inclusion of a cultural clause would prevent such disputes. In this sense, recent South African BITs expressly allow the application of government measures 'designed to promote the achievement of equality or to advance the interests of the previously disadvantaged'.[282] For instance, the 1998 treaty between the Czech Republic and South Africa states that:

> [the guarantees of non-discrimination for foreign investors] shall not be construed so as to oblige one Party to extend to the investors of the other the benefit of any treatment, preference or privilege which may be extended by the Former Party by virtue of . . . any law or other measure the purpose of which is to promote the achievement of equality in its territory, or designed to protect or advance persons, or categories of persons, previously disadvantaged by unfair discrimination.[283]

This clause clarifies the willingness of the parties to fulfil the obligations of the BIT and to maintain a margin of manoeuvre for protecting the rights of disadvantaged groups. Exceptions protecting morals and/or public order can also be interpreted so as to include selected cultural concerns.

## 7.9 Cultural impact assessments

A cultural impact assessment is a technical device which identifies the effects of a proposed activity on cultural values and identifies methods to avoid, remedy, or mitigate adverse effects. A cultural *heritage* impact assessment is a more specific 'process of evaluating the likely impacts, both beneficial and adverse, of a proposed development on the physical manifestations of a community's cultural heritage including sites, structures and remains of archaeological, architectural, historical, religious, spiritual, cultural, ecological or aesthetic value or significance'.[284]

[282] See L. E. Peterson, 'US–Southern Africa Negotiations Stall: Race Based Affirmative Action an Obstacle?', IISD, 22 July 2004.

[283] Agreement Between the Czech Republic and the Republic of South Africa for the Promotion and Reciprocal Protection of Investments, Article 3(3)(c), 14 December 1998.

[284] See Secretariat of the Convention on Biological Diversity, Akwé: Kon *Voluntary Guidelines for the Conduct of Cultural Environmental and Social Impact Assessments Regarding Developments Proposed to Take Place on, or which are Likely to Impact on, Sacred Sites and on Lands and Waters Traditionally Occupied or Used by Indigenous and Local Communities* (Montreal: Secretariat of the Convention on Biological Diversity, 2004) ¶ 6(b).

Both cultural impact assessments and cultural heritage impact assessments are instruments of cultural governance that ensure that the cultural implications of decisions are taken into account before the decisions are made. At the international level, under the Council of Europe Framework Convention on the Value of Cultural Heritage for Society, the states parties are required to undertake cultural heritage impact assessments and adopt mitigation strategies where necessary.[285] While investment treaties and free trade agreements rarely, if ever, require such assessment,[286] *de lege ferenda*, the introduction of this specific mechanism in investment contracts between the host state and foreign investors might help to reconcile the different interests at stake.

*De lege lata*, cultural heritage impact assessments may be deemed to be a component of environmental impact assessments (EIAs). These assessments are already required by over one hundred national laws and a number of international treaties. In this sense, EIA is an appropriate tool which may also take cultural considerations into account. Several projects financed by the World Bank have been modified as a result of an EIA; for example, the developers of the Botswana Tuli Blocks Roads project had to reroute a road in order to preserve an archeological site.[287] Under the World Bank's Operational Policy OP 4.11 (Physical Cultural Resources),[288] the borrower is required to address impacts on physical cultural resources in projects proposed for Bank financing, as an integral part of the environmental assessment process.[289] Therefore, EIAs may represent a useful method of dispute avoidance,[290] ensuring that the cultural implications of decisions are taken into account before such decisions are made and contributing to the 'external' monitoring of the

[285] Council of Europe Framework Convention on the Value of Cultural Heritage for Society (Faro Convention), 10 October 2005, C.E.T.S. No. 199, Article 8.

[286] For instance, Articles 2 and 10.7 of the NAAEC mandate environmental impact assessments. See North American Agreement on Environmental Cooperation (NAAEC), 13 September 1993, 32 ILM. 1480.

[287] A. Barannik and V. Okaru, 'Harmonization of EA Procedures and Requirements between the World Bank and Borrowing Countries', in R. Goodland *et al.* (eds.), *Environmental Assessment (EA) in Africa: A World Bank Commitment* (Washington D.C.: World Bank, 1996), p. 40.

[288] World Bank, Operational Policy OP 4.11 (Physical Cultural Resources), July 2006, available at www.worldbank.org.

[289] *Ibid.* Article 4.

[290] See F. Francioni, 'Dispute Avoidance in International Environmental Law', in A. Kiss, D. Shelton and K Ishibashi (eds.), *Economic Globalization and Compliance with International Environmental Agreements* (The Hague: Kluwer Law International, 2003), pp. 229–43.

relevant UNESCO instruments.[291] More recently, the International Council on Monuments and Sites has elaborated a specific methodology for heritage impact assessment of activities taking place in World Heritage sites; such method specifically focuses on the outstanding and universal value of the given properties.[292]

However, a few investment treaty disputes have questioned the very rationale of imposing an environmental impact assessment. For instance, in *Maffezini v. Spain*,[293] Mr Maffezini, an Argentine investor, complained that the Spanish authorities had misinformed him about the costs of the project, alleging that they had pressured his company into making the investment before the EIA process was finalized, and before its implications were known.[294] Thus, according to the claimant, the Spanish authorities were responsible for the additional costs resulting from the environmental impact assessment.[295] The Arbitral Tribunal dismissed the claims, affirming that 'the environmental impact assessment procedure is basic for adequate protection of the environment and the application of appropriate environmental measures'.[296] In addition to referring to national law, the Tribunal referred to the relevant EEC directives and international law.[297] In sum, it was the Tribunal's perception that 'the investor, as happens so often, tried to minimize this requirement so as to avoid additional costs or technical difficulties'.[298] By contrast, the Tribunal held that Spain had simply required compliance with its environmental laws in a manner consistent with its investment treaty commitments.[299]

In the *Clayton and Bilcon v. Canada* case, a family and their US company objected to the manner in which an environmental assessment was conducted.[300] The EIA recommended rejection of the project to mine basalt in the coastal Canadian province of Nova Scotia and then ship it by tanker to their New Jersey site due to 'the significant adverse environmental effects that [it] would cause to the ... biological and

[291] C. E. Di Leva, 'The World Bank's Policy on Physical Cultural Resources', in B. T. Hoffman (ed.), *Art and Cultural Heritage, Law, Policy and Practice* (Cambridge University Press, 2006), pp. 245–8.

[292] ICOMOS, *Guidance on Heritage Impact Assessments for Cultural World Heritage Properties* (Paris: ICOMOS, 2011).

[293] *Emilio Augusto Maffezini v. The Kingdom of Spain*, ICSID Case No ARB/97/7, Award of the Tribunal, 13 November 2000, 5 ICSID Reports 396.

[294] *Maffezini* Award ¶ 44. [295] *Ibid.* [296] *Ibid.*, ¶ 67. [297] *Ibid.*, ¶ 69.

[298] *Ibid.*, ¶ 70. [299] *Ibid.*, ¶ 71.

[300] *Clayton/Bilcon v. Government of Canada*, Notice of Arbitration, ¶ 9.

human environment on Digby Neck, including on the "core community values" of the affected communities'.[301] While the claimants acknowledged that an EIA was required for their project, they claimed that the process was unusually protracted, discretionary, and ultimately politically motivated, alleging, *inter alia*, violations of NAFTA Article 1105 (fair and equitable treatment).[302] In particular, the claimants allege that the EIA reliance on the concept of 'core communities values' was a 'flagrant departure from the rule of law'.[303]

In its Counter-memorial, Canada contended that its actions in initiating and administering the environmental assessment were 'reasonable, fair and fully within the applicable legislative and regulatory regime'.[304] Canada argued that 'the modern concept of environment encompasses both biophysical components like air, land, water, flora and fauna, and human components' including the 'cultural heritage of a place'.[305] In fact, due to the special relationship existing between the local communities and their surrounding environment, Digby Neck is included in a biosphere reserve designated by UNESCO to reconcile the conservation of biodiversity with its sustainable use.[306] Finally, legislation in Nova Scotia expressly requires consideration of broad socio-economic effects in EIAs.[307] Canada concluded that 'it is not the job of this Tribunal to second guess these heavily based and scientifically grounded decisions'.[308] As the case is in an early phase of the proceedings, it is not possible to foresee how it will be settled.

As explained above, a number of investment treaty arbitrations have centered on EIA processes. In abstract terms, detecting the cultural consequences of a project before it is implemented and ensuring that planned activities are compatible with sound cultural management may lower the risk of damage and promote the reconciliation of private and public interests. However, such assessments must respect international standards of transparency and fairness. In conclusion, the fact that to date EIA procedures have not prevented investment treaty disputes does not mean that they may not do so in the future. They clearly have such potential if they follow adequate procedural standards.

[301] *Clayton/Bilcon*, Statement of Defense of the Government of Canada, 4 May 2009, ¶ 66.
[302] *Clayton/Bilcon*, Notice of Arbitration, ¶ 12.
[303] *Clayton/Bilcon*, Counter-memorial, ¶ 378. [304] *Ibid.*, ¶ 304. [305] *Ibid.*, ¶ 22.
[306] *Clayton/Bilcon*, Statement of Defense, ¶ 10.
[307] *Clayton/Bilcon*, Counter-memorial, ¶ 378. [308] *Ibid.*, ¶ 17.

## Conclusions

The recent flourishing of investment treaties poses a challenge for international lawyers, as it raises the question as to whether or not investment law is clinically isolated from public international law. The question is clearly linked to the debated topic as to whether public international law is a fragmented system or not. Adopting a unitary approach, this chapter advocates the importance of the unity of international law and of achieving coherence among the different sources of international law within investment treaty arbitration.

This chapter has investigated a number of legal tools that both *de lege lata* and *de lege ferenda* may help arbitrators and policy-makers to reconcile the different interests at stake. *De lege lata*, investment treaties should not be considered as self-contained regimes, but as an important component of public international law. Thus, international investment law has to be consistent with international law. In many circumstances, international law is the law applicable to investment disputes according to the arbitral clause or the relevant treaty provision. Even in those cases where the applicable law is the law of the host state, it is worth recalling that national legal systems are permeated by international law, be they monist or dualist systems. Therefore, when arbitrators apply national provisions that reflect international law norms, the boundaries between the international and the national planes become blurred. Where peremptory norms of international law matter in the context of an investment treaty arbitration, arbitrators have to take these fundamental norms into consideration. International investment law must also be interpreted in accordance with customary rules of treaty interpretation. Traditional tools of treaty interpretation may contribute to reconciling foreign investment and cultural heritage in a harmonious fashion, as well as to the gradual and smooth *humanization* of international investment law. *De lege ferenda*, *ex ante* or legislative approaches to cultural heritage protection can be envisaged. It is in this sense that this chapter has considered the inclusion of cultural exceptions and cultural impact assessments in investment treaties and contracts respectively.

# Conclusions

Cultural heritage can be an engine of growth and welfare, being central in wealth creation and people's lives, enriching their existence in both a material and immaterial sense. Cultural heritage is real wealth, something humans value in life, reflecting the diversity of cultures to which all peoples contribute, and enriching the fabric of the international community as a whole. It is a legacy for everyone as it reveals the past and yields a sense of identity for present and future generations. The effective protection of cultural heritage can benefit all humanity. Governing cultural resources in their diversified forms, international cultural law includes extremely diverse components and constitutes a good example of legal pluralism. The almost universal ratification of certain UNESCO instruments indicates that the international community perceives the protection of cultural resources as an important public interest.

In parallel, international investment law has become one of the most developed and sophisticated fields of public international law. International investment law provides extensive protection to investors' rights in order to encourage foreign direct investment and to foster economic development. Unlike the situation that prevailed immediately after World War II, foreign investors are now protected primarily by international investment treaties, rather than by customary international law alone. Investment treaties aim at establishing a level playing-field for foreign investors and a sort of shield against their discrimination and mistreatment by the host state. Investment treaties have ensured foreign investors direct access to international arbitration. The use of the arbitration model is aimed at depoliticizing disputes, avoiding potential national court bias and streamlining procedures.

The aim of this book has been to explore the interaction between international cultural law and international investment law. In abstract terms, there may be a positive synergy between the protection of cultural resources on the one hand and FDI on the other. International cultural law and international investment law may be seen as complementary because cultural resources can foster human development and economic growth, and foreign direct investment is aimed at promoting development. Furthermore, by leading to more choices for people, foreign direct investment in the cultural sector may enhance cultural diversity and media pluralism, thus facilitating free speech, the free flow of ideas, and constant exchanges and interaction between cultures.

However, the enhanced interaction between cultures can endanger cultural diversity. Due to economies of scale, the current asymmetry in flows and exchanges of cultural goods at the global level can lead to cultural homogenization. At the same time, foreign direct investments can affect the cultural policies of the host state and conflicts of norms may arise. In general terms, international disputes relating to the interplay between cultural heritage and FDI are characterized by the need to balance the legitimate interest of a state to adopt cultural policies on the one hand and the economic interests of the investor on the other. While the inter-relationship between cultural heritage and FDI may be studied from a variety of different perspectives and institutional settings, this book has adopted an 'internal' approach with respect to international investment law and arbitration. The choice of this approach is not meant to imply that the institutional setting of international investment law and arbitration is to be preferred to other approaches to reconcile the relevant interests. Instead, looking at the linkage between cultural heritage and FDI from an inside view of international investment law allows a reflection on the pressing issues posed by the emergence of investment treaty arbitration as a tool of global governance.

Due to the lack of a world heritage court, disputes with cultural elements have been increasingly adjudicated by investment treaty tribunals and a rich jurisprudence has emerged in recent years. Therefore an analysis and critical assessment of this emerging linkage was necessary. These disputes illustrate a potential 'clash of cultures' between international investment law and international cultural law. As adjudication plays a fundamental – bottom-up – role in the implementation of a given legal regime, this book has analysed the adjudicative patterns of arbitral tribunals in order to test the effectiveness of international investment law and, albeit indirectly, of international cultural law.

This book has surveyed a number of heritage-related investment disputes, showing that, while international investment law has not developed any institutional machinery for the protection of cultural heritage through investment dispute settlement (after all, international investment law is not intended to protect cultural heritage), in recent years a jurisprudential trend has emerged that takes cultural heritage into consideration. Arbitral tribunals have paid increasing attention to cultural concerns and have often referred to international law principles and cases in their reasoning. The survey of the relevant investment treaty arbitrations presents mixed results.

On the one hand, the review of domestic regulation by arbitral tribunals can improve good cultural governance and the transparent pursuit of legitimate cultural objectives. One might expect the field of cultural heritage law to be overwhelmed by the sophisticated web of international investment treaties – in particular due to the fact that arbitral tribunals have limited jurisdiction and thus cannot adjudicate on the violation of other norms of international law outside the realm of international investment law. However, this book illustrates that arbitrators have increasingly taken cultural concerns into consideration in deciding cases brought before them, not limiting themselves to purely economic standards of valuation. The fact that economic standards of valuation are not the only ones that are taken into consideration by arbitral tribunals is distinctive. An inward-looking approach, that is non-consideration of broader cultural concerns, may weaken the wider effectiveness and the perceived legitimacy of adjudicative bodies, and lead to a 'superiority complex' and isolationism.[1] While investor–state arbitration deals with an area at a crossroads between economics and law, the legal dimension of these disputes cannot be neglected or dismissed in favour of purely economical considerations.

On the other hand, the fact that such disputes are adjudicated before investment treaty tribunals may ultimately pinpoint the sophistication of international investment law and arbitration vis-à-vis international cultural law, and – albeit indirectly – some failures of the latter. International cultural law maintains the centrality of the state, as the right-holder and primary bearer of international obligations. The fact that international cultural law remains defined by state interests has implications for the identification of the type of cultural heritage to be protected and the way such heritage is governed. For instance, a monumental understanding of heritage leaves much indigenous and rural heritage vulnerable to economic and developmental interests.

[1] J. Pauwelyn, 'WTO Compassion or Superiority Complex? What to Make of the WTO Waiver for "Conflict Diamonds"', *Michigan JIL* 24 (2003), 1177–207.

Furthermore, from a cultural heritage perspective, it may be questioned whether these tribunals constitute the best available *fora* for settling this kind of dispute. One may wonder whether the fact that cultural heritage disputes are adjudicated before arbitral tribunals raises a sort of institutional bias. Concerns remain that, unlike other bodies – for example, those with adjudicative responsibilities regarding human rights – arbitral tribunals are ill-suited to the task of protecting cultural entitlements. At the end of the day, such tribunals are of limited jurisdiction: they cannot adjudicate on the eventual violation of international cultural law. The hermeneutical pathways adopted by arbitral tribunals may diverge from those adopted by human rights courts due to the different institutional mandate of each forum. There is a risk of arbitrators interpreting international cultural law restrictively, developing lines of arguments divergent from mainstream international law.

At the procedural level, the mechanism is mostly triggered by foreign investors; the affected communities are represented by the host state, but have no procedural rights in the context of the proceedings. Arbitration rules of procedure are not sufficiently developed to adequately protect indigenous peoples' rights. The participation of indigenous peoples as *amici curiae* at arbitral proceedings is not automatically granted, and arbitral proceedings involving cultural heritage have not always been open to the public. Only recently has investment arbitration started to respond positively to requests by public interest groups to make *amicus curiae* submissions and adopt policies concerning transparency and openness that facilitate public scrutiny.

The question as to whether a *lex administrativa culturalis*, or cultural administrative law, has emerged – characterized by the coalescence of consistent narratives, emerging rules and patterns of behaviours by relevant intra-national, national, supranational administrative bodies, adjudicators and private actors – remains open to debate. Certainly, through their constant interactions, international investment law and international cultural law are continuously contributing to the development of international law itself. Arbitral tribunals are building an ongoing dialogue and borrowing of concepts between these two areas of international law, contributing to the current debate on the unity or fragmentation of international law and supporting the argument that international law, albeit decentralized, is not an anarchic amalgam of different norms.

International investment treaties are not closed legal systems but have to be contextualized within international law. In many circumstances, international law is the law applicable to investment disputes according to an applicable arbitral clause or other relevant treaty provision. Even in those cases where the applicable law is the law of the host state, international law permeates national legal systems. Furthermore, according to the principles of systemic interpretation as restated by Article 31(3)(c) of the Vienna Convention on the Law of Treaties, together with the context, any relevant rule of international law applicable in the relationship between the parties should be taken into account. Arbitral tribunals are not courts of general jurisdiction, and cannot adjudicate on the eventual breach of international cultural law, but may analyse the specific investment claims in the light of the relevant rules of international law applicable in the relationship between the parties. Given the fact that UNESCO has an almost universal membership and that the relevant UNESCO conventions are widely ratified, this leads to the conclusion that arbitrators will have to take cultural concerns into account. If one deems that the protection of cultural heritage in times of peace already belongs to customary international law or to general principles of law, the case for such consideration is even stronger.

Certainly, these arbitrations can contribute to the emergence of general principles of international law and customary law with regard to the protection of cultural heritage in times of peace. In this regard, two emerging general principles may be distilled from the examined awards of arbitral tribunals. *First*, states can legitimately govern and delimit private property interest to protect cultural heritage.[2] Arbitral tribunals consider the objective of protecting cultural heritage as a legitimate public policy objective. *Second*, a fair balance between public and private interests needs to be struck when protecting cultural heritage. On the one hand, international cultural law requires the protection of cultural heritage in respect of human rights and fundamental freedoms; on the other, international investment law protects the private property interests of foreign investors within a given country to promote development. In this sense, the regulatory autonomy of the host state must find a balance between individual economic freedoms and the common weal thus complying with the relevant international law obligations of the state.

This analysis contributes to the current discourse on global governance in a twofold fashion. On the one hand, it highlights that

[2] F. Lenzerini, 'Property Protection and Protection of Cultural Heritage', in S. Schill (ed.), *International Investment Law and Comparative Public Law* (Oxford University Press, 2010), p. 564.

international investment law has been increasingly humanized, and that there is room for further humanization. When arbitrators juxtapose the interests of investors and cultural concerns, not only do they contextualize international investment law in the broader framework of international law, but they also highlight the human dimension of investment law and, albeit indirectly, of international cultural law. In parallel, cultural heritage-related investment disputes highlight the need to further democratize both international investment law and international cultural law to better reflect the interests and values of a wider range of actors, including indigenous peoples, minorities and local communities. On the other hand, this analysis strengthens the growing cognizance of the importance of effective protection and promotion of cultural heritage and diversity for sustainable development and peaceful relations among nations.

# BIBLIOGRAPHY

## Books

Adorno, T. W. and Horkheimer, M. *Dialektik der Aufklärung* (1947); trans. E. Jephcott, *Dialectic of Enlightenment* (Stanford CA: Stanford University Press, 2002).

Alberti, L. B. *De Re Aedificatoria* (1485) (trans. J. Rykwert, R. Tavernor and N. Leach), *On the Art of Building in Ten Books* (Cambridge MA: MIT Press, 1988).

Anaya, J. *Indigenous Peoples in International Law* (Oxford: Oxford University Press, 1996).

Baderin, M. A. and McCorquodale, R. 'The International Covenant on Economic, Social and Cultural Rights: Forty Years of Development', in R. G. McCorquodale and M. A. Baderin (eds.), *Economic, Social and Cultural Rights in Action* (Oxford: Oxford University Press, 2007), pp. 3–24.

Ball, D. *The Diana Adventure* (Groningen: Malaysian Historical Salvors Kuala Lumpur and Kemper Printers, 1995).

Bandelj, N. and Wherry, F. F. (eds.) *The Cultural Wealth of Nations* (Stanford CA: Stanford University Press, 2011).

Barannik, A. and Okaru, V. 'Harmonization of EA Procedures and Requirements between the World Bank and Borrowing Countries', in R. Goodland *et al.* (eds.), *Environmental Assessment (EA) in Africa: A World Bank Commitment* (Washington D.C.: World Bank, 1996).

Baslar, K. *The Concept of the Common Heritage of Mankind in International Law* (The Hague: Kluwer Law International, 1998).

Berman, F. 'Evolution or Revolution?', in C. Brown and K. Miles (eds.), *Evolution in Investment Treaty Law and Arbitration* (Cambridge: Cambridge University Press, 2011), pp. 658–72.

Bhagwati, J. *In Defense of Globalization* (Oxford: Oxford University Press, 2004).

Bhagwati, J. 'U.S. Trade Policy: The Infatuation with Free Trade Agreements', in J. Bhagwati and A. O. Krueger (eds.), *The Dangerous Drift to Preferential Trade Agreements* (Washington D.C.: AEI Press, 1995).

Binder, C., Kriebaum, U., Reinisch, A. and Wittich, S. (eds.) *International Investment Law for the 21st Century* (Oxford: Oxford University Press, 2009).

Bjorklund, A. K. 'Investment Treaty Arbitral Decisions as Jurisprudence Constante', in C. Picker, I. Bunn and D. Arner (eds.), *International Economic Law: The State and Future of Discipline* (Oxford: Hart Publishing, 2008).

Blackaby, N. 'Investment Arbitration and Commercial Arbitration (or the Tale of the Dolphin and the Shark)', in J. Lew and L. Mistelis (eds.), *Pervasive Problems in International Arbitration* (Kluwer Law International, 2006), pp. 217–33.

Boesten, E. *Archaeological and/or Historic Valuable Shipwrecks in International Waters: Public International Law and What It Offers* (The Hague: T.M.C. Asser Press, 2002).

Boisson de Chazournes, L. 'Monitoring, Supervision and Coordination of the Standard-setting Instruments of UNESCO', in A. A. Yusuf (ed.), *Standard-Setting in UNESCO: Normative Action in Education, Science and Culture*, vol. I (Leiden: Brill, 2007).

Booth, F. 'The Collision of Property Rights and Cultural Heritage; the Salvors' and Insurers' Viewpoints', in B. Hoffman (ed.), *Art and Cultural Heritage: Law, Policy and Practice* (Cambridge: Cambridge University Press, 2006).

Bosselmann, K. 'Introduction to State Sovereignty, Indigenous Governance and International Law', in J. R Engel, L. Westra and K. Bosselmann (eds.), *Democracy, Ecological Integrity and International Law* (Newcastle upon Tyne: Cambridge Scholars Press, 2010).

Bourdieu, P. *Language and Symbolic Power* (Cambridge: Polity Press, 1991).

Boyle, A. and Freestone, D. 'Introduction', in A. Boyle and D. Freestone (eds.), *International Law and Sustainable Development: Past Achievements and Future Challenges* (Oxford: Oxford University Press, 1999), pp. 1–18.

Brems, E. 'Accommodating Diversity in International Human Rights: Legal Techniques', in P. Meerts (ed.), *Culture and International Law* (Hague Academic Press, 2008).

Brownlie, I. *Principles of Public International Law*, 7th edn. (Oxford: Oxford University Press, 2008).

Cardozo, B. *The Paradoxes of Legal Science* (New York: Columbia University Press, 1928).

Carducci, G. 'Articles 4–7', in F. Francioni (ed.), *The 1972 World Heritage Convention* (Oxford: Oxford University Press, 2008), pp. 103–45.

Carducci, G. 'Introduction to the UNESCO Convention on the Protection of the Underwater Cultural Heritage', in R. Grenier, D. Nutley and I. Cochran (eds.), *Underwater Cultural Heritage at Risk: Managing Natural and Human Impacts* (Paris: ICOMOS, 2006).

Carman, J. *Against Cultural Property: Archaeology, Heritage and Ownership* (London: Duckworth, 2005).

Casanovas, O. *Unity and Pluralism in Public International Law* (The Hague: Martinus Nijhoff Publishers, 2001).

Chapman, A. and Russel, S. (eds.) *Core Obligations: Building a Framework for Economic, Social, and Cultural Rights* (Antwerp: Intersentia, 2002).

Charnovitz, S., Steger, D. and Van den Bossche, P. (eds.) *Law in the Service of Human Dignity: Essays in Honour of Florentino Feliciano* (Cambridge: Cambridge University Press, 2005).

Collier, J. and Lowe, V. *The Settlement of Disputes in International Law: Institutions and Procedures* (Oxford: Oxford University Press, 1999).

Comeaux, P. E. and Kinsella, N. S. *Protecting Foreign Investment under International Law: Legal Aspects of Political Risk* (New York: Oceana, 1997).

Conversi, D. 'Genocide, Ethnic Cleansing and Nationalism', in G. Delanty and K. Kumar (eds.), *The Sage Handbook of Nations and Nationalism* (London: Sage Publications, 2006).

Coombe, R. 'First Nations' Intangible Cultural Heritage Concerns: Prospects for Protection of Traditional Knowledge and Traditional Cultural Expressions in International Law', in C. Bell and R. Paterson (eds.), *Protection of First Nations' Cultural Heritage: Laws, Policy and Reform* (Vancouver: University of British Columbia Press, 2008).

Cotula, L. *Human Rights, Natural Resources and Investment Law in a Globalized World* (Abingdon: Routledge, 2011).

Cowen, T. 'Public Goods', in D. E. Anderson (ed.), *The Concise Encyclopedia of Economics*, 2nd edition (Monterey CA: Liberty Fund Inc., 2005).

Crawford, J. 'International Protection of Foreign Direct Investment: Between Clinical Isolation and Systematic Integration', in R. Hofmann and C. J. Tams (eds.), *International Investment Law and General International Law – from Clinical Isolation to Systemic Integration?* (Baden/Baden: Nomos, 2011), pp. 17–28.

Crocker Chester, A. *et al. Herding Cats: Multiparty Mediation in a Complex World* (Washington D.C.: United States Institute of Peace, 1999).

Cutler, C. 'The Globalization of International Law, Indigenous Identity, and the "New Constitutionalism"', in W. Coleman (ed.), *Property, Territory, Globalization: Struggles over Autonomy* (Vancouver: University of British Columbia Press, 2011).

D'Ayala, D. and Forsyth, M. 'What is Conservation Engineering?', in M. Forsyth (ed.), *Structures and Construction in Historic Building Conservation* (Oxford: Blackwell Publishing, 2007).

Daes, E.-I. 'Indigenous Peoples' Rights to their Natural Resources', in A. Constantinides and N. Zaikos (eds.), *The Diversity of International Law* (Leiden/Boston: Martinus Nijhoff, 2009).

Dahrendorf, A. 'Trade Meets Culture: The Legal Relationship between WTO Rules and the UNESCO Convention on the Protection and Promotion of the Diversity of Cultural Expressions', Maastricht Faculty of Law Working Papers, 2006/11.

Deloria, V. Jr. 'Self-Determination and the Concept of Sovereignty', in J. R. Wunder (ed.), *Native American Sovereignty* (New York: Garland, 1996).

De Vattel, E. *The Law of Nations*, in J. Chitty (ed.) (Philadelphia: T. & J.W. Johnson & Co., 1883).

Di Leva, C. E. 'The World Bank's Policy on Physical Cultural Resources', in B. Hoffmann (ed.), *Art and Cultural Heritage: Law, Policy and Practice* (Cambridge: Cambridge University Press, 2005).

Dirk Moses, A. 'Raphael Lemkin, Culture, and the Concept of Genocide', in D. Bloxham and A. Dirk Moses (eds.), *The Oxford Handbook of Genocide Studies* (Oxford: Oxford University Press, 2010).

Dolzer, R. and Schreuer, C. *Principles of International Investment Law* (Oxford: Oxford University Press, 2008).

Dolzer, R. 'The Notion of Investment in Recent Practice', in S. Charnovitz, D. Steger, N. Rubins and S. Kinsella (eds.), *International Investment, Political Risk and Dispute Resolution* (Oxford: Oxford University Press, 2005).

Donders, Y. 'Culture and Human Rights', in P. Forsythe (ed.), *Encyclopedia of Human Rights* (Oxford: Oxford University Press, 2009).

Donders, Y. 'The History of the UNESCO Convention on the Protection and Promotion of the Diversity of Cultural Expressions', in H. Schneider and P. Van den Bossche (eds.), *Protection of Cultural Diversity from an International and European Perspective* (Antwerp: Intersentia, 2008), pp. 1–30.

Donders, Y. 'The UN Declaration on the Rights of Indigenous Peoples. A Victory for Cultural Autonomy?', in I. Boerefijn and J. Goldschmidt (eds.), *Changing Perceptions of Sovereignty and Human Rights* (Antwerp/Oxford/Portland: Intersentia, 2008).

Donders, Y. *Towards a Right to Cultural Identity?* (Antwerp: Intersentia, 2002).

Douglas, Z. *The International Law of Investment Claims* (Cambridge: Cambridge University Press, 2009).

Dupuy, P. M. 'The Impact of Legal Instruments Adopted by UNESCO on General International Law', in A. A. Yusuf (ed.), *Normative Action in Education, Science and Culture* (Leiden/Boston: Martinus Nijhoff, 2007), pp. 351–64.

Dupuy, P. M. 'Unification Rather than Fragmentation of International Law? The Case of International Investment Law and Human Rights Law', in P. M. Dupuy, F. Francioni and E. U. Petersmann (eds.), *Human Rights in International Investment Law and Arbitration* (Oxford: Oxford University Press, 2009).

Eide, A. 'Economic and Social Rights', in J. Symonides (ed.), *Human Rights: Concepts and Standards* (Aldershot: UNESCO Publishing, 2000), pp. 109–74.

Eide, A. 'Cultural Rights as Individual Human Rights', in A. Eide, C. Krause and A. Rosas (eds.), *Economic, Social and Cultural Rights: A Textbook* (Dordrecht: Martinus Nijhoff, 1995).

Engle, K. *The Elusive Promise of Indigenous Development: Rights, Culture, Strategy* (Durham N.C.: Duke University Press, 2010).

Fisher, R. and Ury, W. *Getting to Yes: Negotiating Agreement Without Giving In* (New York: Penguin Books, 1983).

Forrest, C. *International Law and the Protection of Cultural Heritage* (Abingdon: Routledge, 2010).

Fowler, P. 'Cultural Landscape: Great Concept, Pity about the Phrase', in Kelly, R., Macinnes, L., Thackray, D. and Whitbourne, P. (eds.), *The Cultural Landscape. Planning for a Sustainable Partnership between People and Place* (London: ICOMOS, 2001), pp. 64–82.

Francioni, F. 'Preamble', in F. Francioni (ed.), *The 1972 World Heritage Convention: A Commentary* (Oxford: Oxford University Press, 2008).

Francioni, F. 'The 1972 World Heritage Convention: an Introduction', in F. Francioni and F. Lenzerini (eds.), *The 1972 World Heritage Convention: A Commentary* (Oxford: Oxford University Press, 2008), pp. 3–7.

Francioni, F. 'Culture, Heritage and Human Rights: An Introduction', in F. Francioni and M. Scheinin (eds.), *Cultural Human Rights* (Leiden/ Boston: Martinus Nijhoff Publishers, 2008), pp. 1–15.

Francioni, F. 'Sviluppo sostenibile e principi di diritto internazionale dell'ambiente', in P. Fois (ed.), *Il Principio dello sviluppo sostenibile nel diritto internazionale ed europeo dell'ambiente* (Naples: Editoriale Scientifica, 2007), pp. 41–62.

Francioni, F. 'La protezione internazionale dei beni culturali: un diritto consuetudinario in formazione?', in P. Benvenuti and R. Sapienza (eds.), *La tutela internazionale dei beni culturali nei conflitti armati* (Milan: Giuffré editore, 2007), pp. 3–33.

Francioni, F. 'WTO Law in Context: The Integration of International Human Rights and Environmental Law in the Dispute Settlement Process', in G. Sacerdoti, A. Yanovich and J. Bohanes (eds.), *The WTO at Ten: The Contribution of the Dispute Settlement System* (Cambridge: Cambridge University Press, 2006).

Francioni, F. 'Dispute Avoidance in International Environmental Law', in A. Kiss, D. Shelton and K. Ishibashi (eds.), *Economic Globalization and Compliance with International Environmental Agreements* (The Hague: Kluwer Law International, 2003), pp. 229–43.

Francioni, F. and Lenzerini, F. 'The Future of the World Heritage Convention: Problems and Prospects', in F. Francioni and F. Lenzerini (eds.), *The 1972 World Heritage Convention: A Commentary* (Oxford: Oxford University Press, 2008), pp. 401–10.

Francioni, F. and Lenzerini, F. (eds.) *The 1972 World Heritage Convention: A Commentary* (Oxford: Oxford University Press, 2008).

Francioni, F. and Scheinin, M. (eds.) *Cultural Human Rights* (Leiden/Boston: Martinus Nijhoff Publishers, 2008).

Froehlich, A. 'Cultural Matters in Investment Agreements and Decisions', in A. Reinisch and C. Knahr (eds.), *International Investment Law in Context* (Utrecht: Eleven International Publishing, 2008).

Froehlich, A. 'L'enjeu de la culture dans son contexte économique international', in P. Meerts (ed.), *Culture and International Law* (Cambridge: Cambridge University Press, 2008).

Gaffney, J. P. 'Going to Pieces without Falling Apart: Wälde's Defence of "Specialisation" in the Interpretation of Investment Treaties', in J. Werner and A. Hyder Ali (eds.), *A Liber Amicorum: Thomas Wälde: Law Beyond Conventional Thought* (London: CMP, 2009), pp. 55–68.

Gaillard, E. and Savage, J. *Fouchard, Gaillard, Goldmann on International Commercial Arbitration* (The Hague: Kluwer Law International, 1999).

Gangjee, D. *Relocating the Law of Geographical Indications* (Cambridge University Press, 2012).

Garabello, R. and Scovazzi, T. (eds.) *The Protection of the Underwater Cultural Heritage Before and After the 2001 UNESCO Convention* (Leiden/Boston: Martinus Nijhoff, 2003).

Germann, C. 'Towards a Global Cultural Contract to Counter Trade Related Cultural Discrimination', in N. Obuljen and J. Smiers (eds.), *UNESCO's Convention on the Protection and the Promotion of the Diversity of Cultural Expressions: Making it Work* (Zagreb: Institute for International Relations, 2006).

Gilbert, J. 'Custodians of the Land: Indigenous Peoples, Human Rights and Cultural Integrity', in M. Langfield, W. Logan and M. Craith (eds.), *Cultural Diversity, Heritage and Human Rights* (Abingdon: Routledge, 2010), pp. 31–44.

Goethe, J. W. *Italian Journey (1786–1788)*, trans. W. H. Auden and Elizabeth Mayer (London: Collins, 1962).

Goodale, M. 'Foreword', in G. A. Sarfaty, *Values in Translation: Human Rights and the Culture of the World Bank* (Stanford CA: Stanford University Press, 2012), pp. ix–xi.

Gramsci, A. *Quaderni del carcere* (Turin: Einaudi, 1948–1951).

Greffe, X. 'Heritage Conservation as a Driving Force for Development', in *Heritage and Beyond* (Strasbourg: Council of Europe, 2009).

Hallward-Driemeier, M. 'Do Bilateral Investment Treaties Attract Foreign Direct Investment? Only a Bit... And They Could Bite', Policy Research Working Paper No 3121 (Washington: World Bank, 2003).

Hart, H. L. A. *The Concept of Law* (Oxford: Clarendon Press, 1961).

Herreman, Y. 'The Role of Museums Today: Tourism and Cultural Heritage', in B. Hoffman (ed.), *Art and Cultural Heritage* (Cambridge: Cambridge University Press, 2006), pp. 419–26.

Hippocrates, *Aphorismi Hippocratis* (Amsterdam: Hendrik Wetstein, 1685).

Hirsch, M. 'Interactions between Investment and Non-Investment Obligations in International Investment Law', in P. Muchlinski, F. Ortino and C. Schreuer (eds.), *The Oxford Handbook of International Investment Law* (Oxford: Oxford University Press, 2008).

Hoffman, B. 'A Consideration of Cultural and Natural Heritage Guidelines Applicable to Infrastructure Projects, Mining Operations, and Their Financing', in B. Hoffman (ed.), *Art and Cultural Heritage: Law, Policy and Practice* (Cambridge: Cambridge University Press, 2009), pp. 243–4.

Hofmann, R. and Tams, C. J. (eds.) *International Investment Law and General International Law* (Baden: Nomos, 2011).

Hsu, L. 'Applicability of WTO Law in Regional Trade Agreements: Identifying the Links', in L. Bartels and F. Ortino (eds.), *Regional Trade Agreements and the WTO Legal System* (Oxford: Oxford University Press, 2006).

Huntington, S. P. and Harrison, L. E. (eds.) *Culture Matters: How Values Shape Human Progress* (New York: Basic Books, 2000).

Jackson, J. *The World Trading System* (Cambridge MA: MIT Press, 2002).

Jokilehto, J. *A History of Architectural Conservation* (Oxford/Boston: Butterworth-Heinemann, 1999).

Kaul, I., Grunberg, I. and Stern, M. A., 'Defining Global Public Goods', in I. Kaul, I. Grunberg and M. A. Stern (eds.), *Global Public Goods: International Cooperation in the 21st Century* (Oxford University Press, 1999).

Kawharu, A. 'Participation of Non-Governmental Organizations in Investment Arbitration as Amici Curiae', in M. Waibel, A. Kaushal, K.-H. L. Chung and C. Balchin (eds.), *The Backlash against Investment Arbitration: Perceptions and Reality* (Kluwer Law International, 2010), pp. 275–295.

Kelsey, J. *Serving Whose Interests? The Political Economy of Trade in Services Agreements* (Oxford: Routledge Cavendish, 2008).

Khalfan, A. and Cordonier Segger, M. C., 'Introduction', in A. Khalfan and M. C. Cordonier Segger (eds.), *Sustainable Development Law* (Oxford: Oxford University Press, 2005).

Klein, N., *Dispute Settlement in the UN Convention on the Law of the Sea* (Cambridge: Cambridge University Press, 2005).

Kono, T. and Wrbka, S. 'General Report', in T. Kono (ed.) *The Impact of Uniform Laws on the Protection of Cultural Heritage and the Preservation of Cultural Heritage in the 21st Century* (Leiden/Boston: Martinus Nijhoff, 2010), pp. 1–8.

Koren, G., 'Limitations in Enforcement of International Conventions: Implications for Protection of Monuments and Sites', in *Estrategias relativas al patrimonio cultural mundial. La salvaguardia en un mundo globalizado. Principios, practicas y perspectivas* (Madrid: ICOMOS, 2002), pp. 90–3.

Kowalski, A. 'When Cultural Capitalization Became Global Practice', in N. Bandelj and F. F. Wherry (eds.), *The Cultural Wealth of Nations* (Stanford CA: Stanford University Press, 2011), pp. 73–89.

Kreindler, R. H. 'The Law Applicable to International Investment Disputes', in N. Horn (ed.), *Arbitrating Foreign Investment Disputes* (The Hague: Kluwer Law International, 2004), pp. 401–24.

Lalive, P. 'Réflexions sur un ordre public culturel', in E. Wyler and A. Papaux (eds.), *L'extranéité ou le dépassement de l'ordre juridique étatique* (Paris: Pédone, 1999).

Langfield, M., Logan, W. and Nic Craith, M. (eds.) *Cultural Diversity, Heritage and Human Rights* (Abingdon: Routledge, 2010).

Last, K. 'Cultural Pluralism and the Return of Cultural Heritage', in S. Tierney (ed.), *Accommodating Cultural Diversity* (Aldershot: Ashgate, 2007), pp. 123–43.

Last, K. 'The Resolution of Cultural Property Disputes: Some Issues of Definition', in International Bureau of the Permanent Court of Arbitration (ed.), *Resolution of Cultural Property Disputes* (The Hague: Kluwer Law International, 2004).

Leibniz, G. *Discourse on Metaphysics* (1686) reprinted (2007).

Lenzerini, F. 'Property Protection and Protection of Cultural Heritage', in S. Schill (ed.), *International Investment Law and Comparative Public Law* (Oxford: Oxford University Press, 2010), 541–68.

Lenzerini, F. 'Article 12 Protection of Properties Not Inscribed on the World Heritage List', in F. Francioni (ed.), *The 1972 World Heritage Convention: A Commentary* (Oxford: Oxford University Press, 2008), pp. 201–18.

Lew, J. and Mistelis, L. *Pervasive Problems in International Arbitration* (Kluwer Law International, 2006).

Lew, J., Mistelis, L. and Kröll, S. *Comparative International Commercial Arbitration* (The Hague: Kluwer Law, 2003).

Lowe, V. 'Sustainable Development and Unsustainable Arguments', in A. Boyle and D. Freestone (eds.), *International Law and Sustainable Development – Past Achievements and Future Challenges* (Oxford: Oxford University Press, 1999), pp. 19–39.

Lowenfeld, A. *International Economic Law*, 2nd edn (Oxford: Oxford University Press, 2008), pp. 469–94.

Luxford, D. 'Finders Keepers Losers Weepers – Myth or Reality? An Australian Perspective on Historic Shipwrecks', in B. Hoffmann (ed.), *Art and Cultural Heritage: Law, Policy and Practice* (Cambridge: Cambridge University Press, 2006), pp. 300–7.

Maffei, M. C. 'Culinary Traditions as Cultural Intangible Heritage and Expressions of Cultural Diversity', in S. Borelli and F. Lenzerini (eds.), *Cultural Heritage, Cultural Rights, Cultural Diversity* (Leiden/Boston: Martinus Nijhoff, 2012).

Maffei, M. C. 'Food as a Cultural Choice: A Human Rights to Be Protected?', in S. Borelli and F. Lenzerini (eds.), *Cultural Heritage, Cultural Rights, Cultural Diversity* (Leiden/Boston: Martinus Nijhoff, 2012).

Mainetti, V. 'Le principe du patrimoine culturel de l'humanité: de la république des arts à un ordre public international', in *Alberico Gentili: La salvaguardia dei beni culturali nel diritto internazionale: atti del convegno Dodicesima Giornata Gentiliana* (Milan: Giuffré, 2008), pp. 581–601.

Mann, H. 'The Right of States to Regulate and International Investment Law: A Comment', in UNCTAD, *The Development Dimension of FDI: Policy and Rule-Making Perspectives* (New York/Geneva: UN, 2003), pp. 211–23.

Mann, H. and Von Moltke, K. *Protecting Investor Rights and the Public Good: Assessing NAFTA's Chapter 11* (Winnipeg: IISD, 2003).

Mayer-Robitaille, L. *Le statut juridique des biens et services culturels dans les accords commerciaux internationaux* (Paris: L'Harmattan, 2008).

McLachlan, C., Shore, L. and Weiniger, M. *International Investment Arbitration: Substantive Principles* (Cambridge: Cambridge University Press, 2007).

Meisel, N. *Governance Culture and Development: A Different Perspective on Corporate Governance* (Paris: OECD, 2004).

Meerts, P. (ed.) *Culture and International Law* (The Hague: T.M.C. Asser Press, 2008).

Meron, T. *The Humanization of International Law* (Leiden: Martinus Nijhoff, 2006).

Michelot, A. 'Les Réserves de Biosphère du Programme sur l'Homme et la Biosphère de l'UNESCO: au delà des aires protegégées, un modèle de société durable?', in J. R. Engel, L. Westra and K. Bosselmann (eds.), *Democracy, Ecological Integrity and International Law* (Newcastle upon Tyne: Cambridge Scholars Publishing, 2010), pp. 389–408.

Momtaz, D. 'La Convention sur la protection culturel subaquatique', in T. Malick Ndiaye and R. Wolfrum (eds.), *Law of the Sea, Environmental Law and Settlement of Disputes: Liber Amicorum Judge Thomas A. Mensa* (Leiden/Boston: Martinus Nijhoff, 2007).

Montt, S. *State Liability in Investment Treaty Arbitration: Global Constitutional Law and Administrative Law in the BIT Generation* (Oxford: Hart Publishing, 2009).

Morijn, J. *Reframing Human Rights and Trade: Potential and Limits of a Human Rights Perspective of WTO Law on Cultural and Educational Goods and Services* (Antwerpen: Intersentia, 2010).

Morijn, J. 'The Place of Cultural Rights in the WTO System', in F. Francioni and M. Scheinin (eds.), *Cultural Human Rights* (Leiden/Boston: Martinus Nijhoff Publishers, 2008), pp. 285–316.

Muchlinski, P. *Multinational Enterprises and the Law*, 2nd edn (Oxford: Oxford University Press, 2007).

Muchlinski, P. 'Global Bukovina Examined: Viewing the Multinational Enterprise as a Transnational Law Making Community', in G. Teubner (ed.), *Global Law Without a State* (Aldershot: Ashgate, 2003).

Muchlinski, P., Ortino, F. and Schreuer, C. (eds.) *The Oxford Handbook of International Investment Law* (Oxford: Oxford University Press, 2008).

Nafziger, J. A. R. 'The Present State of Research', in *Le patrimoine culturel de l'humanité: The Cultural Heritage of Mankind* (Leiden: Martinus Nijhoff, 2008).

Nafziger, J. A. R., Paterson, R. K. and Dundes Renteln, A. (eds.) *Cultural Law-International, Comparative and Indigenous* (Cambridge: Cambridge University Press, 2010).

Nafziger, J. A. R. and Nicgorski, A. M. (eds.) *Cultural Heritage Issues: The Legacy of Conquest, Colonization and Commerce* (Leiden: Martinus Nijhoff, 2009).

Neuwirth, R. J. *The Cultural Industries in International Trade Law* (Hamburg: Kovac, 2006).

Newcombe, A. 'General Exceptions in International Investment Agreements', in M. C. Cordonnier Segger, M. W. Gehring and A. Newcombe (eds.), *Sustainable Development in World Investment Law* (The Hague: Kluwer, 2011).

Newcombe, A. and Paradell, L. *Law and Practice of Investment Treaties: Standards of Treatment* (Austin/Boston: Kluwer Law International, 2009).

Nic Craith, M. 'Linguistic Heritage and Language Rights in Europe', in M. Langfield, W. Logan and M. Nic Craith (eds.), *Cultural Diversity, Heritage and Human Rights* (Abingdon: Routledge, 2010).

O'Keefe, P. J. *Shipwrecked Heritage: A Commentary on the UNESCO Convention on Underwater Cultural Heritage* (The Hague: T.M.C. Asser Press, 2002).

O'Keefe, P. J. and Prott, L. V. *Cultural Heritage Conventions and Other Instruments* (London: Institute of Art and Law, 2011).

Orakhelashvili, A. *Peremptory Norms in International Law* (Oxford: Oxford University Press, 2006).

Orellana, M. 'Science, Risk and Uncertainty: Public Health Measures and Investment Disciplines', in P. Kahn and T. Wälde (eds.), *New Aspects of International Investment Law* (Leiden: Martinus Nijhoff, 2007).

Ortino, F. 'Non-Discriminatory Treatment in Investment Disputes', in P. -M. Dupuy, F. Francioni and E. -U. Petersmann (eds.), *Human Rights in International Investment Law and Arbitration* (Oxford: Oxford University Press, 2009).

Ost, F. and Van de Kerchove, M. *De la pyramide au réseau, Pour une théorie dialectique du droit* (Brussels: Publication des facultés universitaires St-Louis, 2002).

Paulsson, J. *Denial of Justice in International Law* (Cambridge University Press, 2005).

Pauwelyn, J. *Conflict of Norms in Public International Law: How WTO Law Relates to Other Rules of International Law* (Cambridge University Press, 2003).

Peterson, L. E. *The Global Governance of Foreign Direct Investment: Madly Off in All Directions* (Geneva: Friedrich Ebert Stiftung Publisher, 2005).

Phares, J. and Guttman, C. *Investing in World Heritage: Past Achievements, Future Ambitions, A Guide to International Assistance* (Paris: UNESCO, 2002).

Picciotto, S. *Regulating Global Corporate Capitalism* (Cambridge: Cambridge University Press, 2011).

Plutarch. *Rise and Fall of Athens: Nine Greek Lives*, trans. I. Scott Kilvert (New York: Penguin Books, 1960).

Porter, M. E. 'Attitudes, Values, Beliefs, and the Microeconomics of Prosperity', in S. P. Huntington and L. E. Harrison (eds.), *Culture Matters: How Values Shape Human Progress* (New York: Basic Books, 2000).

Posner, R. A. *Economic Analysis of Law*, 6th edn (Aspen Publishers, 2003).

Prost, M. *The Concept of Unity in Public International Law* (Hart Publishing, 2012).

Prott, L. 'UNESCO International Framework for the Protection of Cultural Heritage', in J. A. R. Nafziger and A. M. Nicgorski (eds.), *Cultural Heritage Issues: The Legacy of Conquest, Colonization and Commerce* (Leiden: Martinus Nijhoff, 2009), pp. 257–81.

Prott, L. V. 'Cultural Rights as Peoples' Rights in International Law', in J. Crawford (ed.), *The Rights of Peoples* (Oxford: Clarendon Press, 1988).

Puvimanasinghe, S. F. *Foreign Investment, Human Rights and the Environment* (Leiden: Martinus Nijhoff, 2007).

Redgwell, C. 'The World Heritage Convention and Other Conventions Relating to the Protection of Natural Heritage', in F. Francioni (ed.), *The 1972 World Heritage Convention* (Oxford: Oxford University Press, 2008), pp. 377–97.

Redgwell, C. 'Protecting Natural Heritage and Its Transmission to Future Generations', in A. A. Yusuf (ed.), *Standard-Setting in UNESCO, Normative Action in Education, Science and Culture* (Brill: Leiden, 2007).

Reiner, C. and Schreuer, C. 'Human Rights and International Investment Arbitration' in P. M. Dupuy, F. Francioni and E. U. Petersmann (eds.), *Human Rights in International Investment Law and Arbitration* (Oxford: Oxford University Press, 2008).

Reinisch, A. *Standards of Investment Protection* (Oxford: Oxford University Press, 2008).

Romano, S. *L'ordinamento giuridico*, 2nd edn (Florence: Sansoni, 1946).

Rubino-Sammartano, M. *International Arbitration Law and Practice*, 2nd edn (The Hague/Boston: Kluwer Law International, 2001).

Rubins, N. and Kinsella, S. *International Investment, Political Risk and Dispute Resolution* (Oxford: Oxford University Press, 2005), pp. 153–174.

Sadat-Akhavi, S. A. *Methods of Resolving Conflicts between Treaties* (Leiden: Brill, 2003).

Samuels, W. *The Legal-Economic Nexus* (Abingdon: Routledge, 2007).

Sandler, T. 'Intergenerational Public Goods', in I. Kaul, I. Grunberg and M. A. Stern (eds.), *Global Public Goods: International Cooperation in the 21st Century* (New York: UNDP, 1999).

Sands, P. 'Litigating Environmental Disputes: Courts, Tribunals and the Progressive Development of International Environmental Law', in T. Ndiaye and R. Wolfrum (eds.), *Law of the Sea, Environmental Law and*

*Settlement of Disputes: Liber Amicorum Judge Thomas Mensah* (Leiden: Brill, 2007), pp. 313–25.

Sassen, S. *Globalization and its Discontents: Essays on the New Mobility of People and Money* (New York: New Press, 1998).

Sax, J. *Playing Darts with a Rembrandt: Public and Private Rights in Cultural Treasures* (University of Michigan Press, 1999).

Schill, S. W. *The Multilateralization of International Investment Law* (Cambridge: Cambridge University Press, 2009).

Schill, S. (ed.), *International Investment Law and Comparative Public Law* (Oxford: Oxford University Press, 2010).

Schneiderman, D. *Constitutionalizing Economic Globalization: Investment Rules and Democracy's Premise* (Oxford: Oxford University Press, 2008).

Schreuer, C. *The ICSID Convention: A Commentary* (Cambridge: Cambridge University Press, 2001).

Schwebel, S. 'Is Mediation of Foreign Disputes Plausible?', in S. Schwebel, *Justice in International Law* (Cambridge: Cambridge University Press, 2011), pp. 318–22.

Scott Rau, A. 'Mediation in Art-Related Disputes', in Q. Byrne-Sutton and F. Geisinger-Mariéthoz (eds.) *Resolution Methods for Art-Related Disputes* (Zurich: Schultess Verlag, 1999).

Scovazzi, T. 'The Definition of Intangible Cultural Heritage', in S. Borelli and F. Lenzerini (eds.), *Cultural Heritage, Cultural Rights, Cultural Diversity* (Leiden/Boston: Martinus Nijhoff, 2012).

Scovazzi, T. 'Articles 8–11 World Heritage Committee and World Heritage List', in F. Francioni (ed.), *The World Heritage Convention: A Commentary* (Oxford: Oxford University Press, 2008).

Scovazzi, T. 'The 2001 UNESCO Convention on the Protection of the Underwater Cultural Heritage', in B. Hoffman (ed.), *Art and Cultural Heritage: Law, Policy and Practice* (Cambridge: Cambridge University Press, 2006), pp. 285–292.

Sen, A. *Development as Freedom* (Oxford: Oxford University Press, 1999).

Serafini, F. *Musei navali e collezioni marittime nel mondo* (Milan: Gribaudo, 2005).

Shan, W., Simons, P. and Singh, D. (eds.) *Redefining Sovereignty in International Economic Law* (Oxford: Hart Publishing, 2008).

Shelton, D. 'Law, Non-Law and the Problem of Soft Law', in D. Shelton (ed.), *Commitment and Compliance: The Role of Non-Binding Norms in the International System* (Oxford: Oxford University Press, 2000), pp. 4–10.

Simma, B. and Kill, T., 'Harmonizing Investment Protection and International Human Rights: First Steps towards a Methodology', in C. Binder, U. Kriebaum, A. Reinisch and S. Wittich (eds.), *International Investment Law for the 21st Century: Essays in Honour of Christoph Schreuer* (Oxford: Oxford University Press, 2009).

Sinclair, I. *The Vienna Convention on the Law of Treaties* (Manchester: Manchester University Press, 1984).

Singer, J.W. *Entitlement: The Paradoxes of Property* (New Haven CT: Yale University Press, 2000), pp. 95–139.

Slaughter, A.M. *A New World Order* (Princeton N.J.: Princeton University Press, 2004).

Smith, A. *An Inquiry into the Nature and Causes of the Wealth of Nations* (London: Strahan and Cadell, 1776).

Sornarajah, M. *The International Law on Foreign Investment,* 3rd edn (Cambridge: Cambridge University Press, 2010).

Sornarajah, M. 'A Coming Crisis: Expansionary Trends in Investment Treaty Arbitration', in K. Sauvant (ed.), *Appeals Mechanism in International Investment Disputes* (Oxford: Oxford University Press, 2008).

Sornarajah, M. *The International Law on Foreign Investment,* 2nd edn (Cambridge: Cambridge University Press, 2004).

Sornarajah, M. 'Right to Regulate and Safeguards', in UNCTAD, *The Development Dimension of FDI: Policy and Rule Making Perspectives* (New York/Geneva: UN, 2003), pp. 205–10.

Spiermann, O. 'Applicable Law', in P. Muchlinski, F. Ortino and C. Schreuer (eds.), *The Oxford Handbook of International Investment Law* (Oxford: Oxford University Press, 2008).

Stamatopoulou, E. 'Taking Cultural Rights Seriously: The Vision of the UN Declaration on the Rights of Indigenous Peoples', in S. Allen and A. Xanthaki (eds.), *Reflections on the UN Declaration on the Rights of Indigenous Peoples* (Hart Publishing, 2011).

Stamatopoulou, E. *Cultural Rights in International Law* (Leiden and Boston: Martinus Nijhoff, 2007).

Stavenhagen, R. 'Cultural Rights and Universal Human Rights', in A. Eide, C. Krause, and A. Rosas (eds.), *Economic, Social and Cultural Rights: A Textbook* (Dordrecht: Martinus Nijhoff, 1995).

Stern, B. 'In Search of the Frontiers of Indirect Expropriation', in A. Rovine (ed.), *Contemporary Issues in International Arbitration and Mediation* (Leiden/Boston: Martinus Nijhoff, 2008), pp. 29–51.

Stiglitz, J. *Globalization and Its Discontents* (New York: WW Norton & Company, 2002).

Subedi, S. *International Investment Law: Reconciling Policy and Principle* (Oxford: Hart Publishing, 2008).

Throsby, D. *The Economics of Cultural Policy* (Cambridge: Cambridge University Press, 2010).

Throsby, D. *Economics and Culture* (Cambridge: Cambridge University Press, 2001).

Tienhaara, K. *The Expropriation of Environmental Governance* (Cambridge: Cambridge University Press, 2009).

Tudor-Knoll, I. 'The Fair and Equitable Treatment Standard and Human Rights Norms', in P. M. Dupuy, F. Francioni and E. U. Petersmann (eds.), *Human Rights in International Investment Law and Arbitration* (Oxford: Oxford University Press, 2009), pp. 310–43.

Vadi, V. *Public Health in International Investment Law and Arbitration* (Abingdon: Routledge, 2012).

Vadi, V. 'The Protection of Cultural Landscapes and Indigenous Heritage in International Investment Law', in L. Westra, C. Soskolne and D. Spady (eds.), *Human Health and Ecological Integrity – Ethics, Law and Human Rights* (Earthscan: London, 2012), pp. 250–261.

Van Damme, I. *Treaty Interpretation by the WTO Appellate Body* (Oxford: Oxford University Press, 2009).

Van den Bossche, P. *Free Trade and Culture* (Amsterdam: Stichting Boekmanstudies, 2008).

Van den Bossche, P. and Schneider, H. (eds.), *Protection of Cultural Diversity from a European and International Perspective* (Antwerp: Intersentia, 2008).

Van Den Kerchov, M. and Ost, F. *De la Pyramide au réseau? Pour une théorie dialectique du droit* (Brussels: Publications des facultés universitaires Saint-Louis, 2002).

Van Harten, G. *Investment Treaty Arbitration and Public Law* (Oxford: Oxford University Press, 2007).

Van Woudenberg, N. *State Immunity and Cultural Objects on Loan* (Leiden: Martinus Nijhoff, 2012).

Van Woudenberg, N. 'Immunity from Seizure: A Legal Exploration', in S. Pettersson, M. Hagedorn-Saupe, T. Jyrkkio and A. Weij (eds.), *Encouraging Collections Mobility* (Brussels, 2010), pp. 184–95.

Varmer, O. 'RMS Titanic', in R. Grenier, D. Nutley and I Cochran (eds.), *Underwater Cultural Heritage at Risk: Managing Natural and Human Impacts* (Paris: ICOMOS, 2006), pp. 14–16.

Veenstra-Kjos, H. E. 'Counter-Claims by Host States in Investment Dispute Arbitration "without Privity"', in P. Kahn and T. Waelde (eds.), *New Aspects of International Investment Law* (Leiden: Martinus Nijhoff Publishers, 2007), chapter 14.

Von Moltke, K. 'Discrimination and Non-Discrimination in Foreign Direct Investment Mining Issues' (Paris: OECD, 2002).

Von Schorlemer, S. 'UNESCO Dispute Settlement', in A. A. Yusuf (ed.), *Standard-Setting in UNESCO: Normative Action in Education, Science and Culture Essays in Commemoration of the Sixtieth Anniversary of UNESCO* (Leiden/Boston: Martinus Nijhoff, 2007), pp. 73–103.

Voon, T. *Cultural Products and the World Trade Organization* (Cambridge University Press, 2007).

Vrdoljak, A. F. 'Self-Determination and Cultural Rights', in F. Francioni and M. Scheinin (eds.), *Cultural Human Rights* (Leiden/Boston: Martinus Nijhoff Publishers, 2008), pp. 41–78.

Vrdoljak, A. F. 'Reparations for Cultural Loss', in F. Lenzerini (ed.), *Reparations for Indigenous Peoples: International and Comparative Perspectives* (Oxford: Oxford University Press, 2008).

Waibel, M. 'International Investment Law and Treaty Interpretation', in R. Hoffman and C. Tams (eds.), *International Investment Law and General International Law: From Clinical Isolation to Systemic Integration* (Baden Baden: Nomos, 2011).

Waibel, M., Kaushal, A., Chung, K.-H. and Balchin, C. 'The Backlash against Investment Arbitration: Perceptions and Reality', in M. Waibel, A. Kaushal, K.-H. Chung and C. Balchin (eds.), *The Backlash against Investment Arbitration: Perceptions and Reality* (Netherlands: Kluwer Law International, 2010), pp. xxxvii–xlix.

Waibel, M., Kaushal, A., Chung, K.-H. and Balchin, C. (eds.), *The Backlash against Investment Arbitration* (Netherlands: Kluwer Law International, 2010).

Wälde, T. W. 'Interpreting Investment Treaties: Experiences and Examples', in C. Binder, U. Kriebaum, A. Reinisch, and S. Wittich (eds.), *International Investment Law for the 21st Century: Essays in Honour of Christoph Schreuer* (Oxford: Oxford University Press, 2009).

Westra, L. *Environmental Justice and the Rights of Indigenous Peoples: International and Domestic Legal Perspectives* (London: Earthscan, 2008).

Whitby-Last, K. 'Article 1 Cultural Landscapes', in F. Francioni (ed.), *The 1972 World Heritage Convention* (Oxford: Oxford University Press, 2008), pp. 51–62.

Wiessner, S. 'Indigenous Self-Determination, Culture, and Land: A Reassessment in Light of the 2007 UN Declaration on the Rights of Indigenous Peoples', in E. Pulitano (ed.), *Indigenous Rights in the Age of the UN Declaration* (Cambridge: Cambridge University Press, 2012), pp. 31–63.

Wouters, J. and Vidal, M. 'International Normative Action for Cultural Diversity: The Contribution of UNESCO', in M.-C. Foblets, J.-F. Gaudreault-Desbiens and A. Dundes Renteln (eds.), *Cultural Diversity and the Law: State Responses from around the World* (Brussels: Bruylant, 2010), pp. 779–90.

Yescombe, A. E. *Principles of Corporate Finance* (San Diego/London: Academic Press, 2002).

Yusuf, A. A. (ed.), *Standard-Setting in UNESCO: Normative Action in Education, Science and Culture* (Leiden: Martinus Nijhoff, 2007).

## Articles

Abramovich, V. E. 'Courses of Action in Economic, Social and Cultural Rights: Instruments and Allies', *International Journal of Human Rights* 2 (2004), 180–216.

Acheson, K. and Maule, C. 'Convention on Cultural Diversity', *Journal of Cultural Economics* 28 (2004), 243–56.

Affolder, N. 'The Private Life of Environmental Treaties', *AJIL* 103 (2009), 510–525.

Affolder, N. 'Mining and the World Heritage Convention: Democratic Legitimacy and Treaty Compliance', *Pace Environmental Law Rev.* 24 (2007), 35–66.

Akinsanya, A. 'International Protection of Foreign Direct Investments in the Third World', *ICLQ* 36 (1987), 58–75.

Alston, P. 'Resisting the Merger and Acquisition of Human Rights by Trade Law: A Reply to Petersmann', *EJIL* 13 (2002), 815–844.

Alston, P. 'U.S. Ratification of the Covenant on Economic, Social and Cultural Rights: The Need for an Entirely New Strategy', *AJIL* 84 (1980), 65–393.

Alston, P. and Quinn, G. 'The Nature and Scope of States Parties' Obligation under International Covenant on Economic, Social and Cultural Rights', *HRQ* 9 (1987), 156–229.

Andreeva, Y. 'The Tribunal in Malaysian Historical Salvors v Malaysia Adopts a Restrictive Interpretation of the Term "Investment"', *Journal of International Arbitration* 25 (2008), 503–8.

Anglin, R. 'The World Heritage List: Bridging the Cultural Property Nationalism-Internationalism Divide', *Yale J. L. & the Humanities* 20 (2008), 241–75.

Aniakor, C. C. 'Cultural Objects as History and National Patrimony: A Moral Challenge', *Proceedings of the Annual Meeting of the American Society of International Law* 89 (1995), 434–8.

Appleton, B. 'Regulatory Takings: The International Law Perspective', *NYU Environmental L.J.* 11 (2003), 35–48.

Ashe, M., Jernigan, D., Kline, R. and Galaz, R. 'Land Use Planning and the Control of Alcohol, Tobacco, Firearms, and Fast Food Restaurants', *American Journal of Public Health* 93 (2003), 1404–8.

Bainton, N. A., Ballard, C., Gillespie, K. and Hall, N. 'Stepping Stones across the Lihir Islands: Developing Cultural Heritage Management in the Context of Gold-Mining', *International Journal of Cultural Property* 18 (2011), 81–110.

Balasubramanyam, V. N., Salisu, M. and Sapsford, D. 'Foreign Direct Investment and Growth: New Hypotheses and Evidence', *J. Int'l Trade and Economic Development* 8 (1999), 27–40.

Baltag, C. 'Precedent on Notion of Investment: ICSID Award in MHS v Malaysia', *TDM* 4 (2007), 1–5.

Barelli, M. 'The Role of Soft Law in the International Legal System: The Case of the United Nations Declaration on the Rights of Indigenous Peoples', *ICLQ* 58 (2009), 957–83.

Barrera-Hernández, L. 'Indigenous Peoples, Human Rights and Natural Resource Development: Chile's Mapuche Peoples and the Right to Water', *Ann. Surv. Int'l & Comp. L.* 11 (2005), 1–28.

Barsch, R. L. 'Indigenous Peoples in the 1990s: From Object to Subject of International Law', *Harvard Human Rights Journal* 7 (1994), 33–86.

Battini, S. 'The Procedural Side of Legal Globalization: The Case of the World Heritage Convention', *International Journal of Constitutional Law* 9 (2011), 340–68.

Bauer, A. A. 'New Ways of Thinking about Cultural Property: A Critical Appraisal of the Antiquities Trade Debate', *Fordham Int'l L. J.* 31 (2007–2008), 690–724.

Bell, C. 'Protecting Indigenous Heritage Resources in Canada: A Comment on Kitkatla Band v. British Columbia', *International Journal of Cultural Property* 10(2) (2001), 246–63.

Bénassy-Quéré, A., Coupet, M. and Mayer, T. 'Institutional Determinants of Foreign Direct Investment', *World Economy* 30 (2007), 764–82.

Benvenisti, E. 'Margin of Appreciation, Consensus and Universal Standards', *NYU JIL & Politics* 31 (1999), 843–54.

Bhagwati, J. 'Why Multinationals Help Reduce Poverty', *World Economy* 30 (2007), 221–8.

Bianchi, A. 'Human Rights and the Magic of Jus Cogens', *EJIL* 19 (2008), 491–508.

Bianchi, R. and Boniface, P. 'Editorial: The Politics of World Heritage', *International Journal of Heritage Studies* 8 (2002), 79–80.

Biondi, A. 'The Merchant, the Thief and the Citizen: The Circulation of Works of Art within the European Union', *CMLR* 34 (1997), 1173–95.

Bjorklund, A. 'The Emerging Civilization of Investment Arbitration', *Penn State L. Rev.* 113 (2009), 1269–1300.

Blake, J. 'On Defining the Cultural Heritage', *ICLQ* 49 (2001), 61–85.

Böckstiegel, K. H. 'Enterprise v. State: the New David and Goliath?', *Arbitration International* 23 (2007), 93–104.

Boer, B. W. 'World Heritage Disputes in Australia', *Journal of Environmental Law and Litigation* 7 (1992), 247–79.

Boyle, A. 'Dispute Settlement and the Law of the Sea Convention: Problems of Fragmentation and Jurisdiction', *ICLQ* 46 (1997), 37–50.

Braun, M. and Parker, L. 'Trade in Culture: Consumable Product or Cherished Articulation of a Nation's Soul?', *Denver J. of Int'l Law & Policy* 22 (1993), 155–91.

Brower, C. H. 'NAFTA's Investment Chapter: Initial Thoughts About Second Generations Rights', *Vanderbilt Journal of Transnational Law* 37 (2003), 1533–66.

Brower, C. N. and Schill, S. W. 'Is Arbitration a Threat or a Boon to the Legitimacy of International Investment Law?', *Chicago JIL* 9 (2008–2009), 471–98.

Brunetti, M. 'Introduction', *International Law Forum de Droit International* 5 (2003), 150–4.

Bryant, C. R. 'The Archaeological Duty of Care: The Legal, Professional, and Cultural Struggle over Salvaging Historic Shipwrecks', *Albany Law Rev* 65 (2001–2), 97–145.

Burri-Nenova, M. 'Cultural Diversity as a Concept of Global Law: Origins, Evolution and Prospects', *Diversity* 2 (2010), 1059–84.

Burri-Nenova, M. 'Trade and Culture in International Law: Paths to (Re)conciliation', *Journal of World Trade* 44 (2010), 49–80.

Cabrera Ormaza, M. V. 'Re-thinking the Role of Indigenous Peoples in International Law: New Developments in International Environmental Law and Development Cooperation', *Goettingen JIL* 4 (2012), 243–70.

Carducci, G. 'New Developments in the Law of the Sea: The UNESCO Convention on the Protection of Underwater Cultural Heritage', *AJIL* 96 (2002), 19–434.

Caron, D. D. 'Investor State Arbitration: Strategic and Tactical Perspectives on Legitimacy', *Suffolk Transnat'l L. Rev.* 32 (2009), 101–12.

Carpenter, K. A., Katyal, S. K. and Riley, A. R. 'In Defense of Property', *Yale Law Journal* (2009), 1022–125.

Carter, B. and Grimwade, G. 'Balancing Use and Preservation in Cultural Heritage Management', *International J. of Heritage Studies* 3 (2007), 45–53.

Casini, L. 'Italian Hours: The Globalization of Cultural Property Law', *International Journal of Constitutional Law* 9 (2011), 369–93.

Cavarello, D. T. 'From Penn Central to United Artists' I & II: The Rise to Immunity of Historic Preservation Designation from Successful Takings Challenges', *Boston College Environmental Affairs Law Review* 22 (1994–1995), 593–622.

Chapman, A. R. 'A "Violations Approach" for Monitoring the International Covenant on Economic, Social and Cultural Rights', *HRQ* 18 (1996), 23–66.

Chapman, T. 'Corroboree Shield: A Comparative Historical Analysis of (the Lack of) International, National and State Level Indigenous Cultural Heritage Protection', *Macquarie J. Int'l & Comp. Envtl. L.* 5 (2008), 81–96.

Choudhury, B. 'Exception Provisions as a Gateway to Incorporating Human Rights Issues into International Investment Agreements', *SIEL* Working Paper No. 2010/13 (2010).

Claeys, E. R. 'The Penn Central Test and Tensions in Liberal Property Theory', *Harvard Environmental Law Review* 30 (2006), 339–69.

Cline, C. P. 'Pursuing Native American Rights in International Law Venues: A Jus Cogens Strategy after Lyng v. Northwest Indian Cemetery Protective Association', *Hastings L. J.* 42 (1991), 591–633.

Coase, R. H. 'The Lighthouse in Economics', *Journal of Law and Economics* 17 (1974), 357–76.

Coffey, W. and Tsosie, R. 'Rethinking the Tribal Sovereignty Doctrine: Cultural Sovereignty and the Collective Future of Indian Nations', *Stanford L. & Policy Rev.* 12 (2001), 191–221.

Cogan, J. K. 'The Regulatory Turn in International Law', *Harvard ILJ* 52 (2011), 321–30.

Conforti, B. 'Unité et Fragmentation du droit international: Glissez, mortels, n'appuyez pas!', 111 *RGDIP* (2007), 5–18.

Coombe, R. 'The Expanding Purview of Cultural Properties and Their Politics', *Annual Review of Law and Social Science* 5 (2009), 393–412.

Coombe, R. 'Legal Claims to Culture in and against the Market: Neoliberalism and the Global Proliferation of Meaningful Difference', *Law, Culture and the Humanities* 1 (2005), 32–52.

Cordero Moss, G. 'Is the Arbitral Tribunal Bound by the Parties' Factual and Legal Pleadings?', *Stockholm Int'l Arb. Rev.* 3 (2006), 1–25.

Cottrell, A. M. 'The Law of the Sea and International Marine Archaeology: Abandoning Admiralty Law to Protect Historic Shipwrecks', *Fordham Int'l. L. J.* 17 (1993–1994), 667–725.

Criddle, E. J. and Fox-Decent, E. 'A Fiduciary Theory of Jus Cogens', *Yale JIL* 34 (2009), 331–87.

Cycon, D. E. 'When Worlds Collide: Law, Development, and Indigenous Peoples', *New England L. Rev.* 25 (1991), 761–94.

Daly, B. W. 'The Potential for Arbitration of Cultural Property Disputes: Recent Developments at the Permanent Court of Arbitration', *The Law and Practice of International Courts and Tribunals* 4 (2005), 261–80.

D'Amato, A. 'It's a Bird, It's a Plane, It's Jus Cogens!', *Connecticut JIL* 6 (1990–1991), 1–6.

Dattu, R. 'A Journey from Havana to Paris: The Fifty Year Quest for the Elusive Multilateral Agreement on Investments', *Fordham ILJ* 24 (2000–2001), 275–316.

De Cesari, C. 'World Heritage and Mosaic Universalism', *Journal of Social Anthropology* 10 (2010), 299–324.

Deneulin, S. and Townsend, N. 'Public Goods, Global Public Goods and the Common Good', *International J. of Social Economics* 34 (2007), 19–36.

De Vietri, R. 'Incorporating Humanity and the Global Economy: The Law of International Investment and Human Rights', *Int'l Trade & Business L. Rev.* 15 (2012), 211–29.

Dolzer, R. 'Fair and Equitable Treatment: A Key Standard in Investment Treaties', *International Lawyer* 39 (2005), 87–106.

Dolzer, R. 'Indirect Expropriations: New Developments?', *NYU Environmental L.J.* 11 (2003), 64–93.

Douglas, Z. 'The Hybrid Foundations of Investment Treaty Arbitration', *BYIL* 74 (2003), 151–289.

Dromgoole, S. '2001 UNESCO Convention on the Protection of the Underwater Cultural Heritage', *The International Journal of Marine and Coastal Law* 18 (2003), 59–108.

Dunoff, J. L. and Trachtman, J. P. 'Economic Analysis of International Law', *Yale JIL* 24 (1999), 1–59.

Du Plessis, A. A. and Rautenbach, C. 'Legal Perspectives on the Role of Culture in Sustainable Development', *Potchefstroom Electronic L. J.* 13 (2010), 27–71.

Dupuy, P.-M. 'Some Reflections on Contemporary International Law and the Appeal to Universal Values: A Response to Martti Koskenniemi', *EJIL* 16 (2005), 131–7.

Efrat, A. 'A Theory of Internationally Regulated Goods', *Fordham Int'l L.J.* 32 (2008–2009), 1466–523.

Egger, P. and Merlo, V. 'The Impact of Bilateral Investment Treaties on FDI Dynamics', *World Economy* 30 (2007), 1536–49.

Ellickson, R. C. 'Bringing Culture and Human Frailty to Rational Actors: A Critique of Classical Law and Economics', *Chicago Kent L. Rev.* 65 (1989), 23–55.

Epstein, R. A. 'Law and Economics: Its Glorious Past and Cloudy Future', *University of Chicago L. Rev.* 64 (1997), 1167–74.

Flecker, M. 'The Ethics, Politics, and Realities of Maritime Archaeology in Southeast Asia', *The International Journal of Nautical Archaeology* 31 (2002), 12–24.

Fletcher-Tomenius, P., O'Keefe, P. J., and Williams, M. 'Salvor in Possession: Friend or Foe to Marine Archaeology?', *International Journal of Cultural Property* 9(2) (2000), 263–314.

Forrest, C. 'Art on Loan: The Role of Immunity in Dispute Resolution', *Transnational Dispute Management* (2013).

Forrest, C. 'Has the Application of Salvage Law to Underwater Cultural Heritage Become a Thing of the Past?', *Journal of Maritime Law and Commerce* 34 (2003), 309–349.

Forrest, C. J. S. 'Defining Underwater Cultural Heritage', *The Journal of Nautical Archaeology* 31 (2001), 3–11.

Fortier, L. Y. and Drymer, S. L. 'Indirect Expropriation in the Law of International Investment: I Know When I See It, or Caveat Investor', *ICSID Review-FILJ* 19 (2004), 293–327.

Foster, G. K. 'Foreign Investment and Indigenous Peoples: Options for Promoting Equilibrium between Economic Development and Indigenous Rights', *Michigan JIL* 33 (2012), 627–91.

Francioni, F. 'Public and Private in the International Protection of Global Cultural Goods', *EJIL* 23(3) (2012), 719–30.

Francioni, F. 'Access to Justice, Denial of Justice, and International Investment Law', *EJIL* 20 (2009), 729–47.

Francioni, F. 'Au-delà des traités: l'émergence d'un nouveau droit coutumier pour la protection du patrimoine culturel', *RGDIP* 111 (2007), 19–42.

Francioni, F. 'Beyond State Sovereignty: The Protection of Cultural Heritage as a Shared Interest of Humanity', *Michigan JIL* 25 (2003–4), 1209–28.

Francioni, F. and Lenzerini, F. 'The Destruction of the Buddhas of Bamiyan and International Law', *EJIL* 14 (2003), 619–51.

Franck, S. D. 'Development and Outcomes of Investment Treaty Arbitration', *Harvard ILJ* 50 (2009), 435–489.

Franck, S. 'The Legitimacy Crisis in Investment Treaty Arbitration: Privatizing Public International Law Through Inconsistent Decisions', *Fordham L. Rev.* 73 (2005), 1521–625.

Frey, B. S. and Steiner, L. 'World Heritage List: Does it Make Sense?', *International Journal of Cultural Policy* 17 (2011), 555–73.

Frigo, M. 'Cultural Property v. Cultural Heritage: "A Battle of Concepts" in International Law?', *International Review of the Red Cross* 86 (2004), 367–78.

Frost, H. 'Museums from the Depths', *Museum* 137(1) (1983), 11.

Fry, J. D. 'International Human Rights Law in Investment Arbitration: Evidence of International Law's Unity', *Duke J. of Comparative & Int'l L.* 18 (2007), 77–150.

Galis, A. 'UNESCO Documents and Procedure: The Need to Account for Political Conflict When Designating World Heritage Sites', *Georgia J. Int'l & Comp. L.* 38 (2009–2010), 205–35.

Gal-Or, N. 'The Investor and Civil Society as Twin Global Citizens: Proposing a New Interpretation in the Legitimacy Debate', *Suffolk Transnational Law Rev.* 32 (2008–2009), 271–301.

Gangjee, D. 'Geographical Indications and Cultural Heritage', *WIPO Journal* 4 (2012), 92–102.

Gast, K. M. 'Environmental Justice and Indigenous Peoples in the United States: An International Human Rights Analysis', *Transnat'l L. & Contemporary Problems* 14 (2004), 253–80.

Gebert, D. L. 'Sovereignty Under the World Heritage Convention: A Questionable Basis for Limiting Federal Land Designation Pursuant to International Agreements', *Southern California Interdisciplinary L. J.* 7 (1998–1999), 427–44.

Genin, O. 'Les musées maritimes, gardiens d'un patrimoine mondial', *Museum International* 48 (1996), 4–7.

Gerkrath, J. 'Libre-échange et diversité culturelle: de l'antagonisme à la conciliation?' *Légicom* 36 (2006), 21–33.

Gerstenblith, P. 'Identity and Cultural Property: The Protection of Cultural Property in the United States', *Boston University Law Rev.* 75 (1995), 559–688.

Goodwin, E. J. 'The Consequences of Deleting World Heritage Sites', *King's L. J.* 21 (2010), 283–309.

Goodwin, E. J. 'The World Heritage Convention, the Environment, and Compliance', *Colorado J. Int'l Environmental Law & Policy* 20 (2009), 157–99.

Goy, R. 'La destruction intentionelle du patrimoine culturel en droit international', *RGDIP* 109 (2005), 273–300.

Grass, S. 'Inordinate Chill: BITs, Non-NAFTA MITs and Host-State Regulatory Freedom: An Indonesian Case Study', *Michigan JIL* 24 (2003), 893–960.

Guzman, A. 'Explaining the Popularity of Bilateral Investment Treaties: Why LDCs Sign Treaties that Hurt Them', *Vanderbilt Journal of Transnational Law* 38 (1997), 639–67.

Habdas, M. 'My Home is My Castle: But is my Castle Truly Mine? Polish Historical Immovables as Objects of Ownership', *Opinio Juris in Comparatione* 2(5) (2010), 1–19.

Hahn, M. 'A Clash of Cultures? The UNESCO Diversity Convention and International Trade Law', *JIEL* 3 (2006), 515–52.

Hale, R. D. 'Economic Aspects of Historic Preservation', *Journal of Cultural Economics* 2 (1978), 43–52.

Hardin, G. 'The Tragedy of the Commons', *Science* 162 (1968), 1243–8.

Harding, S. 'Value, Obligation and Cultural Heritage', *Arizona State L. J.* 31 (1999), 291–354.

Herold, A. 'EU External Policy in the Audio Visual Field: From "Cultural Exception" to "Cultural Diversity"', *ERA Forum* 6(1) (2006), 93–108.

Holtorf, C. 'What Does Not Move Any Hearts: Why Should it Be Saved? The Denkmalpflegediskussion in Germany', *International J. of Cultural Property* 14 (2007), 33–55.

Hunter, M. and Conde, G. e Silva. 'Transnational Public Policy and its Application in Investment Arbitration', *JWIT* 4 (2003), 367–78.

Janis, M. W. 'Jus Cogens: An Artful Not a Scientific Reality', *Connecticut JIL* 3 (1987–1988), 370.

Jenks, W. 'The Conflict of Law-Making Treaties', *BYIL* 30 (1953), 401–53.

Kaufmann-Kohler, G. 'Arbitral Precedent: Dream, Necessity or Excuse?', *Arbitration International* 23 (2007), 357–78.

Knahr, C. 'Transparency, Third Party Participation and Access to Documents in International Investment Arbitration', *Arb. Int'l* 23 (2007), 327–56.

Kolliopoulos, A. 'La Convention de l'UNESCO sur la protection et la promotion de la diversité des expressions culturelles', *Annuaire Français de Droit International* 51 (2005), 487–511.

Komurcu, M. 'Cultural Heritage Endangered by Large Dams and Its Protection under International Law', *Wisconsin ILJ* 20 (2001–2002), 233–96.

Koskenniemi, M. 'International Law in Europe: Between Tradition and Renewal', *EJIL* 16(1) (2005), 113–24.

Kotzé, L. and de la Harpe, S. 'The Good, the Bad and the Ugly: Using Good and Cooperative Governance to Improve Environmental Governance of South African World Heritage Sites: A Case Study of the Vredefort Dome', *Potchefstroom Electronic L.J.* 11 (2008), 1–53.

Koziol, C. 'Historic Preservation Ideology: A Critical Mapping of Contemporary Heritage Policy Discourse', *Preservation Education and Research* 1 (2008), 41–50.

Kreimer, O. 'Collective Rights of Indigenous Peoples in the Inter-American Human Rights System, Organization of American States', *Proceedings of the American Society of International Law at its Annual Meeting* 94 (2000), 315–16.

Kreindler, R. H. 'Fair and Equitable Treatment: A Comparative International Law Approach', *TDM* 3 (2006), 1–7.

Kreindler, R. H. 'Approaches to the Application of Transnational Public Policy by Arbitrators', *JWIT* 4 (2003), 239–50.

Krisch, N. and Kingsbury, B. 'Introduction: Global Governance and Global Administrative Law in the International Legal Order', *EJIL* 17 (2006), 1–13.

Kryvoi, Y. 'Counterclaims in Investor–State Arbitration', *Minnesota JIL* 21 (2012), 216–52.

Kunich, J. C. 'Losing Nemo: The Mass Extinction Now Threatening the World's Ocean Hotspots', *Columbia J. Environmental L.* 30 (2005), 69–70.

Lalive, P. 'Ordre public transnational (ou réellement international) et arbitrage international', *Revue de l'Arbitrage* (1986), 329–73.

Langford, M. 'Closing the Gap? An Introduction to the Optional Protocol', *Nordic J. of Human Rights* 27 (2009), 1–28.

Lankarani, L. 'La notion de dispersion en droit international des patrimoines culturels (immaterial, naturel et mondial)', *Journal de droit international* 2 (2011), 283–312.

Leal-Arcas, R. 'Towards the Multilateralization of International Investment Law', *JWIT* 10 (2009), 865–919.

Legum, B. 'Defining Investment and Investor: Who is Entitled to Claim?', *Arbitration International* 22 (2006), 521–6.

Lenzerini, F. 'Intangible Cultural Heritage: the Living Culture of Peoples', *EJIL* 22 (2011), 101–20.

Lenzerini, F. 'Sovereignty Revisited: International Law and Parallel Sovereignty of Indigenous Peoples', *Texas ILJ* 42 (2006), 155–90.

Litton, S. 'The World Heritage "In Danger" Listing as a Taking', *NYU JIL & Politics* 44 (2011), 219–266.

Lixinski, L. 'Selecting Heritage: The Interplay of Art, Politics and Identity', *EJIL* 22 (2011), 81–100.

Lo, C.-F. 'The Difference between Treaty Interpretation and Treaty Application and the Possibility to Account for Non-WTO Treaties during WTO Treaty Interpretation', *Indiana Int'l & Comp. L. Rev.* 22 (2012), 1–26.

Long, D. E. 'The Impact of Foreign Investment on Indigenous Culture: An Intellectual Property Perspective', *North Carolina Journal of International Law and Commercial Regulation* 23 (1998), 229–80.

Lowe, V. 'Regulation or Expropriation?', *Current Legal Problems* 55 (2002), 447–66.

Lowenfeld, A. 'Investment Agreements and International Law', *Columbia J. Transnational Law* 42 (2003), 123–130.

Lowenfeld, A. 'The Party-Appointed Arbitrator in International Controversies: Some Reflections', *Texas ILJ* 30 (1995), 59–72.

McDonald, T. A. 'Canada, the FTA and NAFTA: A View from the Negotiating Table', *London Journal of Canadian Studies* 14 (1998–1999), 55–65.

MacKay, F. 'The Draft World Bank Operational Policy 4.10 on Indigenous Peoples: Progress or More of the Same?', *Arizona JIL & Comparative Law* 22 (2005), 65–98.

MacKay, F. 'Universal Rights or a Universe unto Itself? Indigenous Peoples' Human Rights and the World Bank's Draft Operational Policy 4.10 on Indigenous Peoples', *American University Int'l L. Rev.* 17 (2002), 527–624.

Madariaga, Cuneo I. 'The Rights of Indigenous Peoples and the Inter-American Human Rights System', *Arizona J. Int'l & Comp. L.* 22 (2005), 53–64.

Manwaring, A. H. 'American Heritage at Stake: The Government's Vital Interest in Interior Landmark Designations', *New England L. Rev.* 25 (1990–1991), 291–323.

McLachlan, C. 'The Principles of Systemic Integration and Article 31(3)(c) of the Vienna Convention', *ICLQ* 54 (2005), 279–320.

Mann, H. and von Moltke, K. 'NAFTA Chapter 11 and the Environment: Addressing the Impacts of the Investor-State Process on the Environment', *IISD Working Paper* 25 (1999), 1–83.

Marx, R. 'The Disappearing Underwater Heritage', *Museum International* 35(1) (1983) 9–10.

Merryman, J. H. 'Two Ways of Thinking about Cultural Property', *AJIL* 80 (1986), 831–853.

Mezey, N. 'The Paradoxes of Cultural Property', *Columbia Law Review* 107 (2007), 2004–2046.

Milligan, A. 'Targeting Cultural Property; The Role of International Law', *Journal of Public and International Affairs* 19 (2008), 91–106.

Moloo, R. and Khachaturian, A. 'The Compliance with the Law Requirement in International Investment Law', *Fordham Int'l L. J.* 34 (2010–2011), 473–1501.

Nafziger, J. A. R. 'The Evolving Role of Admiralty Courts in Litigation Related to Historic Wreck', *Harvard ILJ* 44 (2001), 251–270.

Nafziger, J. 'The Development of Right of International Cultural Law', *American Society of International Law. Proceedings of the Annual Meeting* 100 (2006), 317–22.

Nathan, H. 'Creating an Ever Closer Union: The European Court of Justice and the Threat to Cultural Diversity', *Columbia J. of Transnational Law* (2008), 166–207.

Newcombe, A. 'The Boundaries of Regulatory Expropriation in International Law', *ICSID Review-FILJ* 20 (2005), 1–57.

Nicholas, G. P. 'Decolonizing the Archaeological Landscape', *American Indian Quarterly* 30 (2006), 350–80.

Nicholson, G. 'The Common Heritage of Mankind and Mining: An Analysis of the Law as to the High Seas, Outer Space, the Antarctic and World Heritage', *New Zealand Journal of Environmental Law* 6 (2002), 177–98.

O'Faircheallaigh, C. 'Negotiating Cultural Heritage? Aboriginal Mining Company Agreements in Australia', *Development and Change* 39 (2003), 25–51.

Ohlin, J. D. 'Nash Equilibrium and International Law', *Cornell L. Rev.* 96 (2010–2011), 869–900.

O'Keefe, R. 'World Cultural Heritage: Obligations to the International Community as a Whole?', *ICLQ* 53(1) (2004), 189–209.

O'Keefe, P. 'Fourth Meeting of Governmental Experts to Consider the Draft Convention on the Protection of Underwater Cultural Heritage', *International Journal of Cultural Property* 11 (2002), 168–72.

O'Keefe, P. J. 'Foreign Investment and the World Heritage Convention', *International Journal of Cultural Property* 3(2) (1994), 259–66.

Olynyk, S. 'A Balanced Approach to Distinguishing Between Legitimate Regulation and Indirect Expropriation in Investor-State Arbitration', *Int'l Trade & Business L. Rev.* 15 (2012), 254–96.

Pardo, A. 'Ocean, Space and Mankind', *Third World Quarterly* 6 (1984), 559–72.

Paulsson, J. 'International Arbitration is not Arbitration', *Stockholm International Arbitration Rev* 2 (2008), 1–20.

Paulsson, J. 'Arbitration without Privity', *ICSID Rev-FILJ* 10 (1995), 232–57.

Pauwelyn, J. 'The UNESCO Convention on Cultural Diversity, and the WTO: Diversity in International Law-Making?', *ASIL Insights*, 15 November 2005.

Pauwelyn, J. 'Bridging Fragmentation and Unity: International Law as a Universe of Inter-connected Islands', *Michigan JIL* 25 (2004), 903–16.

Pauwelyn, J. 'WTO Compassion or Superiority Complex? What to Make of the WTO Waiver for "Conflict Diamonds"', *Michigan JIL* 24 (2003), 1177–1207.

Pavoni, R. 'Mutual Supportiveness as a Principle of Interpretation and Law-Making: A Watershed for the "WTO-and-Competing-Regimes" Debate?', *EJIL* 21 (2010), 649–79.

Peacock, A. 'Preserving the Past: An International Economic Dilemma', *Journal of Cultural Economics* 2 (1978), 1–11.

Peng, S. 'International Trade in "Cultural Products": UNESCO's Commitment to Promoting Cultural Diversity and Its Relations with the WTO', *Int'l Trade & Business L. Rev* 11 (2008), 218–35.

Perry-Kessaris, A. 'Anemos-ity, Apatheia, Enthousiasmos: An Economic Sociology of Law and Wind Farm Development in Cyprus', *Journal of Law and Society* 40(1) (2013), 68–91.

Pfaff, C. 'Alternative Approaches to Foreign Investment Protection', *TDM* 3 (2006), 1–16.

Picciotto, S. 'Lessons of the MAI: towards a New Regulatory Framework for International Investment', *Law, Social Justice & Global Development* 1 (2000), 1–6.

Picciotto, S. 'Linkages in International Investment Regulation: The Antinomies of the Draft Multilateral Agreement on Investment', *University of Pennsylvania JIEL* 19 (1998), 731–68.

Posner, E. A. 'The International Protection of Cultural Property: Some Skeptical Observations', *Chicago JIL* 8 (2007), 213–32.

Pratt, A. 'Cultural Industries and Public Policy: An Oxymoron?', *International Journal of Cultural Policy* 11 (2005), 31–44.

Prott, L. V. and O'Keefe, P. 'Cultural Heritage or Cultural Property?', *International Journal of Cultural Property* 1 (1992), 307–20.

Prows, P. 'Tough Love: The Dramatic Birth and Looming Demise of UNCLOS Property Law', *Texas ILJ* 42 (2007), 241–310.

Puleo, T. J. 'Baroque Disruptions in Val di Noto', *Geographical Review* 100 (2010), 476–93.

Radi, Y. 'Realizing Human Rights in Investment Treaty Arbitration: A Perspective from Within the International Investment Law Toolbox', *North Carolina JIL & Commercial Regulation* 37 (2011–2012), 1108–86.

Rao, K. 'A New Paradigm for the Identification, Nomination and Inscription of Properties on the World Heritage List', *International J. of Heritage Studies* 16 (2010), 161–72.

Ratner, S. 'Regulatory Takings in Institutional Context: Beyond the Fear of Fragmented International Law', *AJIL* 102 (2008), 475–528.

Ratner, S. R. and Slaughter, A. -M. 'Appraising the Methods of International Law: A Prospectus for Readers', *AJIL* 93 (1999), 291–302.

Rau, A. S. 'Integrity in Private Judging', *South Texas L R* 38 (1997), 485–540.

Raustiala, K. 'Rethinking the Sovereignty Debate in International Economic Law', *JIEL* 6(4) (2003), 841–78.

Regourd, S. 'Le projet de Convention UNESCO sur la diversité culturelle: vers une victoire à la Pyrrhus', *Légipresse* 226 (2005), 115–16.

Reisman, W. M. 'Protecting Indigenous Rights in International Adjudication', *AJIL* 89 (1995), 350–62.

Renold, M. -A. 'An Important Swiss Decision Relating to the International Transfer of Cultural Goods: The Swiss Supreme Court's Decision on the Giant Antique Mogul Gold Coins', *International Journal of Cultural Property* 13(3) (2006), 361–9.

Richon, M. 'UNESCO Rural and Vernacular Architecture: An Underrated and Vulnerable Heritage', *Futuropa* 1 (2008), 29.

Roberts, A. 'Clash of Paradigms: Actors and Analogies Shaping the Investment Treaty System', *AJIL* 106 (2013), 45–94.

Rodríguez-Garavito, C. 'Ethnicity.gov: Global Governance, Indigenous Peoples, and the Right to Prior Consulation in Social Minefields', *Indiana J. Global Legal Studies* 18 (2011), 263–306.

Rose-Ackerman, S., and Rossi, J. 'Disentangling Deregulatory Takings', *Virginia Law Rev* 86 (2000), 1435–95.

Salacuse, J. W. 'The Emerging Global Regime for Investment', *Harvard ILJ* 51 (2010), 427–74.

Salacuse, J. 'Is There a Better Way? Alternative Methods of Treaty Based, Investor-State Dispute Resolution', *Fordham ILJ* 31 (2007–2008), 138–85.

Salacuse, J. and Sullivan, N. 'Do BITs Really Work? An Evaluation of Bilateral Investment Treaties and Their Grand Bargain', *Harvard ILJ* 46 (2005), 67–115.

Samuelson, P. 'The Pure Theory of Public Expenditure', *Review of Economics and Statistics* 36 (1954), 387.

Sanders, A. B. 'Of All Things Made in America Why Are We Exporting the Penn Central Test?', *Northwestern JIL and Business* 30 (2010), 339–82.

Sands, P. 'International Law in the Field of Sustainable Development', *BYIL* 65 (1994), 303–81.

Sarfaty, G. A. 'Why Culture Matters in International Institutions: The Marginality of Human Rights at the World Bank', *AJIL* 103 (2009), 647–83.

Sarfaty, G. A. 'The World Bank and the Internalization of Indigenous Rights Norms', *Yale L.J.* 114 (2005), 1791–818.

Satterwhite, M. and Hurwitz, D. 'The Right of Indigenous Peoples to Meaningful Consent in Extractive Industry Projects', *Arizona JIL & Comparative L.* 22 (2005), 1–6.

Sattorova, M. 'Denial of Justice Disguised?: Investment Arbitration and the Protection of Investors from Judicial Misconduct', *ICLQ* 61 (2012), 223–46.

Sattorova, M. 'Defining Investment under the ICSID Convention and BITs: Of Ordinary Meaning, Telos and Beyond', *Asian JIL* 2 (2012), 267–90.

Sauer, C. O. 'The Morphology of Landscape', University of California Publications in Geography 2 (1925), 19–54.

Sax, J. L. 'Heritage Preservation as a Public Duty: The Abbe Gregoire and the Origins of an Idea', *Michigan Law Rev* 88 (1990), 1142–69.

Sax, J. L. 'Takings and the Police Power', *Yale LJ* 74 (1964–1965), 36–77.

Scafidi, S., 'Intellectual Property and Cultural Products', *Boston University Law Rev.* 81 (2001), 793–842.

Schill, S. 'Enhancing International Investment Law's Legitimacy: Conceptual and Methodological Foundations of a New Public Law Approach', *Virginia JIL* 52 (2011–2012), 57–102.

Schill, S. 'W(h)ither Fragmentation? On the Literature and Sociology of International Investment Law', *EJIL* 22 (2011), 875–908.

Schill, S. 'Glamis Gold v. United States', *AJIL* 104 (2010), 253–9.

Schreuer, C. 'Conversations across Cases: Is There a Doctrine of Precedent in Investment Arbitration?', *TDM* 5 (2008).

Schreuer, C. H. 'The Concept of Expropriation under the ETC and Other Investment Protection Treaties', *TDM* 2 (2005), 1–39.

Sedlak, D. 'ICSID's Resurgence in International Investment Arbitration: Can the Momentum Hold?', *Penn St Int'l L Rev* 23 (2004), 147–71.

Shany, Y. 'Towards a General Margin of Appreciation Doctrine in International Law?', *EJIL* 16 (2005), 907–40.

Shelton, D. 'Common Concern of Humanity', *Iustum Aequum Salutare* V(2) (2009), 33–40.

Sheppard, A. 'Public Policy and the Enforcement of Arbitral Awards: Should There Be a Global Standard?', *TDM* 1 (2004), 1.

Simma, B. 'Foreign Investment Arbitration: A Place for Human Rights?', *ICLQ* 60 (2011), 573–96.

Simma, B. 'Universality of International Law from the Perspective of a Practitioner', *EJIL* 20 (2009), 265–97.

Singer, J. W. 'The Ownership Society and Takings of Property: Castles, Investments, and Just Obligations', *Harvard Environmental Law Rev.* 30 (2006), 309–38.

Sornarajah, M. 'The Clash of Globalizations and the International Law on Foreign Investment', *Canadian Foreign Policy* 12 (2003), 1–32.

Spain, A. 'Integration Matters: Rethinking the Architecture of International Dispute Resolution', *University of Pennsylvania JIL* 32 (2010–2011), 1–55.

Ssenyonjo, M. 'Reflections on State Obligations with respect to Economic, Social and Cultural Rights in International Human Rights Law', *International Journal of Human Rights* 15 (2011), 969–1012.

Stamatopoulou, E. 'Monitoring Cultural Rights: The Claims of Culture on Human Rights and the Response of Cultural Rights', *HRQ* 34 (2012), 1170–1192.

Steger, D. 'The Culture of the WTO: Why It Needs to Change', *JIEL* 10 (2007), 483–95.

Steiner, L. and Frey, B. S. 'Imbalance of the World Heritage List: Did the UNESCO Strategy Work?, University of Zurich Department of Economics, Working Paper No. 14 (2011), 1–30.

Stern, J. S. 'Smart Salvage: Extending Traditional Maritime Law to Include Intellectual Property Rights in Historic Shipwrecks', *Fordham L. Rev.* 68 (2000), 2489–542.

Stigler, G. J. 'Law or Economics?', *Journal of Law and Economics* 35 (1992), 455–68.

Strati, A. 'The Implications of Common Heritage Concepts on the Quest for Cultural Objects and the Dialogue between North and South', *Am. Soc'y Int'l L. Proc.* 89 (1995), 439–43.

Street, J. 'Music, Market and Manifestos', *International Journal of Cultural Policy* 19(3) (2013), 281–97.

Syed Mustapa, S. A. H. B. 'Showcasing Maritime Heritage Artefacts for the Benefit of the Tourist Industry in Malaysia', *International Journal of Nautical Archaeology* 34 (2005), 211–15.

Symonides, J., 'Cultural Rights: A Neglected Category of Human Rights', *International Social Science Journal* 158 (1998), 559–572.

Te Heuheu, T., Kawharu, M. and Tuheiava, R. A. 'World Heritage and Indigeneity', *World Heritage* 62 (2012), 8–18.

Throsby, D. 'Cultural Capital', *Journal of Cultural Economics* 23 (1999), 3–12.

Tjetje, C. 'The Changing Legal Structure of International Treaties as an Aspect of an Emerging Global Governance Architecture', *GYIL* 42 (1999), 26–55.

Tobin, J. and Rose-Ackerman, S. 'Foreign Direct Investment and the Business Environment in Developing Countries: The Impact of Bilateral Investment Treaties', *Yale Law and Economics Research Paper* No. 293 (2005), 1–52.

Tribe, K. 'Adam Smith: Critical Theorist?', *Journal of Economic Literature* 37 (1999), 609–32.

Urueña Alvarez, R. 'La protección del patrimonio cultural en tiempo de guerra y de paz', *Cuadernos de Estudios Empresariales* 14 (2004), 245–60.

Vadi, V. 'Culture Clash? World Heritage and Investors' Rights in International Investment Law and Arbitration', *ICSID Foreign Investment Law Review* 28 (2013), 1–21.

Vadi, V. 'Converging Divergences: The Rise of Chinese Outward Foreign Investment and Its Implications for International (Investment) Law', *Yearbook of International Investment Law* (2012), 705–24.

Vadi, V. 'Culture Clash: Investors' Rights v. Cultural Heritage in International Investment Law and Arbitration', SIEL Working Paper, June 2012, 1–25.

Vadi, V. 'Through the Looking Glass: International Investment Law through the Lenses of a Property Theory', *Manchester JIEL* 8 (2011), 22–64.

Vadi, V. 'When Cultures Collide: Foreign Direct Investment, Natural Resources and Indigenous Heritage in International Investment Law', *Columbia Human Rights Law Review* 42 (2011), 797–889.

Vadi, V. 'Critical Comparisons: The Role of Comparative Law in Investment Treaty Arbitration', *Denver Journal of International Law & Policy* 39 (2010), 67–100.

Vadi, V. 'Investing in Culture: Underwater Cultural Heritage and International Investment Law', *Vanderbilt Journal of Transnational Law* 42 (2009), 853–904.

Vadi, V. 'Fragmentation or Cohesion? Investment versus Cultural Protection Rules', *JWIT* 10(4) (2009), 573–600.

Vadi, V. 'Cultural Heritage & International Investment Law: A Stormy Relationship', *Int'l J. Cultural Property* 15 (2008), 1–23.

Vadi, V. 'Intangible Heritage, Traditional Medicine and Knowledge Governance', *Journal of Intellectual Property Law and Practice* 2 (2007), 682–91.

Van Harten, G. 'The Public-Private Distinction in the International Arbitration of Individual Claims against the State', *ICLQ* 56 (2007), 371–94.

Van Harten, G. and Loughlin, M. 'Investment Treaty Arbitration as a Species of Global Administrative Law', *EJIL* 17 (2006), 121–50.

Van Krieken, R. 'Cultural Genocide Reconsidered', *Australian Indigenous L. Rev.* 12 (2008), 76–81.

Varmer, O. 'The Case Against the "Salvage" of the Cultural Heritage', *Journal of Maritime Law & Commerce* 30 (1999), 279–93.

Vecco, M. 'A Definition of Cultural Heritage: From the Tangible to the Intangible', *Journal of Cultural Heritage* 11 (2010), 321–4.

Velasquez, M., Andre, C., Shanks, T. and Meyer, M. 'The Common Good', *Issues in Ethics* 5 (1992), 1.

Vierdag, E. W. 'The Legal Nature of the Rights Granted by the International Covenant on Economic, Social and Cultural Rights', *Netherlands YIL* 9 (1978), 69–105.

Viñuales, J. 'Foreign Investment and the Environment in International Law: An Ambiguous Relationship', *British Yearbook of International Law* 80 (2010), 244–332.

Von Schorlemer, S. 'Compliance with the UNESCO World Heritage Convention: Reflections on the Elbe Valley and the Dresden Waldschlösschen Bridge', *GYIL* 51 (2009), 321–90.

Voon, T. 'UNESCO and the WTO: A Clash of Cultures?', *ICLQ* 55 (2006), 635–51.

Wagner, D. 'Competing Cultural Interests in the Whaling Debate: An Exception to the Universality of the Right to Culture', *Transnat'l L. & Contemp. Probs.* 14 (2004), 831–64.

Waibel, M. 'Demystifying the Art of Interpretation', *EJIL* 22 (2011), 571–88.

Wälde, T. 'The Umbrella Clause in Investment Arbitration: A Comment on Original Intentions and Recent Cases', *JWIT* 6 (2005), 183.

Wälde, T. and Kolo, A. 'Environmental Regulation, Investment Protection and "Regulatory Taking" in International Law', *ICLQ* 50 (2001), 811–48.

Waldron, J. 'Indigeneity? First People and Last Occupancy', *New Zealand Journal of Public and Int'l Law* 1 (2003), 555–82.

Wangkeo, K. 'Monumental Challenges: The Lawfulness of Destroying Cultural Heritage during Peacetime', *Yale JIL* 28 (2003), 183–274.

Ward, T. 'The Right to Free, Prior and Informed Consent: Indigenous Peoples' Participation Rights Within International Law', *Northwestern Journal of International Human Rights* 10 (2011), 54–84.

Weiler, T. 'Balancing Human Rights and Investor Protection: A New Approach for a Different Legal Order', *TDM* 1 (2004), 1–15.

Weiler, T. (ed.) 'Intersections: Dissemblance or Convergence between International Trade and Investment Law', *TDM Special* 3 (2011).

Wiessner, S. 'The Cultural Rights of Indigenous Peoples: Achievements and Continuing Challenges', *EJIL* 22 (2011), 121–40.

Wiessner, S. 'The Rights and Status of Indigenous Peoples: A Global Comparative and International Legal Analysis', *Harvard Hum. Rights J.* 12 (1999), 57–128.

Wouters, J. and De Meester, B. 'The UNESCO Convention on Cultural Diversity and WTO Law: A Case Study in Fragmentation of International Law', *JWT* 42 (2008), 205–40.

Xanthaki, A. 'Indigenous Rights in International Law over the Last 10 Years and Future Developments', *Melb. JIL* 10 (2009), 3–27.

Yupsanis, A. 'The Concept and Categories of Cultural Rights in International Law: Their Broad Sense and the Relevant Clauses of the Human Rights Treaties', *Syracuse JIL & Commerce* 37 (2009–2010), 207–66.

Zacharias, D. 'The UNESCO Regime for the Protection of World Heritage as Prototype of an Autonomy-Gaining International Institution', *German Law Journal* 9 (2008), 1833–64.

Zacharias, D. 'Cologne Cathedral versus Skyscrapers: World Cultural Heritage Protection as Archetype of a Multilevel System', *Max Planck Yearbook of United Nations Law* 10 (2006), 273–366.

## Newspaper Articles

'A Holy Journey: Church Moved to Make Way to Coal Mine', *Spiegel Online*, 24 October 2007.

Bearak, B. 'For Some Bushmen, a Homeland Worth the Fight', *New York Times*, 4 November 2010.

Bohlen, C. 'Joyous Design Defies Nature in Sicily', *International Herald Tribune*, 1–2 June 2013.

Carter, H. 'English Heritage Lodge Formal Objection to Liverpool Waterfront Development', *The Guardian*, 23 February 2012.

'Clarification on Aboriginals and Canada's Investment Treaties', *Investment Law and Policy Weekly News Bulletin*, 11 June 2004.

Cleary, P. 'Heritage Status for WA Ochre Mine Site', *Australian*, 8 March 2011.

Dalrymple, W. 'Mes Aynak: Afghanistan's Buddhist Buried Treasure Faces Destruction', *The Guardian*, 31 May 2013.

'Debate over N.W.T. Caribou Hunting Goes Public', *CBC News*, 9 February 2010.

Godsiridze, V. 'Restoration Threatens Georgian Medieval Masterpiece', *Georgian Daily*, 2 January 2012.

Graham-Harrison, E. 'Mes Aynak Highlights Afghanistan's Dilemma over Protecting Heritage', *The Guardian*, 23 May 2013.

Hodson, P. 'How to Invest in Sunken Treasures; Salvage Stocks Offer High Returns, but Big Risks', *National Post*, 31 May 2007.

Jack, I. 'Who Owns What Lies Beneath?', *The Guardian*, 20 October 2007.

Lester, S. 'Trade and Investment in French Chateau Wine', *International Economic Law and Policy Blog*, 26 September 2012.

Lloyd, G., 'Wilgie Mia Mine Site Will Test China's Iron Will', *Australian*, 4 January 2011.

'New Plan for Canadian Bathurst Caribou Herd Management', *Eye on the Arctic*, 2 June 2010.

Peterson, L. E. 'In Policy Switch, Australia Disavows Need for Investor–State Arbitration Provisions in Trade and Investment Agreements', *IAR*, 14 April 2011.

Peterson, L. E. 'Majority Awards Damages for Lost Tenders', *IAR*, 11 April 2011, 4.

Peterson, L. E. 'Investor Warns Poland of Arbitration Unless Permit is Green-Lighted for Resumed Construction of Libeskind-Designed Tower in Warsaw', *IAR*, 28 August 2010.

Peterson, L. E. 'International Investment Law and Media Disputes: A Complement to WTO Law', *Columbia FDI Perspectives* 17 (2010), 1–3.

Peterson, L. E. 'Majority Finds that Failure to Examine Wide Definition of Investment in UK–Malaysia BIT was Manifest Excess of Power on the Part of Earlier Arbitrator', *IAR*, 20 April 2009.

Peterson, L. E. 'Tribunal Selected to Hear NAFTA Claim between Canada and US Investors in Proposed Quarrying and Shipping Scheme', *IAR*, 10 February 2009.

Peterson, L. E. 'Bush Administration Sets Process in Motion to Amend BITs with Eastern and Central Europe', *Investment Law & Policy Weekly News Bulletin* 16 (2004), 7–8.

Peterson, L. E. and Bonnitcha, J. 'New Government in Peru Confronts Recent Arbitration Loss and New Claims by Foreign Investors in Electricity Transmission, Construction, and Port Sectors', *IAR*, 4 August 2011.

Ripinsky, S. 'Venezuela's Withdrawal from ICSID: What it Does and Does Not Achieve', *ITN*, 13 April 2012.

Sackur, S. 'Australian Resources Key to Booming China', *BBC News*, 12 April 2011.

'Studio Daniel Libeskind, 'Zlota Tower Moves Forward in Warsaw', 12 January 2012, available at http://daniel-libeskind.com/news/zlota-tower-moves-forward-warsaw.

'UNESCO Removes Oman Oryx Sanctuary from Heritage List', *Reuters*, 30 June 2007.

Vis-Dunbar, D. 'Underwater Salvaging Firm Fails "Investment Test" in ICSID Case Against Malaysia', *ITN*, 30 June 2007.

Von Staden, A. 'Deference or no Deference, that is the Question: Legitimacy and Standards of Review in Investor-State Arbitration', *ITN* 4 (2012) 3.

## Documents of International Organizations

African Commission on Human and Peoples' Rights, Resolution on the protection of indigenous peoples' rights in the context of the World Heritage Convention and the designation of Lake Bogoria as a World Heritage site, 5 November 2011, ACHPR/Res. 197 (L)2011, available at www.achpr.org/english/resolutions/Resolution197_en.htm.

Agenda 21, Report of the UNCED, I (1992), UN Doc.A/CONF.151/26/Rev.1, (1992) 31 ILM 874.

Committee on Economic, Social and Cultural Rights, 5th Sess., *General Comment 3: The Nature of States Parties Obligations (Art. 2(1))*, 14 December 1990.

Council of the European Union, Resolution of 16 November 2007 on a European Agenda for Culture, 2007/C 287/01, OJEU, 29 November 2011.

Council of the European Union, Council Conclusions on the Promotion of Cultural Diversity and Intercultural Dialogue in the External Relations of the Union and its Member States, Brussels, 20 November 2008 at 4. http://ec.europa.eu/culture/documents/icd_external_relations_en.doc.pdf.

ICSID, *The ICSID Caseload-Statistics 2012-1* (Washington D.C.: ICSID, 2012).

ICSID, Press Release, 'Glamis Gold v. United States of America, Hearings on the Merits', 13 August 2007.

International Council on Mining and Metals, Position Statement: Mining and Protected Areas, Commitment, 20 August 2003, at www.icmm.com/document/43.

ICMM, Sustainable Development Framework, available at www.icmm.com/our-work/sustainable-development-framework/10-principles.

International Finance Corporation 2012 Performance Standards, available at www.ifc.org/wps/wcm/connect/c8f524004a73daeca09afdtf998895a12/IFC_Performance_Standards.pdf?MOD=AJPERES.

International Law Commission, Draft Articles on Diplomatic Protection (2006), Official Records of the General Assembly, Sixty-first Session, Supplement No. 10 (A/61/10).

International Law Commission, Fragmentation of International Law: Difficulties Arising from the Diversification and Expansion of International Law, Report of the Study Group (Martti Koskenniemi) UN Doc.A/CN.4/L.682 (13 April 2006).

OECD 'Multilateral Agreement on Investment, Consolidated Text and Commentary, Draft DAFE/MAI/NM(97)2.

OECD, 'Indirect Expropriation and the Right to Regulate in International Investment Law', Working Paper on International Investment No. 4, 2004.

Pillay, N. Statement by the United Nations High Commissioner for Human Rights, United Nations, New York, 9 August 2011, available at www.ohchr.org/en/NewsEvents/Pages/DisplayNews.aspx?NewsID=11284&LangID=E.

Secretariat of the Convention on Biological Diversity, *Akwé: Kon Voluntary Guidelines for the Conduct of Cultural Environmental and Social Impact Assessments Regarding Development Proposed to Take Place on, or which are Likely to Impact on, Sacred Sites and on Lands and Waters Traditionally Occupied or Used by Indigenous and Local Communities*, 6(b) (Montreal: Secretariat of the Convention on Biological Diversity, 2004).

UNCTAD, *Bilateral Investment Treaties: 1959–1999* (Geneva: UNCTAD, 2000).

UNCTAD, WIR 1996, *Investment Trade and International Policy Agreements* (New York and Geneva: UN, 1996).

UNESCO News, 'Eight New Sites from the Straits of Malacca, to Papua New Guinea and San Marino added to UNESCO's World Heritage List', available at http://whc.unesco.org/en/news/450.

UNESCO, *Operational Guidelines for the Implementation of the World Heritage Convention*, WHC 12/01 (July 2012) (Paris: UNESCO, 2012).

UNESCO, *Operational Guidelines: Articles 7, 8 and 17 of the Convention on the Protection and Promotion of Cultural Expressions, Measures to Promote and Protect Cultural Expressions* (June 2009).

UNESCO, *Recommendation concerning the Safeguarding of Contemporary Role of Historic Areas*, 26 November 1976.

UNESCO, *Recommendation concerning the Preservation of Cultural Property Endangered by Public or Private Works*, Paris, 19 November 1968.

UNESCO, *Recommendation concerning the Safeguarding of the Beauty and Character of Landscapes and Sites*, 11 December 1962.

UNESCO World Heritage Comm., *Report on the Mission to Kakadu National Park, Australia 26 October to 1 November 1986*, 1, WCH-98/CONF. 203/INF.18 (29 November 1998), available at http://unesdoc.unesco.org/images/0011/001175/117512e.pdf.

United Nations, Commission on Human Rights, Sub-Commission on Prevention of Discrimination and Protection of Minorities, *Principles and Guidelines for the Protection of the Heritage of Indigenous* Peoples, (by E. I. Daes, Special Rapporteur) UN Doc. E/CN.4/Sub.2/1994/31, 8 July 1994.

United Nations, Commission on Human Rights, Sub-Commission on Prevention of Discrimination and Protection of Minorities, *Study on the Protection of the Cultural and Intellectual Property of Indigenous Peoples*, (by E. I. Daes, Special Rapporteur), UN Doc. E/CN.4/Sub.2/1993/28, 28 July 1993.

United Nations Commission on the Elimination of Racial Discrimination (CERD), *General Recommendation No. 23: Indigenous Peoples*, UN Doc. A/52/18, Annex V, 18 August 1997.

United Nations Conference on Environment and Development, *Report of the United Nations Conference on Environment and Development: Agenda 21*,

UN Doc. A/CONF.151/26/Rev.1 (Vol. I) Annex 1 (12 August 1992), (*Agenda 21*).

United Nations Development Program, Human Development Report 2004, *Cultural Liberty in Today's Diverse World* (New York: UNDP, 2004).

United Nations, Economic and Social Council, Committee on Economic, Social and Cultural Rights, *General Comment No. 21, Right of Everyone to Take part in Cultural Life* (art. 15, para. 1(a), of the International Covenant on Economic, Social and Cultural Rights), 21 December 2009, E/C.12/GC/21, 2–20 November 2009, available at http://www2.ohchr.org/english/bodies/cescr/docs/gc/E-C-12-GC-21.doc.

UN Economic and Social Council, Commission on Human Rights, Final Report of the Special Rapporteur of the Sub-Commission on Prevention of Discrimination and Protection of Minorities on the Realization of Economic, Social and Cultural Rights, (D. Türk) UN Doc.E/CN.4/Sub.2/1992/16, 3 July 1992.

UN Economic and Social Council, Sub-Comm'n on Prevention of Discrimination and Protection of Minorities, Rapporteur on the Rights of Indigenous People, *Study of the Problem of Discrimination Against Indigenous Populations*, UN Doc.E/CN.4/Sub.2/1986//7/Add.4 (1987), by José R. Martínez Cobo (Martínez Cobo Report).

United Nations, Economic and Social Council, Human Rights Commission, *General Comment No. 23: The Rights of Minorities* (art. 27), UN Doc. CCPR/C/21/Rev.1/Add.5, 8 April 1994.

UN Human Rights Council, *Guiding Principles on Business and Human Rights: Implementing the United Nations "Protect, Respect and Remedy" Framework*, 21 March 2011, A/HRC/17/31.

UN Human Rights Council, Special Rapporteur on the Situation of Human Rights and Fundamental Freedoms of Indigenous People, *Promotion and Protection of All Human Rights, Civil, Political, Economic, Social and Cultural Rights, including the Right to Development*, UN Doc. A/HRC/9/9 (11 August 2008), available at www.un.org/ga/search/view__doc.asp?symbol=A/HRC/9/9 (Anaya, *Promotion and Protection*).

UN Human Rights Council, *Protect, Respect and Remedy: A Framework for Business and Human Rights*, Report of the Special Representative of the Secretary General John Ruggie on the Issue of Human Rights and Transnational Corporations and Other Business Enterprises A/HRC/8/5 (2008).

United Nations Industrial Development Organization, *Public Goods for Economic Development* (Vienna: UNIDO, 2008).

United Nations, Office of the High Commissioner for Human Rights, Expert Mechanism Advice No. 2 (2011) Indigenous Peoples and the Right to Participate in Decision Making, available at www.ohchr.org/Documents/Issues/IPeoples/EMRIP/Advice2_Oct2011.pdf.

United Nations Press Release, 'General Assembly Adopts Declaration on Rights of Indigenous Peoples; Major Step Forward Towards Human Rights for All, Says President', GA/10612, 13 September 2007, available at www.un.org/News/Press/docs/2007/ga10612.doc.htm.

World Bank, *The World Bank Operational Manual* (2005).

World Bank Group, *Striking a Better Balance: Final Report of the World Bank Independent Extractive Industries Review* (2003), available at http://irispublic.worldbank.org/85257559006C22E9/All+Documents/85257559006C22E985256FF6006843AB/$File/volume1english.pdf

World Bank, *The Quality of Growth* (Washington D.C.: WB, 2000).

World Commission on Culture and Development, *Our Creative Diversity* (Paris: UNESCO, 1996).

World Commission on Environment and Development, *Our Common Future* (Brundtland Report), 4 August 1987, UN GA Res A/42/427 (1987).

# INDEX